# Queen of Bohemia Predicts Own Death

Frontispiece, Fig. 1: Zoe in a 1909 *East Side* advertorial for Kosmos Electric Runabout wicker cars, meant for tootling around resorts. Author's photo (Oberhardt family collection, N-YHS)

# QUEEN OF BOHEMIA PREDICTS OWN DEATH

## Gilded-Age Journalist Zoe Anderson Norris

Eve M. Kahn

EMPIRE STATE EDITIONS

AN IMPRINT OF FORDHAM UNIVERSITY PRESS
NEW YORK 2025

Copyright © 2025 Fordham University Press

All rights reserved. No part of this publication may be reproduced, stored in a retrieval system, or transmitted in any form or by any means—electronic, mechanical, photocopy, recording, or any other—except for brief quotations in printed reviews, without the prior permission of the publisher.

Fordham University Press has no responsibility for the persistence or accuracy of URLs for external or third-party Internet websites referred to in this publication and does not guarantee that any content on such websites is, or will remain, accurate or appropriate.

Fordham University Press also publishes its books in a variety of electronic formats. Some content that appears in print may not be available in electronic books.

Visit us online at www.fordhampress.com/empire-state-editions.

For EU safety / GPSR concerns: Mare Nostrum Group B.V., Mauritskade 21D, 1091 GC Amsterdam, The Netherlands, gpsr@mare-nostrum.co.uk

Library of Congress Cataloging-in-Publication Data available online at https://catalog.loc.gov.

Printed in the United States of America

27 26 25     5 4 3 2 1

First edition

*To my daughter Alina Kulman, a star in telling people's stories in their own words*

*In memory:
Anna Armstrong, tireless historian of Harrodsburg, Kentucky
Lorianne Oberhardt Kelly, steward of her artist father
William Oberhardt's legacy*

## CONTENTS

Prologue: Weep No More xi

A Tribute to Enslaved People xv

Methodology: Why Zoe, and How, and Why Me? xix

Caption and Footnote Abbreviations xxiii

Sibling Guide xxv

1. A Sort of Waif, 1860–1873  1
2. Mineralogy and Constitutional Law, 1874–1878  13
3. Of the Best Families, 1878–1887  23
4. To Nourish the Temperament, 1887–1893  33
5. She Has a Halo, 1893–1895  41
6. Norris vs. Norris, 1896–1898  49
7. Beetles in Her Biscuits, 1898–1899  57
8. Champagne or Skyrockets, 1899–1900  65
9. A Wealthy Silk Merchant, 1900–1901  73
10. Sisters of Misery, 1901  79

## CONTENTS

11. Threat to Pretty Girl Novelist, 1902   89
12. The Useless Tears, 1902–1903   101
13. On the Rim of Manhattan, 1904–1906   107
14. Those Were Hungry Days, 1906–1907   121
15. That Great Uncertain Chasm, 1907–1909   129
16. Dear Children, 1909–1910   139
17. A Raggeder Edge than We, 1910–1913   159
18. The Best in the Land, 1910–1913   171
19. Lest They Fade from Affection's Bliss, 1913–1914   191
20. Land of the White Lilies, 1914   199
21. To Break Through the Silence, 1914–2000s   209
22. You Wouldn't Believe What's Going to Happen, 2018 Onward   219

Acknowledgments   231

Appendices   235

Notes   241

Selected Bibliography   267

Index   269

Fig. 2: 1910 *East Side* portrait by William Oberhardt of Zoe reporting undercover posing as a blind immigrant musician, begging on Lower East Side curbs. AC, Nicole Neenan photo

## PROLOGUE

### Weep No More

SOMETIME IN THE spring of 1910, a woman who was nothing that she seemed was seen wheezing an accordion's keys, wafting laments through Manhattan's Lower East Side. She squatted on a stool, wore blue goggles to feign blindness, and draped herself in a checked shawl and flowered headkerchief. She recognized some rich passersby, who considered themselves "especially philanthropic"; they ignored her. Other beggars dropped pennies into a cup attached to her instrument.

Her name was Zoe Anderson Norris, a Kentucky belle turned Kansas housewife turned New York writer. She took notes while immersing herself in the experiences of desperately poor immigrants and then published her passing thoughts, like a modern-day blogger. She wanted to right the world's wrongs with her writing.

In her two-decade career, she published hundreds of short stories and articles, three autobiographical novels, and virtually every word in the five-year run of her own bimonthly magazine, *The East Side*. She was one of few women of her time to found her own periodical, and one of fewer who did so with minimal training and connections, no staff, no major financial backer—just outrage, friends, and pawned diamond jewelry. She wrote about trying to control every facet of her magazine—illustrations, typefaces, bindings—and printed her fan mail and hate mail alike. She was brave and foolhardy, in and out of disguise. She called herself "prone to evil as the sparks fly upward,"[1] as she railed against forces that remain pernicious: undermining of women's narratives, gaping disparities in wealth, demonization of immigrants.

For her 1910 undercover reportage playing accordion at the curb, one of the few tunes she could play was "My Old Kentucky Home," an 1850s composition by Stephen Foster from the viewpoint of an enslaved man being sent to a worse fate further south. (The song was later reinterpreted as a eulogy for the Confederacy.) As Zoe emitted "dismal sounds from the sighing instrument," her own incompetence at the keyboard left her "well nigh brought to tears," as she later mocked herself in her *East Side*. A boy gave her a quarter, just for trying to play "My Old Kentucky Home." When a chocolate seller offered her a candy, "Like a lunatic I took it," Zoe wrote—and the vendor "laughed and went back to her tray," upon realizing the musician could see. Friends called out "Oh, you Zoe!" while dropping worthless buttons into her cup. Her performance in disguise netted about $1.50, which she "distributed carefully among the poor of my neighborhood for fear of bad luck." She pitied the disabled street musicians newly arrived in America whom she had impersonated, yet realized, "They make more money than I do."[2]

Many of her friends strolling past were members of her hard-partying, intentionally disorganized organization called the Ragged Edge Klub. They knew that she was a Kentuckian and almost broke. Many clubgoers were hiding their own pasts, on the run from scandals, cut off from conservative families in small towns. During the Klub's weekly dinners, as ragtime and booze flowed, Zoe handed out her magazines. Known as the Queen of Bohemia, she used a wine bottle as her scepter to grant knighthoods to her favorites: Baron Bernhardt of Hoboken, for instance, and Lady Betty Rogers of the Bronx. For *East Side* articles, she harvested her friends' antics, her male editors' abuse of underlings, her East 15th Street apartment's views of skyscrapers with "windows flashing back the fire of the sun." But few of even Zoe's intimates would have understood that her accordion tune's lyrics, urging listeners to "weep no more" over homelands left behind, were so applicable to the impostor musician.

She grew up impoverished amid intellectuals, abolitionists, and Confederate enslavers. By the time she birthed *The East Side*, she had escaped two bad marriages and was largely estranged from her enormous family (she had 14 siblings). She covered up parts of her background with lies and felt at home nowhere until, in middle age, she settled among millions of strangers in New York—"the people who, since she could find no happiness elsewhere had become her people."[3]

The first (and only) 1914 issue of *The East Side* described her recent dream that her death was imminent; the warning had been conveyed at her bedside by her mother, who had died nearly two decades before at an insane asylum in Kentucky. Days after Zoe mailed the print run, she died of heart failure. The news of her accurate premonition made headlines in hundreds of newspapers across the U.S. and Canada. Then she fell into obscurity.

Her heirs stored her minimal memorabilia in a Kentucky closet. A few friends' memoirs mentioned her. A granddaughter who never knew her drafted a biography titled *Zoe*. My title, *Queen of Bohemia Predicts Own Death*, quoting her obituaries, is not of course the one Zoe would have chosen. But she would have wanted her biography to appear under whatever title would sell the most copies. I intend it as a dramatic hook to draw in readers—like you—to her fight for the poor with her pen.

What did any unsuspecting passersby in 1910 think of that supposedly blind, immigrant accordionist playing a Southern anthem? The impostor was committing details to memory during those performances (and during the subsequent giveaway of her musical earnings), to fill her bimonthly with material that drew both fan mail and hate mail—which filled more pages. How did she end up on that curb, another beggar in a sea of relentless poverty, but the first to record the experience in print?

Fig. 3: Nancy Cole, who worked as a servant in Zoe's Kentucky hometown. Author's photo, Dedman family collection

# A TRIBUTE TO ENSLAVED PEOPLE

ZOE'S CULTURED UPBRINGING, which made this book possible, was only possible because of her family's erudition—which in turn was only possible because enslaved Black people performed much of her relatives' hard work for centuries before the Civil War. I offer this list of names—a fraction of the population—with deepest gratitude and awareness that nothing can compensate for these people's brutal treatment in captivity and inhumane family separations.

Kentucky:
> In Hopkinsville area:
>> Enslaved by Zoe's uncle Robert Anderson's family: Rachel (who remained in the family's employ as Rachel Anderson after the war), Peter, Maxey, Polly
>> Enslaved by Zoe's maternal Ducker relatives: Andrew, Charles, Harriet, Henry, Julia Ann (Charles's mother), Julian, Louisa
>> In Versailles and Midway, enslaved by the McIlvain family, hired out to the Andersons' home (where she died in a fire in 1861, as a teenager): Mary McIlvain
>> In Glasgow and Lexington area, enslaved by Zoe's Tompkins relatives: Daphne, Frederick (a violinist and coachman), Hetty, Nelson Tompkins (farm foreman) and his sons John Scott and Isaac Newton

Virginia:
> Enslaved by Zoe's Tompkins and Anderson relatives: Cato, Judith, Moses (who sued for his freedom and then escaped), Randolf, Scipio, Seaser, Syrus

Missouri:
> Enslaved by Zoe's Spenny and Norris in-laws (with postwar surnames): Addison Diggs, Amanda, Augustus Joplin, Catherine, Charles, Charlotte, Daniel, Eliza Diggs Tyman, George, Henry Diggs, Jane Diggs Hall, Lucy Wright, Phillip Diggs, Sandy Diggs, William Plaiter, and Winnie Diggs.

I am grateful for, and deeply indebted to, research by the historian Dr. Traci Wilson-Kleekamp.

Fig. 4: Author seeking graves of Zoe's relatives in a Kentucky cornfield. Yvette Holmes photo

## METHODOLOGY

### Why Zoe, and How, and Why Me?

I FIRST MET the Queen of Bohemia in a windowless basement. It was the fall of 2018, and I was part of a scholarly group touring a trove of American magazines amassed by the historian and neurologist Steven Lomazow. In the suburban New Jersey townhouse that he shares with his artist wife Suze Bienaimee, shelves and racks are piled with magazines by the thousands, accumulated over decades and spanning three centuries. The tour was organized by the Grolier Club, a museum, library and bibliophile society on East 60th Street, founded in 1884, and Steve was gearing up for his 2021 exhibition there of a fraction of his collection. For our group he brought out pre-Revolutionary War calls for free speech, 1942 magazines with American flags incorporated into the covers, and 1960s issues of *Life* with unmemorable pleasant covers that had to be scrapped in mid-print-run when news broke of assassinations. Steve rattled off backstories of the publications' owners and contributors, steering or wrecking the companies while influencing how Americans thought, voted, protested, dressed, and partied. We had just settled into the cellar lined alphabetically in 19th- and 20th-century treasures when Steve handed me Zoe's bimonthly *East Side*, produced at her Manhattan apartment from 1909 to 1914.

He explained that he had long been intrigued by Zoe, an underrated innovator. I noticed that throughout her magazine, she published her own name in large spiky letters and portraits of herself, elegantly coiffed or disguised as a panhandler. Sympathetic sketches of Jewish peddlers and synagogue worshippers also recurred on her pages, as well as calls for alleviating immigrant poverty. As a Jewish New Yorker, I was fascinated by such uncaricatured portrayals from virulently antisemitic times. My mother's Ukrainian-born, Yiddish-speaking parents, aunts and uncles trod the Lower East Side streets where Zoe lived and reported. And given my decades as a journalist and historian, I could not believe I had not heard of this nervy, open-minded woman and her magazine.

*The East Side* still in hand, I scrolled through my cellphone for scholarship about Zoe. Virtually nothing, not even a Wikipedia stub. I set out to research her, never expecting that my CV for her and other Andersons would surpass 350 pages and 235,000 words, dating back to 14th-century British royalty and tied to the history of slavery, religion, social justice crusades, restaurants and ragtime. I had no idea how much Zoe wrote would have contemporary resonances, how much unbridled fun she had, and how many people whose ancestors knew Zoe would begin conversations with a similar refrain: "You know, she predicted her own death."

I based this book, as detailed in Chapter 22, on wide travels, archival scourings, eBay sprees, and undercover reporting. Some sources, such as legal proceedings and diaristic writings, put klieg lights on moments in her life, but elsewhere I have interpreted evidence crumbs to settle on the balance of probability of what happened. I have tried to maintain a steady pace, not weighting the book toward times for which there is a sea of documentation. I clarify what she fictionalized, as a self-described "scribbler who mixed up her imagination with facts." She was not always honest in her journalism, while her fiction teemed with so much autobiography that she was publicly scolded for "making copy out of her friends."[1] Few letters by or to her have survived—she cut off many family members and was an enthusiastic telephone customer. And there are impenetrable archival silences from her immigrant neighbors and the people enslaved by her relatives, among other subjects of her writings.

I call her Zoe (rather than Norris or Mrs. Norris), because that's how she was best known, and what she called herself, emblazoning just her first name even on her stationery. When a critic mangled her full name in print, leaving out the Norris part, a friend was reassuring: "You are the only Zoe."[2] Her descendants pronounce it to rhyme with foe, and that's how I pronounce it, rather than zo-ee. But over the years, in her correspondence, book inscriptions, and published work, it appears as Zoé, Zoë, and Zoé. I generally use first names for women and surnames for men, as she typically did, and I am largely maintaining the idiosyncratic capitalizations Rampant in her self-published Work.

To keep this book to a manageable length, I am quoting her most memorable and revealing writings, without engaging in full-blown literary analysis—that herculean task awaits, perhaps, an annotated Zoe anthology. She described some assignments as "miles of nonsense," produced pragmatically by a "penny-a-liner," and she unapologetically recycled plots and metaphors. But her phrasings can be inventive and gorgeous, even when she was not trying that hard. She considered *The East Side* her masterpiece—and I concur. Miles of her unbylined work remains to be identified, particularly in the New York *Press* and *Sun*. At times it has seemed like I am shining a flashlight into an overstuffed attic, basing this book on whatever jewels of texts glinted most brightly here and there. This biography is just a first pass.

I am supplying quantities of profiles of Kentuckians, Kansans, and Manhattanites in her circle, to highlight how connected she was to major and minor figures and movements of her time, making copy out of them. I am noting many Manhattanites' birthplaces, to show how many of them, like Zoe, were immigrants. I only touch on her siblings, aunts, uncles, in-laws, and their descendants. They deserve a book of their own. I myself sometimes had trouble keeping their names straight, as did some of Zoe's fictional characters with huge families, as my readers surely will—but that blur is a crucial piece of Zoe's story, how she stood out from a huge crowd. Her relatives were so scattered and in so little contact that they would not have known each other if their paths crossed at Gold Rush mines in California, World War II battleships, or Manhattan subway platforms.

Zoe's Kentucky childhood shaped her worldview in ways that, in our time, intensive therapy might have helped her parse. I often joke that my last book will be *That'll Fuck You Up*, about experiences that irrecoverably sear people and distort perceptions and reactions. In Zoe's millions of words, a few brief passages about ethnic groups are unacceptable by contemporary standards. Yet there are vastly more passages in which she identified with those same ethnic groups, praised their achievements, bled for their plights, and urged her readers to do likewise. We do not know what she might have rewritten, retracted or apologized for, had she lived longer or worked with trusty advisers. "Before I have laid down my pen I shall perhaps take back everything I have ever written," she suggested in 1911. I started this book project wishing that she had been a saint, wringing my hands that she wasn't, but I've come to find her unsaintliness more interesting and important. Sometimes when I reread something maddening, I realized that she was mocking swaggerers, grandstanders, and hypocrites, including herself. And I always found compensatory compassionate prose nearby, campaigning against bigotry. Zoe considered herself impossibly contradictory: "Some day I'm going to offer a prize for the best guess as to what I am. I'd like to know, myself."[3]

People ask why I relate so strongly to her. It is not just her concern for my Ukrainian-born ancestors, trying to forget pogrom bloodshed. Like her, I am not a native New Yorker but do not feel at home anywhere else. Like her, I had an idealistic father in failing health, requiring coverups of secrets, and I was made aware early on that my existence (the third of three children) threatened the household's limited rations. I have written nonstop since college, sometimes for money or distraction, producing some works categorizable as "miles of nonsense." I recognize men I know whenever I read how Zoe "roasted the men" for public and private abuse going unpunished after making headlines. My husband's mother was born at an institution for unwed pregnant teenagers, like the charity hospitals that Zoe wrote about, based on the birthplace of her grandson Robert Morris, full of shunned, desperate girls whose experiences caused generational trauma (much like their counterparts in American red states today). I have visited the unmarked graves of mistreated newborns near one of those institutions. I also recognize myself in Zoe's commitment to fixing what cannot be fixed; I have many unattainable goals, including telling her story perfectly.

But this is her book, not mine. So here goes, as I follow the advice from one of *The East Side*'s ever-changing mastheads, where a normal magazine would have listed its contributors: "If You Want To See What She Is, Start Something."

## CAPTION AND FOOTNOTE ABBREVIATIONS

| | |
|---|---|
| AA | Anna Armstrong collection, Harrodsburg, KY |
| AC | Author's collection |
| *Beacon* | *Wichita Beacon* newspaper |
| *Democrat* | *Wichita Democrat* newspaper |
| *Eagle* | *Wichita Eagle* newspaper |
| HTA | Zoe's father Henry Tompkins Anderson |
| JWT | ZAN's 1913 correspondence and memoir essay in John Wilson Townsend collection, Eastern Kentucky University |
| MCJ | Zoe's granddaughter Mary Chelf Jones's 1980s interviews and writings |
| MSB | Mary S. Breckinridge's early 1900s correspondence with Alexander Graham Bell and Anderson relatives and friends, researching Zoe's uncle Robert Anderson's mid-19th-century school for the deaf. A. G. Bell Association, Washington, D.C. |
| NDC | Norris descendants' collection |
| N-YHS | New-York Historical Society (its name at the time of this book's writing) |

| | |
|---|---|
| NYPL | New York Public Library |
| NYT | *New York Times* |
| QPL, *Locke* | ZAN's 1902 novel *The Quest of Polly Locke* |
| *Soul* | ZAN's 1902 novel *The Color of His Soul* |
| TES | ZAN's bimonthly magazine, *The East Side* |
| TKCS | ZAN's 1904 and 1905 stories for the New York *Sun*, published in book form as *Twelve Kentucky Colonel Stories* (J. S. Ogilvie). |
| Wingfield | Marshall Wingfield, *A History of Caroline County, Virginia* (Baltimore: Regional Publishing Co., 1975). |
| *Wind* | ZAN's 1911 novel *The Way of the Wind* |
| ZAN | Zoe Anderson Norris |

## SIBLING GUIDE

Offspring of Henry Tompkins Anderson and his wives Jane and Henrietta:

Zoe's half-siblings (Jane's children):
Clarence (1835–1902), photographer in Harrodsburg then Hopkinsville, KY
Lelia Trabue (1837–1901), wife of physician Benjamin Trabue in Glasgow, KY

Zoe's siblings (Henrietta's children):
Two girls who died in infancy or childhood, Mary (born 1848) and Lily/Lillie (born 1855)
Jessamine "Jessie" Rue (1842–1926), portrait painter, wife of photographer Archibald B. Rue
Henry "Harry" Tompkins Anderson Jr. (1844–1917), rancher, farmer, politician in Ellsworth, KS
Martha "Mattie" Thompson (1845–1909), violinist, wife of Harrodsburg politician and distiller John Burton Thompson
Lucy Cheeks (1847–1877), first wife of Federal veteran, minister, government clerk Peter Cheeks (1844–1894)
Henrietta "Nettie" Cheeks (1850–1911), government clerk, second wife of Peter Cheeks
Louis (1852–1882), musician, musical instrument retailer, bandleader, politician, homesteader with Henrietta in Ellsworth, KS
William (1854–around 1879), known as Willie

Nannie Cardwell (1858–1937), government clerk in Louisville after husband Samuel Creed Cardwell was murdered by moonshiners

Zoe (1860–1914)

Cornelia Pickett Timmins (1861–1943), known as Pickett, portrait painter in Kansas, Kentucky and then Chicago, wife of British-born businessman Harry Timmins

Charles (1864–1881), known as Charlie, homesteader with Henrietta in Ellsworth

# Queen of Bohemia Predicts Own Death

Fig. 5: A fraction of Zoe's large family: top row: father Henry, mother Henrietta; 2nd row: left, 1870s photo taken in Harrodsburg by Zoe's half-brother, Clarence, of unknown sitter with well-behaved pet; right, Zoe's brother Harry; 3rd row, from left: Zoe's sister Mattie Anderson Thompson, pastel portrait of toddler Zoe, and Zoe's sister Pickett as photographed by their sister Jessie's husband Archibald Rue. AC (Henry, Pickett, photo by Clarence), NDC (Henrietta, Zoe), MSB (Harry), AA (Mattie), Nicole Neenan photo

# 1

# A Sort of Waif, 1860–1873

ZOE POPULATED HER family tree with fictions: a pirate, a frivolous Frenchwoman, British vicars tending the poor. She thereby explained her inherited interest in outsiders and outcasts. The truth was just as interesting as the inventions.

She was the 11th of 13 children of Henry Tompkins Anderson (1812–1872) and Henrietta Ducker Anderson (1819–1897). The couple married in western Kentucky in 1841, when Henry, a Virginia native and the youngest of about 10 children, was a widower with two small children, Clarence and Lelia. (His Virginia-born first wife Jane died in 1840, likely in childbirth.) Henrietta was the second oldest of about eight siblings, and her family, immigrants from Maryland, were landowners and businesspeople. (Duckers, a central Kentucky hamlet, was named for them.) One of Henrietta's brothers, William, an industrious undertaker, estimated that he had buried 10,000 Kentuckians.[1]

Henry descended from some of Virginia's earliest white settlers (and that family tree trunk extends back to Britain's 14th-century king, Edward III). During the American Revolution, Henry's grandfather Garland Anderson served as a Virginia legislator, and Henry's maternal grandfather Robert Reade Tompkins (a cousin of George Washington) was a militia captain. Generations of this family branch, men and women, were known for sparkling wit, good looks, talents for music and chess, and impractical passions for literature, "which impaired, nay, sometimes destroyed the influence and powers of ambition."[2]

One of Zoe's short stories imagined her colonial Virginia ancestors, living in a "cottage nestled in a clump of cedars" and recruited for Revolutionary War service. But the majority of her autobiographical writings claimed descent "from a hundred vicars" in Britain's Northumberland, many named Henry T. Anderson. They tended the poor while writing "beautiful sermons . . . in early English, published by order of kings." Some were persecuted for siding with 16th-century Scottish rebels—"Am a Rebel myself," she mused in 1913.[3] All she had inherited from her mother's supposedly French mother was "an inclination to dance," and because of "a distant renegade Uncle, who was a Pirate on the High Seas," she swiped restaurant dinnerware as souvenirs.[4] No evidence backs these pedigree claims—I cannot find, for example, any Northumberland vicars named Henry T. Anderson. Did relatives feed her these tales when she was young? Or were they useful fabrications for her readers and interviewers? Did she want to create an illusion of inevitability as she invented herself?

Henry and his brothers Benjamin, Albert, John, and Robert became respected teachers and leaders of Protestant congregations—"fine looking men, six feet tall or over," at times lacking in business acumen. Henry was so loftily absent-minded that en route to his first wedding, he walked atop some rickety flour barrels and fell in, ruining his suit.[5]

Enslaved labor made such antebellum unworldliness possible. For generations of Zoe's family in Maryland, Virginia, and Kentucky, the highest priced "possessions" were often human beings. Yet many of these slaveholders were paradoxically emancipationists and considered themselves humanitarians. A cousin's 1870 memoir (undoubtedly self-flattering) recalled relatives regarding the system of "forced servitude" as a deplorable, doomed, "festering sore." They protected the enslaved from the "unmeasured vengeance" of the typical slaveholder's lash, agreed in "cheerful concurrence" to manumissions, and supported "gradual but universal emancipation." The contradictory behavior of Zoe's ancestors can be head-spinning. Henry's sister Ann married Thomas Lipscomb, a Virginia slave dealer, who earned abolitionists' praise for helping a kidnapped Black child, Sidney Francis, return to his free family in Massachusetts. (Lipscomb realized that the child had been kidnapped from the North upon hearing him read handbills posted in a Fredericksburg barbershop—a boy born enslaved in Virginia would likely have been illiterate; to testify against the kidnapper, Lipscomb traveled to Massachusetts despite a broken arm in a sling.)[6]

Henry's brother Robert and his wife Martha ran an innovative school for the deaf in a western Kentucky hamlet. They stocked their library with books about theology, science, economics, and world history (but no fiction) and equipped classrooms with terrestrial and celestial globes. Robert tried to benefit "suffering humanity," teaching students from as far away as Texas and Wisconsin to speak "*audibly*, and *distinctly*!" People enslaved by Robert and Martha included a couple, Peter, who served as the farm foreman, and Rachel, who oversaw housekeeping. Rachel adopted the surname Anderson after the Civil War, remained in the family's employ, and "enjoyed the respect of all who knew her."[7] Did Zoe draw any inspiration on the Lower East Side from this Anderson branch, who helped the deaf tell their stories, giving voice to the silenced? Did anyone see the antebellum paradox of enslaving Black people, while benefiting disabled white humanity?

Henry, as a young man, converted to the Disciples of Christ, one of many new evangelical sects taking hold in the South. The Disciples advocated sweeping away clerical hierarchies and bureaucracy, to adhere more closely to Biblical directives and God's unfiltered word. Henry traveled to teach, preach at camp meetings, and baptize adults by full immersion. At the banks of streams and rivers, he promised to raise converts from the waters "free from sin as an angel." He occasionally stayed in a town long enough that congregants paid homage by painting his name on stained-glass church windows. Henrietta focused on raising their brood, often with no relatives nearby for assistance. Zoe's journalism aggrandized her nomadic family's antebellum quarters into a plantation with "marble halls," a grand piano, and a large enslaved population "voluntarily freed" by Henry.[8] (Did anyone ever ask her how those Northumberland vicars had turned into Southern grandees?) Henry and Henrietta did farm at times, but they did not seem to set down deep roots anywhere, nor earn enough to "possess" many human beings. And they never grew Deep South crops like sugar or rice, which demanded quantities of enslaved workers—those deathtrap fields were the destiny of the narrator of "My Old Kentucky Home."

Henry and some of his brothers wrote for religious periodicals, the now-obscure likes of *The Millennial Harbinger* and *The Herald of the Future Age*. New ones kept emerging, similar to the surge of magazine debuts in Zoe's time. Henry sparred with colleagues in print over dogma and ritual, just as Zoe would retort to her critics in *The East Side*. At one point Henry announced plans, apparently unrealized, to publish his own monthly, *The Christian Disciple*. It would cover topics such as prophecy fulfillment, church leaders' responsibilities, and "the sowing of the incorruptible seed" of faith. The annual subscription price, $1, was what his daughter would charge for *The East Side*.[9]

Henry's voluminous prose scarcely mentioned Henrietta and their children, but some passages revealed his emotional extremes, of compassion, foreboding, and fury. He predicted that as Europe was engulfed in antimonarchist uprisings of "the lower and despised classes of society," God would soon "shake the earth," toppling empires and rooting out "Popery" and Islam: "woe to those who have no wisdom to fly the impending eruption." Theologians attacking Henry or publishing errors were "certainly barbarians" who would "add darkness to darkness." When one of his brothers showed a religious independent streak, Henry urged this straying sheep to "unite with me, and with me, hold the Head of Christ. The Lord knoweth I would clasp you to my heart with tears of joy." Henry believed that new schools for Black children would aid "the way of God's word" and signal that the cosmos was "improved by the lapse of ages." (Many of his Disciples colleagues and congregants were abolitionists, who educated and manumitted their enslaved people, "choosing poverty with a good conscience." They also aided the Underground Railroad, trained Black men as pastors, and enabled numerous freed families to resettle in Liberia.)[10]

Henry sometimes heard from "those who, though dead, yet have the power to speak." He had premonitions: "a ray from a better world flashes upon the future and lights it up for the lonely soul that is to sail out upon an uncertain sea." These supernatural phenomena would recur throughout Zoe's writings. He considered "the nation of Israel . . . designed for some grand purpose," akin to Zoe's envy of devout Jewish immigrants.[11] But oddly, Henry little mentioned a driving force of her career: Jesus's mandate to help the poor, to live among them and alleviate their pain.

When Zoe was born on a farm at the bluegrass outskirts of Harrodsburg in central Kentucky—"a little old dog kennel town," in her words[12]— Henry was giving classes in ancient languages (he was fluent in Hebrew, Latin, and Greek) and feeling like "a caged bird." He left steady teaching jobs to focus on translating the New Testament from early Greek texts, "with a zeal that seemed to absorb his every thought and feeling." While his manuscript for *The New Testament Translated from the Original Greek* was in progress, at some point the Andersons were literally homeless. Some of Henry and Henrietta's older children still living under their nonexistent roof were sent to a nearby school for orphans. The couple brought their youngest—including Zoe—to live at Daughters College, a campus of colonnaded buildings in Harrodsburg (Zoe's alma mater, see Chapter 2). The elite girls' boarding school was run by John Augustus Williams, a Disciples scholar who helped Henry with translation work, and John's wife Mary. On a rainy night, when the Andersons arrived unannounced at the Williamses' doorstep, Henry "carried his little babe on one arm, a roll of manuscript under the other, and an uncorked inkstand in his hand, safely stoppered with his thumb."

Mary Williams adapted the school tearoom into quarters for the Andersons. Henry focused on writing, "heedless of the sleepy fretfulness of the babe and the noisy romp of the other children." John Williams, despite his close friendship and proximity with the Andersons, never pinned down the headcount of their "large family—I think of ten children." Henry sometimes headed outdoors, spreading his reference books on the grass. Henrietta never failed "to relieve him of all domestic care, and to cheer him in his literary and ministerial labors." The Williamses were eventually able to settle the Andersons in a rented cottage, and Henrietta "called all her children to come home and gather under her wings once more." Through the bouts of chaos and poverty that Henry caused, he never wavered from "his divine call to the work"—just as Zoe would rely on no major benefactors while unprofitably tilting at windmills with words.[13]

Henry, overcoming "many adverse circumstances," issued editions of his translation through printers in Cincinnati, Louisville, and Birmingham, England. The books are still considered a scholarly achievement, especially coming from "an obscure village school teacher" who lacked institutional backers and "access to hoary libraries, opulent in ancient manuscripts and modern learning." Henry was grateful for praise from colleagues who "hold up my hands" (Zoe applied that phrase to her Ragged Edgers), defending his choices of pronouns, verb tenses, and prepositions, defying opponents engaged in "suicidal criticism." Henry rhetorically asked, upon verbally slaying a naysayer, "Shall I leave him to die, a spectacle for the people?" But he could not compete with editions from major distributors like the American Bible Union, and sales were slow. The translation's proceeds might someday "enable me to buy a horse," Henry wryly predicted.[14]

Zoe described her father as renowned for "difficult translations from the original Greek" as well as "exquisite sermons, delicately worded, masterpieces of style but sad, sad." His 15 children resulted from a desire to prevent "race suicide," undeterred by "the little matter of a scarcity of rations." She pitied her mother birthing and raising 13 children, "a fatal and most unlucky number, egad!" A number of her short stories, written in thick Southern accents, portrayed large families in rural Kentucky. One patriarch has "so many chillun he couldn't count 'em" and lives amid thick blackberry patches on the Cane Run Pike (a road of that name ran past Zoe's real-life birthplace). One narrator wonders (as did Zoe in the slums) why God sends so few children to "rich people what's got money to burn" but so many "to a man what ain't got half enough money to feed and clothe 'em." The fictional parents lose track of their offspring. A son drowns during a picnic and goes unmissed "till they got home and counted noses." A daughter is mistaken for a different child "whut had bin misbehavin'" and is slapped by her mother—the girl stops speaking to her mother for three months but "her mothah nevah noticed it a tall." One brood of 16 children are named, like Zoe's siblings, "Lucy and Mary and Net and Nan and Will" and are close in age, "under your feet everywhere, one a little higher than the other, like stair steps."[15]

In April 1861, at the Civil War's outbreak, tragedy struck at Henry and Henrietta's home. Henrietta was about to give birth to her 12th child, Zoe's only younger sister, Cornelia Pickett, known as Pickett. An enslaved teenager, Mary McIlvain, had been hired out to the Andersons by a neighbor. On a Sunday evening, the teenager returned from church and "threw herself upon the bed which took fire from a candle. Badly burned and much frightened," she leapt out a second-floor window to her death.[16] She was the first of two young housekeepers named Mary killed by flames at Zoe's homes (see Chapter 5).

Further horrors unfolded in wartime, as the Andersons' relatives and friends enlisted. Kentuckians hoped at first to maintain "armed neutrality," but the border state soon teemed with guerrillas, scouts, rumormongers, deserters, and refugees—tattered, parched, freezing, mutilated, sick, dying. Civilians drove carriages past each other, headed somewhere safe that might be nowhere, clinging to "valuables and trumpery that the fleeing gathered up as people do things wildly in a fire." Zoe's brothers Harry and Clarence joined the Federal forces, tasked with shooting at their own Confederate cousins; Harry served in a blur of cavalry and infantry companies from Kentucky, Ohio, and Indiana. Among other Kentucky cousins were Robert Anderson, who led the Federal forces at Fort Sumter, and Stephen Gano Burbridge, a slave owner turned Federal commander, who executed Confederate prisoners en masse and recruited Black troops, targets of Confederate atrocities. Women, whether slaveholding housewives or Catholic nuns with nursing training, helped out along the Kentucky roads. They supplied beasts of burden, food, clothing, bandages, and hiding places, sometimes washing the unshaven faces of foe and friend alike. Mothers recognized each other's sons among the bedraggled drummer boys and buglers. Wounded soldiers crawled under blackberry bushes to die. Homes, schools, hotels, and churches were converted into makeshift hospitals, piled with amputated limbs, blood seeping into the floorboards. Unidentified corpses were shoveled into mass graves.[17]

Henry's wartime writings barely mention the hellish conditions, as if his New Testament labors blotted out all else. He did consider emancipation a Christian necessity: "The Almighty has been at work here with the sword, and the way for truth is open." But he lamented, "the war swept away what little I had." Zoe wrote that her religious father "was opposed to slavery on the face of it," yet in the war's "hideous ravages" on supposedly neutral Kentucky, her family's plantation became a battlefield. Federal forces dragged away the parlor's "splendid grand piano . . . and made kindling wood of it." Was that a more dramatic soundbite to offer her mostly Northern readers, rather than Henry's unprofitable commitment to eradicating theological errors and her brothers' Federal service? Yet she also described Abraham Lincoln as "the Greatest Man in the Nation's History," martyred while rising to "heights transcendent." By 1900, she had shaved years off of her age and claimed to have not witnessed wartime at all, born "considerably after the last gun had been fired" and raised amid only "the smoke of reminiscence."[18]

During and just after wartime, Henry officiated at some of his children's weddings—it must have been a blur of ceremonies for nearly youngest Zoe. Her half-brother Clarence married Mary Spilman, from a prominent Harrodsburg family, and set up photography studios in Harrodsburg and then hundreds of miles westward in Hopkinsville (where Henry had married Henrietta and pastored for years, near his brother Robert's school for the deaf). Lelia married a physician, Benjamin Trabue, and moved westward to Glasgow, Kentucky (about halfway between Harrodsburg and Hopkinsville). Harry decamped to homestead in Kansas with his Pennsylvania-born teenage bride, Sarah Hughes—they married on horseback and lived at first in a turf dugout. Zoe's sister Jessie, who had let a Confederate hide in a mansion near Harrodsburg where she spent part of the war, became a portrait painter in Harrodsburg after studying at a Cincinnati art school. She married the photographer Archibald B. Rue, a Federal veteran, and displayed her paintings "imbued with life" at his studio.[19] Zoe's sister Lucy married Peter Cheeks, a Federal veteran from New Jersey who had worked as a newspaper editor and minister (he converted from Methodism to Henry's Disciples). Zoe's sister Mattie briefly taught music (she was an accomplished violinist) and sought a government clerkship in Washington, reminding President Andrew Johnson that her famous scholar father had supported abolition "at great pecuniary sacrifice."[20] But then she made her fortune by marrying John Burton Thompson, a charismatic Confederate veteran, lawyer, and whiskey maker in Harrodsburg.

(The Thompsons' wealth and unhappiness would make many appearances in Zoe's journalism and fiction.)

By 1870, Henry managed to acquire acreage in the hamlet of Guinea Station in eastern Virginia, in battle-scarred lands just south of Fredericksburg, near farmland owned by his physician brother Benjamin and Benjamin's second wife, Tabitha. During the war, Benjamin's son Robert, a Confederate soldier, caught a fatal disease at a Federal prison in Washington. Benjamin's daughter Anne's in-laws, Thomas and Mary Chandler, owned a nearby plantation where Stonewall Jackson died in 1863, after being accidentally mortally wounded by his own men. The site had not yet become a Lost Cause shrine, and Northerners were buying local farmland at bargain prices. At times Zoe roamed unsupervised and uncomforted there. A sobbing Italian immigrant girl reminded adult Zoe of shedding tears during girlhood, "quite as bitterly over the little troubles of life as she had done later on over the great." Her 1902 novel heroine Polly Locke went joyously barefoot in girlhood, "wading in streams, paddling in mud-puddles, squeezing up the mud between your toes" and ending up "sore fingered in the woods of Virginia," after harvesting prickly chinkapins (a chestnut relative). Mattie played a favorite hymn on violin in Virginia, the rest of the large family "sitting around in the twilight listening, the circle of them." But Zoe felt restless and out of place, critiqued by so many sisters, as if surrounded by unflattering mirrors: "each look and act was hideously reflected."[21]

It is unclear where Zoe was educated during her peripatetic childhood, but she was not intellectually stimulated. For people like her, who had "slept away the days of their youth in a country town," New York "never loses its interest," she wrote in 1912. In one of her fictional huge Kentucky families, one daughter is the smartest offspring and her father's favorite; she refuses to help with housework "or comb the little childern's curls of mornin's," preferring instead "to read and write and add up sums." One-room schoolhouses dotted the countryside in Virginia and Kentucky, and songbirds accompanied Zoe on her twice daily walks of "a sun-flecked mile to school." She fictionalized coed classrooms, where female teachers use guns and birch rods to discipline "half baked, ovah grown boys." Girls were teased for excelling in class: "the boys cried: 'Look at her! Don't she think she is smart?' . . . they punished us for being 'smart' by leaving us out of their games. . . . Often we failed in our lessons purposely so that they could 'go ahead' and smile on us once again." During her childhood Sundays stuck in church, she prayed not for salvation but rather for the end of "inane and lifeless sermons . . . that send you to sleep, from sheer disgust and weariness." She felt "disconsolately alone" after church services, when the rest of the family napped.[22]

Henry, as his health failed (due to neuralgia and "a disordered action of the heart affecting the brain"), nonetheless traveled to preach and teach. He turned down an Iowa college's offer of its presidency, although Henrietta was "inclined to that region." He started translating another version of the New Testament, based on an 1860 transcription of the fourth-century Codex Sinaiticus, which the German scholar-explorer Constantin von Tischendorf had discovered at St. Catherine's Monastery in Egypt. "Send me money, my brethren," Henry begged other Disciples, since the next translation would certainly make his fortune and "defy all the efforts of the fault-finders."[23]

One of Zoe's heroines prays for success as a writer, to follow in her long-dead theologian father's footsteps. "I have been a sort of waif from my childhood," she reminds God. She carries her father's picture always, lest she forget his face. She had tried to comfort him as he ailed:

> His life had not been a happy one. I knew that, young as I was at the time of his death. Once they left me to watch at his bedside, fanning. His eyes were closed, but his lips moved, murmuring half unconsciously: 'I am tired. Let me die.' I must have heard many of his words, but those are the only ones that remained with me.[24]

President Andrew Johnson helped Henry find a last salaried post in Washington, where one congregant, the politician James Garfield, fled from Henry's droning sermons full of "intolerable denominational bigotry, arrogance and egotism." Colleagues deemed Henry "doomed to utter dependence," his Virginia farmland "impossible to sell," his mind irreparably damaged by depression, "poverty and loneliness." His death, on September 19, 1872, was attributed to "inflammation of the lungs." Henrietta buried him in Washington's Glenwood Cemetery. She bought three plots. (Alongside his unmarked grave would come the unmarked graves of his daughters Lucy and Nettie.) Obituarists lauded his stainless character and "unwavering faith," maintained through "dark and troublesome" days of toil, "reckless of health and fame and fortune . . . in the midst of noisy, and sometimes hungry, children." He had completed his Codex Sinaiticus translation, which John Williams futilely tried to publish (Henry's youngest daughter Pickett would become its torchbearer, see Chapter 21).[25]

Henry visited Zoe thereafter in dreams during her "most terrible crises," as the gossamer veil "separating this world and the next . . . blows aside." He appeared as a radiant angel, reassuring her that earthly pain "is not worth grieving about; it is not worth a sigh, it is not worth a tear."[26] It is not known why Henrietta's ghost, by contrast, came to Zoe only a few times, including in the last dream warning of imminent death.

Henrietta in widowhood joined her son Harry in central Kansas, homesteading with her daughter Pickett and sons Louis and Charles (known as Charlie)—another son, William, known as Willie, somehow ended up in Wisconsin. Zoe was sent to Daughters College in Harrodsburg, where her infant cries had not distracted her father from translating.

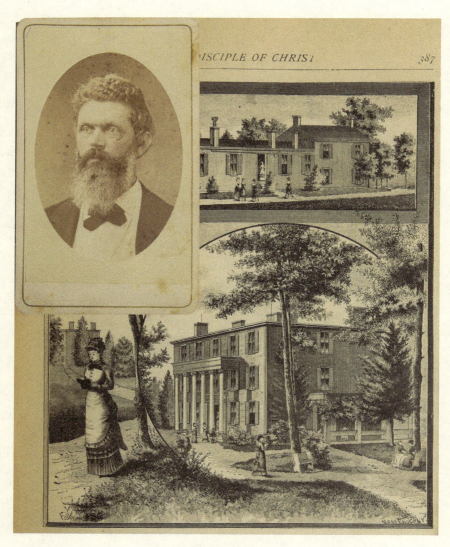

Fig. 6: Zoe's alma mater, Daughters College (1884 engraving from *Disciple of Christ* magazine); 1870s photo of the school's head, John Augustus Williams, by Zoe's half-brother, Clarence Anderson. AC, Nicole Neenan photo

# 2

# Mineralogy and Constitutional Law, 1874–1878

HARRODSBURG, "A LITTLE old dog kennel town," was one of three places where Zoe lived for any substantial length of time, along with Kansas and Manhattan. She based reams of writings on her hometown's gossipy provinciality, unhurriedness, hospitality, colonnaded mansions, bluegrass landscape (which she called "God's country"), natty raconteurs calling themselves colonels, Black servants, feudists, and vigilante mobs (and their victims). Wherever she wandered in adulthood, she met fellow Kentuckians who "never get quite weaned from home."[1]

Founded in the 1770s by frontiersmen led by the hunter and explorer James Harrod, Harrodsburg is considered the first permanent settlement for American colonists west of the Appalachians. (Daniel Boone, among other explorers, sheltered in the region's caves.) During clashes with Native Americans, seized land became "dark and bloody ground"—both sides committed atrocities, including scalping. Fieldstone slabs, marking settlers' graves, slumber today in overgrown pastures. *The East Side* sympathized with the battles' losing forces: "The natives of this country, the American Indians, we have driven into the sea."[2]

Many early white arrivals had, like the Andersons, roots in Tidewater Virginia, and brought enslaved people westward as they "braved dangers, cold, hunger and wild animals." Log cabins came as shocks compared to Virginia's "regal halls . . . where air and sunshine flowed." Among the town's famous early settlers was Rachel Donelson Robards; in the 1790s, while married to Lewis Robards, an abusive plantation owner, she fled to

Tennessee with the young lawyer Andrew Jackson. Zoe fictionalized the lovers first meeting when Jackson took shelter from a snowstorm at the Robards cabin. Illuminated by firelight and "curious, shining candlesticks of brass brought from Virginia," the future president and Rachel whisper to strategize the rescue of "a noble woman wedded to a clod." (Zoe published these words in 1898, upon rescuing herself from a suboptimal husband.)[3]

At the town outskirts, Shakers farmed on thousands of acres in a community called Pleasant Hill. Destitute non-Shakers sometimes took temporary vows for refuge in its dorms. Sunlight gave the buildings' scrubbed windowpanes "diamond-like brilliancy as if in mockery of the asceticism of these quaint people," as Zoe wrote in a story about an impoverished married couple spending miserable months at Pleasant Hill. The pair cannot bear celibacy and modest dress, so they flee by moonlight (as did a number of Pleasant Hill's real-life lovers). "We will starve together," the wife resolves, relievedly tossing away her bonnet, silhouetted on the gravel turnpike back to Harrodsburg.[4]

Teenage Zoe also saw the ruins of James Harrod's fort and early 19th-century resorts, where enslaved men had waited on tables and played ballroom music. A sprawling antebellum hotel complex was built atop medicinal mineral springs by Dr. Christopher Columbus Graham, a swashbuckling entrepreneur. He marketed Harrodsburg as "the Saratoga of the West," curing everything from rheumatism and neuralgia to "female weakness." Dr. Graham sent his most popular enslaved musicians to perform off-season around the region, and a trio of liveried teenagers seized the opportunity to escape by steamboat to Canada. (The doctor futilely pursued them and then sued the steamboat owner for his losses—not just the human beings, but also their instruments.) A magnesian spring courses through hotel acreage that, in 1856, was turned into Daughters College, one of several ambitious single-sex schools in the area (including ancestors of the University of Kentucky). Daughters College had stayed in session during the Civil War, "the sound of distant artillery sometimes mingled with the voices of the devoted teachers."[5]

Zoe remembered the school as "a magnificent college of rare stateliness, of Colonial build, of Doric columns much be-ivied, of sloping lawns richly carpeted with grass of a velvety green."[6] Room, board, and tuition cost $150 or more per year—at a time when all the worldly possessions of a local businessman might have been valued around $1,000. Zoe may have received a scholarship, in her father's honor, and lived with relatives nearby—day students received substantial discounts. (Hospitality was a regional norm, after all; when a Bronx farmer invited midcareer Zoe to join him for strawberries on his veranda, she remembered a Kentuckian "who went to a house to spend the day" and stayed 23 years.) Mattie's husband John Thompson may also have helped with Zoe's school fees; she fictionalized him visiting her in New York, complaining that after Henry's death he had supported "the whole posse" of Andersons, "a raft of tow-headed, big-eyed kids, knee high to ducks." (This Thompson avatar also financed burials, divorces, and clothing for the flock.) Was Zoe considered so intellectually promising that she deserved the luxury of private schooling? Jessie and Pickett had some brief formal training in art, but no records have surfaced of higher education for any other Anderson siblings.[7]

Harrodsburg was prosperous as well as heavily intermarried. Zoe's brother Clarence's Spilman in-laws worked in medicine and photography. Jessie's photographer husband Archibald Rue was an Anderson and Spilman business partner. Nannie married Samuel Creed Cardwell, whose family was involved in Harrodsburg politics and publishing and ran the opera house. Mattie and John Thompson's Greek Revival brick mansion from the early 1800s, called Clay Hill, overlooked Daughters College. Zoe stitched her girlhood dresses with Mattie's help: "We used to sit upstairs together in her beautiful old Colonial home in a wide airy sunny room and sew." Like many antebellum Harrodsburg landmarks, Clay Hill contains elaborate woodwork carved by the cabinetmaker Matthew Lowrey (the father of Zoe's future mother-in-law, Mariah Meaux Lowrey, see Chapter 3).[8]

Harrodsburg's Protestant congregations, including descendants of Henry's Disciples, built impressive masonry churches. Anderson relatives' day trips, vacations, business dealings, parties, weddings, illnesses, injuries, and funerals made local headlines. Hard feelings subsided among men who had shot at each other in wartime. Dr. Graham's resort was converted into an asylum for aged and invalid soldiers and then abandoned—Zoe described the grounds as "weird with horrors." Her brother Clarence advertised his drugstore and photography studio in a newspaper, *The Kentucky People*, run by Henry's brother John's daughter, Florence Anderson Clark (who also published fiction and poetry), and her Harvard-educated husband James B. Clark—a Confederate veteran and lawyer who worked with the Thompsons. The lawyer and politician Philip B. Thompson Jr., known as Phil, the twin brother of Mattie's husband John, was pardoned for his Confederate service by President Andrew Johnson. Phil served as a Democratic congressman in Washington, boasting about his Confederate adventures and helping Zoe's brother-in-law Archibald Rue maximize his Federal military pension. Zoe fictionalized an aged, deafened, pensioned Federal veteran of an 1862 battle at Perryville, about 10 miles from Harrodsburg, in which 8,500 men were mowed down in a matter of hours. He repeats his confusing war stories, "overflowing with ardor," without mentioning that his brother had served with the Confederacy.[9]

Daughters College's founder John Williams became a father figure for Zoe. In 1903, at his deathbed, he and his late wife Mary came as haloed ghosts to her Manhattan bedside, "their fine white heads of hair just tinged with the left-over gold of their youth." Zoe was pleased to sense that "all was well" in the afterworld with her youthful protectors. John's ghost was sighted outside his Harrodsburg home, too, which made sense to Zoe in New York: "a man of such strength of character, such beauty of nature, can do as he pleases."[10]

The Williamses marketed the school as homelike, "rather than a boarding house." Their three daughters had died as children, and they treated students as "adopted members of our family." Instead of imposing uncomfortable uniforms, they required "a neat plain style of dress" made of green wool, "pink lawn, gingham or calico." No unchaperoned shopping trips in town, no "contraband" packages of sweets from home, no pocket money, no bribing servants for extra work, no "*superfluous* jewelry" were allowed, so girls could focus on achievement rather than their appearance and inheritances.[11]

Among the school's servants was a couple, Abram and Lucy Williams, who had been enslaved by John Williams' family and neighbors. John, as a teenage plantation slaveowner, had snuck away in the evenings and taught Abram to read, using the New Testament as a textbook. Abram Williams was inspired to evangelize to other enslaved people, and after the war he worked as a minister, preaching at congregations in Kentucky and Chicago.[12] Many local laborers similarly came from formerly enslaved families who adopted the enslavers' surnames after the war. Zoe fictionalized—and of course idealized—the postbellum ties. Her last novel, *The Way of the Wind*, opens with the newlywed Celia Lawson leaving Harrodsburg for the Kansas frontier after tearfully embracing her childhood "mammy," who offers blessings "musical with tenderness."

Zoe's high-school classmates were mostly Kentuckians, some daughters of alumnae. The faculty, from as far away as New York and New England, taught subjects as varied as Zoe's future writing topics: zoology, philosophy, theology, art criticism, and constitutional law. Ancient languages were optional—did the Williamses reminisce with Zoe about Henry's polyglotism, her infant time in the tearoom? The school "kept progress with the age" by offering pragmatic electives such as telegraphy, taxidermy, and bookkeeping—did Zoe apply the latter to her one-woman magazine company? A department trained teachers; John Williams deemed that a woman's "*natural vocation.*" Classrooms were equipped with mineralogical and botanical specimens as well as mastodon bones found on Shaker farmland.

Parents were asked to provide "a full supply of good shoes," so the girls could explore "in the fields and forests," observing "the strange fossil, the painted beetle, and the new song bird." They visited engineering marvels as well. A new four-mile rail line, connected to interstate trunklines, was speeding up transport of Harrodsburg's products such as Old Jordan whiskey made by Zoe's brother-in-law John Thompson (a teetotaler himself). Shipping by turnpike in the region was hindered by old-fashioned tollgates with live-in toll-keepers. Daughters College students were escorted on the rail line's 1877 maiden passenger voyage by Mary E. Whittington, a teacher whose specialties included taxidermy. When a worldly teenager from Lexington, Kentucky, ridiculed a younger classmate who "confessed never to have been on a railway train," Mary Whittington retorted that the younger student's geometry prowess "is more honor than to have traveled on railroads." The line, fondly known as the "Great South Western" or "Little Dinky" or "Jerk Water," could handle a few cars at a time—lengthy circus trains required shift after shift to unload.[13] *Wind*'s hero Seth Lawson, as he slinks back to Harrodsburg on foot from his failed Kansas farm, passes through a tollgate run by a woman (her husband prefers smoking his pipe on the porch) and then finds backbreaking work hauling baggage for the Great South Western.

Daughters College students crossed the Kentucky River via High Bridge and Brooklyn Bridge, newly laid between forested palisades. High Bridge's stone bases were built according to plans from New York's Brooklyn Bridge designer John Roebling. Did adult Zoe know about these hometown connections as she traversed "bridges like great opal necklaces" spanning the East River? She considered the Kentucky River's banks the "most beautiful spot in the Universe, the Blue Danube of America," but she kept catching poison ivy while picnicking there (yet another reason she felt most at home in Manhattan).[14]

The teachers banned the "sham or cram" of memorizing and regurgitating in "the *rote* or *parrot system*" and encouraged students "to think for themselves on all subjects," developing sound judgment, taste, "confidence and power." To maintain work-life balance and "invigorated constitutions," the school mandated daily exercise and forbade studying after 9 p.m. Saturday afternoons were reserved for "repairing wardrobes and writing letters." Loneliness, homesickness and restlessness nonetheless were widespread.

Zoe sometimes "slipped away from the class; and, out under some tree, wept and laughed" with her bonneted friends. Girls dressed in drag to perform mock weddings, and they used diamond rings to graffiti-etch their names into the college's windowpane glass.[15]

John Williams detested the era's typical public "exhibitions or parades" of learned girls, lest they start craving "the strong drink of the popular applause." Instead of becoming bejeweled, "purposeless butterflies," graduates should pursue charity work and emulate "the stars set high in the heavens—lustrous and beautiful . . . all unconscious of the world's gaze and admiration." In times of "sorrow, or disappointment or temptation," his protégées should remember the teachings of Jesus and the apostles, which would slake "your thirsty soul like sweet waters from the smitten rock."

Zoe prayed in her darkest times, and she urged *East Side* readers to follow suit, although she belonged to no church congregation in adulthood. She absorbed John Williams' lessons in truth-seeking and independent thinking—she wrote about pretensions and hypocrisies—but she had soft spots for roués and posers, and she audaciously covered up her own past. She detested vain, rich women, "in silk and velvets," yet prided herself on her youthfulness. As early as her teens, she sang in public, and her performance of a tune about starry skies led a Harrodsburg reporter to call little Miss Anderson "brighter than any star that shines."[16] From her 30s, Zoe was fascinated by female stage performers basking in "popular applause," and no amount of writing ever brought her quite enough "gaze and admiration."

John Williams repeated another warning that she ignored: do not leave your childhood home, do not marry, until you have developed enough workplace skills that you can support yourself and possibly your family "under every reverse of fortune"—if your male breadwinners or inheritances fail you:

> Dear girls, keep at home, be useful to others, be sensible and practicable—good and pure. And should you consent, at last, to leave your father's house to go to your own home, do not leave it—*do not go till you are able, **if necessary**, to support a husband!*[17]

*The East Side* urged employment on all women—"Work is your only Salvation"—yet contradictorily decried working women who neglected their children. Antebellum southern men, "the most immoral men in the Universe, barring a few million here in New York," had protected their inherently lazy wives from needing to earn money. But then in postwar desperation, the women ran boardinghouses, while their husbands whiled away time "sitting around on wiggly drygoods boxes." Zoe told *East Side* subscribers, "I never worked a lick in my life till I came to New York," where orders came from God: "Now root, little hog, or die."[18] Did she think her readers expected such untrue reminiscences—she had worked for years as an art teacher and then prolific writer before settling in Manhattan—from a Kentucky boarding-school belle?

On Sundays, chaperones brought Daughters College girls to church services in town, and would-be male suitors attended just to stare. Some young men descended on campus, "gloriously drunk and behaving very ungentlemanly."[19] Male relatives or friends could ask girls' parents for permission to visit. Otherwise, "calls from gentlemen, especially cousins" were forbidden—and in a region full of intertwined families, countless men could call the girls kin. How often did Zoe's relatives stop by? Did Henrietta ever make the trip from Kansas?

John Williams gave eulogies for some of Zoe's relatives. Deaths in the family during her student years included nieces and nephews and her sister Lucy Cheeks, who fatally hemorrhaged in childbirth. Family burial plots accumulated at Spring Hill, near a mass grave for Civil War dead. The sound of gunfights echoed around Harrodsburg, as generations of feuding white men went unpunished for murdering each other in broad daylight, justified since their honor had been insulted. The narrator of a dozen of Zoe's short stories, a garrulous Kentucky Colonel based on Phil Thompson, reminisces about feuds around Harrodsburg, "a pretty lively town in the shootin' line." The stories spell out his heavy local accent: "cote house" for courthouse, "cyahs" for cars, "theah" for there. He names native sons, "ahmed to the teeth," who notched their sticks to tally killings yet managed to die "a natchul death." This narrator based on a Thompson calls the Thompson twins "the very loveliest of charactahs" and "the mos' interestin' men," who had perfected their marksmanship while roaming with Confederate guerillas. The Colonel tells his anecdotes to a female writer who grew up in Harrodsburg. He teases her for being "mighty keerless" about remembering feuds, especially since she had witnessed one as a girl: "you was comin' down the main street . . . all scared to death, backin' up against the wall of a house. . . . It's a blessed wondah you didn't get shot." Manhattan gun violence and anarchists' bombings would help Zoe feel at home, reminding her of Kentucky feud outbreaks when everyone unarmed "dropped to the floor at the sound of firing, and lay there, face down, until it was over."[20]

Zoe may well have cowered along Main Street's walls in late November 1873, when a gunfight broke out during a trial at the courthouse. The

Thompsons and an enemy clan, the Daviess family, were among the litigants and witnesses in a debt dispute. As the day's proceedings wound down, someone fired first, which turned into a fusillade. Law officers and onlookers dove for cover. The violence spilled out into the street. The Thompsons suffered minor bullet injuries while mowing down two young Daviess brothers and their father. The Thompsons claimed that they had acted in "dire necessity" of self-defense, and lawmen agreed. But the Daviess tombstone near Zoe's grave in Harrodsburg calls the young men "martyrs to the assailed honor of their Father."[21]

Just before the shootout, Zoe's fictional Colonel recalls, there had been a "ca'm befo' the sto'm" on Main Street, with passing schoolchildren "laffin' and talkin'" and ice skaters twirling on a rink. Zoe and her future fiancé may have been out on the ice, as mass murder played out. Her courtship with Spencer William Norris began during her teens, when he became "her most handsome favorite skating partner."[22]

Fig. 7: Top: Zoe's first husband, Spencer Norris; below, their children Robert and Mary Clarence, known as Clarence. Wichita-Sedgwick County Historical Museum (Spencer), NDC (Robert and Clarence), Nicole Neenan photo

# 3

# Of the Best Families, 1878–1887

ON JUNE 11, 1878, Zoe broke a Daughters College cardinal rule. She married a few days after she "graduated with Honors!"—long before she could support a household, and "like an idiot," as she wrote in 1913. Her schoolmaster, John Williams, officiated for her and Spencer William Norris, whose nicknames over the years included Spenny, Spenney, Spenie, Spennie, Spinny, and Spinnie. The match seemed promising, with bride and groom "both of the best families."[1]

Spencer's version of their 19.5-year marriage is not recorded, but the archival trail and Zoe's recollections do not flatter him. As she bore two children in Harrodsburg and he worked in the hospitality trade, her relatives went through tragedies and scandals. What did he know about his own family's antebellum catastrophes? Did he commiserate with Zoe about witnessing wartime chaos, premature death and financial ruin? Was Spencer ever told that was not his name at birth?

By the time he was born in Missouri in 1856 as Weedon Spenny Norris, his father, William Walker Norris, a Virginia-born farmer and storekeeper who went by Walker, was on his fourth marriage. Walker had buried three previous wives and three children. The first two wives, Mary and Sarah Spenny, were daughters of Weedon Spenny, a widowed miller from Virginia. One of Mary and Walker's two sons lost in infancy had already been named Weedon. Sarah and Walker's daughter Mary, known as Mollie, long lived with her grandfather Weedon Spenny and more than a dozen enslaved people. (The human beings were "valued" at up to $1,000 each—

Mollie "inherited" them while not yet in her teens.) It is unclear whether Walker brought Mollie to live with him during his subsequent marriages.[2]

In 1854, Walker married for a fourth time, to Mariah Lowrey, a Harrodsburg-born teenager. (The couple had likely been introduced by family members of Walker's Kentuckian third wife, Fannie Morton, who was a Lowrey relative.) Mariah's cabinetmaker father, Matthew Lowrey, had died during her infancy. Mariah's mother, Martha Meaux Bush Lowrey McAfee, known as Patsy, was a granddaughter of John Meaux, a Kentucky farmer who knew Andrew Jackson. In the 1820s, during Jackson's presidential campaign, Meaux provided eyewitness testimony that in the 1790s, Rachel Robards had "sustained an unblemished character" when the future president rescued her from an abusive marriage. (Meaux also made headlines with his humanitarian will, which emancipated more than 60 enslaved people and granted them land, farming equipment, and cash. When his white heirs fought the will's provisions, the freed people took their case to court and won.[3])

In Boonville, in central Missouri, Walker farmed and co-owned a store, Norris & Keyser, offering clothing and housewares "at uniformly low prices." In 1857, he and Mariah had their second child, Sarah, known as Sallie—firstborn Spencer's only full sibling. Late that year, the headlines blared "Extensive Rascality" when Walker was revealed to have fraudulently borrowed tens of thousands of dollars and fallen into hopeless debt. He had obtained the loans with fake signatures on paperwork—he could imitate supposed lenders' handwriting "so as to deceive even the person whose name he forged." Among his victims were widows, orphans, and "wealthy and cautious capitalists," including his dead wives' relatives. He was not considered malicious or greedy, just desperate "to sustain both reputation and extravagance." His first father-in-law, Weedon Spenny, set off an "investigation and consequent exposure." Walker fled eastward and southward with lawmen in pursuit. He stopped running in Brownsville, Texas, and died there on October 3, 1858, during a yellow fever outbreak. He had "devoted himself to the care of the sick with untiring zeal" before succumbing to the disease.[4]

Walker's heirs spent years sorting out his estate quagmire in courtrooms. By 1860, Mariah was farming in western Missouri with little Spencer and Sallie, her brothers Matthew Jr. and James, and their mother Patsy, relying on labor from enslaved people. Mariah's sister Sarah Moberley and her husband Curtis also farmed in Missouri, aided by enslaved people. In the Norris court filings, there is a heartbreaking line from July 1860: Spencer's sister Sallie had died, so the toddler no longer needed to be included in the addressees for paperwork. By 1862, as war broke out, Mariah's sister Sarah and her son Willie had died of diphtheria—Sarah's obituarist wrote that death brought her "from the midst of the commotions of the time to that peaceful clime where rumors of wars are never heard." By 1864, Mariah's brother Matthew had joined his relatives in that peaceful clime. A sheriff auctioned some of Walker's remaining real estate for $2.50. By the 1870s, most of the family returned to Harrodsburg (Spencer's half-sister, Mollie, remained in Missouri).[5]

When was little Weedon Spenny Norris renamed Spencer? What did he know in Harrodsburg of his disgraced storekeeper father and all else that was lost to him in Missouri by the time he was a schoolboy: the infant siblings, aunt, uncle, cousin, farmlands and enslaved people? How did he feel as a fatherless only child in a small town where ancestry, "who your people were," mattered so much? Which townspeople whispered snidely or pityingly about his family? Did he first notice Zoe amid schoolgirls at a church service? He was working as a confectioner when he married—did Zoe, a scholar's daughter and star student, have forebodings of incompatibility?

Their son, Robert Grimes Norris, known as Rob, was born less than a year after the marriage. *The East Side* often observed that motherhood makes for indelible bonds: "nothing holds the note of Eternity so much as Maternity," whereas fathers could easily forget paternities. Zoe's matriarch neighbors on East 15th Street starved themselves to keep food on the table: "you never see an East Side mother flying the coop when the Stork comes along." But *The East Side* only hinted at how Zoe herself felt as a teenage mother, in a crowded household in a small town, longing for more genteel pursuits than changing diapers: "I'd rather maul rails than take care of a baby."[6] The growing Norris family lived in Harrodsburg with Spencer's mother, Mariah, and his grandmother, Patsy (much marital happiness in Zoe's fiction is undermined by such in-law arrangements). Mariah was a pillar of Harrodsburg's Presbyterian church, and Zoe left her father's Disciples to join the Norrises' congregation.

Zoe and Rob, apparently without Spencer, also spent months with her mother, Henrietta, and other Andersons homesteading in Kansas. The 1880 census lists Zoe and her baby living with the Andersons near Ellsworth, a bustling cow town in north-central Kansas. Henrietta's crowded household included not only her children Zoe, Louis, Pickett, and Charlie but also their brother Willie's widow Kate—it is unclear where and when he died—and Kate's toddler, Stella, and infant son, Willie Jr. (Stella would die in Pennsylvania just a few weeks after the census-taker counted her.)[7] Zoe's brother Harry and his wife Sarah homesteaded nearby and raised seven children, the firstborn named Henrietta. Immigrants from Ireland, Germany, Switzerland, Sweden, and, yes, Bohemia were among the neighbors. Land seized from Native Americans was free or cheap for anyone willing to make improvements. The Andersons added stables, fencing, and a fishpond—salmon spawn was imported from Maine to the prairie.[8]

The Andersons grew comfortable enough in Kansas to buy pianos, and Louis became a well-known musician and teacher in various boomtowns. By 1880 he styled himself "Prof. L. H. Anderson" and lived in one frontier town's Delmonico Restaurant (the New York eatery's name was often loftily borrowed in Kansas). Louis led "a first-class orchestra" and a choir, performing at fundraisers and dances. He retailed and repaired musical instruments that soothed children and filled homes with "mirth and friendship," according to his newspaper ads. He also helped the poor, for instance delivering food and money to a destitute widow and her sickly children.[9] (That is, he would have made an ideal Ragged Edger.)

Zoe often wrote about people battling to stay alive and sane on monotonous prairieland, where danger lurked "from horizon to horizon." At night, "little lonely lights in the windows" of the nearest homes glowed like distant galaxies. Zoe's Kansas characters fend off rattlesnakes and wolfpacks and are killed by cyclones and disease. Grasshoppers descend, "blackening the earth, eclipsing the sun," denuding plants and clotheslines. Sparks from passing trains, "out of pure fiendishness," set off wildfires that suffocate occupants of dugouts. Summer winds, with "a hissing sound as of flames," ruin corn crops. Pioneers' burial mounds are erased when subsequent property owners plow the fields. Seth, the protagonist of *Wind*, ends up too crippled by grief and poverty to keep homesteading, although he grows to love "the little wild things . . . in the prairie grasses"—he sees himself reflected in "the prairie dogs . . . sitting on their haunches at the doors of their little dugouts." His friend Cyclona rocks his sleepless infant, Charlie, as the wind "stormed tempestuously, fretfully; it raved, it grumbled, it groaned" and then faded with "little sad remorseful penitential sobs." Zoe spent enough nights in her family's wind-shaken frontier homes that it took her years in big cities to grow accustomed "to sleeping in a bed that didn't rock." Bad days at her Manhattan apartment left her shivering with memories of "the cold and unhappiness of those desert plains of Kansas."[10]

Her family in Kansas coped with human invaders as well. Her brother Harry, hardened by Civil War service, bragged about capturing and killing robbers on his property, part of which is still called Horsethief Canyon. He escaped conviction for assault after helping lead a gang who nearly lynched a neighboring immigrant farmer accused of stealing some pistols and ammunition. (Harry was overheard taking credit for the nonfatal crime, but he still talked his way out of a guilty verdict.) Among the celebrities patrolling Ellsworth's untamed outskirts was the lawman Bat Masterson, who became one of Zoe's *New York Times* interviewees when they both resettled in Manhattan. His gun was said to be notched with Wild West killings, but he preferred to be known for his frontier exploits as a "cowboy, buffalo hunter, ranger, ranchman, Indian scout . . . runner of gambling houses, of poolrooms, of boxing clubs, and vaudeville shows."[11]

By 1879, risk-taking had made Harry notorious statewide. He was elected to the Kansas state legislature, with a platform focused on helping farmers combat railways' freight tariffs, "to show the railroad companies that there is a mightier power than theirs in the land." He was ousted after a few months, deemed "unworthy to occupy seats in this House," after allegedly attempting to bribe colleagues for votes. He admitted to carrying fistfuls of cash around a Topeka hotel, supposedly gathering evidence of illegalities by opponents determined "to rule or ruin." He tried to live down the scandal with his prowess as an irrepressible raconteur, "one of the liveliest men in the west," decrying his enemies' "insinuations and fanaticism," remaining at the fringes of local politics and angling to serve as sheriff. He drank and gambled away much of his earnings from ranching and farming. In newspaper op-eds, the theologian's son defended his sins—unlike some hypocritical critics, "I deny nothing that I do." When his luck held, farmhands did his hard work: "he neither holds plow or drives and yet he thrives." In *The East Side*, Zoe gently chided an unnamed "eldest brother," who had broken the (fictional) centuries-long line of Anderson vicars tending the poor and "left the carrying on of the work to me."[12]

Soon after Harry's Topeka misdeeds forced him out of office, he paid a visit to Washington. "The fellow would do well to hide his face for the future," Kansas newspapers cautioned. He likely visited his sister Nettie, a government clerk who had married their sister Lucy's widower, Peter Cheeks, and was caring for the children, Eglina (known as Lena) and Charles Ewing Cheeks. Lucy had fatally hemorrhaged in 1877, seven days after giving birth to a girl who did not survive. Peter, who had contracted tuberculosis during Civil War service, was eking out a living in Washington with government posts and disability handouts. As his condition worsened, Nettie wrangled some breadwinning clerkships, with recommendations from politicians, including her father's congregant James Garfield and Mattie's brother-in-law, Phil Thompson. By 1881, the Cheekses' relationship had deteriorated in public. Nettie accused Peter of physical and emotional abuse—after a beating, "she bore the marks of his cruelty many days." He countered that she had undergone abortions, "a sin against God and man." He obtained custody of the children, despite his destitution and terminal illness, and brought them to northern California, likely for its healthful climate. He briefly worked there as a postmaster and as "Prof. P. C. Cheeks," distributing quack medicine guidebooks. Nettie, although never divorced, became so estranged from her Cheeks relatives that in 1894 she was surprised to learn that Peter had died, entitling her to his pension (which her nephew-turned-stepson Charles hoped to claim). "Communication between us had been interrupted," she euphemistically wrote to pension bureaucrats.

Zoe fictionalized Nettie's humiliations as a Kentuckian alone in Washington, freezing in a "dismal boarding-house," nothing but streetcar tickets and want ads in her purse, pleading for civil servant posts. Congressmen scorn her as a quarrelsome "government rat"; when she stops by a restaurant seeking their help, they dodge behind the curtains and bribe the waiter for silence. They accuse her of pretending to mourn her debilitated husband, whose ailments predated his wartime service anyway. One of Zoe's East 15th Street neighbors, a violent abuser married to his dead wife's sister, stirred up Zoe's "old and hideous memories" as she shouted at him to stop the nightly beatings. "I have often thought that I should come back and haunt a husband who had married my beautiful younger sister . . . A beaten woman suffers a thousand deaths in humiliation and despair."[13]

While the Cheeks family was being torn apart, Zoe's brothers Charlie and then Louis died. They share a grave marker, a sheared stone column, in a tiny cemetery near their homestead. Ellsworth obituarists called teenage Charlie "loved and respected by all who knew him" and Louis "one of the most generous hearted men we ever met." A familiar funeral hymn's lyrics were published with Charlie's obituary: "Go to thy rest in peace . . . For soon, with a celestial smile, / We meet to part no more." With Louis's obituary, an unbylined original poem described goodbye as "the saddest word," which "opens the future's door" and separates "the past from what's before." Its rhymed musings on fate and the afterlife are characteristic of Zoe's *East Side* poetry—might it be her first published writing?[14]

Between the deaths of Charlie and Louis, Zoe gave birth to a daughter, Mary Clarence, known as Clarence. By age 22, Zoe had finished her last recorded pregnancy and outlived six siblings among so many other relatives. "I must tell you of my family," she wrote in *The East Side*'s last issue. She was sure that Henrietta's ghost was warning of imminent death because of the terrible numerical pattern of the deaths of Lucy, Willie,

Charlie, and Louis, "always two years apart." The sequence had ominously restarted, the last *East Side* pointed out, with the loss of Mattie in 1909 and Nettie in 1911....

Zoe used the name Charlie for multiple boys in her fiction, including the Lawsons' son in *Wind*, who dies of disease and malnutrition in a dugout. Kansas farm widows in Zoe's stories, after losing young sons, can barely withstand prairie life alone. One fears the wind "will get into my brain and addle it."[15]

Henrietta Anderson, after outliving all of her sons except problematic Harry, sold the homestead. She moved to downtown Ellsworth with her youngest surviving child, Pickett, who tried to make a living as an artist and art teacher. Pickett took out newspaper ads for her classes, landscape paintings, and portraits "taken from life or photographs." She had polished her skills with help from her artist sister Jessie in Harrodsburg. (Of Jessie's six surviving children, a son, Insco, was named for her painting instructor in Cincinnati, J. Insco Williams, and a daughter was named Zoe.) Pickett studied at the Corcoran Gallery of Art in Washington as well—how did the family finance her travel and tuition? Pickett set up her easel in the Corcoran halls after earning her "copyists' card," by painting a landscape. With card in hand, she replicated an 1870s portrait of French Revolution assassin Charlotte Corday, imprisoned and stoically anticipating the guillotine.[16] Zoe fictionalized a Kentucky teenager studying at the Corcoran, trying to render Charlotte Corday's "pathetic wistfulness." The teenager commiserates with a classmate from rural Virginia, struggling to capture "purplish boughs laden with sun-flecked leaves" in an 1870s scene of cows fording a stream by James McDougal Hart (a painting that Zoe herself would copy in Wichita—see Chapter 4). The two Southern students fall in love, although the Virginian is only selling paintings to "some idiot of a tourist . . . I might as well be mauling rails."[17]

Ellsworth newspapermen lauded Pickett as "a first-class artist among us." But not enough potential portrait sitters had yet settled in the cow town, so she headed to the larger market of Topeka—her studio was near the hotel where Harry's bribes ended his statehouse career. Her venture was short-lived, despite Topekans' praise for her "unusual genius" in the application of "pleasing and harmonious" palettes.[18] Zoe's fictional female artists likewise flounder while supporting themselves. They inhale noxious paint fumes while applying floral motifs to porcelain vessels, and they cannot afford meals more nutritious than "flapjacks composed principally of leather." One painter heroine stays neatly dressed at her failing Kansas studio, lest her corpse end up treed by a cyclone "with a hole in her stocking." (Zoe often brought up being well-dressed in case of sudden death, even in her last *East Side* premonition.) Newspaper ads attract no clients for Zoe's artist heroines except philistines, dressed in purple, yellow and flaming red, "the fantastic fashion of western country-women," scarcely able to distinguish "a vanishing point from an antelope."[19]

Zoe, with two small children underfoot, somehow learned enough about art in Harrodsburg to paint "strikingly life-like" portraits of subjects including her mentor John Williams and the politician Grover Cleveland. Daughters College, where her high school chaperones were still on the faculty, hired her to teach drawing and painting. The student body had somewhat diversified, with Choctaw teenagers from what is now Oklahoma. Zoe's protégées created "beautiful plaques, panels and banners," displayed at venues including the Norrises' "brilliantly lighted" home. Zoe hosted parties for "fair ladies and gallant beaux," who indulged in waltzing "until the wee sma' hours."[20]

During her early married life, Harrodsburg's Confederate veterans kept getting away with murder over "affairs of honnah." In 1883, her in-law politician Phil Thompson became convinced that his wife Mollie had been seduced, while drunk, by a Harrodsburg grocer, Walter H. Davis, a young married father of two and longtime friend of the Andersons and the Thompsons. As Walter boarded a train at Harrodsburg, Phil felled him with a single shot to the head. Mollie insisted Walter was innocent: "I wish Phil had shot me instead." Jurors agreed with Phil's claim of justifiable homicide: Walter "ruined my household" and had to be punished, to protect "the virtue of our wives." His twin, John, testified that Mollie drove besotted "through the streets of Harrodsburg." After the murder, Phil was viewed as unelectable and left Congress.[21] Zoe remained friendly with her "beloved Kentucky Colonel"—did his storytelling skills outweigh his misogyny and homicidal temper?

Harrodsburg's outdated firefighting equipment could not keep pace with arson and accidental blazes, which destroyed buildings, including churches and a Thompson mansion. Whenever a fire broke out, "it never knows when to stop." Disheveled crowds shouted "fire!" and gathered helplessly, "the spread of flames lighting up myriads of frightened faces." In 1883, a fire badly damaged Spencer's store, which was topped in a huge bronze eagle salvaged from a hotel destroyed by a different fire. As he recovered from the blaze, he expanded his inventory from sweets to turkeys, watermelons, succotash, hammocks, cigars, fireworks, and shotguns. With a one-horsepower steam engine imported from Cincinnati, he offered freshly ground coffee and peanuts. His newspaper ads hyped "everything at bottom prices" available through "Norris! Norris!! Norris!!!" He also ran a restaurant, aggrandized into "Harrodsburg's Delmonico's," and catered parties with "oysters on the half shell—a rare dish in Harrodsburg" and canvasback ducks imported from the east.[22]

In June 1886, Spencer took a new high-profile job, managing a hotel at Cumberland Falls, a 65-foot cascade in southern Kentucky woodlands. The resort was recovering from reputational setbacks; there were reports that its plumbing system spread deadly diseases. Spencer brought along Zoe and the children, and relatives visited, including Zoe's sisters Mattie Thompson from Harrodsburg and Nannie Cardwell from Lexington. (Nannie and her husband Creed, a government revenue collector, who had two small children—their daughter was named Henrietta—were recovering from near disaster. After he became embroiled in a politician's failed presidential bid, Nannie was said to have attempted suicide "by the laudanum process."[23])

In Zoe's fiction, resort-goers ride in oxcarts for hours between Cumberland Falls and the nearest train station, jostled along "steep gullies that threatened every moment to dump them out." One of her male characters rows close to the falls in a wooden boat, falling in love with the nervous Harrodsburg belle aboard. As they are about to be sucked into "the current, swollen, rapid, dangerous, plunging madly," he embraces the damsel and rescues them both by grabbing some ropes close to shore. They are dragged to safety just as his "calmly regal" fiancée arrives at the riverbank and spots them. She returns his engagement ring with a knowing smile and wishes him well. He is stunned—"manlike, he never once doubted her love for him"—and regrets his choice of the sweet, vapid Harrodsburg girl.[24]

Spencer's job at the falls, for unknown reasons, ended after only a few weeks.[25] He was soon, like many Kentuckians, exploring opportunities in booming Wichita, Kansas. Among the thousands of new buildings there was a school where Zoe would exaggerate how much she knew about teaching art.

Fig. 8: Spencer Norris's Wichita store. Wichita-Sedgwick County Historical Museum

# 4

# To Nourish the Temperament, 1887–1893

ZOE MADE AN impression on Wichitans with her beauty, Kentuckian hospitality, and "many talents in music, art, literature and even in housekeeping."[1] While she gave art lessons, played piano, and shepherded her children to parties and recitals, Spencer marketed his grocery store's increasingly exotic fare. Newspaper reports and family reminiscences reveal how Zoe furnished her parlors, where her pets slept, and which of Spencer's products sold best. Her public persona apparently gave no hint of how much she chafed at marital chains.

*The Way of the Wind* quoted Wichita's 1880s boosters, who marketed it as "the Magic City, the Windy Wonder of the West, the Peerless Princess of the Plains." At the confluence of the Big and Little Arkansas Rivers, where Native Americans (including the Wichita tribe) had pitched tents, "Colleges and Palaces and Temples and Watch Factories" were mushrooming. *Wind* portrays its hero Seth Lawson as the area's earliest homesteader, convinced that "Wise Men from the East" will someday build on his desolate claim. He reassures his Kentuckian wife, Celia, that Native Americans consider it safe, "unvisited by cyclones." Seth devises the name "Wichita" for his anticipated wonderland, "after the old witch who had driven the winds from the forks of the rivers."

The city's name of course has no connection to the supernatural, and no single visionary's homestead was urbanized during the 1880s real estate boom. But Zoe's novel only slightly exaggerates "the mad whirl of speculation," as planned subdivisions "reached half way to Denver." The mixed-use developments were meant to be crisscrossed by streetcars and aglow in electric lights "that twinkled at eventide like big pale blinking fireflies." Cottonwood saplings, which "grew so magically, thrusting deep roots into the moist black soil," could help subdue prairie winds.

Seth, at the novel's end, commits suicide in Harrodsburg without knowing that his dreams have come true. His friend and heir, Cyclona, builds the mansion that Seth had envisioned at his claim, clad in pink stone and staffed by liveried valets, "maids, mantua-makers and milliners." The new millionairess, with an "excess of insanity," invests in gilded furniture and solid-gold doorknobs.

By the time the Norris family moved into a series of gingerbread-trimmed clapboard houses in the new subdivisions, it was clear that not enough Wise Men from the East would come to sustain all the colleges, churches, factories, banks and stores: "Fortunes were made in a day and lost before midnight." In one of Zoe's short stories, a delirious murderer on the lam is found dead in a "gaudily frescoed" empty mansion at Wichita's outskirts, built on spec, "rapidly going to ruin, the abode of owls and bats." Many real-life Kentuckian émigrés in Kansas gave up and went back to their hometowns, finding themselves "perfectly satisfied" or even "better pleased" with their old Kentucky homes.[2]

Spencer nonetheless optimistically started selling groceries and sundries from his "showy and most elegantly appointed" storefront on Main Street. His crates and stacks of sweets, nuts and a "tropical fruit paradise" spilled out onto the sidewalk. (A previous tenant in his Main Street space was a pawnbroker, useful in a town where finances were in flux.) Spencer splurged for a gleaming soda fountain, "a fancy, but formidable contraption" temptingly visible just inside his shop window. The taps bore a kaleidoscope of labels: "vanilla, lemon, orange, nectar, sarsaparilla." In a Magic City flaunting its sophistication, hardly anyone ever ordered plain seltzer; that tap remained "in perpetual disuse and in perpetual readiness." Patrons noticed Spencer's "rare manly beauty" at the cash register and ranked him among Wichita's "handsomest men." He came across to customers as "florid, bustling, clean and pleasant." But in private, he was miserly. His underpaid employees, some of them from Kentucky, sometimes lived with the Norrises or overnighted at the store. They further scrimped by dining on his inventory's "cast-off fruit and candy."

Spencer financed Zoe's basic household expenses, including for a carriage and a cook's wages. But he allotted her no other spending money. At some point, he started sharing the store profits with his mistresses. *The East Side* described Zoe's friend, suspiciously similar to Zoe, whose adulterous husband only financed "a home, servants, a dog-cart and pony, bills at the shop, this for show . . . She had to go among friends absolutely penniless. . . . he was giving his money to other women."[3]

Kansas and Kentucky newspapers announced that Zoe had been hired as an art teacher at Wichita's Lewis Academy, a Presbyterian school in a brick Romanesque building with creamy stone accents. (That architectural mode was adapted citywide, especially for schools including Garfield University, named after the slain president who had fled Henry Anderson's sermons.) Established "to honor Christ through a sanctified education," the academy channeled many graduates into ministry and missionary careers. It advertised Zoe as "an accomplished scenic and portrait painter" with an "attractive personal presence," who had earned "flattering credentials" in Washington, D.C. (Zoe indeed may have absorbed lessons from her sister Pickett's studies at the Corcoran Gallery.) She was said to have expertise in "freehand and mechanical drawing, drawing from life, from casts, from flat surface, crayoning, landscape and portrait painting, decorative work upon China, pottery, satin or velvet." Listing herself as an artist in Wichita directories, she painted portraits and copied the Corcoran's dappled cattle tableau by James McDougal Hart. In a portrait of a Lewis Academy student named Maude English (a real estate tycoon's daughter), Zoe "ignored the conventional" by giving "an intimation of perspective" that the *Eagle* deemed "hard to describe"—was she showing maverick tendencies already, or did she not know that much about perspective? She inspired conscientious, "creditable progress" among her students, who included her daughter Clarence; Victor Murdock, a member of the *Eagle*'s founding family; and Joseph Lemon, an artist whose writer mother, Margaret, would foster Zoe's career and whose brother Courtenay would nearly ruin Zoe (see Chapter 11).[4]

Zoe spent three semesters on the academy faculty, which she fictionalized in a 1902 short story, "After Long Years," about a former art teacher, Gabrielle, reuniting with a student named Courtney Griswold. (Did Zoe pick that name to taunt Courtenay Lemon, her nemesis by 1902?) Gabrielle had reluctantly withdrawn from studies at an art school in Washington, "the most beautiful of cities," to follow an unnamed, unfaithful fiancé to an unnamed "little western town all plank walks and windstorms and dust and cyclones." She found work at a strict religious academy that expelled students for drinking beer or playing cards. In Gabrielle and Courtney's "rollicking old days" in the classroom, her spiky curly hairdo (which was Zoe's actual Wichita coiffure) had discouraged him from kissing her. She had pretended to understand mechanical drawing, although she had barely heard of the subject before she was hired. Her conscience still twinges at this audacious bluff "perpetrated upon an unsuspecting public"—that is, Lewis Academy may have been the first place where Zoe worked in disguise and took notes on the experience. Courtney long ago secretly fell in love with his teacher Gabrielle, forgiving her for assigning problems "impossible to solve" and then standing over the desks "trying hard to look wise!" After Courtney left the school, she had broken off her engagement, unable to mold her fiancé into "my ideal man . . . knowing him all the time to be false."[5]

Zoe took long vacations in Kentucky with her children, but not Spencer. An 1888 news item (which she clearly planted) about her plans for summer weeks in Harrodsburg expressed hopes that "she may find the cooling shadows and velvet blue grass swards of her former home as delightful as they have seemed in imagination while away." Henrietta made trips from Kansas to Kentucky, too, and in 1888, Harry—gambling and mired in controversy as usual, "with his little three card monte (political) game"—escorted his mother to visit the Norrises in Wichita.[6] These were Henrietta's final travels. She would spend the rest of her life institutionalized. Her psychiatric symptoms must have been severe, or else surely one of her many children or stepchildren would have cared for her at home.

In Harrodsburg, a courtroom full of men declared Henrietta a lunatic "since her birth" (which made no sense, since she had run Henry's underfunded households and a Kansas homestead). Then a courtroom full of men in Lexington attributed her mental illness to a recent "spell of fever." Newspapers eventually falsely declared that she had "lost her mind" shortly after Henry's death. Zoe's sister Nannie Cardwell escorted the theologian's widow to the Eastern Kentucky Lunatic Asylum in Lexington. Founded in the 1820s, it was poorly maintained, fetid, overcrowded, and racially segregated. Inmates suffered from epilepsy, morphine addiction, gangrene, syphilis, senility, and Civil War wounds. The staff tried to suppress news of violence and suicides.[7]

Did any relatives visit the asylum? Did Zoe want her mother institutionalized? She wrote many times about her fear of degenerating into madness, with "a twist in my brain." *Wind*'s Seth Lawson dreads "the bewildered and weakened brain" torn from its pedestal, "the nothingness of the vacant eye." After his friend Cyclona suffers a breakdown, her pupils shrink to pinhead size, and she retreats to her pink downtown palace, considered too "gentle and mild" to be institutionalized. *The East Side* raged against sanitariums where greedy or inconvenienced spouses and heirs locked up "helpless and ill-treated" sane patients, "to become gradually insane through contact, or die of heartache and grief." Manhattan newspapers' reports of drunken asylum staff, "insane with cruelty," reminded Zoe of "like instances stored in the brain . . . a subject I hardly dare speak of." Was she referring to her mother's ordeals, or her own Manhattan hospital experiences (see Chapter 14), or both? *The East Side* prayed for the Lord to "keep us sane enough to roam at large to the last."[8]

Around the time that Henrietta was sent away, Zoe stopped teaching, for unknown reasons—had she been outed and ousted for her mechanical drawing ruse? She busied herself as a wife, mother, and hostess, decorating her home "with bamboo, wicker, satin pillows, lace curtains, paintings, portraits and family objects." Wichitans took note of "the fascinating pride of southern breeding" of this plump, soft-voiced, dark-eyed, "extraordinary beautiful woman." Spencer's business branched out into oysters from Virginia and "the finest olives in America." He invited customers to compare his store's pickles and condiments to memories of their "grandmother's gifts" on childhood pantry shelves. The Norrises pampered their pets: "Nip, a sleek, small Italian greyhound who had the privilege of the house"; Mable, a turkey; and "Toodles, the dearest little black and tan dog that ever breathed the breath of life." On a cold March day, after Toodles breathed her last, she was wrapped "in a blue silk baby blanket" and laid in an unmarked grave under a Kansas cherry tree. Long after leaving Wichita, Zoe thought of the faded fabric enfolding "the poor little shivery thing . . . without a slab or a flower or even a bit of upright board above her with her name."[9]

Zoe and Spencer, at first, socially cut a swath together in Wichita. Their home accommodated "merrie companie," staying up late and sharing "many a sparkling jest." They joined in the antics elsewhere of the Dew Drop Serenading Club and the Time Kil'n Club's dance hops. They befriended other former Kentuckians, including Will Lowe, a Harrodsburg native who went into Wichita's dicey real estate trade (see Chapter 6 for his role in the Norrises' divorce). *Wind* aggrandizes Will into one of the new millionaires, trading his dugout for a masonry palace and donning "raiment fashioned by hands Parisian." Zoe learned to bicycle with friends in "perilous places" and stitched costumes for her children's stage performances. Bewigged Rob played a rag doll, and Clarence danced around maypoles and dressed as Bo Peep in "orange and white silk with a girdle of gold."[10] (The little Norrises trod the same stage boards as the talented teenage singer Libbie Arnold, a future Ragged Edger.) The press noted the comings and goings of Norris relatives, as Spencer's mother Mariah visited Wichita—one of Zoe's fictional Southerners in Kansas longs for "the aid of an opiate" to survive a summer with her mother-in-law. In 1890, "An Artist's Marriage"[11] was among the headlines on Kentucky and Kansas reports on Pickett's wedding at beflowered Clay Hill, with John Williams as officiant. Pickett moved with her British-born groom Harry Timmins to Chicago, which Zoe added to her own travel roster.

Zoe's sister Nannie and brother-in-law Creed Cardwell visited the Norrises in 1891, when Creed had just been promoted in the government revenue ranks. A year later, he was felled by ambushers' buckshot in southern Tennessee; one headline read "Killed by Moonshiners."[12] His group of officers had been lured to a remote forest by an anonymous tip that barrels of untaxed brandy were buried there. The assassins emerged from behind a fallen tree. In widowhood, Nannie scrounged for civil servant jobs, like Nettie in Washington. Nannie raised her children Henrietta and Samuel Creed Jr. while working as a customs clerk in Louisville, occasionally fending off men vying for her post (see Chapter 14).[13] Zoe's writings are silent on Creed's assassination, although *The East Side* did excoriate male bureaucrats who resented and tormented female underlings.

Zoe's Wichita circle expanded, foreshadowing her multiethnic Ragged Edgers. She befriended the Levys, among the first Jewish immigrant businesspeople in Kansas's Sedgwick County—they assimilated to the point that one scion was named Sedgwick Levy. But Zoe could not gain a foothold with the "brightest and most cultivated ladies," members of Wichita's Hypatia Club. The group, founded in 1886, was named after a female scholar-martyr of ancient Alexandria.[14] It hosted talks on topics as varied as women's property rights, chrysanthemums, the history of philanthropy, and "Is the world growing better?" Many members were suffragists—in freewheeling frontier Kansas, women were already voting in municipal elections and even serving as mayors and police matrons. Temperance was another Hypatian cause; although the state was technically dry, Wichita only minimally enforced prohibition. Hypatia's leaders included the firebrand Populist orator Mary Elizabeth Lease; the writers Sallie Toler, Rea Woodman, and Margaret Lemon; and Dr. Nannie Stephens, one of the Peerless Princess's first female physicians—all of whom would figure in writings by or about Zoe.

Spencer's store drew newspapermen's attention as he caught a shoplifter pocketing nuts, installed an electric fan, and found an impressive eight-lobed strawberry. Yet the business kept grazing the guardrails of bankruptcy and was at times for sale through the sheriff's office. He still paid the household servants' wages, so Zoe could avoid everyday drudgery; if the cook did not arrive in the morning, Zoe would fetch her by pony cart.

To help "Nourish the Temperament in a small town," Zoe bowered her rooms with yellow roses for parties and served hot chocolate, "the latest thing in New York." She gave piano recitals, sometimes as fundraisers as Wichita's economy worsened. "Mrs. Norris is approaching the top of the ladder rapidly" in music, one critic noted. Clarence took up piano as well, playing with Wichita's Mozart Club, and Zoe painted on porcelain with Wichita's Ceramic Club. She served as the club's treasurer, her loftiest organizational title before her coronation as bohemia's Queen.[15]

In summer 1893, Zoe and fellow porcelain painters put on a show at the World's Columbian Exposition in Chicago. In the Kansas pavilion's gallery devoted to women's achievements, the ceramists "excited the attention of all the visitors" by packing a vitrine with "plaques, platters, plates, pictures, jardinieres, bonbons, bowls, cups and saucers." Displayed nearby were frontierswomen's folk-art feats: the phrase "Sun Flower State" fashioned from dried sunflowers, a giant Grecian urn woven from oats. Kentucky distillers hawked products in Chicago—waggish whiskey advertisements from Zoe's brother-in-law John Thompson announced that despite Old Jordan's ancient-sounding name, his machinery and formulas were cutting edge. James Harrod's 18th-century pioneers had never tasted Harrodsburg's medicinal Thompson brew nor "felt the inspiring influences of its glow—a sad and melancholy fact which entitles them to the sympathy of all." In August, Spencer joined his family at the fair, said to have disliked being alone and "experiencing bachelordom again."[16]

Zoe was dazzled by the Chicago exposition's electric lights, which "marvelously illumined palace after palace, upon beach and lagoon, until the whole gleamed fairylike." One of her fictional writers, while delirious, hospitalized and dying, remembers strolling the Chicago fairgrounds with a beloved, as an orchestra played Chopin's funeral march and tuberoses perfumed "green arbors covered with gourd vines." The story's heroine had prolifically contributed to magazines until her brain shattered—"It couldn't stand the pressure"—while her success had made her the subject of envy, alienated, "not often surrounded by sympathetic souls."[17]

Which is where Zoe ended up, a few months after returning from the fair.

Fig. 9: 1895 *Midland Monthly* author photo. AC, Nicole Neenan photo

# 5

# She Has a Halo, 1893–1895

WITH A PSEUDONYMOUS *Wichita Eagle* column intended to offend, Zoe introduced her firehose of prose about outcasts, overzealous reformers, snobbish cultural arbiters, and overoptimistic fiancées. And she verbally struck a pose, as a confident yet self-mocking provocateur.

Around 1893, she carved out space for a typewriter as she and Spencer settled into their last gingerbread-trimmed clapboard house, on a double lot in a subdivision near her former employer Lewis Academy and Spencer's store. The home had been moved there from somewhere else, probably a failed subdivision—it was floated on a river for part of the journey.[1]

Zoe's friend Margaret Lemon, an Illinois-born suffrage activist (who knew and admired Susan B. Anthony), had set a precedent with a weekly column in Wichita's *Journal*, "Woman's Tidings," which ran from 1888 to 1890 under the fairly generic byline "Mrs. M. Lemon." Like newspapers nationwide, the *Journal* and its advertisers increasingly targeted women readers as decision-making consumers.[2] "Woman's Tidings" reported on female professionals worldwide, for instance writers and editors in big cities "making a good living with their pencils," without neglecting their responsibilities as homemakers and charity volunteers. Women could outdo men in some fields, "Tidings" predicted: as architects and interior designers creating attractive kitchens that "lighten the humdrum . . . of dishwashing and potato peeling," or as skeptical jurors who could "see through a blackmailing scheme of a designing female." The column died when Margaret moved to New York with her husband William, a Federal veteran and jack-of-various-trades including hotelkeeping, and their sons Joseph and Courtenay. She reported back to the *Journal* from Manhattan about her experiences as a writer and clubwoman. At a Delmonico's dinner, she met P. T. Barnum, and her descriptions of faraway Kansas sent even the jaded showman into "a sort of wonderment." She marveled at apartment house clotheslines with "pullies and ropes" attached in tiers to telephone poles, and she contrasted urban millionaires' pampered dogs with tenement children "ill fed and shivering"[3]—the same topics that Zoe would cover from East 15th Street.

In late 1893, Zoe adopted the pseudonym "Nancy Yanks" for a weekly *Eagle* column—was she jokingly pretending to be a Yankee, or warning that she would be yanking at people's egos and heartstrings? Or was she cryptically referring to Nancy Hanks, Abraham Lincoln's mother, whose family had lived in the Harrodsburg area? (See Chapter 21 for Zoe's family's role in preserving the Lincolns' traces in Kentucky.) The *Eagle* promised that Yanks, "a society leader in Wichita, who attends all the pink teas and afternoon receptions, and hears herself abused on all sides," would "pour hot-shot" on foibles. Each column ended with short zingers—"Wichita needs a society for the punishment of people who turn and scowl when a baby cries in church"[4]—and notes on travels and parties enjoyed by "the four hundred of Wichita." (Gilded Age readers knew that 400 was the maximum headcount for elite Manhattan spots like Delmonico's and the Astors' ballrooms.) Zoe ran news of her friends, her children, and herself: "Mrs. S. W. Norris entertained at cards." At a Hypatia meeting, Nancy Yanks reported, a club member read Margaret Lemon's recent *Godey's* magazine article about a trip from New York to St. Augustine, at times sailing on rough seas akin to an "untamed beast, with her rampant paws unfolded in her fury." (That is, Margaret, in publishing a travelogue, was blazing yet another trail from New York that Zoe would follow.)[5]

Yanks mocked Wichita's "World of Swelldom" while chatting at her fireside with a sleepy cat, describing mediocre local musicians who "wrangle and fight and scratch" and enviously descend on any pretty competitor: "they tear her to shreds and throw the fragments to the four winds." An upwardly mobile young woman returned "brilliantly plumaged" but crestfallen from a fancy tea, snubbed by intellectual women whose glances "would have frozen a volcano." Yanks listed female literary lights—"Cleopatra, Juliet, Desdemona and Rosalind"—who would have made for better company. The columnist pleaded with eligible bachelors, "in the interest of humanity," to pursue homegrown brides rather than flock to "the dim farawayness of mystic splendor" exuded by haloed new arrivals, liable to bring along "a regiment of hungry relations." One young man told Yanks that, "owing to the financial stringency" of Wichita's post-boom economy, he could not afford to repair his ripped clothing—during the "almost heaven" of waltzing with belles, he was stabbed by pins ornamenting their gowns. Bartenders could not concentrate on formulating any "real scientific cocktail," since saloons were besieged by female temperance activists, "weeping and wailing. . . . Men hate to see women weep, though they keep right along doing a thousand things to make them weep." Yanks wondered if women brought on some of their marital problems by being desperate enough for marriage to wed alcoholics, whose sons inherited the vice.[6]

Yanks spied a fiancé dodging in and out of a downtown store, "stealing time that should have been spent with his betrothed." When the frantic young woman came seeking him, a clerk lied that the man had been nowhere sighted—after all, falsehoods "come easier to most men" than truths. The man's "dire and sinister" reasons for slinking around would likely be exposed someday: "nothing ever happens in this rustling, dashing, hurrying world of ours that somebody doesn't find it out." Was Zoe spying at Spencer's store, as he slunk around the gossipy town? Local husbands enjoyed "the gay, laughing, rollicking world," while their well-educated wives stuck by hearths and babies' cradles, expressing "unutterable longings" in lullabies, stitching "regrets, disappointments, sorrows and tears" into embroidery. Just as boys in Zoe's childhood classrooms ostracized smart girls, and ancient Alexandrian men dismembered Hypatia "because she dared to be learned," Kansas men were shredding the reputations of accomplished women. The orator Mary Lease was accused in "Base calumny!" of having affairs with male politicians on the campaign trail, all while she "dodged decayed eggs" tossed at the podiums by misogynistic enemies. Yanks theorized that would-be lovers would be put off anyway by Mary's "gaunt, spare, majestic figure," thin mouth and "small and piercing eyes."[7] (In 1904, Mary Lease, six feet tall and unflappable, became one of Zoe's New York *Sun* interviewees; by then, both women felt most at home in New York.[8])

Yanks reported on the joys of starting to write, too, with a tall tale of a depressed middle-aged wife who weeps so much that she is used to irrigate neighboring croplands. Whenever she starts to cheer up, locals fear drought and elicit fresh tears, reminding her "of the unhappiness of her having married the wrong man." The woman gathers strength to "have revenge on the world" by combing a dictionary for rhymes to use in poetry. When newspapers publish the results, "news being scarce," she becomes known as a "dreamy-eyed poetess with the blighted life." *Eagle* readers made "frightful accusations" that the Yanks pseudonym belonged to Mary Lease, or to a poetess—"Could anything be worse?"—from Kentucky. To try fending off the Kentuckian charges, the columnist claimed to pronounce at least some of her r's and "ing" word endings. She stereotyped her homeland's men, "too busy shooting or too lazy to work," apt to slay or be slain "in an affair of 'honnah,'" while their exhausted wives dreaded bullet-riddled corpses "brought home on a shutter."

After four months of weekly appearances, a last Yanks column lambasted "pious ladies," better off "at home taking care of the children." The prudes tried to discourage vice by tearing down posters depicting scantily clad ballerinas on horseback. But the damaged advertisements became all the more alluring for impressionable boys—"everything prohibited gains a twofold interest"—and for the writer herself: "show bills haunt me sleeping or awake . . . the first thing you know I shall be running away with a circus." An unfunny aphorism was buried in that last column's society news: "nearly every married woman has thought seriously of leaving her husband."[9]

One outraged reader suggested Yanks should consider that the community "may grow more cultured" with age and wondered, "have you ever had any acquaintance with the best men?" It is not recorded whether such humorlessness persuaded the *Eagle* to silence Yanks, and how Zoe felt about losing her stand-in. Wichita papers gave the Norrises friendly coverage for years thereafter, and the family socialized with the Murdocks, the *Eagle*'s owners. During Zoe's New York years, it was reported that she first "got herself disliked" by revealing which eminent Wichitans had previously lived in dugouts or worked as tailors. In 1910, *Eagle* contributor (and Hypatia pillar) Sallie Toler attended a Ragged Edge party and reminisced about Zoe's early writings that "cruelly caricatured" and alienated friends. But only in Zoe's obit did the *Eagle* officially unmask her as Yanks, whose "snappy gossip column" relieved the boredom of the provinces: "Wichita was too small a field for such an ambitious spirit."[10]

Zoe laid low for some post-Yanks months, painting violets on china and taking up mandolin. In late summer 1894, after ominously bloodying her nose when her carriage pony stumbled and threw her and Clarence into the street,[11] she visited Pickett in Chicago. On that trip, she would receive news of a fatal fire at her home.

While packing for the train journey back to Wichita, Zoe had sent an alert of her imminent return to the family washerwoman, Mary McEachran. The servant started putting the house "in apple pie order," airing out rugs and curtains on a backyard clothesline and melting paraffin for floor wax in a shallow pan on the gas stove. An explosion of "burning grease" set her aflame. She ran to an empty lot across the street, rolled in the grass, and collapsed. Firemen "tenderly carried" the victim back into the Norrises' house. She died the following day at her own home, surrounded by her husband, "an honest and industrious Scotchman" who worked for a coal company, and their small children. The *Eagle* found the bereaved living in "honest poverty," their rooms "destitute of any comfort," the kind of conditions that many Wichitans did not know were in their midst: "one-half of the world don't know how the other half lives." What did Zoe know then about the other half, who would become her Manhattan raison d'être?[12]

A day or so before the tragedy, she had recounted a nightmare to Pickett, of seeing Mary McEachran "stretched upon a cheap iron bedstead" in an uncarpeted room, bandaged and anesthetized into a stupor, her long hair splayed on the pillow and strangely unharmed despite gruesome mortal wounds elsewhere. When Zoe found out that the dream had been an accurate premonition, she was left "on the verge of nervous prostration." Well-meaning friends told of similar experiences, "until the whole world seemed on fire and filled with poor, screaming creatures fleeing from the flames." She never felt "another moment of happiness" in the clapboard house; it seemed accursed, "filled always with terrible visions of the burning woman." During her *East Side* interviews with families of the victims of the Triangle Shirtwaist Factory fire (see Chapter 18), Zoe remembered the 1894 nightmare in Chicago followed by "the horror in my own eyes at the sight of Mary" and guilt over "the tragedy of her death in my service."[13]

The blaze did not much visibly scar the Norrises' house. Zoe kept throwing themed parties, offering candy-making lessons, and her repertoire of motifs painted on porcelain expanded to arrow-wielding cupids. When she visited family in Kentucky, Spencer held a stag party (guests included his future betrayer, Will Lowe of Harrodsburg) with mandolin music for entertainment.[14] All the while, Zoe geared up to publish fiction about the destitute in national publications. How did a provincial housewife build up the nerve, dream up the plots and characters, and find the mailing lists to submit her work so widely?

Her first known outlet outside Wichita was *The Midland Monthly*, a short-lived, Iowa-based publication. It combined travelogues, historical essays, support for progressive causes including women's suffrage, and fiction about midwestern rural misery. A gilded cornstalk striped the cover of the issue with Zoe's story "Janet," illustrated with a photo of the author in a wicker chair. Janet, a sunburned Kansas cowgirl, is reduced to poverty as her father attends Populist rabblerousing sessions in town and neglects farm work. (Was Zoe remembering her own father's idealism?) The Populists rant "against noblemen, monopolists, money-holders, and swells in general," while Janet's family battles insect infestations, "the hopeless heat of the burning prairie," and cyclones reddening the skies with "lurid light" and setting off cattle stampedes. Janet roams her pastures with a beloved, an Englishman from Runnymede, a real-life, short-lived colony of British expats about 50 miles southwest of Wichita. (They were notorious for inflating their aristocratic titles and frittering away time on polo matches and steeplechase races.) Janet, who dreams of escaping to his homeland's breezy oak groves and "shadowy meadows," is killed in a cyclone while trying to protect him from a falling tree bough. Kansas newspapers praised Zoe's "pathetic tale of love, ending in a horrible tragedy," which accurately depicted Runnymede's ineffectual, "inexperienced and impractical people."[15]

In late 1895, she syndicated "The Sunshine Within," the first of many sentimental poems about accepting fate and maintaining optimism to ward off "bitter winds with wailing moans and sighs."[16] Wichita's *Mirror* ran "Two Waifs," the first of her stories about homeless people starving and freezing. Tatters and Jimmy, the title characters, wait for handouts during a yuletide banquet at a city mansion, "where long icicles hung from the eaves like fringes." Orchestra music and "savory odors" waft out as the boys drowse in a portico, ignored by departing guests carrying souvenir roses. Some angelic-seeming girls complain about party details: insufficiently waxed floorboards, outdated waltz tunes. When one girl estimates that the floral arrangements cost enough to feed "an army of the poor," Tatters mistakes her for a charitable soul and pleads: "we're freezin' ter death." But she sends her carriage driver to threaten the "horrid little beggar" with a whip. Tatters imagines "heart-shaped lumps of ice" within the girls' satin bodices, as the boys sink into a fatal "slumber of infinite peace." Money wasted on extravagances, witnessed by children abandoned to the elements—Zoe was laying *East Side* groundwork.[17]

Over the next two years, she broadened her writing repertoire with happier endings, characters of varied social strata, and ever more autobiography. Kansas reporters grumbled about her unflattering views of prairie life, and Wichitans snubbed her, as she prepared to leave the accursed house.

Fig. 10: 1897 *Home* magazine author photo. AA

# 6

# Norris vs. Norris, 1896–1898

ZOE QUICKENED HER pace of throwing parties and mailing out manuscripts as her marriage and Spencer's finances deteriorated. The couple buried their mothers, without much shared grief, yet maintained enough semblance of "a happy home" that their divorce caught Wichitans by surprise.

By 1896 Zoe was offending Wichitans without pseudonyms. At a coed banquet, newspapermen overheard her wondering why doctors stayed healthy despite late-night drinking, mince-pie meals, and fast carriage rides, yet "prescribe to their patients light suppers, early to bed and a drive behind a slow horse." She led weekly gatherings of her new club, Conversazione, Wichita's first association aimed at "the cultivation of refined and interesting conversation." Attendees prepared "humorous, moral, and ficticious stories" on topics "from X rays to the New Woman." When Conversazione called for atrocious puns on book titles, "Allover Twist" was a crowd favorite. One guest, costumed in a black flowing robe, unmasked himself as John F. von Herrlich, an Episcopalian priest (who would follow Zoe to Manhattan)—he had ennobled his working-class German immigrant family by adding a "von" a few years before arriving in Wichita. Conversazione members played ragtime on pianos and discussed Wichita's successful women writers, including Zoe.[1]

She contributed to a growing list of short-lived, general-interest monthlies, which combined culture, fashion, politics, sports, and travel articles with fiction, often in multipart series—a genre that Zoe never seems to have attempted. She fictionalized freelancers whose rejected manuscripts return "disfigured by file-punched holes" and editors' sarcastic regrets. One of her heroines, Sara Charleton (a name similar to charlatan that Zoe granted to several puffed-up characters), feels "ravishing vistas of unalloyed bliss" when a periodical called *The Frog Stool* runs her submission. The acceptance letter comes addressed to Dear Sir, "for contributors, you must know, have but one gender the world over."[2]

*The Symposium* in Northampton, Massachusetts, which lasted a few months, published Zoe's tale of an upwardly mobile frontierswoman in Kansas bragging about her untalented daughter and recalling dugout life: "I tell you these prairies is cruel, they've cost many a woman her life or her senses."[3] *The New Bohemian* in Cincinnati, which lasted less than a year despite congratulating itself for "instantaneous and phenomenal" success, ran Zoe's story of a young female mandolinist wandering a moonlit Kansas town while brokenheartedly in love with a young Catholic priest (the first of many handsome clerics in Zoe's writings). A mannish Hypatia harridan neglects her ailing baby while speechifying at clubhouses against "the Slightest Cruelty to Animals," in Zoe's story for *Boston Ideas*, a general interest weekly. (Some contributors paid to be published, to build their reputations for "conscious literary vigor.") The Daughters of the American Revolution in Washington, D.C., mocked themselves in their *American Monthly Magazine* with Zoe's "A Daughter of the Revolution." The story's narrator, craving a shiny membership scroll from the "so swell, so exclusive" DAR, sets out to document her militiamen ancestors. But she abandons the project after having a disturbing dream that her great-grandfather in Virginia had been a sniveling coward, the "creeping embodiment of fear," who was executed for deserting his Revolutionary regiment. His wife conceals his fate from their sleeping toddler, the narrator's future grandmother: "She shall never know, if I can help it." (No evidence has surfaced that Zoe's forebearers were wartime shirkers.)[4]

Newspapers noticed that Zoe, "a keen delineator of character," had begun "commanding literary fame in the east." But not all Kansans liked seeing themselves in her mirrors. She had little right to write about homesteaders, "being a Kentuckian and no pioneer woman," one critic griped—not realizing how much the wind had shaken her bedsteads at the frontier.[5]

In early 1897, Zoe called off a Conversazione meeting, slated to focus on writings about Kansas sunsets. She was left "almost prostrated" by the news that Henrietta had died of heart failure—during her asylum deathwatch, her spirit had paid a visit to Wichita. "My poor little mother stood by my bedside out there in Kansas the morning she died," Zoe told her daughter Clarence years later. The theologian's widow was "conscious of her approaching death" and anticipated her place in heaven. The obituaries reminded readers that Henry's New Testament translation remained popular "in theological institutes all over the country."[6]

Soon after Henrietta's death, Zoe took a month-long trip to, of all places, Texas. (She may have visited Spencer's niece Celeste Ewing, who was living in San Antonio—Celeste's mother was Spencer's half-sister Mollie, the only other surviving child of oft-married fraudster Walker Norris.)[7] Zoe explored the Texas seashore and rode trains through miles of prairies blanketed in wildflowers "sweet as sweet." The Gulf of Mexico was the largest body of water she had ever seen. Her 1902 novel's heroine Polly Locke fearfully arrives at Rockport's shores in dense mist, "stinging my face. And the boom, boom, boom of that old Gulf! I nearly died that night of the horrors." But then Polly has "the time of my life" traveling to nearby Mustang Island, where Zoe set her 1897 short story "A Starlit Sail," starring an ocean-loving woman "doomed to live in an inland city." The character is the only female passenger on a mailboat full of men playing poker and exchanging tales of fish catches. One young local on deck, "brimming over with life," entrances her by explaining the sunset scenery: "waves prismatically radiant," half-circles of seagulls aloft, "big-throated pelicans skimming close to the water." As he admires her worldliness and luminous beauty, "phosphorescent jets sparkled in the waves that oozed from the sides of the slowly moving boat." She longs to slough off her unnamed "other ties" and stay with him in Rockport, "near to nature . . . to go barefoot and dabble in the waves." He whispers lovingly to her in Spanish that she does not understand, and the two part regretfully when the sailboat reaches the wharf. They keep indelible memories of each other's voices, just as a seashell, "held close to the ear, brings back the moan of the ever-complaining sea."[8] How many other married American women in 1897 published such vivid descriptions of traveling unchaperoned and feeling requited desire for someone not their husband?

Zoe returned to her fraying other ties in Wichita in time to prepare for summer weeks with her mother-in-law, having just published caricatures of Spencer and Mariah. The heroine of *The Home Magazine*'s "Aliens from God's Country" is an unhappily married Kentuckian named Josephine, stuck in Wichita. (*Home*, founded in 1893 as a fundraiser for an upstate New York home for indigent traveling salesmen, published two dozen of Zoe's stories, although *The East Side* would savage its editor Arthur T. Vance—see Chapter 16.) Josephine's elderly Kentuckian friend and distant relative, Charles Montgomery, loses his fortune in Wichita's real estate bust and is starving and freezing, "on the ragged edge." At his deathbed in a shabby apartment, moneylenders "swarmed from every direction, their mouths watering for the feast." Josephine's insensitive husband Jack—"she had long since given up trying to make him understand her"—jeers that she should write a book about this stranger's straits since she cares so much: "Your imagination is certainly lively enough to furnish the material." Zoe's equally obnoxious avatar for Spencer was Mr. Leland, the title character in "Her Only Son," for the new Chicago-based magazine *Four O'Clock* (which lasted until 1902, offering "sincerity, beauty, ease, cleverness," and lavish illustrations hand-glued to its pages). Mrs. Leland, a Kansas housewife from the South married to a spoiled and cold only child, reluctantly tends a garden full of nasturtiums grown from seeds sent by his widowed mother in the South. The flowers take luxuriantly to "loamy Kansas soil." Visitors gush over them and cluelessly wonder why the Lelands do not invite the munificent mother-in-law—"How sweet she must be!"—to live with them. The younger Mrs. Leland, viewed as "a villain of the deepest dye," longs for "the aid of an opiate" to survive time with her mother-in-law. Scolding nasturtiums aloud has become her habit, "born of a life of loneliness," and she rips them out by the roots. They remind her how the jealous mother-in-law has poisoned a "beautiful rose-colored marriage," reducing it to "a dull, hideous drab."[9]

Mariah arrived at her only son's house in early June, 1897—did she read the magazine stories about her family? Days later she caught pneumonia. She rallied briefly and then fell into fatal decline. Zoe knelt by her deathbed around midnight (Spencer's whereabouts at that moment are unclear), wishing John von Herrlich had been there to pray with them, since Mariah was a devout Presbyterian. The following day, when the clergyman saw the Norrises' door creped in black, he stammered out that at midnight, he had dreamed of Zoe pleading at his bedside: "There is somebody dying. I wish you could be here." Mariah, while failing, asked for a burial under Kentucky bluegrass. Her body was sent by train to Harrodsburg. Spencer returned to his childhood home to inter his mother, "the saddest trip of his life."[10]

Zoe, instead of joining him in mourning, headed off for weeks of travel, with stops including Chicago and Colorado. And she published more fiction about disastrous betrothals and marriages, some escapable only through suicide. A violent abuser's wife drinks a fatal dose of painkiller. An upstanding young Kentuckian, entrapped into marriage by a blonde blackmailer, fires his revolver into his skull. A wealthy young Kansan's British fiancé from Runnymede is unmasked as a fake aristocrat—his gifts of diamond jewelry are "paste, paste, paste, like his English home, his title, himself!"[11]

Men mocked Zoe as she traveled unchaperoned, which inspired her first nationally known feat and travelogue. In a newspaper feature prophetically calling her Miss Zoe Anderson Norris, she was named "the first educated woman" to attempt the ascent of Pikes Peak on foot. (That title inaccurately left out, of course, countless Native American women climbers as well as white female hikers who had written about exploring Pikes Peak since the 1850s.) Zoe had been sewing and relaxing on a Manitou hotel's veranda when she overheard two male hikers dismiss her for bothering to visit with no plans to climb: "She's from the South and lazy." To prove them wrong, she set out to scale the peak, "or die." She traipsed for miles, tearing apart her thin silk footwear, fainting and recovering, as the foothills and plains "waved and settled" under clouds "nebulous and shining. I could see their silver lining—for once." One of her fictional heroines screams to her heart's content while scaling the Rockies, "waking the echoes" and burning off years of frustration. When Zoe "dropped down out of the clouds" by train back to the hotel, men crowded around her "in amazement and admiration." If any doubts remained about her journey above the silver-lined clouds, the slippers "silenced them—the shoes were literally in rags."[12]

During her absences, Spencer's ever wordier newspaper ads targeted "the best men" with Baltimore oysters, Colorado peaches ("Best on Earth"), and "the only pure Ice Cream ever made in Wichita." And he grew careless about concealing his extramarital activities. By early January 1898, Zoe and Harrodsburg-born Will Lowe had seen Spencer in flagrante with a blonde. The divorce was finalized on January 15, despite local burghers' last-ditch attempts to foster reconciliation between the grocer and "an unusually bright woman whose articles published in magazines have attracted a good deal of attention." Spencer did not show up in the courtroom. Reporters and gawkers did. Zoe, upon arrival, "took a chair in the back part of the room and rested her head on her hand, as if in deep trouble." Will Lowe testified that Spencer had admitted adultery. Zoe was deemed "the proper person" for custody of Clarence. (Rob, finishing high school and no longer a minor, could decide his own fate.) When the judge finalized the breakup of "what most people considered a happy home, a cloud seemed to pass from Mrs. Norris' face, and the sunshine spread over it like a summer day." Spectators came away with "no doubt . . . that she desired to be free."[13]

Living with an adulterer had felt like being "nailed to the Cross," she wrote in *The East Side*. She invited readers to "come look at the print of the nails" caused by cohabitation "with a man whom I knew to be false, whom I knew to be giving me the Judas kiss fresh from the red and tainted lips of the Other Woman." She realized that she had married a beast, when she was "too young to recognize horns and hoofs." Zoe's advice to any wives vulnerable (that is, in her view, all of them) to a "Judas kiss," which dishonors children as well: put your name on the house deed, so you can "grasp him by the collar of his coat and pitch him out. He will come shiveringly back on bitter days, promise to be good, and beg to be admitted, but throw him out again. Don't believe a word he says." Spencer was required to pay alimony and cover Zoe's legal fees. Her name was not on the Wichita deed. He signed over his mother Mariah's home in Harrodsburg to his ex-wife, who promptly sold the property.[14]

By late summer 1898 Spencer was bankrupt (see Chapter 7) and never sent Zoe money: "got alimony but didn't got it," she recalled in 1913. She stewed over the American government "failing to enforce" its court decree on his payments. One of her fictional writers marries badly as a teenager— "He bored me to extinction. I forgive him everything but that"—and receives none of the mandated child support: "I was all at once thrown to the wolves with this little girl. Well, I have fought the wolves and defeated them." *The East Side* warned female readers not to rely on alimony but instead pursue dependable trades such as plumbing, upholstering, dressmaking, or hod-carrying ("It's better to carry a hod than a husband"). Rather than live humiliatingly with a breadwinning adulterer again, Zoe would have taken on impossible chores: "I would carry armsful of fog from the roof; I would dust the twilight from the clouds and replace it with dusk; I would buy me a long light broom and sweep the rain from the skies on cloudy mornings."[15]

Wichita friends gave Clarence an inscribed spoon at her farewell party, as she and Zoe returned to their people in Kentucky. Rob found work in Wichita as an office boy for a railroad line, starting a lifelong career in train ticket sales. Deeply distressed by the divorce, he likely saw his mother only once more. By the time she founded *The East Side*, she did not know where he was living. Over the years she fictionalized a few rocky mother-son relationships, with incompatibilities and inadequate maternal warmth. Her journalism does not mention Rob. *Wind*'s Celia so despises the Kansas frontier that she abandons her infant Charlie there, barely misses him while back in Kentucky, and shows no emotion when informed of his death.

On Zoe's way eastward, she published one more potshot at Wichita's music scene, a story about two women attending a numbingly dull provincial recital, one whisperingly begging the other to "faint and let me carry you out." *Home* profiled her as "one of the most popular and most promising writers of western stories of the day." The editor Arthur Vance had asked her to find a literary friend to provide a fuller biography, but she had become literarily and literally friendless: "if there is anything good to be said of me I shall have to say it myself." Her career had already been a rollercoaster, and she was committed to the ride:

> I have wept over rejected manuscripts, and laughed, through tears sometimes, too, when others were accepted. I have been paid well for poor stories and nothing at all for good ones. I have been asked for stories and made enemies by refusing; indeed, I think I never made so many enemies in my life—many of them unconsciously—as I have done since I commenced to write. I have trembled at the approach of the postman, and spent all my pin money on stamps; and there are times when I have wondered whether it was all worth while. . . . But whether it is or it isn't, the fever is on me and I must keep it up. It is a kind of madness that gets into the brain and stays there. I have no will in the matter.

The same *Home* issue ran her lightweight tale of Gerald, a Kentuckian reluctantly spending New Year's Eve in dry Kansas, serving mint juleps to his young Kansan friend Lenon. Gerald pities Kansas teetotalers who "refuse to keep vanilla in their houses" and never experience juleps, which make fireplace coals "shine with brilliant promises for the future." Yet he hopes that Lenon, "a weak and foolish youth," would not start overindulging. Is Lenon a play on Lemon? Did Zoe already know about her teenage friend Courtenay's weakness for alcohol?[16]

By the time the New Year's story was in print, Zoe was preparing to join the Lemons in New York and discover slum life, while Clarence suffered deprivations worth writing about at boarding school.

Fig. 11: 1899 *Puritan* magazine illustration for Zoe's tale of a freelance writer's woes. AC, Nicole Neenan photo

# Beetles in Her Biscuits, 1898–1899

BLENDING INTO CROWDS in Manhattan, where newspapers paid little heed to anyone's whist parties or pony cart stumbles, suited Zoe immediately. She typed up observations of the metropolis and sent word westward that she was thriving. She received plaintive letters from Clarence at boarding school, and dire news of Spencer's finances.

With Margaret Lemon as her sponsor, Zoe joined the Woman's Press Club of New York. It was founded in 1889 by the British-born editor, writer and women's rights activist Jane Cunningham Croly—a "splendid pioneer woman," Zoe called her. The club welcomed authors along with artists, lawyers, doctors, teachers "and women who sympathize in these pursuits."[1] At hotels and Carnegie Hall, the club hosted lecturers as prominent as Mark Twain as well as classical musicians and lighthearted entertainers, including a woman whistler who imitated birdsong. Some club pillars shared Zoe's Southern roots, public unhappiness in love, and recent self-reinvention. Alice Chenoweth, a Virginia-born lecturer, writer and suffragist, had fled the Midwest with her married lover and then renamed herself Helen Hamilton Gardener. The Louisiana-born publishing tycoon Mrs. Frank Leslie gave herself that fake name based on her third husband's fake name and later elevated herself to the imaginary Baroness de Bazus.

While networking through the Press Club, Zoe placed more fiction in general-interest periodicals, as well as publications targeted at women or focused on music. She did not deign, however, to work in the lucrative genres of self-help, fashion, homemaking, gardening, or childrearing. Her love stories usually ended unhappily because the beloveds were abusive drunks, adulterers, or skinflints. "I'd starve before I'd ever ask you for another cent," one Kansas farmwife tells her prosperous husband, as her clothes and parlor curtains fall into tatters. A Kansas teenager's British émigré suitor is a pompous deadbeat, yet his blond head stays imprinted in her mind like "the dazzling loop of the incandescent upon the retina after the light is out." An icy widower, evocatively named Ashton, regrets mistreating his sensitive wife, Janie: "He had thought her discontented, dissatisfied, hysterical." He is (like Spencer the grocer) her intellectual inferior: "his family had not been so brilliant as hers and she had dared to say so." Janie's ghost, like Zoe exulting in her Manhattan freedom, basks in "love, satisfying, immortal, undying" in the afterlife, her miseries with Ashton amounting to "a small dark speck in the whiteness of the joy in which I now live." Did anyone show these magazines to Spencer?[2]

Zoe started setting stories in New York. At a "musty and shadowy" downtown bookstore, lovers reunite a year after a quarrel—he finds her diary for sale in the store's bins, recording her undying love for him, and she arrives seeking the journal, misplaced when her impoverished family broke up their library. Zoe, by that point, owned few heirlooms. Much of what she salvaged from Wichita was left behind in Kentucky: "when I decided to come to New York, my sisters, numbering me among the Lost, parted my raiment and knives and forks and plates and spoons." Comfortless boardinghouses in New York inspired her tale of a young artist from Kansas, hoping to make her fortune as "a full-fledged bachelor maid" (a euphemism that was replacing "old maid" and "spinster" in Zoe's time), barely able to afford her brownstone garret. The artist, foreshadowing *The East Side*, tries to fathom teeming New Yorkers, "each so full of his own troubles and worries and so indifferent to the troubles and worries of all the rest." The heroine recognizes some of herself in "those ragged little children who hunt in the ash-barrels for the leavings of apple-cores."[3]

Grim headlines influenced Zoe as well. As typhoid devastated Spanish-American War regiments in the tropics, and her nephews enlisted, she fictionalized a soldier's fiancée who ominously dreams of muddy waters and then glimpses her beloved in a movie-theater newsreel about the troops. He marches in formation onscreen, gaunt, exhausted, with "hollow eyes peering straight into hers in all the sadness of a last farewell," and she discovers that he was filmed just before his death. As lynch mobs committed atrocities on Black people dragged from prisons, Zoe set a brutally realistic *Home* story in a southern hamlet ironically named Acordia, where a Black boy is burned alive, falsely accused of murdering a little white girl gone missing. Acordia's white mob draws "conclusive evidence" of the terrified boy's guilt as he "contradicted himself over and over" under interrogation. When the girl reappears unharmed, her mother, who had lit the lynching pyre, collapses with guilt and grief.[4]

Zoe syndicated her work, bylined and unbylined, through publishing empires run by Major Orlando J. Smith, Samuel S. McClure, and Frank A. Munsey (whose company would keep running her fiction after her death). Smith and McClure came from Indiana farm backgrounds, and Munsey was a carpenter's son from Maine—like Zoe, self-reinventors from the provinces. Newspapers were supplied with ready-to-print, illustrated stories, on a variety of topics with some constraints: nothing too sensational, controversial, or depressing.[5]

She started syndicating collections of quotes, the first one focused on women's premonitions and telepathy. One interviewee had dreamed of her "unworthy husband" irritably adjusting his necktie in a room with lace curtains and oak furniture. When she told him about the dream, he blanched and fancied her "half a witch"—he had just left his mistress's home, with décor matching that description. It was "a good dream," empowering the wife to leave him, having stumbled upon his secret long concealed "through the mistaken kindness of friends." Zoe quoted herself about her 1894 nightmare in Chicago, foretelling the housekeeper Mary McEachran's death, and John von Herrlich's 1897 dream that he was needed at the deathbed of Spencer's mother Mariah. Zoe also quoted herself describing a string of "seemingly trivial" supernatural incidents in New York. She walked past a shoe store, thinking that her "little girl at boarding school," known as Sis, might need new shoes, then was startled to find evidence of telepathy at home. A letter from the girl had arrived: indeed, "her shoes were worn to tatters." (Zoe by then was telling new friends and readers that Clarence was her sister, known variously as Sis, Cis, Cissy, or "the girl.")[6]

Clarence's footwear was failing near Bardstown, Kentucky, at Nazareth Academy, a Catholic institution founded in the 1820s. It is unclear why she was not sent to Daughters College, since so many relatives lived in or near Harrodsburg. Nor is it known how the family, Protestants for centuries, reacted to the choice of Catholic school. Henry Anderson had raged against "Popery" and Catholics, "bound, body and soul, to their miserable superstition." Nazareth Academy promised steam-heated dorms and classrooms and nuns in "constant solicitude," offering "a thorough English and classical education" with strengths in "music, painting in oils, water colors, woodcarving," French, and Latin. Zoe's sister Nannie Cardwell's daughter Henrietta studied at the academy with Clarence, but despite a first cousin

Fig. 12: Zoe's daughter Clarence (right) at Nazareth Academy near Bardstown, KY. NDC

on campus, Clarence suffered "the shock of separation" from family. She arrived as "a slip of a girl," wearing long braids and short dresses (typical of girlhood in her time, when women's garments reached the ground), and then donned the academy's uniform of a bulky black gown and pale sunbonnet. Despite receiving an award for cleanliness, she found the school unclean as well as rigid: "Clarence was frightened when the Mother Superior came around at night and sprinkled holy water and then closed the curtains around her tiny bed. She pleaded with her mother to take her out of this bondage and wrote that there were beetles in her biscuits." Zoe's response from New York: "Never mind, I found a fly in my roll, here." Clarence, for years thereafter, suffered pangs of "boarding school hunger."[7]

A child's misery was Zoe's necessary sacrifice on the road to becoming "more than ordinarily successful," as *The Writer* described her. (The

Boston-based monthly, meant "to interest and help all literary workers," is one of her few outlets to survive into the 21st century.) Coming from "a long line of writers" in Virginia and Kentucky had not much eased her professional path, she told *The Writer*: "a literary career is bought by your very life blood . . . it has cost me so much—you would never believe how much." She defended outraging people with her truthfulness: "Nearly everything I write is taken from life. Strange enough things happen around you. It is hardly necessary to invent." One of her writer heroines deforms her thumb while typing autobiographical stories. She can barely afford the postage for her oft-rejected manuscripts, based on exhausting vigilance: "the real enjoyment of life is marred by being obliged to turn it into a story. Your every thought, sentiment, emotion, passes in review beneath a sort of microscope. . . . You pass your life in an eternal search for copy." A reliable suitor comes to this writer's rescue, promising "rest from her labors"—one of Zoe's few happy endings for authors in her romances. Another workaholic writer heroine, "actually rolling in wealth," barely sleeps: "I would work at night, only I am afraid of going blind." She befriends a magazine publisher, whose business is "pretty well on the ragged edge," and he storms out of her apartment, after enviously scorning her popular stories as "pessimistic, morbid, decadent."[8]

On July 4, 1898, six months after the Norrises divorced, Spencer made a milkshake at his store for an Irish American farm boy named Charles Driscoll, age 12. The boy's family had promised the icy treat as compensation for his weeks of labor "in the frying sun, planting, hoeing, and scratching out potatoes." (Driscoll would go on to study at Lewis Academy and have a distinguished writing career in the East, penning a syndicated column, "New York Day by Day.") The July 4th delicacy, served under the breeze of Spencer's electric fan, ended up stored in the boy's "rusty memory files," along with rumors about Zoe that swirled around Wichita in 1898. Spencer's hand-cranked machine jounced the boy's milkshake in a glass container "at a dazzling rate of speed. And the people pointed to Norris and said, 'His wife is a literary woman. . . . She has gone to New York and she is famous.'. . . There was a glamor about Zoe that lighted up that modest little refreshment parlor back in Wichita."[9]

Spencer's coffers were drained, despite his ads promising that his frozen drinks of "pure Jersey cream . . . will make you feel good for a long time." In late August, "Norris Fails, Considerable Litigation Is Likely to Follow" read the headline, as news spread to Kentucky that the sheriff had seized the store, sunk at least $4,000 into debt. Perishable inventory was sold off. Spencer disappeared for a few days, amid confusion over which creditors were entitled to his money and possessions—reminiscent of his father's absconding in the 1850s. Spencer deeded away the accursed house where Zoe threw parties, stitched her children's dance costumes, prayed at her mother-in-law's deathwatch, and mourned the housekeeper killed by paraffin aflame. While the store was mired in legal wrangling, the *Eagle* announced that oft-published Zoe in New York "expects to go to Europe this winter"—did she time that news item for when her ex was at risk of homelessness? A competing grocer hired him as a salesman, and his business was taken over by a former employee, Ray W. House, son of a Kentucky tollgate keeper, who marketed the confections on the shelves to boys seeking "a treat for your best girl."[10]

Zoe prepared for her only trip overseas, which would last nearly two years, while syndicating stories about farmwives stitching, ironing, gossiping, and commiserating over unhappy marriages and widowhoods. One widow encourages a younger counterpart to marry a knock-kneed, pigeon-toed, unambitious suitor—at worst he can serve as a scarecrow-protector, warding off lawyers and other unscrupulous "hawks on the lookout for widder women, waitin' to peck 'em to death." Zoe's folksy stories along these lines were syndicated for years, as the farm communities that she depicted were shrinking. She profited from her own unhappy homesteading memories, easily marketed to nostalgic editors and readers.[11]

For her first professional bridge-burning in New York, she excoriated male editors in a feature for *The Writer*. She described visiting the headquarters of an unnamed newspaper on Park Row—she gave details of the office layouts, so it would have been recognizable to the villains and their competitors. Her manuscript for "a timely and rather interesting article" had gone missing, and she tried to determine whether it had ever been published. Workers stonily bounced her from hall to hall. Hours of leafing through back issues left her as depleted as any modern-day web-surfer: "sheet after sheet unfolded itself before me in dazzling, many-colored pictures, flaring headlines, and unlimited columns," scrambling her brain "with the wildly variegated mass of matter." When she "timidly broached the subject of pay" for her unbylined newspaper work, editors were thunderstruck. As she recalled in *The East Side*, "I got in bad from the start. . . . it was the only way I knew of to earn money. Was that my fault?" Yet she prided in her stream of uncredited prose, particularly in the New York *Sun*, whose "Big Chief" welcomed her into "the happy family" of regular contributors: "the glory goes to the paper you love."[12]

In late January 1899, she gave her first and only talk for the Woman's Press Club, at a Carnegie Hall tea. *The New-York Tribune* listed her lecture title as "Fiction in the East and West," but according to the club's minutes, she spoke on "Friction in the East and West." How one wishes to know which title was a typo! Alas no transcript has surfaced of her "spicy and refreshing talk. . . . She showed the necessity of mental alertness and direct energy in the woman Journalist who would succeed."[13]

Around the time of the Carnegie Hall presentation, Zoe rescued Clarence from the Kentucky nuns. The teenager had metamorphosed into a poised, regal beauty, stared at by men. Zoe told Wichitans that she was horrified when Clarence reached New York, "calling me 'Mamma' right out loud, when I had told everybody that I was expecting my younger sister."[14] Was Clarence never warned to hide Zoe's age, or was the schoolgirl simply uncomfortable with deception? Zoe fictionalized a number of women whose engagements break up when pretty young relatives, "commencing to play with hearts," return from boarding school. Even aged men prefer "to hang around a girl that's jest about fryin size." One fictional suitor refuses to live with his beloved's schoolgirl daughter, and when the brokenhearted mother comes to hug her drowsy child, the girl mocks her parent's "silly spells" of suffocating emotionality, "always either laughing yourself to death or crying."[15] How did Clarence react to these unflattering avatars?

After less than a year in Manhattan, Zoe sailed with Clarence for Europe. As she recalled in 1913: "was doing so well concluded to go to England—like an idiot—thinking I could do better." The Woman's Press Club was instructed to send her mail to Margaret Lemon.[16] Zoe packed a steamer trunk with her remaining finery, which also fit Clarence.

THE COS-
MOPOLITAN
CROWD
WATCHING

A PROCES-
SION OF
SOLDIERS
FROM A
BRIDGE

# A WOMAN AT THE PARIS EXPOSITION

### AN IMPRESSIONISTIC SKETCH OF THE GLORIES AND SHORTCOMINGS OF THE WORLD'S GREATEST FAIR

## By Zoe Anderson Norris

*With Illustrations from Photographs by the Author*

THE Exposition Universelle, this great Exposition of 1900, is well placed. It occupies a central position and a beautiful one. Entered by the Place de la Concorde, splendid with statues and and gold domes, turrets, minarets and towers, on beyond the Tour Eiffel, and finishes with the electrical palace, an immense structure containing the exquisitely decorated Salle des Fêtes, where the inauguration was held at the Champ-de-Mars.

If you succeed in crossing the Place de la Concorde, an intricate network of cabs, voitures and omnibuses pouring out of the Champs Elysées and the Place de la Madeleine, and escape being torn to shreds by the ticket sellers, swarming like bees, outstretching imploring hands

Fig. 13: Zoe provided photos for her 1900 *Home* story about the Paris Exposition. Author's photo

# 8

# Champagne or Skyrockets, 1899–1900

ZOE AS A European nomad took notes on lustful or callous boardinghouse dwellers, moonlit scenery, and her travel companion Cis, for stories starring unencumbered, naïve American women voyagers, willing to try anything.

During the ocean crossing, seasick Zoe fainted in the washroom, "striking her head on the lavatory bowl. She lost a lot of blood." Or so Clarence told her daughter Mary decades later. Zoe fictionalized herself instead as a seaworthy caregiver in a *Home* story, "The Passing of Rebecca." The title character, an unattached Southerner, travels by ocean liner from New York to Europe with her unnamed teenage daughter, newly released from boarding school. The girl, formerly "a most unruly child," is at first agonizingly seasick and then, upon recovering, vows to serve as her mother's nurturer. (The girl calls herself the n-word, which appears in about a dozen of Zoe's works; she put it in the mouths of white Southern racists, and she used it to refer generally to menial laborers—including herself.) The oceangoing girl dons Rebecca's outfits, shoes, and jewelry, abandoning schoolgirl clothes and a plain handkerchief bearing her school room number "marked in indelible ink." On the ship's piano, she plays her mother's favorite pieces, "diamonds sparkling on her dimpled hands," drawing throngs of men. A handsome Englishman tells Rebecca, "Your sister plays well," then walks away at the reply: "She is my daughter." The mother's loneliness swells as passengers pair off in deck chairs, under lifeboat shadows "flinging themselves aslant across the deck." Rebecca finds herself "a faded likeness" of the teenager, "dimmed by the shadow of the sorrowful years lived in between."[1] How did Clarence react to her mother's published envy of her own child?

In London, Zoe and Clarence rented rooms in a boardinghouse near Russell Square and beelined for the nearby British Museum. Its library owned Henry Anderson's New Testament translation, "that precious work for which he labored so long." Zoe claimed that the museum also possessed many of her ancestors' "beautiful sermons," commissioned by kings. She dreamed of having her own writings on the shelves, "side by side with that of all those vicars." As discussed in Chapter 1, was she misinformed in her youth? Did she mistake some other Anderson theologians for her ancestors, as she reverently leafed through the museum's "great index book"? Or did she just invent a literary pedigree? (Copies of her *East Side* did at last join Henry's work on the library's shelves in 2008.) At London's National Gallery, a Renaissance altarpiece's angel, "peaceful with the patience of grief, yet radiant with hope," reminded her of Henry's comforting spirit in her dreams. Zoe spent mornings at her typewriter, "to scribble for a living" for American clients, updating Wichitans and thanking those "who were kind to me when I most needed kindness."[2]

She started covering celebrities for *The Criterion*, a lavishly illustrated literary weekly based in New York and run by women. (The owner, Grace L. Davidson, masculinized herself in print as G. L. Davidson, and she did not name her financial backer, St. Louis newspaper heiress Ellen McKee.) Zoe jostled crowds at the Adelphi Theatre as Sarah Bernhardt conveyed Hamlet's grief, with "frail little hands trembling against the darkness." The American actor Nat Goodwin told Zoe that he did not mind when his cowboy jokes fell flat among British playgoers; they brooded in "ominous stillness" while he and his third wife Maxine Elliott starred in a comedy about love and murder in a Colorado mining town. (*The East Side* would deem aging Sarah Bernhardt "supreme, preeminent and sufficient unto herself" and Nat Goodwin "a homely brute," whose by-then-ex-wife Maxine ran her own Manhattan theater, "beautiful as she is.") Hypocritical British authorities censored shows to protect Londoners' "chaste eye," yet the newly minted baronetess Lillie Langtry was admired in "deliriously shimmering" couture, starring in a risqué play about an aging woman jealous of her blossoming daughter. At Rudyard Kipling's retreat along the southern British coast, Zoe peered into his walled orchard, longing for a souvenir, even just a chicken feather or leaf, to induce "every symptom of a poetess."[3]

She fictionalized American women expats scraping by in rigid, depressing, gossipy British boardinghouses. One landlady posts signs everywhere forbidding practically anything fun: "Butter must not be eaten with meat or marmalade or cheese." Servants snub a young boarder whose money is running out, as she evades the clutches of a wealthy European cad, "burdened with ancestral vices." A dying chorus girl pleads for a doctor to be sent to her boardinghouse garret, piled with stage finery and publicity photos, "a strange mixture of splendor and poverty." But the other boarders stay downstairs, barely looking up from their whist game. Zoe observed that "too long habitation" in boardinghouses inured people to suffering, wringing out any "shreds of sympathy."[4]

On July 4, 1899, a coach passed Zoe's Russell Square boardinghouse, full of Americans shouting and blowing horns. Zoe explained to an inquiring Englishman that her countrymen were celebrating the anniversary of "the day we licked you," and he responded with red-faced paroxysms. (British newspapermen accused her of practicing "happy-go-lucky journalistic fiction" with that anecdote, since no Englishman nor "well-bred American lady" could possibly have interacted that way—the first of many times her verbatim quotes would be disputed.[5]) She received career advice from a Russell Square neighbor, "the Professor the Star Boarder." A former editor, of German ancestry, he ranked America among "primitive nations," its natives speaking "broken English." Any writer in London who had "the misfortune to be a woman" should try "painting barbed wire fences," he suggested, rather than expect editors to pay for bylined stories. British publications plagiarized Zoe's prose, and she slogged for miles in the rain to pin down the perpetrators and get paid. At office after office, flunkies and bosses posing as their own flunkies sent her away. She envied pigeons, easily finding crumbs, and imagined herself a streetsweeper, a shoestring peddler, "a vender of old clothes, a seller of rags." London's ubiquitous beggars were worse off, "grimy as the city itself, with its soot and its fog," and its slums were packed with "soiled children strung in rows, like small black pearls, hand in hand." The Professor, planting a seed for her *East Side* undercover work, envisioned Zoe begging on street corners: "hold out your hand . . . you are apt to get a few pennies dropped into it now and again."[6]

By late fall 1899, Zoe had given up on "the millions of thieving London Magazines" and headed off to Paris. She and Clarence were tempted to rent a room on the Left Bank, convenient for Zoe's planned studies of "poor out-at-the-elbows artists." An aspiring painter from Alabama offered the Norrises a sublet in her flat at the American Girls' Club, an 18th-century building adapted into a single-sex expat refuge. But tenants were not allowed to hire housekeepers, and extra fees were imposed for light and heat. Zoe dreaded further surcharges for wallpaper, cornices, "and the air we would breathe." She and Clarence moved into a pension run by Mademoiselle Jaunt, wizened at about age 60 and stingy with food portions: "the courses consist principally of plates." She feigned politeness, but her cold craftiness showed through, "like a cloven foot beneath a cloak." Mademoiselle intimidatingly told her renters that she had eaten rats to survive the Franco-Prussian War. Zoe rented a piano for her quarters and hung an American flag over the bed, "a great and beautiful stars and stripes"; while she was unmoored for years, "everything American grew so beloved." One of her fictional Americans in Paris develops an acute homesickness variant: "Newyorkitis."[7]

Zoe's American heroines at Mademoiselle's pension, prefiguring the Queen of Bohemia, like attention. One has never been "a good background . . . If I can't star, I retire." Another is "ready to do almost any ridiculous thing to make people laugh." Zoe's other recurring pension characters included Froken, a tall, gawky, Swedish stenographer, and some Scandinavian musicians, flirting in "abominable English." One "cheerful liar" from Norway tells all eligible women in residence, including Froken and stand-ins for Zoe and Clarence, that he loves only her. Paris merchants saddled Zoe with worthless coins. Cart drivers cursed her while swerving around her. If she accepted a Frenchman's free dinner but then "refused to go with him to his rooms," she ran the risk that he would have her arrested for alleged prostitution.[8]

Zoe struggled to master French: "the harder I studied the less I knew." She and Clarence sat through meals "dumb as oysters" (and on the Lower East Side, memories of that "awfully helpless" feeling helped her empathize with immigrants). When the Norrises bunglingly spoke French to the pension's maid, asking for fires in their hearth, they might instead receive "clean towels, or a bottle of ink, or a match." Mademoiselle rented a room to William Dodsworth, a young Milwaukeean working as an agent for American Express. He pretended to understand French dinner conversations, leaving the Norrises in stitches by interjecting deadpan non sequiturs in English: "And did the teacher send a note to his father?" Doddy, as Zoe called him, escorted the Norrises to tourist attractions. Zoe was surprised that museums charged no entry fees, and at every church with spectacular stained glass, she gladly put sous in a velvet pocketbook held agape by "the dearest little modest-faced nun." Zoe downed absinthe at Cabaret du Néant, a macabre-themed nightclub in Montmartre, where the light fixtures were made from bones and "waiters dressed as devils served the meal on coffins." Zoe saw Latin Quarter students, determined to "starve heroically in the cause of art," keeping warm by day in Louvre galleries, sleeping on park benches, "bravely keeping up appearances till the last."[9]

In Zoe's syndicated story set at an American reading room on Rue Scribe, a Kentuckian mother and her daughter named Cis (of course) meet a Harrodsburg-born exile, Will Thompson (of course). The three expats commiserate over longings for Black cooks' comfort food: "we never get quite weaned from home." He has fled his hometown after a "babble of lying tongues" had accused him of killing a friend in a feud over a belle's affections. Zoe's proxy tells him about Harrodsburg's modernizations, with tollgates abolished and "newfangled shops" revitalizing downtown streetscapes damaged by fires and nearly rivaling Parisian counterparts. He asks after the town's ice pond—does he mean the one where Spencer first wooed Zoe, as "her most handsome favorite skating partner"? News of new faucets on Harrodsburg's communal water pump so wounds him, "you might have supposed that pump to have been a personal friend."[10] Had travel in Europe made ambitious Harrodsburg look absurdly provincial to Zoe? Was she nonetheless homesick for her hometown, which she likely visited only once more?

Doddy returned to Mademoiselle's pension one day with a clean-shaven head. He had asked a barber for a haircut, "but then he did not know enough French to get him to stop." Zoe recounted the amusing story without his permission to a *Wichita Eagle* editor, who published it, and it spread virally to newspapers worldwide. Doddy found himself "the joke of Paris," and then she syndicated his furious reaction. He called her "a penny-a-liner," always taking notes, remorselessly profiting from "the private affairs of people." She begged forgiveness. She had never meant for the *Eagle* letter to be printed, and she earned "not a red cent" as it proliferated. He tearfully accepted her apology, although he did not believe what any writers said: "They mix their imagination up so with facts that they get so they can't tell the truth." She soon proceeded to fictionally kill him off, with a syndicated story about a New Yorker named Celeste Ewing (the name of Spencer's only niece), writing unanswered letters to her Paris-based beloved Doddy, unaware that he has died of typhoid.[11]

One night, after a stingy pension dinner, Zoe suddenly announced that she was headed by train alone to elsewhere in Europe. She would leave Clarence behind, "in the safe hands of Mademoiselle Jaunt." (The teenager's reaction to yet another family separation is not recorded.) One of Zoe's traveling narrators carries a "miniature of a girl I love" in her luggage and displays it in her temporary quarters. Zoe's heroines scrimp on the road, repairing old clothes, and one riskily accepts meals from a wealthy man, so that the hotel staff will not eye her askance as "a petty thief, perhaps, or a downright burglar." At a pension in Lausanne, overlooking sparkling lakes and Alps veiled in mists "volatile, subtle, ethereal," one of Zoe's avatars meets a Swiss embroideress, futilely awaiting the return of a tourist cad from Harrodsburg who has promised undying love. Zoe sent word to Rob in Wichita that she planned to climb Mont Blanc, its opalescent clouds "melting to nothingness," as well as "the Matterhorn and other European peaks." They did not seem "more difficult of ascent" than Pikes Peak, where she had shredded her slippers in 1897.[12] She roamed with a camera and became "a kodak fiend of the rankest description. . . . It is strange the hold a kodak gets on you." She hid expensive chemicals for developing and printing film under her bed, but a housemaid managed to break and spill a vial of dissolved gold.[13]

Zoe mastered the equipment enough to provide images for a *Home* feature on the 1900 Exposition Universelle (she would briefly return to photography in her *East Side* days). Studded with light bulbs and oldfangled "little gas lamps containing candles," it was noticeably less "marvelously illumined" than Chicago's 1893 spectacle. Sculptures, paintings, and tapestries in the Continental pavilions would leave any sensitive soul "paralyzed with a sense of your own insignificance." In the American pavilion, of "most excessive plainness," Zoe admired a portrait of President William McKinley signing the treaty ending the Spanish-American War, but she tired of stereotypical images of Native American men: "We rake him up on all occasions. We won't let him rest." American dignitaries appalled Parisians with extravagant parties, the décor simulating the Arctic or tropics. Multicourse meals were served on "gold plates of different patterns, so that you knew they couldn't have been just washed and put back." No one could say how much taxpayer money "went up in champagne or skyrockets." Zoe was still tempted to bribe her way into a fairgrounds audience with a prince from India, to show off her hand afterwards: "It has shaken the hand of a real Prince!" (Did her plan succeed or fail, and either way, did it inspire the Queen of Bohemia's princedoms?) The fair's performers, craftspeople, and chefs from around the world dressed in traditional garb. One of her fictional American expat writers sees the Swedish pavilion's craftswomen making lace, rugs, and tapestries, and she longs to trade her unpredictable freelance workdays for a life of needleworking, "some simple thing the immediate outcome of which it was possible to see." Outside a Turkish musicians' booth, the barker turned out to be a Kansas cowboy, a veteran of a failed Wild West show's European tour. He was living in a Paris garret, homesick and headed home: "There's no life worth talking about" east of Kansas, he told Zoe.[14]

Also strolling the fairgrounds was Harold William Morris, a Londoner in his 20s. Someone inflated his résumé as he won Clarence's heart.

Fig. 14: 1900 *Criterion* portrait of Zoe during her second trip to London, attending Clarence's wedding. Author's photo

# 9

# A Wealthy Silk Merchant, 1900–1901

FEW DETAILS ABOUT Harold William Morris, recorded in newspapers and Norris family lore, are verifiable today. After he married Clarence, Zoe headed off for months of solo travel and was shocked at the depths of poverty in southern Europe. When the marriage collapsed, her pregnant teenage daughter required an emergency rescue.

The *Eagle*'s wedding announcement—how much was Zoe's hype?— appeared ten days after the London ceremony on July 5, 1900. Zoe's son Rob just received the news. Clarence and Harold had begun "a casual acquaintance" at the Paris fair that "ripened into love." Wichitans had never forgotten pretty Clarence nor Zoe, who had been her daughter's Wichita costumer, a Hypatia member, "bright and ambitious . . . a caustic critic, a woman of many talents in music, art, literature and even in housekeeping." (Did that last phrase suggest Wichitans knew Zoe hated to cook and hired servants, even on Spencer's budget?) Clarence could have chosen from among "counts, lords and dukes" in Europe, since all knew "she would never return single." Harold, descended from "Spanish nobility," surpassed an aristocrat "from a practical standpoint"; he was the "chief heir" of a silk company, "one of the greatest merchants in London," distributing its textiles worldwide. Zoe and Spencer's families were both said to have owned "many slaves in the good old days of Dixie."[1]

Zoe and Spencer's ancestors did not in fact possess "many slaves" in old Dixie, but she was known in Wichita as a "caustic critic," particularly of Hypatia members. Nothing in archives or publications backs up any claims about Harold's Spanish ancestry and his family's conglomerate; he is not mentioned in the British press, which surely would have reported on the eligible multimillionaire and his American bride. The marriage certificate listed Zoe as a witness and gave Harold and Clarence's address as an unprepossessing London boardinghouse. His father was described as a deceased silk merchant, and hers as a deceased wholesale grocer. (Spencer was newly remarried to a young Methodist, Ruth Crook, and working as a grocery company's "genial traveling man.")[2]

Zoe used Clarence's wedding as a business opportunity, reporting for *The Criterion*. Americans were supporting the British in the Boer War, so London flowerbeds were planted in American flag patterns, and shops carried American flags and products "calculated to coax the least nimble of pence from your inside pocket." American theater productions "convulsed the audience with jokes they understood and a good many they didn't." At a pet cemetery in Hyde Park, Zoe studied the epitaphs, noting causes of death. The fate of a cat named Chinchilla: "Poisoned!" Zoe wondered if human neighbors annoyed by loud mewing "had done the deed," concealing toxins for Chinchilla in mouse corpses or bowls of milk. She remembered her dog Toodles, in an unmarked grave under a Kansas cherry tree, shrouded in a blue baby blanket "all faded by now."[3]

Clarence was likely already pregnant, and Harold already falling behind on boardinghouse rent, by the time Zoe headed back to Paris and started packing for months of sightseeing from Marseilles to Pompeii. She adapted the contents of her little black travel notebook for journalism and fiction, including her second novel, *The Quest of Polly Locke*. She did not conceal that she was mining every waking moment for publication. In her syndicated short story set on an English Channel ferry, a handsome Scotsman urges an American woman writer to try not taking notes—"always the story! Drop it and live"—as she admits to earning her bread "but not always the butter" by pounding her typewriter. Zoe's telepathic connection with Clarence, while they were "indefinitely separated," rivaled the era's wireless communication systems. On a lonely Friday afternoon, Zoe cried out her daughter's name twice, and Clarence's letter soon arrived from "across the seas"; she had heard her mother call her name twice at that exact moment. She wrote to Zoe, "I ran to the head of the stair, expecting every moment to see you come up to me." One of Zoe's fictional Paris pension residents cries out "Oh, sister, sister!" in longing for "a little girl I love," and then receives a letter confirming that the message was received.[4]

Polly Locke closely resembles Zoe: she is a brunette whose dark eyes "glowed moodily," she carries a little black notebook and a Kodak camera, descends from "generations of sturdy pioneers" (but the novel does not mention vicar forebearers), has grown up lonely in a deeply religious family, spent childhood years in Virginia, visited the dramatic Texas seacoast, mourns a long-dead tan-and-black dog named Toodles, and "wasted ten precious years of her life" in cyclonic Kansas. The novel opens with Polly informing fellow Paris pension residents that she is fleeing the decadent city's "nauseating atmosphere," in pursuit of "my ideal man." Mademoiselle and the Scandinavian bachelors sneeringly feign despair at Polly's plan to "go forth alone and unprotected out into the cold, cold world." The Scandinavians fall far short of her ideal beloved: "foremost, he must be the opposite exactly of what I have known. There must be no trickery in him. . . . yes, he must be truthful! It is this eternal deceit which goes more than any other thing to wreck the lives of women." Polly's other essentials include chastity, mercy, gentleness, "nobleness of heart and serenity."

She crosses the Continent feeling "irresponsibly reckless," like men from small towns "foot-loose in large cities." She sees Riviera peddler stands full of "fresh sardines that eyed her reproachfully." While leaning out of a railcar at the Mediterranean rim, she spots "her own two startled eyes reflected in the shallow liquid of the blue." She hikes to Vesuvius's molten edge and rows into a Capri grotto dripping with blue stalactites. She jostles Roman mourners at the tomb of assassinated King Umberto and escapes from murderously drunk sailors in Genoa. This lapsed Protestant kneels in prayer for God's protection in Catholic sanctuaries and fends off homesickness and loneliness: "she must brace up and be a man if she would travel alone." Polly/Zoe had become a New Yorker at heart, stretching her arms eastward at Mediterranean beaches, wishing "she might see across to the tall gray towers of her beautiful Manhattan, encircled by the sea."[5]

*Locke* was a crucial step toward *The East Side*'s focus on the poor. Beggars with devastating injuries and birth defects follow Polly. She wishes for enough pennies to fill all of their "wrinkled, shriveled, trembling, outstretched hands." She pities "my miserable sisters": little girls earning pennies by making coral beads, peasant women hauling carts and tottering under bundles on their heads. An elderly beggar's eyeless face "fixed itself upon her memory for all time." In Neapolitan slums, underfed families crowd into "cave-like rooms cut into the walls," yet keep "little lamps burning steadily to the Virgin." A Genoese senator grows fond of Polly, and she imagines marrying him and drafting and enforcing legislation: "First, she would do away with the beggars, or try." She envisions herself immortalized for charitable deeds as a statue "on a tall and stately column," although she sees few likenesses of real women atop pedestals on Italian piazzas.

Polly stops caring what anyone thinks of her outspokenness, which shocks both locals and expats and prefigures the unfiltered *East Side*. Polly learns to "kick and scream" when thronged by tour guides and carriage drivers demanding tips. After she asks a Monte Carlo casino worker how often unsuccessful gamblers blow their brains out, "she became known as the American who was waiting patiently to see somebody shoot himself at play." She sees no men in Italian churches' confession booths: "They know better than to give themselves away." She compares a landlady's attempt to shush her with Paul the Apostle's "command of silence laid upon women," a blow from which women are "only just now recovering." (*The East Side* would attribute apostolic misogyny to Biblical printers' typos.) At a Florentine palazzo, a Presbyterian pastor from America keeps contradicting Polly, and she excoriates him for bullying his parishioners, "bleatless lambs shorn of their fleece." He storms away, calling her a heathen and heretic, but later asks for her card so that they can stay in touch. A chivalrous German escorts her around Venice, and the shreds of her Christian faith stop her from spending the night with him at their otherwise empty hotel. Away from prying eyes, aware that no one else "in all the world" would know or care, she suppresses her "heart hunger" while hearing his footfalls just outside her hotel room door. (Some of the novel's reviewers would condemn Polly's behavior as "unspeakable," either for blaspheming or honestly expressing female desire.)

Plot spoiler: a young French tour guide named Leon, seemingly shapeable into an ideal man, covertly and loyally follows Polly throughout Italy. At the novel's end she resolves to bring him to New York and find ways "to support him as he should be supported." Zoe herself did not find any malleable foreigners worth importing. Nor did Clarence.

In November 1900, Zoe wrote to Rob from Venice, intimating that she would soon visit him. "If she does not the son will be greatly disappointed, as he is counting on this as his principal Christmas gift," according to a wistful *Eagle* item. Zoe intended to return alone, but Clarence "was so frightened and lonely she begged her mother to take her back to New York." Harold was devoting his evenings to his "noticeable vice of gambling," leaving his pregnant expat wife alone, and when his mother-in-law returned to London, he was six months in arrears on rent. The boardinghouse landlady "foamed at the mouth" and demanded Zoe's "handsome solitaire" diamond ring as payment for Harold's bill. "I am leaving you her husband," Zoe replied. A "star boarder" (that is, probably the landlady's lover) suggested a ruse instead: Zoe would pacify the landlady by handing her the ring, and he would give it back to Zoe that evening. But then he cunningly went into hiding. Mother and daughter were due to sail the following morning. At dawn, Zoe found a policeman on the foggy streets, who was somehow able to retrieve the ring. Harold was left "in pawn and that's the last I've seen of him," Zoe wrote in *The East Side*. She listed herself as "married" on the ship's paperwork, adding another official falsehood to her résumé, and she somehow distracted the shipping line's staff from noticing Clarence's advanced pregnancy. A pregnant American living abroad, married to an Englishman (and thereby likely losing her U.S. citizenship), risked being denied steamship passage or deported at Ellis Island, categorized as an "alien" who would burden the American economy with her baby—officially designated "LPC," short for "likely public charge."[6]

Zoe took notes on navigating back to the city where she felt most at home—and would scarcely leave again.

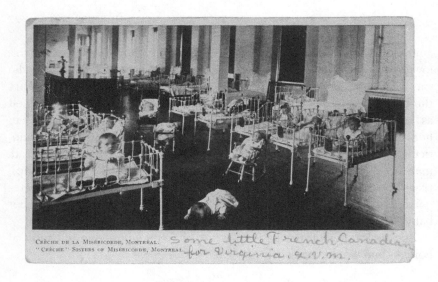

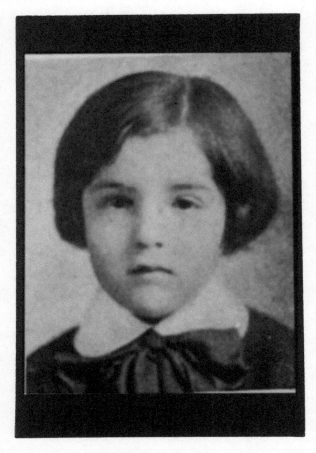

Fig. 15: Zoe's grandson Robert, born at a Manhattan charity hospital (and orphanage) for unwed mothers run by nuns; postcard from nuns' Montreal orphanage. AC, Nicole Neenan photo

## 10

## Sisters of Misery, 1901

WEEKS AFTER HAROLD Morris was left alone to face his London landlady, Clarence gave birth at a Manhattan charity hospital, where Zoe then set an entire novel. While accelerating on the literary speedway, she extended her subject matter to icemen, rabblerousers, and the Lemons.

Zoe and pregnant Clarence came home in January 1901 on the *Vaderland*, a Belgian-American steamer with rich Americans onboard—some had worked on the extravagant 1900 Paris exposition displays. About 180 immigrants, mainly from Italy, Russia, and Scandinavia, were in steerage. Zoe fictionalized Atlantic crossings through "the biting teeth of storms of hail, of snow, of sleet"; when U.S. lighthouses come into view, homesick passengers brave winds on the foredeck, "wet eyes fastened on the flicker of the lights." One of her heroines, Molly Seawell (a pun on oceangoing, or powers of observation, or in homage to the Virginia-born writer Molly Elliot Seawell?), descends belowdecks during an ocean voyage, curious about the men who stoke the ship's furnaces. She is startled to see them blackened with soot, exhausted, dressed in rags, desperate for beer and coins. One is a college student, earning his passage back to a sweetheart, and Molly comforts him as he dies, "burned out with the heat of the furnace." He is buried at sea, with only seagulls marking his grave.[1]

According to 1901 newspaper reports, Zoe and Clarence checked into the Waldorf-Astoria hotel to await the baby. Zoe was at the bedside when her nine-pound grandson was born at the New York Infirmary for Women and Children on East 15th Street (steps from *The East Side*'s future headquarters), according to Clarence's daughter Mary. Harold Anderson Morris's birth certificate, however, lists his birthplace as the New York Mothers' Home, an imposing turreted building on East 86th Street run by nuns, the Sisters of Misericorde.[2]

It took in unmarried patients as young as their early teens, destitute, "hitherto respectable," and shunned by family and friends. Malnutrition, alcoholism, and sweatshop labor worsened the mortality rates for mothers and babies. No girl was turned away, at any hour, if beds were available. Some arrivals, suffering from syphilis or tuberculosis, "had been refused admittance to other institutions." Unwanted children were left in the nuns' care, sometimes for years.[3] Why did Clarence, whose mother still had at least a diamond ring to her name, end up among such desperate teenagers? What is known is that they inspired reams of Zoe's fiction and journalism.

Dolly, the heroine of Zoe's first novel, *The Color of His Soul*, a Southern-born freelance writer living in Harlem, escorts her teenage friend Elsie, a pregnant seamstress, to the East 86th Street facility. (Zoe, around 1901, moved to 57 East 126th Street.) Elsie, an uneducated country girl, has been seduced and abandoned by an intellectual who spouts Voltaire. Despite his atheism, he is "the first to treat her as a sinner" upon impregnating her. The nuns—*Soul* called them "the Little Sisters of Misery"—give Elsie a berth in the main ward, with "a vista of beds alike as peas, stretching indefinitely." But then Dolly pays for a semiprivate room partitioned with screens, where Elsie whiles away anxious hours stitching dainty baby clothes. The corridors echo with the nuns' footfalls and "low-toned voices humming in every direction . . . tender as the voice of a mother singing to her child . . . now resonant and seemingly near, now liltingly far away and soft and sweet." (Was Clarence reminded of her Catholic boarding school days?) Many patients conceal their faces with slatted sunbonnets. Dolly acidly wonders whether the men who impregnated them "were going about in slatted sunbonnets, ashamed to be seen."

Dolly envies the sisters, "shut away from the world and its temptations, away from some happiness, maybe; but happiness that must be paid for with one's life blood." The nuns, "serenely aloof from the companionship of man," help girls "paying the penalty" for some short-lived happiness. The sisters kneel in rows in their chapel, "as if grown to the floor," praying for mothers and babies in extremis or past hope, lighting candles to illumine the passing of souls, the damage wrought by "the loving weakness of woman, the perfidy of man." Elsie overhears girls "grieve and grieve," given no chance to see their unnamed newborns whisked away to a dormitory upstairs.

The dormitory's lines of cribs and cots, "stretching indefinitely," housed 85 foundlings, as old as four or five. They dozed or wailed, tended by a changing roster of hired nurses with "strange cold eyes . . . and apathetic ears, dull, insensible." Mother St. John, the nun in charge, a toddler clinging to her rosary bead belt, told Zoe that the ward's inhabitants would be taught a trade by age 10 or so: "At the age when children with names played in the dawn of rosy futures those nameless children would begin laboriously the work of life. Homeless, placeless, they would start out on difficult paths toward futures doubly darkened by the flush of shame." But when Zoe offered editors a report on this traumatizing place, she was told that such tales of "the dregs of life" belonged only in "the flaunting sheets of yellow journalism."[4]

Elsie, in labor, sends a telepathic cry to Dolly's Harlem boardinghouse. By the time the writer reaches the East 86th Street home, the child is dead and Elsie is failing. The baby's unremorseful father shows up at the candlelit deathbeds. Dolly suppresses her "wish to grapple at his throat" and spits out disgust at his ugly soul and "double crime." She recognizes him as Cecil Mallon (a name too close to Courtenay Lemon, as Chapter 11 will explain), her Harlem neighbor, a Socialist orator who had intrigued her as a subject. She weeps over Elsie's handmade baby clothes and her own dashed hopes of breadwinning as a writer to help raise the child.

The birth certificate for Clarence's healthy newborn lists the absent British father's profession as "soap merchant." Zoe, at first, had little chance to help raise the child. When he was a few weeks old, Clarence brought him to Wichita, visiting Rob and staying with friends including the *Eagle*-owning Murdocks. Zoe may have sent money westward, sometimes copyrighting multiple short stories in a single day. Around this time she syndicated a story about a writer pleading with God to bring her "out of the reach of want" with just a little literary fame: "Never in all my life have I even so much as touched the hem of the garment of happiness."[5]

Zoe and her *Soul* proxy, Dolly, dash off stories, stuff batches into envelopes, and then "addressed them promiscuously," sometimes retyping an old manuscript that then sells "for a dandy price." The typescripts in transit sent telepathic messages, Zoe wrote in a short-lived new monthly, *The Manuscript*, run by Princeton-trained scholar Marion Mills Miller (who would become her lifelong cheerleader). Anything mailed off with soaring hopes would be rejected and returned: "they let me know exactly when they are coming back." When Zoe showed a friend her draft of a story expected to "Electrify the World," the friend deemed it only "very Nice," so Zoe tore the pages "into Tiny Bits . . . and kneeling over them

Wept." Editors scolded her for not paying for her own return postage; she wanted to hear that refusing her work left them "bowed down with grief." She dreamed of replying with letters that began "Dear Madame," so men could share her rattling experience of receiving correspondence addressed "Dear Sir . . . half the time I'm not quite sure whether I'm a man or a woman." Her 18th submission of a manuscript might result in its publication, followed by reviews in the 17 rejecting outlets "that hung upon the ragged edge of compliment. So there!"

A male gatekeeper's harsh evaluation of her short fiction survives in Houghton Mifflin's files at Harvard. "A feeble attempt at an emotional story," an editor jotted down for her submission "The Whirl of the Wheel." (No published or manuscript version is known.)[6]

*Soul*'s Dolly seeks career advice from a Park Row newspaperman, who begins reassuringly: "Your style is exquisite," with every line "finished to perfection." She attributes those virtues to her talented ancestors and "the labor of copying and recopying." (Zoe's typescripts in family hands show that she indeed sent them off polished, with minimal revisions in pencil, pen, or typewriter restrike.) But he critiques her plots as lacking in twists essential to fiction, and she weeps; her mentor's "chill breath of discouragement" would induce weeks of writers' block, taking away "all power to work." She points out that her realism—"I write of life as I see it . . . pen pictures of real people"—has nonetheless appeared in print: "the pictures have been acceptable to many." She imagines sticking pins into all the editors who stabbed pinholes into her rejected manuscripts and wishes "those who had willfully discouraged me might burn." (*The Manuscript* excerpted *Soul*'s chapter about the Park Row conversation under the misleading title "The Editor as Friend.")[7]

Zoe's female characters, even in agony, are not tempted to rely on male breadwinners. For *The Smart Set*, a year-old monthly "magazine of cleverness," she fictionalized a widowed American writer scrambling for work in New York after long travels in Europe. The character feels relieved to be single after dining with a friend unhappily married to a successful, adulterous lawyer: "a widow knows where her husband is of nights."[8] (*The Smart Set*, which would last three decades, published luminaries like the Liverpool-born writer Richard Le Gallienne, who was one of Oscar Wilde's lovers and would join the Ragged Edge Klub.) For *Vanity Fair*, a short-lived monthly focused on theater (unrelated to its celebrity-driven 20th-century namesake), Zoe's story "A New Woman" stars Dr. Nannie Stephens, "the best physician" in a progressive Kansas town, whose sisters serve as mayor and police chief. The doctor's husband, Samuel, is boring, balding, "fat and frowsy," overfond of trashy novels, whiningly tending the couple's four children, "sunk to the commonplace level of housekeeper." Dr. Stephens, in following "the natural order of things," runs off with her ravishing male typist, who has pearly teeth and "yellow ringlets upon his alabaster forehead." The townsmen denounce the doctor, but the townswomen blame Samuel for not even trying "to rise to the doctor's high ideal of perfect manliness." In real life, Dr. Nannie Stephens of Wichita's Hypatia circles had been denounced in the 1890s for divorcing her underemployed husband Ralph. Under headlines like "A New Woman's Way," newspapers called her a "nuisance," and Ralph claimed that the "infernal she-doctor" devoted "too much time to clubs" and adultery (she counter-accused on that latter count). She lost custody of one of her two young sons, who had sobbed on the witness stand.[9] Did Zoe obtain permission to make copy out of the she-doctor's divorce?

The general-interest monthly *Ainslee's* ran Zoe's fluffy story about a buffoonish small-town tightwad who attracts "all the neighbors a-gapin'": he inserts a squawking live goose into his clogged chimneystack, rather than pay for a chimneysweep's services. (*Ainslee's* was owned by New York publishing juggernaut Street & Smith, which would keep Zoe afloat in hardest times, see Chapter 14.) She made a few appearances in *Frank Leslie's Popular Monthly* (with a circulation over 200,000), headed by Mrs. Frank Leslie, a Woman's Press Club pillar self-ennobled as the Baroness de Bazus. In a *Leslie's* tale set in Kansas, Zoe fictionalized a farm widow hoping to retire comfortably in her native Kentucky on the profits from a promising last harvest. But hot winds, "with a hissing sound," blacken the ripening cornstalks, and they rattle hoarsely, "premonitory of death." Her property's next owner plows over her unmarked grave in the cornfields.[10]

Zoe occasionally distracted herself from the typewriter with parties. At a restaurant near Madison Square Park, she joined "more than 200 of the well-known literary people" for a banquet honoring the Illinois-born philosopher and tastemaker Elbert Hubbard (a future *East Side* subscriber). A former soap salesman, he ran an Arts & Crafts mini-empire called Roycroft in East Aurora, New York, and had solemnized himself into Fra Elbertus. The Roycrofters' workshops produced rustic-looking but costly furnishings as well as publications; *The Philistine*, Hubbard's "periodical of protest," attracted 100,000 readers. Zoe sat through his talk on "work is for the worker," his creed that artisans making "beautiful things at a great price" derived more joy from the process than buyers did from owning the wares. The evening's other speeches, many by future Ragged Edgers and *East Side* readers, dragged on far longer than the Queen of Bohemia would tolerate. The poet Edwin Markham "deplored the commercialism of the age," as Americans degenerated into "automatic cash registers." (Markham was nicknamed "The Man with the Dough" because of his best-selling poem, "The Man with the Hoe," an homage to Jean-François Millet's portrait of a downtrodden farmhand.) Richard Le Gallienne giggled while imagining that baby Hubbard had been the offspring of "two trains that fell in love." The Irish-born writer Michael Monahan teased Hubbard for writing about "failures in life, and then making a success of it." Zoe sat near Markham's invitee, the Black pastor and writer James D. Corrothers, who had studied at Northwestern University and published stories and poems in outlets as elite as *The Century Magazine*. She recognized Corrothers only after mistaking him aloud for Booker T. Washington and then Paul Laurence Dunbar. Corrothers forgave her for calling him a "darky minister" and grew deeply fond of "the friend of 'Ragged-Edgers' . . . and notwithstanding her Southern birth and rearing," he numbered her among his "warm personal friends." She soon invited him to a Woman's Press Club tea. How one longs to know how he felt at that event, and how the clubwomen reacted to Zoe's maverick choice of invitee![11]

Cecil Mallon, Dolly's Harlem neighbor in *Soul*, escorts her to bohemian parties where speakers rage against capitalism. Cecil is ambitious, slick, preening, and tall, with a head proportionately small for his body. His cat-like eyes have pupils rounded at the top and pointed at the bottom. Dolly compares him to "a snake uncoiling, capped by the little head, lighted by its strangely glittering, peculiarly pupiled eyes." He has quit a low-level job and lives with his parents, while building his reputation as a "great boy orator." Throngs attend his firebrand Socialist speeches with "hifalutin pyrotechnics," urging violent uprisings to unchain "wage slaves . . . huddled into tenements, bowed in sweatshops . . . ground to the earth by the iron hand of the Almighty Dollar." Cecil thunders at his audiences that their clothes have been stitched by half-starved women, their meat "cut up by half grown boys, standing ankle deep in the blood of slain animals." The orator's mother, a former journalist, has become an unpaid "wage slave" dejectedly distracted by housework. She longs for the days when she loved her work and was "making money hand over fist." Cecil's father supports the family as a traveling salesman for an ink company, and Dolly, an ink-stained wretch herself, wonders about the "quantities of ink" required to finance Cecil's underemployment.

It would be difficult to overstate how much the Mallons (Zoe had Irish-born neighbors of that name on East 126th Street) resemble the Lemons, former Wichitans living at 270 West 119th Street. The 1900 census lists

William as "traveling salesman" and Courtenay as "office clerk." No profession is given for Margaret, a former contributor to newspapers and magazines nationwide. William Lemon indeed worked for the ink manufacturer Sanford over the years. Courtenay was over six feet tall, "with a small head and cat eyes," charismatic, lazy, irresponsible, and "forever in debt." He had been a chess prodigy in the 1890s, playing at future Ragged Edge haunts like Café Boulevard, eliciting citrus puns for his "thoroughly ripe and juicy" chessboard moves. The poet Ella Wheeler Wilcox (who would excoriate *The East Side*) declared Courtenay "one of the rising young men of the day," his brain and heart "filled with worthy ambitions and ennobling purposes."[12]

Among Courtenay's real-life Socialist mentors was the minister, writer, and activist George D. Herron; *Soul* likewise ranked Cecil Mallon among Herron's "most zealous followers." Herron had scandalously abandoned his first wife Mary and their four children in Iowa to marry a younger, wealthier woman, Carrie Rand, whose family approved of the match. The Rands gave Mary Herron about $50,000 from their lumber fortune, "to compensate for the loss of the husband's affection." Cecil defends Herron's behavior as "the natural order of things," suited to a post-religious age. After all, Mary had aged and fallen to "a lower intellectual plane" than her husband, and prim disapprovers should remember how many Old Testament figures kept concubines "by the dozen hanging around on trees." Dolly sarcastically retorts that only by dying young could wives expect to retain husbands' love: "What woman should dare to survive her first wrinkle?"

Cecil mocks Dolly's Christian faith, her Bible as a "moth-eaten fable," and says that no woman could understand his high-level economic analysis. He rails against President Theodore Roosevelt as "a cat's paw for the rich," violently suppressing worker strikes. For Dolly/Zoe, who had lived through the murders of Abraham Lincoln, James Garfield, William McKinley, and Italy's King Umberto, the boy orator's rhetoric is "in atrocious taste." Dolly calls Roosevelt "a magnificent president" (though the Queen of Bohemia would sour on him) and remembers McKinley's "splendid picture" displayed at the Paris fair in 1900. In late September 1901, while finishing *Soul*, Zoe had joined New Yorkers gathering silently in Herald Square for news of the wounded president's worsening condition. Church bells rang in the night when his death was announced, "a heartache in every note, a sob in every peal."[13]

Cecil flirts with Dolly, despite the scorn in her "big black eyes." She lends him money, knowing it will never be repaid. He borrows from teenage Elsie as well, and from a writer and bon vivant named Tucket—the character is undoubtedly based on John Francis Tucker, an NYU-educated lawyer, writer, and bon vivant (and future Ragged Edger). Tucker was a pillar of the Pleiades Club, Quaint Club, and Twilight Club, nomadic organizations that prefigured the Ragged Edgers by hosting coed, multiethnic dinner-lectures at restaurants and hotels. They offered an openminded, affordable alternative to the city's men-only organizations like the Century Association and University Club, which had built themselves grand, freestanding headquarters. Emma Goldman, the reformer, writer, publisher, and editor, considered Tucker "one of the wittiest men in New York."[14] *Soul*'s Dolly gossips with Tucket at restaurants and lecture halls, as members of groups including the left-leaning Sunset Club sing, argue, recite literary passages, smoke, booze, and dance in "a whirl of arms and legs." (The real-life Sunrise Club, which would ignore Zoe's 1910 accordion tunes, was indeed left-leaning—see Chapter 17.)

Dolly considers herself a kind of "wage slave," lashed by editors wielding "little deadly printed slips" to reject stories. She is a refugee from Southern lands impoverished by the Civil War's "hideous ravages." But she can afford the comforts of a Harlem boardinghouse, staffed by maids, overlooking backyards full of rosebushes, time's passage marked by church bell chimes. (A Gothic brownstone church was just down the street from Zoe's Harlem townhouse.) Dolly decides to study actual wage slavery by interviewing laborers, starting with her boardinghouse neighbors. The landlady has barely stepped outside in 15 years, maintaining darkness and silence for her railroad engineer husband who works night shifts. An iceman describes dealing with time-consuming deadbeats—one elderly customer hallucinatorily insists that she had obtained George Washington's autograph from the man himself. A chorus girl tells Dolly what the bald male audience members cannot see onstage as they "smile and giggle and nudge each other and ogle." The scantily clad performers wear "symmetricals" as underlayers—the seductive body parts are fake. The dancers help each other with top-speed costume changes between numbers; when time runs out, a bodice might be left "wide open in the back as the dried skin of a grasshopper."[15]

Dolly starts navigating Lower East Side slums, "where babies rolled in gutters and scrambled away from under the crushing wheels of carts." It cannot be overstated how much these *Soul* portions prefigure *The East Side*. Dolly peers into tenements "where children bent over sewing, over tubs, over cook-stoves." A janitress's redheaded parrot, "a deceitful wretch," tries to bite Dolly as she tours fly-specked rentable rooms, "reeking with uncleanliness." She hopes to help "disseminate refinement" and eradicate slums, as Polly Locke imagines herself combating Genoese poverty by imposing laws. But Dolly cannot yet martyr herself in "the land of unhappiness," with laundry strung across dingy airshafts, mattresses blocking rusty fire escapes, and "forlorn windows stuffed with pillows and newspapers and breeze-blown rags." Still, she admires the energy and resourcefulness of the poor. Peddlers adapt cellar doorways into thriving stands for pickles and herring. In a public-school classroom, kindergarteners collaborate to build a bridge out of wooden blocks, "bordering upon magnificence." Dolly finds no evidence for Cecil's tales of slaughterhouse boys trudging through animal blood. He refuses to believe her observations of immigrant wage slaves "laughing and chatting," playing, flirting, happier than back in Europe.[16]

The unhappiest person Dolly meets while wandering downtown slums, where she cannot bear to rent a home, where Zoe would settle for nearly a decade, is Elsie, left homeless and unemployable by pregnancy, the repulsive Cecil's "natural prey." Courtenay, upon seeing those words in print, would dig his claws into Zoe.

Fig. 16: Editions of Zoe's first novel: in black and white in 1902 (Funk & Wagnalls); in color in 1903 (Fenno); with cover illustrations by her second husband, Jack Bryans. AC, Nicole Neenan photo

## 11

# Threat to Pretty Girl Novelist, 1902

WHILE CRITICS WERE still typing reviews of Zoe's first novel, and literati were toasting her, she was professionally kneecapped by men. She grasped for the hem of marital happiness instead.

In January 1902, Clarence briefly returned to New York with her baby, then still named Harold, on her way from Wichita to London. The boy's father had been "begging his wife to return to him" (not mentioning that he was living with another woman). While still in Wichita, Clarence had mailed updates to Zoe in Harlem. One unsent letter was lost on a downtown street, according to an *Eagle* news brief (guaranteed to madden future biographers): Clarence dropped the unsealed envelope and "is quite anxious to have it returned to her."[1]

Days after an ocean liner steamed away with Clarence and baby—Zoe called them Madonna and Bambino, nicknaming him the Bam—publishing giant Funk & Wagnalls released *The Color of His Soul*, "very lovingly dedicated to my Madonna col Bambino." (Harold Sr. never showed up to meet his American family at the London train station, leaving Clarence to scramble for work—she eked out a living as a backup dancer and piano accompanist, onstage with Sarah Bernhardt and other divas.) Funk & Wagnalls, founded in the 1870s by Lutheran ministers, was known for reference books and risk aversion. In the 1890s, as a budding Wichita freelancer, Zoe had an unpleasant experience with the company. It accepted her tale of Kentucky prohibitionists for *The Voice*, a magazine focused on temperance, but then returned the work to her unpublished albeit "corrected and ready for the press." She attributed the last-minute rejection to the staff's fear of shotgun reprisals from "some big burly Kentuckian."[2] By 1902, Zoe's friend Marion Miller, Funk & Wagnalls' literary adviser, had persuaded the editors to take on *Soul*, and they also accepted the manuscript of *The Quest of Polly Locke*. That is, without having published anything longer than a few thousand words, Zoe nervily had two novels in the works.

She was dating *Soul*'s cover illustrator, John Kennedy Bryans, known as Jack, a pale, narrow-faced, brunet, bespectacled, self-taught New Yorker, 12 years her junior. The eldest of about seven children of an Irish American shoe merchant, Jack was freshly divorced on grounds of "obstinate desertion." (He evicted his pregnant first wife, Ada Brown, from their Manhattan apartment after a few months of cohabitation, since he did not want children and considered her inferior to his bohemian friends—he icily called her "of no use to him." He squandered her savings, and his own relatives damningly testified against him in the divorce proceedings.) For newspapers and periodicals, Jack sketched silhouette comics about goofy characters misunderstanding each other or getting into scrapes. Among his series titles were "In Silhouetteville" and "In Black-and-Whiteville." He had failed at previous jobs as a shoe salesman and bookkeeper, since he could not resist temptations "to scribble caricatures" of customers and colleagues on ledger pages and wrapping paper. *Soul* was his first book assignment, along with Funk & Wagnalls' *The Black Cat Club*, "character studies of Negro life," written by Zoe and Jack's friend James Corrothers, about upwardly mobile Black clubmen in Chicago who share tall tales in thick dialect.[3]

Zoe fictionalized her attempts to please Jack, relying on his "excellent taste" while shopping; if he disapproves of her hat purchase, "life will be hardly worth living." Younger suitors, for a number of her fictional widows and divorcées, help burnish old sadness "into something like radiance." But glimpses of themselves in mirrors, or reflected in their lovers' eyes, bring reminders of sufferings that carve the "insidious trail" of wrinkles and foretell "untold tortures" of comparison to younger women.[4]

Funk & Wagnalls marketed *Soul* as "brilliant sketches of newspaper and Bohemian life," apt to "seize upon the heart of every reader and move it profoundly." It was priced at $1, typical for the era's hardcover novels. Press releases boasted that she descended from Northumberland vicar-scholar-translators named Henry T. Anderson, whose works were on British Museum shelves. She was dubbed "perhaps, the most widely known writer of newspaper sketches in the country"; a member of "America's

Fig. 17: Zoe's second novel, *The Quest of Polly Locke*, with a portrait of her second husband and examples of his humorous postcards. AC, Nicole Neenan photo

aristocracy of brains"; and the Pleaides Club's "rising star," with wit scintillating in "magazines of cleverness."

Her Pleaides book party at a restaurant near Madison Square Park attracted about 150 bohemians, including Marion Miller and Jack Bryans. Female guests' exquisite gowns came as surprises to observers expecting "eccentricity of attire." John Francis Tucker, the club's president (and *Soul's* "Tucket"), introduced the banquet host Lee Fairchild, an orator and writer (who would soon be best man at Jack and Zoe's wedding). Zoe was not yet accustomed to audience reactions as she scintillated aloud: "the hits she intended produced a silence like the grave while totally unintentional sallies on the other hand resulted in prolonged and vociferous laughter and applause."[5]

*Soul* reviews left her equally perplexed. They ran by the dozens, in publications from *The Christian Register* to *The American Hebrew* and *Good Housekeeping*. Kentucky and Kansas newspapermen noted that she had once lived among them with relatives including her father Henry and ex-husband Spencer. She had strung vignettes "loosely together" into a novelette rather than a novel, as she headed "off to the crowded literary speedway," *Literary Digest* opined. She was lauded for "vivid touches of metropolitan color," typeset in ragged right columns on pages with untrimmed edges, all "daintily bound" in white vellum. (It is unclear why Jack designed twin potted trees for the cover and title page.) Readers fell outright in love with Dolly, a role model for newspaperwomen "who cleverly and patiently and independently try to do things up to the limit of their strength." *Soul*, as a "strong force against evil humanity," exposed the dangers of Socialists like George Herron's "shallow, mouthy, idle and shameless" protégés, agitating for violent uprisings and whitewashing their insidious pleasure-seeking with altruistic rhetoric. The book could help protect young working women newly resettled in "the hurrying city," vulnerable to becoming "the victims of all-devouring lust." Zoe did want to help "better the world," partly by warning that Cecil Mallon represented an increasingly common type of egotistical poseur, "to be eyed askance," as she wrote in *Soul*'s preface. But she hoped that readers would be most captivated by her sharply delineated "pen pictures," not the kind of shrill moralizing that had annoyed Nancy Yanks as Wichita prudes ripped down circus posters. *Soul*'s reviews left Zoe looking "long and earnestly into my mirror, wondering if, unbeknownst to myself, I had really blossomed into a humanitarian, and why."[6]

Some critics called the book not depressing enough, full of "irrelevancies and flippancies." Or too depressing, focused on "ignorance, degradation and extreme destitution." Or not as amusing as James Corrothers' Bryans-illustrated collection of tales in "Negro dialect," whose Chicagoan narrators call each other "genamun" and sometimes break into song—one of their audiences' favorites is "My Old Kentucky Home." (For college-educated Corrothers, writing in dialect was unfamiliar and uncomfortable, but his editors persuaded him that it would be marketable—just as Zoe's bosses pressed her for saleable cheerfulness.) *Soul*'s white vellum cover was deemed "oddly in contrast" with the grim topic, and the ragged-edge typesetting in "eccentric style" seemed plagiarized from Elbert Hubbard's Roycroft publications (a criticism also lobbed at *The East Side*).[7]

Courtenay Lemon publicly identified himself as the model for *Soul*'s Cecil. Insisting that he had never impregnated any innocents who died at charity hospitals, he stormed into Funk & Wagnalls' office and threatened a libel suit. Zoe compared the staff's reaction to Kentuckians cowering during feuds: "at the sight of this tall boy of the brilliant eyes, they fell all over themselves getting under chairs and tables out of the way. They covered themselves with Sunday school books and standard dictionaries, crying out: 'We'll suppress it! We'll suppress it!'" They so feared a dilettantish, angry young man, despite his thin résumé, that they threw a vastly more accomplished woman under the bus. They withdrew *Soul* from the market and destroyed the warehouse inventory. (A handful of copies survive, including two that I snapped up on eBay and one at the Library of Congress.) Herron himself was said to have tracked down a first-edition collector's item, "at a fancy price."[8]

Zoe went on a public warpath (which would last until 1914). She called Funk & Wagnalls "white about the gills," cowardly, "very rich and very careful of their money." Their frantic last-minute censorship efforts had led to debacle before, she noted. In 1884, they announced with fanfare an English translation of Alphonse Daudet's *Sappho*, about a licentious artists' model in Paris. But the project was called off, and Daudet handed thousands of dollars in damages, after a Funk & Wagnalls executive read the first few chapters in print. "He had a couple of inward spasms and screamed," Zoe told her readers in 1902. Courtenay had agreed to his fictionalization, according to Zoe, but then he reneged upon realizing that she would not share royalties. She had not known that everyone would want percentages: "the Office Boy, the scrubwoman, the man who swept off the front stoop." After all, the novel did not give Courtenay's real name, it just described him well: "am I responsible," Zoe asked, "for all the tall boys, with small heads and cat eyes?"[9]

Rumors swirled that she had unrequited feelings for Courtenay. *The Papyrus,* a sporadic magazine published by her friend Michael Monahan, detected signs of "the strong acid of a woman's love turned to hate" in *Soul.* Her friend Lee Fairchild praised her writings as "remarkable stuff" but based on friends, "thus reducing the number of her friends." Zoe hired a Polish American Jewish lawyer from Virginia, Melvin G. Winstock, to defend her. (He also worked as a politician, editor, and writer; his unsuccessful novels and plays had portentous titles like *The Fatal Horoscope.*) Winstock threatened to countersue Courtenay and Funk & Wagnalls for suppressing *Soul* "without just cause." Courtenay had voluntarily unmasked himself as the inspiration for "a wrecker of homes and several other unmentionable things," Winstock told reporters. He compared Zoe to authors as celebrated as Thackeray, Dickens, and Ouida (the pen name of British novelist Maria Louise Ramé), who had "a perfect and undeniable right to draw characters from real life."[10]

The press feasted on the controversy, under headlines like "Squeezed Lemon" and "Threat to Pretty Girl Novelist"—never mind that she was a grandmother in her 40s. Pleiades Club members and other bohemians were said to resent *not* being fictionalized, "passed over for a Lemon." Courtenay's mentor George Herron, "openly named" in *Soul,* was not suing, so why was Courtenay coming forward as the inspiration for a contemptible "prig and pimp"? *The Mirror* in St. Louis, which published Zoe's fiction (alongside works by Kate Chopin, Theodore Dreiser, and Paul Laurence Dunbar), suggested that if Courtenay really resembled Cecil, "he should go drown himself, and not go to court."[11]

By spring 1902, Zoe's friends persuaded her to compromise rather than spend years entangled in court proceedings that would mostly profit Winstock—"that's what lawyers are there for," she sighed. Funk & Wagnalls, caught "between two fires" of threats from her and Courtenay, gave her *Soul*'s printing plates but no other compensation in exchange for her promise not to sue. "That was extremely generous of them," Zoe mused, "seeing the plates belonged to me in the first place." *Locke* was taken out of the company pipeline. So she was saddled with two unpublished novels simultaneously. She immediately began seeking to reprint *Soul,* even if it led to arrest and incarceration: "It should live. It shall live."[12]

She pleaded for help from Edwin Markham, "the poet of the people," author of the bestselling "Man with the Hoe," newly transplanted from California to Staten Island with his third wife Anna. He was a friend of Herron, Courtenay, and Funk & Wagnalls' Marion Miller. Zoe typed a frantic letter to Markham on cheap onionskin paper: *Soul* had been unjustly suppressed, despite "splendid reviews" and earnings potential. "You know the boy who suppressed it, Courtney [sic] Lemon. He has no case." She admitted to "making up a type" based on friends, but "no name was used. No injury has been done him." With the printing plates in hand, she sought "a publisher who will dare to take it up, branded as it is." Markham's recommendation letter, just "something nice" in print, could make a book: "Make mine. Won't you?" It is not known whether he replied.[13]

She mailed her letter from 45 West 27th Street, an aging rowhouse partitioned into furnished rented rooms. The same address was listed for her and Jack on their March 26, 1902, marriage certificate. The cohabitating bride and groom were married at the Metropolitan Temple, a Methodist Episcopal sanctuary on West 14th Street. (Known as "the Church of the Open Door," it offered surprisingly secular public programs, such as movie screenings and Dickens readings.) Zoe perjured herself on the marriage's legal documents, shaving four years off her age. (Did Jack ever know her real age, and did she find out how he had treated his pregnant first wife, who miscarried after he evicted her?) Jack—raised Presbyterian—and Zoe had planned on an Episcopal ceremony at the Church of the Transfiguration at 1 East 29th Street, but the rector backed out upon learning that "both parties had incurred previous ties, sundered legally." After the ceremony, the newly re-wed divorcés served "a sumptuous supper" at the boardinghouse, with "Who's Who in Bohemia" at the table.[14]

The best man, Lee Fairchild, was an Illinois-born fraternity brother (Lombard College, Phi Delta Theta, class of 1886) who had spent a decade on the West Coast, working as a minister, teacher, newspaper editor, and orator, known as "the Prince of the Platform." He was considered "fun loving, flowery, frolicsome, fragrant, fair" as he eked out a living in New York, "slinging ink" for periodicals, "hitting strong drink too hard," campaigning for Republicans including McKinley, and "swapping lies" with Pleiades Club members and other bohemians. His listeners could rely on tears welling up whenever he delivered his usual "glowing word picture of the beauties of a sunset on Puget Sound." When he witnessed Zoe and Jack's Metropolitan Temple ceremony, he was drawing rave reviews for his new poetry collection about alcohol's ruinous temptations, *The Tippler's Vow*, an update of medieval Persia's *Rubáiyát of Omar Khayyám*. Zoe contributed to Fairchild's short-lived monthly magazine *The Thistle*, "a journal of opinion, aggressive and digressive," which genially lacked the thistle's "pricking, unkind, traumatic tendencies."[15]

The Bryanses' matron of honor, Grace Miller White, like Zoe, had reinvented herself in New York after shedding an unimpressive ex-husband in the West. Grace, a native of Ithaca, New York, had been married to Homer White, a housepainter in Butte, Montana. She ran a charity home there, which took in orphans and indigent women abandoned by "idle, worthless . . . good for nothing" men. By 1900 or so, Grace had become a Manhattanite, supporting three children, claiming to be a widow (as did most of Zoe's divorcée friends) and working on McKinley's campaign. Her stemwinder speeches urged women to keep an "eagle eye" on their menfolk at risk of voting for William Jennings Bryan. His progressive stance would embolden anarchists and Socialists and drive the middle class into "hovels full of misery and unhappiness," Grace thundered. In her own short-lived newspaper, *The Reasoner*, she used "cold reason and logic" to analyze Bryan's policies "and dash them into atoms." (Grace may have been mainly Jack's and not Zoe's friend, since she made no further appearances in Zoe's writings. Jack illustrated Grace's first book, *A Harmless Revolution*, about proper punctuation use.)[16]

No out-of-town guests, apparently, attended the Norris-Bryans nuptials, although the couple sent out announcement cards, "handsomely engraved," even to Kentuckians. Some relatives would not have been welcome. Zoe had stopped visiting her family (her writings do not mention the deaths, in 1901 and 1902 respectively, of her half-siblings Lelia and Clarence). During Zoe's last trip to Harrodsburg, Mattie Thompson had treated her coldly, and the sisters were estranged. The day after Zoe became Mrs. Norris-Bryans, *The Mirror* ran her story about Elizabeth, a lonely Southerner making ends meet in "the great rumbling overcrowded city" during "pitiless years" of family separation. Tired of Manhattan's kaleidoscope of strange faces, she longs for her sleepy hometown's "old unchanging hills" and fragrant flowerbeds. There she could "break bread with kindred" and not have to pay for it. She takes a two-day train ride southward in the autumn and receives a chilly reception from her sister Margaret, "who had seemed to love her in the old days." Margaret's column-fronted hilltop mansion is so closely based on Mattie's Clay Hill that both real and fictional front lawns slope steeply upward from a high stone retaining wall at the roadside. When Elizabeth's luggage is delivered, containing her winter cloak (she hopes for a prolonged stay), she overhears Margaret irritably speculating to the servant Jemima that the New Yorker's visit could last "all winter long." Elizabeth rushes back northward, preferring the nameless urban masses to "a familiar face grown cold." *The Mirror* also ran Zoe's story about Dolly, a Manhattanite from the South, recently married but still impoverished, dining at a luxurious hotel with a brother-in-law clearly based on John Thompson. He grumbles about supporting Dolly and his wife Cappie's many other sisters, "the whole posse of you," a burden since they were "knee high to ducks . . . If your husbands die, I bury them. If you conclude that you want a divorce, I get it." He plans to cut off his "lazy, trifling," hard-drinking son, age 26, who is running out of money at Harvard while Cappie lives near campus, attempting "to keep him straight," splurging on her own violin lessons. The brother-in-law resents having bought Dolly not only a velvet cloak but also her hotel meal. Dolly replies, in Queen of Bohemia fashion, "I'm so interesting . . . that most people are very willing to pay for my dinner to hear me talk." He remains entranced by Cappie's blonde, blue-eyed queenliness, although she has evicted him from her bedroom at their home, called Pleasant Hill. Dolly reminds him that evidence of adultery—a girl's picture and lock of hair—have surfaced. At the hotel table, Dolly watches him rip up his angry letter-in-progress to his son, resigning himself guiltily to financing the extravagances of "Cappie's boy," who might manage to "drink up all the whiskey in the Union."

Mattie was a blonde, blue-eyed violinist, reigning "supreme in society," viewed even by long-estranged Zoe as "a great strong fine woman always . . . the head of the family to me." John Thompson was indeed among the Harrodsburg area's "great ladies' men." Pleasant Hill is the name of the nearby Shaker community—that is, Zoe named Cappie's sin-plagued mansion after a celibates' colony. John cruelly treated his unemployed son Philip, who spent one year at the University of North Carolina and another at Harvard (class of 1894, D average, Southern Club member). By 1900, Philip's alcoholism was so severe that he was found unconscious in a Harrodsburg cemetery, his leg broken, with no idea how he got there. How did the Thompsons feel about Zoe's characterizations of them in print? (John Thompson, after Mattie's death, did become a supporter of *The East Side*.)[17]

During Zoe's early married life, *Soul*'s suppression somewhat narrowed her professional options, a number of magazine editors "having some fear of libel suits also." Courtenay kept denouncing her as unscrupulous in the bohemian world, which left her feeling "almost friendless." But he painted his own soul unflatteringly in public, with speeches and writings advocating free love and freely available contraception ("affinities" was his circle's euphemism for lovers). "Polygamy is not only natural, but essentially necessary," he told *The Washington Times*.[18]

Remarried Zoe kept writing about unmarried women writers, churning out words, trying robotically to "cover one side of a paper with letters and present it to editors." They are sidetracked by long-winded neighbors and landlords bemoaning their own troubles, because everyone knows when freelancers are working at home: "If someone would only invent a noiseless rubber-tired typewriter!" Zoe imagined herself failing to syndicate a weekly New York society newsletter, "spicey, but not too spicey," for imaginary newspapers including *The St. Paul Blizzard* and *The Kentucky Six Shooter.* She added to her range of characters: a boardinghouse family's violently abusive patriarch, with "murderous blue eyes"; Black dancers competing in cakewalking competitions; a lighthouse keeper haunted by sightings of "wrecks and broken bones and dead bodies." In her stories set in small towns, aged narrators mock self-indulgent young New Yorkers for wasting time at the gym and having faces and limbs "cut to pieces" with cosmetic surgery. One widow's farm falls into ruin as her only son contorts himself on expensive bodybuilding equipment, recommended by a New York instructor, although thrashing wheat "would be jest every bit and grain as good exercise."

Zoe hated writing about "the favored class," against backdrops with "judicious touches of moonlight, fireflies, and stars," she confessed in *The Writer.* Given her alleged pedigree of "a hundred vicars, accustomed to hasten to the relief of the poor," she pulsated with desire to tell of the oppressed masses' "ghastly necessity of grappling for bread." But editors attached little paper addendums to their rejection letters: "Give us something cheerful.... What we want is not the dregs of life, but its cream." With clothes frayed and rent unpaid, Zoe caved to her bosses' demands: "I must dance to the music. I am a literary harlequin. My hands are tied." On her darkest days, she walked for miles seeking a church with an open door, "some dim-stained windowed place," where she could plead for solace from "a great mysterious silent Somebody who doesn't weigh down my soul with wordy advice at a time when I can't stand to hear a single syllable."[19] But she did not apparently join any congregation; would that have been too reminiscent of her stifling childhood Sundays?

By summer 1902, she began experimenting with undercover reporting, with a four-part exposé of servants' miserable lives—the only multi-parter of her career. Did she know about trailblazers like Nellie Bly, undergoing painful experiences for professional advancement and public good? Zoe had originally sold the articles to *Good Housekeeping*, but they were shunted to a sister trade weekly, *American Agriculturist,* and wedged between ads for grain threshers and cider presses. Zoe had grown curious about women servants, who were forming unions, after her boardinghouse's maid quit and fled "without so much as 'Good-day.'" Zoe took boardinghouse jobs under the Irish-sounding pseudonym Jane Higgins; a male friend (perhaps Jack?) posed as Jane's reference. She commuted at dawn amid streams of workmen, "lunches protruding from bulky pockets, frantic for fear they might get there late and lose their job." Young male boarders in residence, with "soft and alluring" eyes, flirted with Jane/Zoe—"they would have waited on the table for me"—as she served dinners cooked in a rat-infested kitchen. Mounds of towels and sheets, "malignantly waiting" to be ironed, brought her to the brink of screaming. She fled her first post when assigned to sleep in the kitchen; the curtainless windows unnerved her, as did a leering colleague toying with his knife while promising to keep her company. At another live-in job, she catered to a family of five from New Orleans, former slaveholders, with oaken furniture "left over from palmier days." The patriarch was an invalid, reliant on earnings from his two stenographer daughters, expected to "pound typewriters till the end of time and die at the desk." The family was pleased at the efficiency of Jane/Zoe, who eradicated kitchen cockroaches "with the slap of deadly wet rags" while cooking, bootblacking, mending and ironing clothes, polishing silver, washing windows and lugging rugs to the roof to beat out dust. Zoe remembered her childhood amid thrifty sisters—"It always makes me homesick to sew"—and she realized what her own family's overworked housekeepers in Kentucky and Kansas had endured as their arms "moved rustily on their hinges." The mother from New Orleans piled on demands: "I could fancy a whip in her hand as she stood over me." In the maid's tiny bedroom, "all the steam pipes in the building running through it," the family stored moldy carpets and refuse "in a rank and disheartening heap." Rather than sleep there, Zoe bolted back to her own well-staffed boardinghouse. She could understand why good help was hard to find: the worst-off peddlers "prefer the independence of the curb." Although the *Agriculturist* report was "corking stuff," she wrote in *The East Side*, she was paid less than "a Slave in a Kitchen."[20]

She meanwhile found a publisher for *Locke*. She added a line to her old manuscript, dedicating the book "very affectionately . . . to Jack, who approaches as nearly as could be expected to my ideal man." She would regret those words within months.

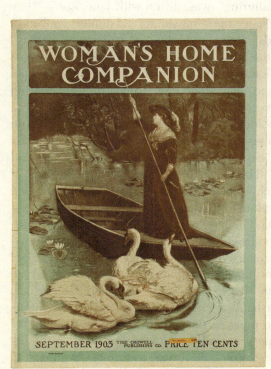

Fig. 18: Examples of magazines that Zoe contributed to as her second marriage failed: *Woman's Home Companion* (Sept. 1903), *The Smart Set* (Oct. 1903), *The Munsey* (April 1905). AC, Nicole Neenan photo

# 12

## The Useless Tears, 1902–1903

WHILE CRITICS IGNORED or savaged Zoe's second novel, she reunited with her daughter and grandson and fictionalized her failing marriage and a last meeting with her son.

Zoe agreed to pay J. S. Ogilvie (which had also published works by her matron-of-honor Grace White) to run 1,000 hardcover *Locke* copies. The cover price, $1, was at the company's higher end; it was known for paperback dime novels and play novelizations. Jack provided *Locke*'s cover silhouette of Polly, musing at Vesuvius's base. A few dozen reviews appeared, most of them brief, some penned by her friends.

Her best man Lee Fairchild told *Thistle* readers, "you would better buy this book," since Polly's encounters with "many interesting folk" could substitute for European travels. *The Mirror* predicted that Polly had "sufficient nonchalant impertinence to fascinate every lord of creation with the right sort of lump beating in his chest." *The Writer* praised Polly's vivacity as well as the suppressed *Soul*'s "especial value for collectors." Other reviewers familiar with *Soul* noted that Zoe kept demonstrating "a strong and real sympathy with the poor," as *Locke* teemed with "the lame, the halt and the blind . . . painted in tender colors." Polly was called "decidedly American" in her unconventionality, triumphing over situations "sufficiently risky to satisfy the most sensational taste," and unlikely to find the French tour guide Leon sufficiently ideal for the long term.

Moralists described Polly's behavior as impulsive or "unspeakable," whether because she blasphemed at a Presbyterian or lusted after a German. A Chicagoan snidely wondered why Polly sought an ideal man in Southern Europe, when better options could have been found "at home in Kansas." A Californian only liked the frontispiece photo of "the rather pretty young author." One Minnesotan summed up *Locke* as "neither bad enough nor good enough to be interesting." Nitpickers pointed out "decidedly weird" versions of Italian and French terms.

Zoe knew the book had been minimally marketed and poorly printed and proofread. Ogilvie, "the cheapest of the cheap," turned out only 100 copies, and she ignored his dunning after paying $210 of his $450 charge: "His typesetters were criminals, fit for Sing Sing." She expected that male critics would dislike *Locke*'s roasting of men, its mirrors reflecting them in "too lifelike a manner," but not that they would call the book not worth writing. The author of a smear in the *Sun* was "paid by Funk & Wagnalls," she was told. She had been a *Sun* contributor since her escape from Wichita, so she was stung at the betrayal from her "parent in a literary way." (Zoe, after all, had not enjoyed much parenting as a child nor much mentoring as a working woman.) A *Sun* editor called her work "good enough for anything or anybody," so perhaps the office had ended up "divided against itself." Zoe told Wichitans that even with books suppressed or dismissed on her résumé, "the author is unsuppressible."[1]

In December 1902, she spent a final week in Wichita. After the "hurried trip to the West, with sleepers and transportation free, or I wouldn't have taken it" (her son Rob probably obtained gratis tickets through his railroad job) she barely left New York again and wondered why anyone would. "Mrs. J. K. Bryans" gave interviews upon arrival at a Wichita hotel, not far from the homes and offices of her son and ex-husband. (Did she cross paths with Spencer's pregnant wife Ruth?) Zoe did "not look a day older" than at her 1898 divorce proceedings as she sugarcoated Clarence's status in London for the press: "Her husband is a fine young man." Zoe asked to go off the record upon revealing that she was a grandmother—"for pity's sake, don't put that in the paper"—but the *Beacon* had no such pity. The *Eagle* preened that it had published her writings before she headed off to the literary speedway, famed on two continents for European travelogues "as good as a play," character sketches "of a rare quality," and evocative depictions of "nooks and corners in New York." She lied that "her love for Wichita has never waned," and that wherever she traveled, she defended Kansas when anyone disparaged it as full of wallowing buffalo and devoid of trolley lines and electricity. Kansans were adventurous, brilliant, sometimes freakish—"your hatchet woman, for instance," she told the *Beacon*, referring to the temperance advocate Carry Nation, who was taking axes to bars. (Had no one read Polly Locke's regrets for wasting "ten precious years" in the cyclonic state?) Mrs. Bryans described New York itself as "provincial in many respects," since horses pulled some trolley cars.[2]

But one of her syndicated stories[3] starred a liar from New York named Mrs. Charleton, who visits the unnamed Western town where she has outlived her first husband and left behind their teenage son. She publicly declares the town much improved since her departure years before, and she professes unwaning love for the wide-open West, contrasting with eastern cities "crowded to suffocation." But rumors soon spread via "very intimate friends" that she is privately sneering at farm wagons trundling through downtown, women covering their heads with provincial knitted shawls, and "giant telegraph poles" blocking views. (Manhattan by then had largely submerged such infrastructure.) Mrs. Charleton reunites delightedly with her handsome brunet son—she looks young enough to be his sister—"but he has committed one crime": he is engaged to a nouveau riche woman from a farm family. The snobbish widow recoils from the fiancée's grammatical errors and family home full of garish paintings. The widow, who is newly remarried herself, insists on postponing her son's wedding. "My mother thinks I am too young," he tells his weeping beloved. But then a telegram arrives from Mrs. Charleton's second husband, lonesome in New York, and she tremblingly rushes to board the next train eastward. The brokenhearted fiancée brings homemade candies to the station, and the widow's heart melts. "Love is scarce," she tells her son. "Marry her. What am I that I should dare to separate you?"

As the Charletons' story was going to press, Rob was preparing to marry Eva Leighton, whose Illinois farm family was newly resettled in Wichita. They were prospering in businesses, including Spencer's old store. Rob had minimal contact thereafter with his mother. By 1909 she did not know his whereabouts. Did the fictional Mrs. Charleton's condescension finish off whatever remained of newly affianced Rob's affections for the globetrotting mother he had not seen since his parents divorced when he was a teenager?

Zoe, once back in New York, prepared a nest for her daughter Clarence and toddler grandson. With $200 from Harold Morris in hand, Clarence escaped London with the boy, his name newly changed from Harold Anderson Morris to Robert Melvin Morris. Zoe and Jack by then were living in a decade-old, boxy brick apartment building at 78 West 82nd Street (her last uptown address).[4] Jack, who still did not want children (as he had insisted to his pregnant first wife), refused to live with his stepdaughter and step-grandson: "They are not coming here!" Zoe's reply: "Then you get out!" She had tired anyway of married life, "cooped up the livelong day with a humorist." When they separated, she turned him into story fodder. "It's a deadly thing to see people grind out fun," she wrote in the *Times*. "I used to know a comic artist. I had to sit by and watch him try to match his jokes to pictures!"[5]

In her fiction about mediocre and bad relationships, she used Jack's name and incorporated his youth, impracticality, constant criticisms, and dislike of children. "Jack nags me so about everything," one Manhattan heroine says about her controlling, unpleasant spouse. A farmwife falls into a fatal fever after her second husband refuses to live with her unhappily married daughter, blocking his stepdaughter's return "like a great, dark wall of stone. Like bars to a jail." The farmwife's neighbor can only understand why anyone would marry once, "puttin' her hand in the fire before she knows how it burns." A Manhattan artist sheds "useless tears" upon losing her freelance newspaperman husband, who had complained when "she insisted upon eating regularly." Upon regaining her footing and creativity—"friends had nursed her back to life"—the artist pays for her disheveled ex's dinner tab, thanking "the hand of God that took him from me." Another Manhattan artist's husband bitterly resents that she took in her orphaned younger sister, known as the Girl (one of Zoe's pet names for Clarence). For a Manhattan writer named Nona (Robert Morris's name for his grandmother), her younger suitor does not mind that she lives with her widowed daughter and toddler grandson. Nona adores the angelic boy, although being a grandmother "seems to put you in the Paleozoic age." She makes rounds of late-night parties to insure "brilliant up-to-date work," terrified of ending up faded, toothless, shawled and ignored in a corner: "Hopeless brains can't bring money."

No record has been found that Jack and Zoe went through the costly and time-consuming process of divorcing, which might have required official documentation of one spouse's adultery. One of her fictional estranged husbands only grumblingly agrees "to pay a detective to have myself caught." ("Widow" was Zoe's census status.) In an *East Side* short story, a successful drama critic and her improvident younger husband—like Jack he is a pale, bespectacled brunet—separate after a yearlong marriage but never divorce. Her limbo protects her from remarrying. "I am a poor judge of men," she bluntly tells him. He suggests reconciling, flattering her that she has aged well, envying her "thrice blessed work." But then he dredges up old quarrels, "throwing her faults in her teeth." She concludes that she would rather drown in the East River than resubject herself to "the barking of the dogs of yesterday."[6]

Zoe tried to forgive friends who suggested that she return to improvident Jack, who still "spoke very well" of her. In "The Song of the Typewriter," an *East Side* poem, she urged herself to "Work, damn you, Work!" while wondering why she had attempted a second marriage: "Were you Mad or Sane, that you Tried it Again? / When you Knew it would End in the Same Old Way?" Just passing through Upper West Side subway stations left her sobbing: "I lived near here once with a husband."[7]

She reissued *Soul* in 1903, recycling the printing plates from Funk & Wagnalls and Jack's tree silhouette designs and pricing it again at $1. The publisher, R. F. Fenno & Company, was teetering into bankruptcy despite an author list that included Arthur Conan Doyle and Rudyard Kipling. About two dozen critics briefly mentioned *Soul*'s redux, some simply noting that a review copy had arrived. Someone cluelessly, or pot-stirringly, sent one to *The Comrade*, a Socialist monthly with George Herron and Courtenay Lemon on the advisory board. Some critics, remembering the 1902 version and Courtenay's outrage, were either puzzled by the swift reappearance of the suppressed novel or impressed with Fenno's bold rerelease that "deserves a large sale." *The Washington Post*, which had praised the 1902 *Soul*'s "humor and pathos and sympathetic human interest," did no homework in 1903, unsure whether Zoe was "a new literary light or one who has gleaned in journalistic fields before." *The New York Herald* had enthused in 1902 about *Soul*'s "vivacity, originality and picturesqueness," but found the identical 1903 text "spoiled by retouching with conventional sentimentality." Zoe theorized that the newfound distaste for *Soul* was due to Fenno's status as "not quite so rich" as Funk & Wagnalls.[8] By the time *The East Side* marketed *Soul*, Courtenay's censorship became a selling point: "No. It wasn't Erotic," Funk & Wagnalls had just sacrificed her "for fear they might lose a dollar." (She would eventually drop the price to 50 cents in a "reckless manner" and then simply give away signed Fenno copies to new *East Side* subscribers.)[9]

The reissue of *Soul* may have renewed magazine editors' concern that Zoe was a troublemaker. Within a few months, that stream of income largely dried up. Grappling for bread made her ever speedier at the typewriter and more baring of her soul in newsprint.

Fig. 19: 1906 *Bohemian* magazine illustration of Zoe interviewing at Ellis Island. Author's photo

# 13

# On the Rim of Manhattan, 1904–1906

ZOE GAVE EDITORS something cheerful to keep the Norris-Morrises afloat.
 She lost some magazine customers after offending editors or being offended. *Woman's Home Companion* shelved her story with a Jewish character, although she was sure that her Jewish friends would not have minded "a word in it" (the first of several times she came under a cloud of antisemitism accusations). She recycled manuscripts for resubmission to new monthlies like *10 Story Book* ("spicy and clever" fiction) and *The New Age* (targeted at Freemasons). Given the "wild and hilarious uncertainty" of freelancing, a number of unpublished typescripts from this period remain in descendants' hands, suggesting a relatively high rejection rate. Still, she preferred precarity as an author over peddling shoestrings or womaning a cash register. She kept up her Woman's Press Club membership and attended some Pleiades Club events, and "whole-souled cosmopolitan people" occasionally treated her to Welsh rarebit and chop suey.[1]
 Starting around 1904, Zoe had her mail sent to various buildings on 21st Street near Broadway, an area dense with publishers' headquarters. Her fictional characters love the neighborhood's domed towers and "rushing, rushing, rushing" streams of pedestrians. Madison Square Garden's dome was topped with sculptor Augustus Saint-Gaudens' nude bronze figure of "eternal Diana, poised with her bow." At night, the huntress statue "tiptoed duskily," and rooftop advertisements, skyscrapers' windows, and churches' electrified crosses "flamed against the sky apparently bodiless." A Broad-

way fur dealer's sign inspired a pun: "Importers of Skins . . . as if there weren't enough skins in New York without importing any."[2]

Zoe's nomadic family found some joy in "infinitesimal flats," scraping together about $35 in monthly rent. A freelance story could bring anywhere from $9 to $100, and an unbylined joke could bring $2. The Norris-Morrises sought out cheaper places so often that "Moving Tales" was one of Zoe's proposed memoir titles. Yet she treated the Bam, her toddler grandson, to opera and theater tickets, and he charmed storekeepers into philanthropy: "He darted into a flower shop one day and came out with his arms filled with a variety of beautiful flowers."

One of Zoe's fictional freelancers, Nona (the real-life Bam's nickname for Zoe), supports an unmarried younger sister whose young son, the Bambino, is nicknamed the Bam. In a tiny mouse-infested apartment, the sisters entertain "hordes of friends." They serve feasts on a foldout table and roll up rugs afterwards for waltzing, hoping the partygoers "don't guess at our extremity." Departing male guests ply the Bam with dollar bills and coins, "tempting little pieces of silver." The boy accumulates $5, which he stuffs into a pocketbook in his toy cupboard. His mother fears he could become a "hoarding miser," like his cruel and absent father, and bills are piling up from the iceman and gasman—late-night parties, after all, require chilled drinks and illumination. The sisters steal the boy's savings to cover their expenses. He blames mice for the theft and thereafter spends every penny profligately on toys and sweets: "The flat filled with miniature firewagons, engines, automobiles, and Teddy bears, and he waked of nights groaning from the effects of the peppermint-creams and molasses candies."[3]

Did the real-life little Bam have any inkling how close Nona and Cis had come to the ragged edge? And how did Cis react to Zoe's portrayals of unmarried writers feeling suffocated, resentful, and envious while handing over profits and favorite clothes to spoiled, unemployed relatives? One breadwinner half-lovingly calls her Cis "the bane of my life." Another Zoe stand-in chats vivaciously with her younger sister's suitor, as he wonders if the older woman's pale profile had been sketched by "the pencil of sadness." A wealthy farmer woos the daughter of a freelance writer named Momsey (another one of Zoe's family nicknames), a committed urbanite who would only feel contented with her own lot in the countryside "if it were a lot in a cemetery."[4]

A number of Zoe's circa-1904 characters play-act to escape poverty, "bony, merciless and grim." A spendthrift artist masquerades as a tattered bum, cadging handouts from friends with sob stories in snowy Union Square Park. An antiques dealer downtown is actually a French marquis, but after he confides his title to a barkeep, the restaurant staff guffawingly feigns deference with "an obsequious bow." By the time the truth-telling marquis' wealthy daughter arrives from Europe to thank the men for their kindnesses, he has been found dead at his dusty store, one less unnoticed meanderer in New York's "antlike crowd [that] meanders swiftly, restlessly and with apparent aimlessness, though each, as a matter of fact, is bound for the selfsame goal." A heroine of pioneer stock joins America's "aristocracy of brains" (as Zoe did in *Soul*'s press release) by becoming a magazine researcher, reporting undercover as a housemaid at a farm. She falls in requited love with a farmhand who, in turn, unmasks himself as a German aristocrat sent for undercover research on Americans. Zoe typed so rapidly that proofreading fell by the wayside; she described the German count's hair as auburn at the story's start but tawny gold later.[5]

All the while, Zoe kept optimistically revising *Wind*'s manuscript, despite Houghton Mifflin's verdict: the tale of failed Kansas homesteaders was short, mystical, somber, and "not well enough done to bear up under its load of sorrow and blundering."[6]

Zoe's writings do not mention Spencer's death in early 1904, due to typhoid and paralysis—he was out of work, and he and his wife Ruth and their baby Spencer Jr. were living with relatives in Wichita. Rob, by then based in Memphis, attended the funeral. Clarence and little Robert did not. (Rob and Eva, who had no children, eventually lived near his stepmother Ruth and his half-brother Spencer Jr. in Kansas City, but the families had virtually no contact.) Historians and genealogists had begun researching the Andersons, but no one apparently contacted the family's star autobiographer—had she had fallen so far out of touch with relatives? Her brother Harry was interviewed about his hardscrabble early years in Kansas, coping with cattle-borne diseases: "in those days . . . we had no relief." Zoe's photographer brother-in-law Archibald Rue in Harrodsburg published a book about historical sites including Daughters College, the Thompson distillery, and Clay Hill, with boosterish text comparing Kentucky River cliffs to "the Palisades of the Hudson."[7]

Manhattan celebrities, transplanted from the American hinterlands or Europe, gave interviews to Zoe while complaining about how other writers distorted their narratives. The orator Mary Elizabeth Lease, a former Wichitan who was newly divorced, settled in Harlem and converted from Populist to Republican, mused that Republicans now praising her speeches as "the most heavenly music" had despised her "dreadful voice" in her Populist years. Bat Masterson, the Kansas sheriff turned newspaperman, "lapsed into a comatose state of suppressed indignation" while pleading with Zoe not to repeat rumors that he had notched his guns with frontier killings—so Zoe simply wrote in the *Times* that he did not want the rumors repeated. The *Times*'s Irish-born Sunday editor William J. Guard assigned her to report on a pastoral rooftop garden, complete with a windmill and chicken coop, that the Prussian-born theater impresario Oscar Hammerstein had installed atop one of his midtown theaters. Hammerstein was enraged over *Times* coverage of government allegations that his buildings were firetraps, so he threatened to have his outdoor band blast Wagner music toward a top editor's office and "make it impossible for him to write." (See Chapter 14 for how Guard derailed Zoe's newsroom career.)

At the Wall Street office of Ella Rawls Reader, an Alabama-born financier investing in Latin American copper mines and government debt, Zoe outmaneuvered throngs of male colleagues to secure a private interview. Ella explained that her biography had become unrecognizable in the hands of newspapermen, who pried into her love life: "They know more about it than I do. They know more and more every edition." Zoe kept her promise to the sculptor Gutzon Borglum, an Idaho native, that she would "seriously and sympathetically" report on two plaster angels that he proposed to render in stone for the Cathedral of St. John the Divine. The prototypes were rejected as excessively feminine, so he smashed them; Zoe described reverently handling the androgynous shards at his studio. Borglum thanked her with a plaster gargoyle, which she hung on an apartment wall as a "great splendid grinning Ape to mock my loneliness." At the workshops of artist-designers as prominent as John La Farge and Louis Comfort Tiffany, she tried to determine which models had posed for Biblical figures in stained-glass windows. A seemingly soulful young actor who guzzled highballs had inspired "every saint in the calendar" on the windows. Zoe was told that women were inherently angelic, but when she asked where feminine angels could be found on church walls, no workman would give her clearer answers than "It's a ticklish subject" and "I am not at liberty to say."

Waldemar Kaempffert, a *Scientific American* editor (and future *East Side* subscriber), puzzled Zoe with anecdotes about female inventors; why would any woman ease men's path to alcoholism by patenting "a barrel-tapping and emptying device"? Zoe played pollster with prominent men, asking whether Sabbath prohibitions on work and play should be imposed on New Yorkers. Lawyers told her that the cosmopolitan, headstrong residents of "the best town in the universe" could decide for themselves how to rest, but clergymen insisted that only churchgoing should be allowed on Sabbaths. Even the size of Sunday newspapers was deemed sinful, "the work of the devil. . . . With difficulty the reporter refrained from tears. She was one of the devils." Zoe polled 12 women, including Woman's Press Club leaders, about what verdict they would reach if they could serve on a jury (a right not granted until 1937) weighing the death penalty for the showgirl Nan Patterson. She had fatally shot her married lover, Caesar Young, during a carriage-ride tussle, and multiple trials had led to hung juries. "No woman who has never known starvation can judge one who has," the writer and philanthropist Cynthia Westover Alden told Zoe. The suffragist Margaret Ravenhill tried to go off the record: Nan was guilty but not deserving execution, since "Most men ought to be hanged—now, for the goodness' sake don't say that I said that." (Zoe rarely wasted a good opportunity to burn a source.) Zoe's imaginary jury would have been hung, too (in actuality the showgirl soon walked free); an unnamed female philanthropist, living "in the midst of ormolu and gold," told Zoe that Nan "should be electrocuted without further argument."

As a "beautiful and brainy" newspaperwoman, generating "a running fire of fun," Zoe sometimes published multiple features per day. The foggier or snobbier the interviewees, the more fun she had. She found it "impossible to represent" on the page how the Belgian sculptor Paul Nocquet kept his hands in "electric movement" while dreamily describing his hobby of hot air ballooning. Transit tycoon August Belmont Jr. rambled on about international affairs, ignoring Zoe's suggestions that subway tunnels flooded by broken water mains could be adapted into Turkish baths or recreational cave lakes with "stalactites, stalagmites, everything." The British-born poet Oliver Herford scuttled around his apartment, reading his works aloud, dodging Zoe's biographical questions, flattering her taste in poetry; if he had not kept the windows closed, "he might have fluttered out."

Mark Twain was persuaded to sit for Zoe's interview about his cat Bambino, a golden-eyed black beauty who had run away and been recaptured. The reporter waited for hours at the humorist's Greenwich Village mansion, until a steely blue-eyed servant informed her that the great man would not in fact come downstairs. Bambino left Twain's bedside and nuzzled her "desolate skirts," so she interviewed him about the boredom of watching "the alleged humorist . . . grind out fun." She gave the cat her address, in case he wanted to decamp to her tiny apartment. "Bambino licked his chops preparatorily" as she promised feasts of goldfish and canaries and opportunities to sharpen his claws on the *Times* tower's flagpole.

The aftermaths of her profiles were sometimes not pretty. Her Tiffany interviewee "nearly lost his job" for speaking too frankly about women's influence on angel designs. The sculptor Nocquet died in a mysterious balloon crash, and Zoe wondered if her feature might have embarrassed him into suicide. *Times* bosses nearly fired William Guard with "a thundering reprimand" for letting her mock Twain (whose equally unamused secretary Isabel Lyons could not find Zoe's "literary flavor that she thinks she has"). One of her fictional newspaperwomen wrote a gushing profile of a sculptor, but then she overhears him at his studio telling new customers that she is nothing more than "a little penny-a-liner." Zoe's reputation for acidity reached enough profile subjects that when she made initial inquiries, "they trembled and begged me with tears not to interview them."

She had never intended to become primarily a reporter, sticking to the facts. But the *Soul* scandal made newspapering her most viable income source: "not being a born reporter, but having had reporting thrust upon me by the suppression of my book, I never knew when or where to stop. I told it right on." No amount of "the scorn and the contumely," not even a butler's kick down the stairs, would keep her from reportering: "I prefer the fate to that of washing dishes."[8]

She documented her moods and missteps while exploring every inch of her adopted "woeful city," drawn to its "indefinable magnetism." She loved all the streets, "wide, narrow, straight, or crooked . . . She had tried to live elsewhere and had failed." At a Turkish bathhouse, she emulated shopgirls splurging on beauty treatments; a few dollars' worth of massaging and manicures left her turning heads but "dead broke, alas!" Just west of Times Square, she toured the new Hotel Astor's "biggest kitchens in the world," with rooms just for processing squabs or polishing silver salt dishes. Just east of Times Square, she longed for "three pairs of eyes to see it all at once" at the Hippodrome Theatre's mélange of drama, musical and circus, where "crosses between a dragon and a griffin" mingled on Mars with contortionists and elephants. She was irked that the Hippodrome show ended with horses diving into a simulated Confederate lake, during a reenactment of Federal troops freeing Andersonville prisoners: "as if there were no Northern prisons where Southern prisoners suffered a million tortures." On "Decoration Day" (now Memorial Day), her Northern friends teased her while heading off to plant flags at suburban cemeteries: "Come with us to decorate the graves of those who killed off your relatives." She had been born "considerably after" Federal forces looted her family's "plantation," where her abolitionist-preacher father "had voluntarily freed his many slaves," she wrote in the *Times*. The graveyards' planes of grass, studded with mausoleums, looked like starlit skies and "gave her an indefinable sense of the infinite." She planted flags at Federal graves, for she belonged among New Yorkers "who, since she could find no happiness elsewhere had become her people."[9] How improbably rooted she was in a 17th-century city, a Kentuckian turned Kansan homesteader descended from Virginia colonists, as she subtracted from her age and invented Confederate family landholdings.

The *Times* dubbed her "an Inquisitive and Irreverent Feminine Observer" as she picked her way along waterfront marshlands, quarries, and railroad tracks, free-associating about beasts of burden and other New Yorkers in dire straits. "What country is this?" was her reaction to flowered hillsides in the Bronx, where a hospitable farmer offered her strawberries. As she crossed the Brooklyn Bridge by streetcar, the East River mirrored blue skies, "showing kaleidoscopically between criss-cross railings." Brooklyn's weathered wooden statues of tomahawk-wielding Native Americans, advertising stores and restaurants, faced westward "with infinite longing" for the centuries before "the Indians were ignominiously driven forth from New York and the rest of the country." She trekked along the Hudson's Manhattan shore, from uptown's dreamland of "pink and white palaces . . . linked sociably arm in arm" to the southernmost piers and docks, "the Place of Those Who Toil." Workmen delivered "great shining stones for the building of more palaces" and crushed scrap tin, "iridescent balls of light," for recycling into window sash weights. Empty carts idled on their backs, "with helpless arms raised imploringly to high heaven." Mules breakfasted to prepare for pulling canal flatboats, and Texas cattle glared at Zoe through slats on freight cars. Gatherings of immigrants gazed eastward, as if "trying to see across to their own country," as she had done on Mediterranean shores. She rejected a houseboat owner's marriage proposal, although she was tempted to sail away from New York again, "just a little afraid of catching the fever of Wanderlust, of which a microbe already existed in her veins."

She masqueraded as an underpaid needlewoman to wangle a cabin bunk bed on the Deep Sea Hotel, an 1850s merchant ship moored at a Chelsea pier and converted into low-cost housing for laborers. As mist engulfed the waterfronts, "the foghorns screaming out as if in pain," she played ragtime on the ship's piano for the shopgirls aboard, who cakewalked, "tying themselves into hilarious knots." Zoe told her new acquaintances about her equally impoverished friend, a freelance newspaperwoman, who would love writing about ship life, while falling deeper into poverty "when her editors go away on their vacation." On waterfront rocks, Zoe saw old and young gathering wood scraps to sell or to feed into tenement stoves. A boy with a sack already full pointed out where she might obtain her own supply, and she suspected that her cover was blown: "He had seen from her face that she was a free-lance newspaper woman and might be in considerable need of kindling wood." Her visit to the prison on Blackwell's Island (now Roosevelt Island) gave her weeks of insomnia: "wild eyed men in stripes" dragged wagonloads in "human chains of misery, back of them brutal keepers brandishing inhuman clubs." Beneath a bridge, an emaciated man in "clay-colored rags . . . whose home is Nowhere . . . broke into a wan and toothless smile at her look of sympathy, for, being a Woman of Sorrows, acquainted with Grief, she had it in her heart to sympathize."[10]

While interviewing the destitute and disabled, Zoe philosophized about how fate "ruthlessly cuts the crude gem of our lives." Annie C. Ortega, a German-born widow left blind by an operation, described paying neighborhood boys with pennies to escort her on miles-long walks. Annie scrubbed her apartment daily, "to keep from thinking." Zoe was warned that Italian American neighborhoods on the Lower East Side and in East Harlem teemed with brigands and mafiosos "who scuttled ships and cut throats." Instead she met motherless "little mothers" and "little fathers," barely out of toddlerhood, tending infant siblings. She gave nickels to the malnourished children, who played games with crumpled paper balls—they could not afford marbles. They danced "to the shriek of the organ" and helped Whitewings (sanitation workers) hose down the slimy asphalt. She admired (like *Soul*'s Dolly) the resilience of "wage slaves" in neighborhoods where parrots clung to fire escapes, and peddlers hawked wares "from cellar doors, from half windows, from window sills, from doorsteps, from each and every available aperture." The finest-grained details made it into her newspaper reports: "little glittering earrings" glimpsed through mosquito netting on a baby girl's carriage, fish for sale glaring upward with "one blind but reproachful eye." In a tenement near the Brooklyn Bridge's Manhattan anchorage, she spoke with Rocco Pietrafesa, paralyzed and bedridden after being struck by a train. His wife, Angela, minced lemons to make sherbet for sale, and the couple's children served as translators. Zoe assured the family that her writings would bring them charities' attention (a faith she lost in *East Side* times): "my Manhattan of the tall gray towers—she is splendidly rich and good to her poor. She will help you when she knows."[11]

Bread riots were expected to break out on the Lower East Side, as kosher bakers went on strike. Zoe found neighborhood excitement generated instead by "spindle legged children" playing hopscotch, flying kites from fire escapes, and "following the ice wagons, catching greedily at stray lumps." Along Chinatown's "curiously belanterned" byways, she saw cosmopolitan Brooklynites trying out chop suey, and she wondered whether any Chinese-born women had assimilated enough to emulate their white counterparts by hosting "gay little dinner parties" at restaurants. No respectable Chinese immigrant wife, she was disappointed to learn, would eat anywhere but "at home with her husband." Zoe and an artist friend roamed Little Syria, "the land of Omar Khayyam" on the Lower West Side. They fruitlessly tried to order alcohol at Muslim-run restaurants while quoting Omar's medieval Persian odes to wine. The neighborhood's businessmen chatted with Zoe about her Lebanese-born writer friend Ameen Rihani (a Pleiades Club member, *Papyrus* contributor and future Ragged Edger). He had returned to his homeland after offending Little Syrians with calls for tolerance—Maronite Church leaders excommunicated him for criticizing clergy and religious institutions. One of Zoe's fictional heroines, after attending Rihani's farewell party, dines at a restaurant in Little Syria and assimilates a little herself when handed a hookah: "I'll take a puff at one if it kills me."[12]

Some of Zoe's most "pitiful tales" of immigrants went inexplicably unpublished, "rudely extricated by the printer" (a problem *The East Side* would solve). "The more I write for the press the less I comprehend its rules," she mused in "The Common-or-Garden Reporter," an essay in *The Bohemian* ("A Clever Magazine for Clever People," based in upstate New York, issued from 1905 to 1909). She made "pen pictures" while watching thousands of Europeans "tramp, tramp, tramp, tramp" through Ellis Island each day. Russian Jews submitted to rough eyelid exams by "brass-buttoned officers" while still whispering in fear of Cossacks. In the eyes of saber-scarred orphans "who have seen their parents shot or with swords run through them ... there seems still to lurk the reflection of those horrors," memories of hiding in cellars or "darksome, fearful forests from death or from a fate more terrible." One little girl flung out her hands: "I know nothing except that everybody is dead. Everybody is dead." A grayed man "told of the flat roofs from which the Jews were thrown to the pavement to mutilation or death." An elderly rabbi whose family had been massacred sat on his trunk, "afraid that it, too, might be taken away." Yet he steeled himself for the Lower East Side, "with the unflinching strength and character and courage of his race" (a positive stereotype of Jews that recurred throughout *The East Side*). A jeweler whose Odessa store had been pillaged was "helplessly clean ... smiling and serene ... glad to escape fire and sword." He was somehow unrobbed of his fur coat and hat, "of such exceeding radiance you might in the sun have seen it a mile." On some travelers' bent shoulders, suitcases contained potted plants, "as if we had no earth, nor little trees, nor flowers in this country." One Italian toddler lost her grip on a demijohn of red wine, and her family teared up as its contents oozed out in a semicircle, resembling "ink spilled on a blotter.... Could they ever buy such wine this side of Italy?"

Charity workers and bureaucrats escorted Zoe along the processing station's corridors. Alexander Harkavy, the Russian-born head of the Hebrew Immigrant Aid Society's Ellis Island office, tried to guide new arrivals out of "LPC" limbo while fielding Zoe's "innumerable questions" and serving as her interpreter. (He was also a polyglot writer, scholar, and lexicographer, known as "the Noah Webster of the Yiddish language.") Steamship company officials complained about spending 23 cents per head on Ellis Island meals for passengers not yet welcome in the promised land. Zoe saw two young women in floor-length fringed shawls, expecting their suitors to greet them, shunted to a waiting cage with "tall silver bars." They sobbed into their fringe as a matron half-heartedly tried "to find their sweethearts." The matron, a bitter xenophobe (like a number of Zoe's East 15th Street neighbors), would deport the abandoned girls back to Europe "in the steerage.... We must do something to protect the country.... We must draw the line somewhere against this wholesale invasion." The matron's lips only pinched more tightly as Zoe pointed out that a "stampeding herd" of about 2,998 other "invaders" had come through that day. Zoe's conclusion: She was "chronicling history" with her "kaleidoscopic existence," a daily blur of "the bitter and the sweet, the humorous and pathetic, the gaudy brilliancy of color ranging side by side with sad, gray tones."[13]

A *Sun* editor, tired of overexposed celebrities and impressed by Zoe's report on Twain's Bambino, commissioned a four-month series of interviews with high-profile animals. (When she unmasked herself years later as the author of these memorable unbylined features, her friends replied, "They were so clever!") At zoos in Central Park and the Bronx, she eavesdropped on visitors peering into enclosures, mistaking seals for whales and Arctic sled dogs for polar bears. Following journalistic protocol, she telephoned the animals for appointments in advance, handed them her *Sun* business card, and used their real names in print. Zoe promised to vindicate the gray wolf if he told the truth, and he obliged: "Red Riding Hood's grandmother was a cross old dame, who deserved to be eaten." She offered a glittery-eyed serpent the chance to look over the text "before it goes to press," while asking what really happened in the Garden of Eden—"did you tempt that young woman Eve to eat the apple or did she tempt you?"—but the snake was too discreet and gentlemanly to reply.

Central Park's family of hippos named Murphy endured "English sparrows drinking impudently" from their man-made Nile, and having their many relatives sold away. Zoe saw baby Petey still nuzzling his parents Caliph and Fatima Murphy. The patriarch was annoyed by crowds oohing at his yawns: "Can't open my mouth even, without creating a sensation." Zoe, whose own outspokenness had caused controversy, told Caliph he was lucky that he never published a novel, which would have brought on maddening reactions: "You never know what you have meant by a book until the critics tell you." Central Park's rhino Smiles (a survivor of circus abuse) shook with sobs under her cage's hay, "shut off from the companionship of every gentleman rhinoceros in the world." The reporter consoled the thick-skinned bachelorette that if she had been trapped behind "matrimonial bars," she might have rubbed away both horns, "trying to break through." Zoe's *Sun* rhino profile appeared alongside Jack Bryans' silhouette cartoon of a young couple hoping that their infant son would support them in style someday. Did a waggish editor know that Jack was Zoe's unsupportive, child-hating ex?

The Bronx-dwelling giraffes Romeo and Juliet stopped romantically swaying long enough to tell Zoe how much they enjoyed "taking a bird's-eye and scornful view" down at their despised keeper, who called them "such silly creatures." A centuries-old Galapagos tortoise snorted at the fake tortoiseshell combs flooding the market, and his wife would not come out of her home nor her shell since she was, like so many women, "awfully sensitive" about being asked about her real age. The alligator Big Ben, who had an appetite for blue overalls and "tried to eat a keeper the other day" (and a Central Park staffer had indeed just survived such an attack), agreed to a conversation only if Zoe steered clear of the subject of pocketbooks and suitcases made from his friends. A sea lion king, whose companions had become humans' winter coats, ended his interview with a dive and a "watery sneezing wail . . . Alas! Alaska!"

Working animals toured Zoe through their offices, explaining the impact of the city's economic disparities. Calls and letters left a bespectacled stork frazzled at his desk: "this is his busy day," a pigeon assistant warned Zoe (who would post a similar phrase over her *East Side* desk). A fatherless newsboy, breadwinning for a large family on Mulberry Street, pleaded with the stork to deliver yet more siblings by the tenement chimney. But the stork had trouble fostering population growth at uptown doorman buildings, heated by steampipes: "a radiator is no place for me," he told Zoe. A fire station's hound guided her through a veterinary hospital, where he had recovered from a broken neck. Caged purebred dogs were recuperating there from "too rich food, too much luxury, and too little exercise." A circus elephant, forced to play cymbals, drive cars, and walk tightropes onstage, lamented during a dressing-room cigarette break that he hated looking "like a blooming idiot." All it would take to crush his trainer's head, he told Zoe conspiratorially, was "one touch of my pedal extremity."

A softshell clam, dug out of New Jersey estuary mud, insisted on avoiding publicity—even when Zoe squeezed him, he would discuss nothing deeper than "the weather and the scenery." So she got revenge, sprinkling him with pepper and salt and swallowing him. She laughed "in a cannibalistic way" at her first chance "to get even with the interviewed. I have often felt like devouring them, but they always got away. But now! But now!"[14]

Zoe syndicated a dozen *Sun* tales narrated by a Kentucky Colonel, based on Mattie Thompson's murderous politician brother-in-law Phil. In the heavy accent of Zoe's dog-kennel hometown, the narrator exaggerates the feats of the Thompson brothers, among other "kind hahted" community leaders. Generations of men, rich and poor, evade punishment for gunning down or hacking apart real and perceived enemies in broad daylight. The Colonel blames the "putty sassy" intended victims, who had lobbed feud-provoking insults out of "puah devilment." Bystanders felled by crossfire had been stupidly "idlin' about . . . where a fight was liable to occur mos' any minute." Black men clean up the aftermath—one servant sweeps up a hotel floor strewn with what looked like costly Spanish grapes, but were actually feudist eyeballs.

Women are dragged into the violence, in darkly humorous ways. A schoolteacher, after subduing her overaged male students with guns, knives, and swords, ends a generational feud by serving as "a livin' sacrifice," married into an enemy clan "whut had he'ped kill off her relatives." One gunman wounds another's obnoxious mother-in-law "jest in the ahm." Because she is so widely hated for spending her days "studyin' up devilment," and injured but not killed outright, the two clans try to exterminate each other. Entire towns are burned, and dozens of gravestones in mountainside cemeteries bear the same epitaph: "Mahtah to the cause of the mother-in-law!"

The Colonel shares Zoe's love of bluegrass country. He remembers joining a band of drunken horsemen on steeds jumping "sof'ly and swif'ly" over a countryside turnpike's tollgates, to cheat the tollkeeper of a few cents: "You can imagine how putty it must 'a' looked in the moonlight, all of us leapin' me'ily ovah that theah gate and on along the broad white beautiful pike." The Colonel is knowledgeable about Kansas, which needs "cyclone cellahs" for emergency shelter, just as Harrodsburg requires "feud cellahs." John Thompson, a "smooth spoken" ladies' man, is said to be mostly "livin' in Looieville," while his twin Phil "took up his abode up Noath" (meaning Washington, D.C.). The real-life brothers, who often resided at hotels far from their estranged wives, treated Zoe to expensive New York meals as she took notes on their swaggering and cynicism.

J. S. Ogilvie, *Locke*'s publisher, gathered the tales into a dime paperback, *Twelve Kentucky Colonel Stories. Describing Scenes and Incidents in a Kentucky Colonel's Life in the Southland*. The company advertised the collection (even after Zoe's death) in its line of joke books, packed with "laughs to the square inch . . . equivalent to a vaudeville show." It printed 100 copies and kept the proceeds—Zoe still owed the company $240 for the typo-riddled *Locke* run. Other companies ran ads at the back of the Colonel's book, for instance touting "Mrs. Winslow's Soothing Syrup," which soothed children (sometimes fatally) with morphine. Zoe received no royalties as the joke book went into further printings: "my debt, if debt it was, had been canceled again and again and again," she wrote in *The East Side*. She categorized the anthology in her "miles of nonsense," turned out for money, unnoticed by the literary world.

*Brooklyn Life*, a "Home Weekly" full of society news and cartoons, published the unfunniest series of her career: four brief streams of consciousness about single women in agony. They are flayed unconscious by "the knout of pain," chased through slums and pastures by "The Skeleton of Loneliness," or sleepless through "the dense, horrible stillness of the little hours," arms outstretched to "form a cross . . . by way of penance, patiently, uncomplainingly" awaiting dawn's gray streaks on the wallpaper.[15]

Zoe herself was flayed into unconsciousness, as she was falsely accused of antisemitism and ostracized from "the happy family" of newspaper contributors.

Fig. 20: 1907 *Bohemian* magazine illustration of a newspaper editor firing Zoe, after she was falsely accused of antisemitism. AC, Nicole Neenan photo

## 14

# Those Were Hungry Days, 1906–1907

ZOE ALIENATED MORE editors, while she lived apart from her family and was vulnerable to assault.

Her circa 1907 home was "a tiny studio in a skyscraper building, stone floored, stone stepped, aching with loneliness, walls like dungeons, dark and fearsome stairs I had to climb and climb and climb." Her financial precarity brought her 54 cents in arrears on her Woman's Press Club annual dues of a few dollars. She defaulted on rent for a storage unit on the Upper West Side, and its contents were put up for auction—what did she keep there, near her home with Jack Bryans? Madonna and the Bam were taken in by relatives in Kentucky. One of Zoe's fictional Manhattan breadwinners regretfully sends her unemployed younger sister, "so frail, so delicate," to regain health on a farm.[1]

Two of Zoe's sisters, at this same grim time, were frantically protecting their own livelihoods. In Louisville, Nannie Cardwell, breadwinning with a customs clerkship since moonshiners murdered her husband, managed to defend herself from men who envied her salary and accused her of muddling records with erasures or the wrong inks. Nettie Cheeks in Washington begged men for work, even just retyping records destroyed in the 1906 San Francisco earthquake and fire. "You will thereby save me from starvation and death," she wrote to President Theodore Roosevelt, reminding him that his martyred predecessor James Garfield, her father's congregant, had "looked after my interests."[2]

The Panic of 1907 struck late that year, with stock market crashes and bank runs that spiraled into national depression. Ruined businessmen threw themselves into the paths of subway trains; Zoe deemed the transit system "a Morgue, hardly a station in it failing of the terror of such a memory." Among the failed companies were publishers preparing to release *Wind*, which Zoe had rewritten about five times. Ellis Island's halls turned into "a desert waste," as Europeans postponed moves to New York and unemployed immigrants left behind an apparent "sinking ship." A press agent "in silk socks of a lavender hue" paid Zoe a few dollars, which covered her transit fares, to interview businessmen supporting William Howard Taft's presidential campaign. "It promises to be a hard winter, I fear," the publicist unhelpfully warned her, as he syndicated her unbylined work. Aged women beggars cursed Zoe for not giving them pennies: "they wish warts on you. . . . It's a wonder I wasn't all over warts."

A *Smart Set* editor kept piteously borrowing from her, $5 at a time, "saying he had an order for a story but no roof under which to write it." Another male acquaintance borrowed $10 to pay for dinner with his mistress, and then his naïve wife invited Zoe to spend the night at their apartment while he played poker with friends. Zoe "slept fitfully, on account of the clicking of the chips," until it was clear that he was winning. The following morning, she indicated that she would keep his secret, but conditionally: "I reached out my paw . . . That ten, if you please."

She developed "an intense hatred" of President Roosevelt, blaming him for the sufferings of "my beloved poor," including her writer friends: "I know a woman of brains who spent the year of the panic in a Sweatshop . . . whose brains are now defective in consequence." The panic reduced the worth of all brains: "mine were hardly bought at all. . . . I was hysterical over my lack of work. . . . How volatile, unstable, intangible and evanescent a thing it is to have to live by, this brain!"[3]

Powerful men's whims, in addition to the economic downturn, caused newspapers to fire her. Some problematic submission made her *Times* editor William Guard end her "feminine explorer" run: "I wrote something that wasn't fit to print, and he printed it and it was All Over." (Her friendly *Times* coverage of Oscar Hammerstein helped Guard land a post-*Times* job as Hammerstein's press rep, but he never thanked her.) An unnamed editor banned her from his newsroom for excessive honesty: "I unconsciously offended him by writing the truth about someone he feared to offend." The *Sun* canceled her after she was falsely accused of antisemitically reporting on "LPC" ("likely public charge") deportees in detention at Ellis Island. Her friend Alexander Harkavy, a Yiddish translator and aid society rep, had brought her to meet a group of Eastern European Jewish men, deemed too old or young to find work or suffering from "some slight physical defect." They were caged in a steamy "terrible room," piled with filthy grayish blankets and hammocks, "which reeked with uncleanliness." They were nonetheless celebrating Rosh Hashanah, shrouded in prayer shawls, davening with "faces to walls," blowing a shofar. They called out "Happy New Year!" in between wailing funereally, "because they were not permitted to enter the promised land." In the new year, they would be forcibly returned to Cossack territory or stranded elsewhere in Europe, to face even direr poverty and vulnerability to assault. A teenage worshipper in the crowd sobbed and pleaded with Harkavy for government help: "Send a telegram! Beg them to let me stay!" But no breadwinner could be found to remove the boy's "LPC" stigma. "They won't let him land," Harkavy told Zoe. Her *Sun* editors called it "a beautiful story," about unshakeable faith among the doomed.

But her mention of uncleanliness irked a doctor who oversaw Harkavy's aid society. When Zoe stopped by the doctor's Manhattan headquarters, researching another refugee-related topic, he bluntly called her a liar. The detention room had been clean, he insisted—implying that she had smeared it, and by extension the men, out of xenophobia. She had interviewed this bureaucrat before but never named him in print, preferring instead to quote Harkavy's vivid accounts from the immigrant trenches. The doctor's motive for undercutting her was actually envy of Harkavy, she suspected. Her Kentucky blood boiling, she longed to violently defend her reputation. "I am only a woman," she told her insulter. "If I were a man I would knock you down." Afterwards she dashed off a letter to him, warning that she would fight him with her pen, exposing his petty jealousy in print: "I shall take pleasure . . . in teaching you how to call the representative of a distinguished paper a liar to her face. . . . You will wish that I had been a man and merely knocked you down." He responded with a flurry of letters to the *Sun*, alerting editors that she had threatened him and claiming that she had lied about the Rosh Hashanah detention room, which was actually "beautifully clean." The *Sun*—much like Funk & Wagnalls in 1902, fearing Courtenay's lawsuits—unquestioningly accepted a man's version of Zoe's story. The editors who had assigned the Rosh Hashanah piece told the doctor that she was "not their representative" on assignment, merely an occasional contributor gone rogue, powerless to cause further damage in print. She was thus besmirched as "a double liar," who had falsified her *Sun* credentials after antisemitically misrepresenting the Ellis Island room. She was mortified that the doctor's lie about her supposed bigotry could be used as "a cruel weapon with which to hurt me among my Jewish friends." The newspaper's "Big Chief" rejected her manuscripts thereafter; he would not even look at her when she came by the office, hoping for paychecks. He must have recognized himself in print when she savaged the unfairness of her *Sun* firing in *The Bohemian* and *The East Side*, recalling "all my loving work for him . . . my feet had run so willingly in his service." With the quenching of her running fire of words, "the old glad days were over and gone . . . the door forever shut me out and away from the happy family." No newspaperman would have been so readily ostracized: "Heaven help the woman reporter!"[4]

To fool former employers into publishing her again, a young Kentucky-born newspaperman, Albert Edward Ullman, let her use his byline and then gave her the proceeds. Ullman was making his name, as Zoe had attempted, interviewing celebrities, including Mark Twain. Some totally uncharacteristic features appeared under Ullman's name, with distinctive signs of Zoe's hand. One described "a struggling young reporter," on assignment to interview Santa Claus, traveling by dogsled through Arctic forests of Christmas trees where retired reindeer are "eating themselves into gout." Santa, "a very busy man," explains Christmasland's newfangled methods of delivering presents by airship, but he will not disclose his real age: "I keep my heart young by doing good." A Zoe-like Ullman reminisced about a previous Christmas, gratefully receiving charities' turkey dinners, new shoes, and a cot for the night, while "penniless, sick, and out of work . . . the down and outest of the down and out." Real-life Ullman pocketed one of Zoe's freelance checks, so she chased him across City Hall Park, demanding the stolen goods. From an adjacent office, an editor saw her familiar white dress contrasting with the park's greenery, and then he banned her undercover "Ullman" from his pages.[5]

"Pauper wages" from a few unbylined newspaper pieces sustained her at the ragged edge. When clueless friends quoted one of her uncredited witticisms, she retorted, "It doesn't sound funny to me. . . . I wrote it." They looked back askance, as if to say "I'd hate to go about lying like that." One tightwad editor reminded her of antebellum plantation overseers, mercilessly whipping enslaved people: "I wished for a long sharp knife that I might with one swift whack cut off his head." By the time that bloodthirsty thought ran in *The East Side*, "his head was off"—his own writings were being rejected. (God would thus punish a number of powerful men who hurt Zoe: "injustice unravels itself if you wait long enough.")

For a bleak unbylined *Times* piece (reprinted in *The East Side*), she joined a line in the snow for the Bowery Mission's nightly handouts of coffee and rolls. The charity doors opened at 1 a.m., to ensure "no make-believe"—that is, weeding out anyone who could afford someplace to sleep. The breadline stretched for half a mile, noiselessly: "The panic of the rich screams out its pain to the world. The panic of the poor is still." The needy huddled over each other as El trains loosed "furious flurries of snowflakes on their unprotected shoulders." Planks atop the slush did not keep frayed shoes dry. Bonfires served as "footlights to accentuate the wildness of hungry eyes set in the frames of pallid faces." A thousand people grabbed bread with claw-like hands and pressed "trembling lips" to coffee cups. When the mission's supplies ran out, it slammed the doors on block after block of unfortunates, with "the fiendish stare of insatiable and unsatisfied hunger." Zoe wept for "those pitiful outcasts," and for herself.[6]

Her name resurfaced briefly in newsprint as she mourned her friend Katherine Stuyvesant Van Ness Roberts, aka Mabel Tinley, who fatally overdosed on poison to escape lawmen and creditors descending on her Riverside Drive apartment. Although claiming to be a brilliant investor and childless widow, she was a divorced stenographer turned actress and scammer. (Her ex-husband raised their son in a Colorado mining town.) Zoe had mingled at Mabel's soirees with "the most fashionable women and the greatest artists and writers." Reporters thronged the deathbed and then contacted authentic Stuyvesants, who "never had heard of the woman." No mourner "would permit her name to be used" except Zoe (who would fall for Ragged Edgers' fake pedigrees, too); she eulogized bejeweled Mabel as "the dearest, sweetest woman . . . of a fine family."[7]

A few pre-Panic clients—*The Bohemian, 10 Story Book*—kept publishing and sometimes syndicating Zoe's bylined fiction. Some circa-1900 stories were regurgitated for syndication, with identical texts but new titles. She made connections with pulp monthlies—*People's* (from Street & Smith), Munsey's *The Argosy*—and general-interest *Success Magazine* (with "artistic features and fiction," it has survived into the 21st century).[8] Her pulpiest plots revolved around men's hijinks and mix-ups. One accuses his friends of theft after a $100 bill goes missing (it had fluttered into an umbrella stand). A jaded apartment dweller witnesses a violent burglary in progress at a nearby building, but he mistakes it for the set of a movie destined "for some vaudeville house." A Brooklyn patriarch dining with his wife and two daughters is mistaken for a Mormon polygamist, a "foxy old duffer" plying his womenfolk with wine. (*The East Side* would sermonize against "flagrantly unfaithful" Mormons, crisscrossing boroughs to maintain multiple families.)

Zoe resuscitated her circa-1900 scenarios of provincials transplanted to cities, floundering "on a wild-goose chase" for upward mobility. A Virginia teenager draws acclaim in vaudeville shows for whistling in imitation of birdsongs, but then he flees home after Manhattan's cacophonies "of sobs and tears and moanings" blot out his memories of wood thrushes and bobolinks. A bachelorette on a Coney Island outing ruins her glad rags in the rain, while awaiting a date with the monocle-sporting Prince Heliotrope de Saginack. A white Federal veteran turned failing Broadway actor is fired from a bit part, playing an enslaved antebellum Black footman, "grown too old to hold the girandoles." Zoe's icy or caddish fictional suitors drive glittery cars to woo wealthy women like Mabel Tinley, living on Riverside Drive and named Van Ness. One heiress tires of her plutocrat fiancé's gifts of rose bouquets, "in the panic period, when people are begging for bread!" He self-indulgently hires servants with bronze skin to match a favorite hallway blackamoor statue; one lackey is nearly indistinguishable from the sculpture: "One bats the eye and the other doesn't—that is all."[9]

Zoe speculated on the fates of immigrants she had seen newly arrived. The befurred jeweler whose Old Country store had been destroyed, who came through Ellis Island rosy-cheeked and "exquisitely clean," cannot survive in "the seething cauldron of the slums." Unwilling to humble himself to peddling pickles, suspenders, cheap jewelry, or boiled corn ears, he heads homesick back to Odessa, preferring to "face the fire and the sword, and the gunshots." Zoe imagined a Swiss farmwife, stranded at Ellis Island, abandoned by her American husband, going "stark mad" and shouting, "You shall not crucify me!" Zoe's fictional "born again" Polish Jew named Harkavi brought a "weird story" of luck to Ellis Island. In Warsaw, he had been shot into a mass grave with 100 coreligionists and then "burrowed his ghastly way, bit by bit" through the piled corpses to reach daylight. Intoxicated in Manhattan with "an insane desire for untrammeled freedom," Harkavi sets up a chain of newsstands and then rejects his newly emigrated fiancée Rachel. He falls back in love as she reinvents herself as a lace tycoon, headquartered near the Flatiron Building, her eyes "alight with the reflection of the electrics glowing on the Great White Way." (In real life, Zoe's Ellis Island friend Alexander Harkavy was happily married to Bella Segalowsky, whose first fiancé had borrowed her rubles to emigrate and then jilted her when she joined him in the promised land.)[10]

Zoe's undernourished heroines land in charity hospitals, hallucinating that cowbells are calling them back to the countryside. One martyr warns her workaholic architect fiancé that while building mansions and skyscrapers, he neglects "Love's House . . . woven fine of webs . . . from nobody knows where." (That eerie description of a love-nest was improbably printed on a valentine.) An unknown ailment landed Zoe herself at the

Flower Hospital, a gloomy turreted pile on East 63rd Street at the East River's banks. Most patients were charity cases. Medical students trained on them, in crowded wards echoing "with the sighs of the sufferers, with the groans of the dying!" Zoe hallucinated that she was being scrutinized by "the door that turned to a face, the tables whose knobs were eyes to me! . . . I recovered consciousness to find an indifferent, white-clad doctor on either side of my cot, observing my symptoms as if I were an animal, sitting there coldly waiting for me to die." She wanted to murder the physicians and mentees who thumped and prodded her and experimented with "how far they could stretch my cuticle without bursting it." A night nurse "threatened to tie the bandages on my arms with wire." Zoe was convinced that the staff would have given her a "Black Bottle" full of poison to send her across "the Great Divide . . . except that they found out who I was"—still known as a writer.[11]

As she stumbled home from the hospital, a magazine editor "offered to help . . . to talk over my work with me." She accepted his free dinner, despite the risks: "Those were hungry days." Afterwards she let him into her studio. He hung his coat on a chair, uninvited: "It was an indignity, an affront, but I said nothing, for I was in sore need of help. I sat down on a divan. He came and sat by me and put his arms around me. I got up and stood indignantly before him." He replied, "Come . . . None of your airs. I know you newspaper women." Zoe escaped his clutches, handed him his coat, and hustled him out the door, stung that he had "insulted not only me and my calling, but through me every newspaper woman in the world." (By the time *The East Side* ran this story, the attempted assaulter—like so many of her persecutors—had been "torn from his high position.")[12]

Soon after the attack, she scrounged up enough rent to settle for the rest of her life in a sunny literary sanctum, where story ideas poured in through the windows.

Fig. 21: 1908 *Everybody's* illustration of the German band that played out of tune behind Zoe's East 15th Street home (and would provide her funeral dirges). AC, Nicole Neenan photo

# 15

# That Great Uncertain Chasm, 1907–1909

ZOE BRIEFLY SHARED her literary sanctum with her daughter and grandson, taking notes on their reactions to the slums. When they resettled in her hometown, she was left bereft.

What sudden manna financed the family's move to Zoe's last home? The four-room, one-bath unit was on the seventh floor of a nearly new apartment house at 338 East 15th Street. For about $20 a month, the Norris-Morrises enjoyed breezes, sunlight, and the "latest improvements," including a telephone (Stuyvesant 1078 was the number), "closets in plenty," and steam-heat radiators. The brick building, trimmed in stone and creamy terracotta, was sometimes loftily called the Stuyvesant, after the Dutch settlers who had owned acreage in the neighborhood.[1] Their name was also applied to a new all-boys high school across the street from Zoe and a nearby park, laid out in the 1840s and edged in brownstones staffed by liveried servants.

All around, Zoe saw "damnable tenements," a few stories tall, lacking indoor plumbing, "cramped and hideous . . . People live huddled in rooms like rats . . . ten and twelve in a room . . . and only chalk lines to divide them." In winter, immigrants huddled around stoves or fireplaces, fed with coal or kindling. They spent summer heatwaves on rooftops, peering over parapets, "gasping for a breath of air." City workers ignored overflowing trashcans, "reeking of pestilence." Zoe felt fated to live there in relative comfort while documenting privations below, "pushed to it by the superhuman strength of Unseen Hands . . . since there apparently lies my work in life." She somehow afforded the services of Black, Irish, and Italian housecleaners, avoiding drudgery since her Wichita days.[2]

The neighborhood was slowly gentrifying. A *Times* feature by Zoe's journalist friend Kate Masterson deemed it "quite as picturesque and as cheap" as Paris's Latin Quarter and suited to "unattached women." Kate quoted an unnamed woman writer (likely Zoe) who "made the experiment" of moving from a tiny Madison Square apartment to a new "model tenement" at the brink of slums: "Her quick brain saw the advantages and also the possibilities of literary suggestion." Her friends "called on her at first out of curiosity" and then envied "her happy, care-free, and un-harassed way of living."[3]

Zoe's neighbors were mostly from Italy and Eastern Europe's Jewish ghettoes. A few "Stuyvesant" tenants, with tradesmen as patriarchs, climbed enough socioeconomic ladder rungs to have live-in servants. Zoe found the halls redolent with garlic as well as "a literary atmosphere." Her unit had been previously rented by the writer Dorothy Richardson, who went undercover to report on factory conditions for an acclaimed 1905 novel, *The Long Day: The True Story of a New York Working Girl, As Told by Herself*. Zoe speculated that someday people would "stop as they go by and point out the place" as a muse for writers.[4]

From her south-facing windows, sunrises brought pearly backdrops to "my Magic City, Mecca of the Immigrant." (She echoed the hype of Wichita, her first Magic City.) At the horizon loomed "pinnacles, turrets, towers and minarets" of skyscrapers, including the offices of Park Row newspapers that fired her. Rain and mist made the buildings seem "far away as the realization of dreams." At bright noontimes, the towers "glisten gaily, the windows flashing back the fire of the sun." Sunsets unfolded in vermilion, orange, gold, and blue:

> . . . and then these rare colors melt subtly into lavender and the lights come out. It is a Wonder City then of tenderly exquisite gray outlined against the skies. Sometimes it looks to me like a City cut from tissue paper and pinned to the skies, the light in each window a separate pin of pure gold.

The Singer Building, a domed corporate headquarters financed by sewing machine sales and briefly the world's tallest skyscraper, resembled "a beautiful brilliant brooch . . . on the Breast of the Night." When sunsets reddened its brick walls, Zoe thought with horror of the blood of "the little seamstresses who paid for it so dearly, a pittance at a time" and sometimes "died of the loss of their machines."[5]

Her roof had 360-degree views, across Stuyvesant Square Park's venerable elms and the East River's opalescent bridges looming over "pathways of poverty." Chimneys alternated on rooftops with bulkheads, the hut-like entryways to staircases—Zoe called them "little roof houses." Neighbors walked from roof to roof, "the length of a block up there in the air," hosting parties, gossiping, "roasting their Janitors," finding hideaways for flirting, hanging hammocks, or weeping. Laundry was lugged to rooftop or backyard clotheslines by "tiny motherless tots . . . ill fed, ill cared for." The lines' unoiled pulleys chirped "like the song of a bird." Sparrows pecked at the poles, "tall dead posts, the ghosts of trees," sloppily spliced together to reach seventh floors. Pigeons emerged from rooftop cotes for exercise, making joyous circles, "swung hilariously into the ether."[6]

Fire escapes zigzagged down tenement walls, and on rusty landings stuffed with trash and mattresses, children hosted tea parties for dolls. Zoe tried in vain not to watch a neighboring family's Saturday routine, sending two barefooted girls to maneuver along the fire escape and wash the windows. "Special Providence" kept intervening, so the backyard flagstones "don't hold what is left" of the little cleaning crew. Zoe wondered whether the mother "wanted to keep them out of mischief" or was simply careless, "having children to spare." Did immigrant parents coping with huge broods, each child "a stair-step higher" than the next, bring to mind her Kentucky homes teeming with siblings? (Wealthier mothers with few offspring were known downtown as "the Great Unkissed.") She fictionalized a neighborhood parrot, "bright, sleek, well-cared-for," jeering at the poor from his fire escape perch. People's fatal falls over the parapets bring out the vampirical bird's "hoarse, guttural, mocking laughter and cries of 'O Lord!'"[7]

In the backyard bedlam, ragtime and opera arias blared: "phonographs mingled their mad lack of harmony . . . shrieking in competition" with church bells and upwardly mobile children taking music lessons. Buskers—a disabled accordionist barely able to crawl, German oompah musicians playing "terrible untuneful music" (as they would at Zoe's funeral)—pleaded for coins to be tossed from windows, roofs and fire escapes. Foghorn blasts, superior to "the horns of an operatic orchestra," wafted in from the East River, "the little boats begging the big boats not to step on them." The sounds comforted Zoe when she returned late from dinners, "after the elevator has quit running, and I have to climb long, dark stairs to get to the flat, half scared to death."

Some morning wake-up calls came from a telephone lineman, risking his life to shimmy up the spliced poles, offering immigrants their first phones, shouting "Line-up! Line-up! Want a line?" Zoe, while still in her pink kimono dressing gown, leaned out of a window to interview a lineman. He described himself as "worth more dead than alive"—he had insured himself for $75. She barely recognized him later at ground level as he strode through the Lower East Side, "a strange creature seemingly all lines, great strong ropes flung about his shoulders and across and hanging down." She syndicated a supposedly journalistic feature about a lineman who was killed when her backyard pole collapsed, but that seems to have been a morbid invention (accidental electrocution was a more common cause of linemen's deaths in her time).[8]

Human life, she was told, was more disposable on the Lower East Side than elsewhere. One of her Christian avatars visits a neighborhood synagogue during Yom Kippur, pleading with God to stop a sickly Jewish boy from crying "insistently, incessantly" across the space between buildings that Zoe called her "court." He quiets only in death. He was starving, with no medical care, and the Jewish neighbors consider his fate inevitable: "His trouble began with the poverty of his parents." Zoe piled up newspaper clippings at her East 15th Street home about children mowed down by cars, with no consequence for the drivers, which gave her doubts of "the eternal justice of the scheme of things." One janitor responded only "let me sleep!" as a bruised wife, during her husband's nightly beatings, cried out "My God! He's killing me!"[9]

Zoe parodied herself looking for newsworthy woes to write about. A fictional Panic-impoverished newspaperwomen, a Kentuckian living on the "delightfully lawless" Lower East Side, loses out on scoops when "nighthawk reporters" beat her to midnight crime scenes of mafiosos' and anarchists' bombings and kidnappings. She persuades an Italian immigrant family's twin daughters to play with dolls at hèr apartment while posing for photos, which she publishes with articles about the girls' supposed kidnapping and rescue: "Two dollars apiece for the pictures, eight dollars a column for the story, and the rent paid!"[10]

The neighbors, striving or violent or shell-shocked, were silhouetted in Zoe's view of a hundred "living windows . . . a panorama of tumultuous life . . . the seamy side of existence." As an escapee from gossipy Harrodsburg and Wichita, she was relieved to know no one's names, to comprehend no Yiddish or Italian rants from neighbors "with whom I cannot talk or quarrel." Other voyeurs were in sight: a bald old man would pause on his rooftop while hanging laundry, his mouth rammed "full of clothespins," to peep at women getting dressed.[11]

Zoe filtered her sightlines with blue-and-white curtains and potted plants—pigeons nibbled at her geraniums, nasturtiums, ivy, and morning glories—as she settled with her notebook into her windowfront cushions or a wicker "observation chair." She put two ringleted dolls' heads on pedestals at a window, "friends who wait for me . . . and never change color, no matter when I get home." On her blue kitchen's shelves, Delft pottery harmonized with silver vessels, "old pieces of Sheffield Plate left from the wreck of former glory . . . the relics from my Southern home." She bought candles from a blind peddler, to burn in her inherited silver candlesticks and new candleholders made of Russian brass. Among her other treasures was a dried rose from her schoolmaster John Williams' Spring Hill grave, and a copy of her father's "very beautiful translation." She expected his book to be found among her "humble possessions" at her deathbed, open to John 14:1, page 238: "Let not your heart be troubled."

For morning inspiration at the typewriter, Zoe visited the roof, "to let the breeze blow what cobwebs may linger in my brain from over night." She paid in installments for an ebony piano, "a luxury . . . not intended so much for East Side people . . . played only to amuse myself and worry the neighbors and to tune my soul to the pitch of getting to work." A friend teasingly predicted that Zoe would arise one last time in her death throes: "Wait just a minute. I owe a little something yet on my piano." She kept up her fingering skills enough to perform Chopin at a 1908 soiree that the writer and explosives inventor Hudson Maxim hosted at the Brooklyn home he shared with his second wife Lilian, "decorated with cannon, pistols, shotguns, and cartridges." (Maxim was one-handed—he lost the other in a mercury fulminate experiment.) Also in attendance were the illustrator William Oberhardt, Zoe's future staff artist, and the poet Edwin Markham, who probably did not remember Zoe's 1902 pleas for help battling Courtenay Lemon. One of her fictional pianists pounds out a Chopin prelude, the instrument shaking with insistent notes of raindrops, followed by "clap after clap of thunder, pulsing chords in the bass."[12]

For some idyllic months, Zoe lived there with Clarence and Robert Morris: "The Bambino was of such beauty that he lighted the little flat in the great building bordering on the slums." The boy so captivated Zoe that she wondered what games he was playing with friends in the hall: "I wish always to have news of him." In her short story "The Japanese Kimono," a Manhattan breadwinner feels lonely in her apartment and, due to "the fault of my selfishness," retrieves her fragile younger sister from a sojourn at a farm. The younger woman moves "soft-footedly about the flat, amusing herself" or doing chores, dressed in the older sister's gift of a kimono patterned in pink primroses. The older woman, upon returning late from "some festivity," can depend on the kimono wearer's sleepy hands helping unbutton her gown, and chocolate drinks ready in the morning.[13]

Zoe syndicated a story about the Bam using a toy telephone to place a pre-Christmas call to Santa Claus, insuring delivery of the right presents ("338, Iceland" was the North Pole's number, similar to the boy's street address). Zoe and Clarence surprised him with a Christmas tree, "jewel-like with bonbons, balls and gewgaws." It puzzled him that no neighbors had trees, and Zoe explained that instead, candles on Jewish holidays "flickeringly illumined" the court's living windows. Clarence vowed that she and Zoe would instill unshakeable Christian values in him:

> We will make such a man of him . . . that he will compensate for all the imitation men that we have known. We will make him clean, upright, honest. We will teach him to honor women and protect them. . . . I want him to make up to us for every heartache, for every disillusion.

The Bam wept after a Jewish playmate said that Christ was not a real messiah, and Zoe reassured her family that the neighbors still served as excellent role models. They had outlasted "attempted annihilation absolutely unknown to other races," and they were less hypocritical and more religiously observant and charitable than most Christians in New York.[14]

Zoe, who declared herself "champion of the Oppressed of all Races," experienced Jews' philanthropy firsthand in fall 1908 while posing as a stranded tourist, reporting undercover for the *New York Press*. She based the ruse on a true horror story shared by a dinner companion, a "gentle, pure and timid" suburbanite who had made a daytrip to Manhattan, emptied her purse to help a troubled relative, and then missed the last train home. With 29 cents in hand, the distraught young woman was rejected for emergency housing by the YWCA (their minimum charge for a cot was $1). So she spent the night "faint and weak" in Union Square, amid dozing men contorted "like bodies dug from some Pompeii, bodies petrified in misery." Zoe showed up late on a Saturday at a YWCA office near Union Square, pretending to be a shopper from Patchogue who had misplaced her cash except 20 cents and missed the last eastbound train. A bespectacled secretary with "the firmest mouth I ever have seen" said there would be no room for her at any Christian establishment. Zoe was sent to a nearby Hebrew charity, where a whitehaired gentleman's "such genuine pity" tempted the impostor to unmask herself. He directed her to a Rivington Street shelter's 20-cent cots and even gave her a quarter for transit fares (which she considered mounting on velvet to hang in a frame on her apartment wall). Rivington Street blared with "blatant hucksters," organ grinders, and "Socialists going to Socialistic meetings." She paid a few cents for a meal at a rundown but hospitable restaurant—a sign advised, "If U don't C What U want, Ask 4 it." But once she was guided to her dorm cot, she fled, just as she had run away from her 1902 undercover housemaid quarters, unable to bed down in a sea of "terrible figures... the starvation in their faces enhanced by their sleep."[15]

By 1908, Clarence had spent enough time in Kentucky to fall in requited love with Fletcher Creed Chelf, a Harrodsburg farmer of sterling character who also played flute in a local band. (That fall she finalized her divorce and custody arrangement with Harold Morris in Dublin—it is not known whether she traveled for the courtroom proceedings, how Harold ended up there, and what happened to him afterwards.) In "The Japanese Kimono," the younger sister likewise falls in love with a sturdy, wholesome farmer, "fairly quick-witted for a country boy." The older sister has been strengthened through hard times in love and work "that would have crushed to death a weaker woman." She warns her educated, "delicately reared" sibling, "you small frail thing meant for luxury," of the grueling demands of rural life, milking cows at dawn. The younger woman replies that farmwives might be better off than their sleepless urban counterparts, weeping at dawn over husbands out at some "round of gaiety." The younger sister heads back to the country, leaving behind her faded primrose kimono in the apartment's "hollow emptiness." Zoe's morning garb on East 15th Street was a pink kimono; was it Clarence's?

Zoe, aka Momsey, last saw Clarence, aka Cis, Cissy, Madonna, and the Girl, sitting on a couch, "working away at a piece of fine embroidery" at the literary sanctum:

> The Girl was going back home to live, going back to leap into that great uncertain chasm of Marriage, out of which so many come climbing pale faced and painfully to the Well Spring of Divorce. Going to leave me forever alone in my little flat, if all turned out well.

Zoe promised that her "marvelous telepathic sympathy" would extend "across the limitless stretches of country that separate us," that she would sense if unhappiness ever returned to her daughter. The two women embraced, and Zoe prayed for a chance to visit Harrodsburg posthumously "and come and sit by you"—accurately predicting that she would not return to her hometown alive. In late 1908, Zoe helped out at a fundraiser for blind children in Brooklyn—one of the last times she believed that charitable donations made it to the hands of the neediest. Her last known published work from 1908 was a poem, "The Happy Hunting-Ground," in which an insomniac asks nighttime shadows what happens in the afterlife: "will the Almighty Host and the angels help me find my love?"[16]

In Zoe's court of living windows, an elderly couple was silhouetted, "mumbling and toothless," their nest empty except for a black cat. "Your children step out of their cradles and walk out of your life, but if you have found your work, then after all you are not left desolate," Zoe told her readers, upon assigning herself her favorite work of all.[17]

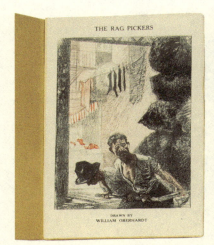
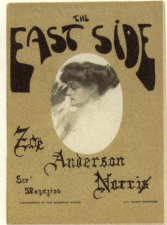

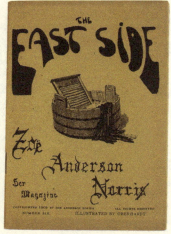
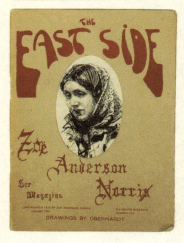

Fig. 22: Examples of *East Side* covers illustrated by William Oberhardt: top row, no. 4 (left), 1 (both 1909); 2nd row: no. 25, left (1913), 6 (1910); 3rd row: no. 10, left (1910), 28 (1913). AC, Nicole Neenan photo

## 16

## Dear Children, 1909–1910

IN AN UNINHIBITED, bimonthly stream of consciousness, *The East Side* recorded its own birth and growing pains as Zoe thanked readers, settled scores, dug into her past, and advertised her other publications. She grew ever rawer in subject matter and angrier at mistreatment of the powerless. She discouraged anyone from pigeonholing her: "I'm going to offer a prize for the best guess as to what I am. I'd like to know, myself."[1]

Marion Miller, who had shepherded *Soul* at Funk & Wagnalls, planted the seed by asking, "Why don't you start a magazine of your own and air your opinions?" Zoe replied, "I didn't think they were worth anything." He unreassuringly assured her, "They are not . . . but they are original." One last encounter with plagiarizers convinced her to give self-employment a try. The monthly *Everybody's* had accepted her undercover report on dressing as a scrubwoman and seeking shelter with the Salvation Army, but then decided to adapt it into a different nonfiction feature, without crediting or paying her. "That cured me of the magazines" owned by anyone else. When she saw an *Everybody's* editor at a party, he expected a snub, but she thanked him: "If it hadn't been for you," *The East Side* might not exist.[2]

She knew the competition would be fierce. According to contemporary scholar Kirsten MacLeod, Zoe was one of hundreds of circa-1900 dreamers founding understaffed, underfinanced, sporadic periodicals known as "magazinelets." Many lasted only a few issues. The editor-owners targeted progressive-leaning readers with irreverent, contrarian, "individualized perspectives on the contemporary scene."[3]

Zoe had already written for this "brotherhood of the little magazines," including Marion Miller's *Manuscript*, "Issued Every Month in the Interest of Book-Builders & Book-Buyers" (April–December 1901), and Lee Fairchild's *Thistle* (March 1902–January 1903). Her New Jerseyan friend Michael Monahan had written about her in *The Papyrus*, "A Magazine of Individuality" aimed at readers "tired of Canned Literature" and sharing "Hatred of Sham and Fake" (1903–1916, with long gaps and a name change to *The Phoenix* along the way). Zoe's friend Bruce T. Calvert, who lived in a rural Indiana shack called "Pigeon-Roost-in-the-Woods," issued *The Open Road* (1908–1940, with long gaps), "A Sane Sweet Toned Magazinelet of Faith" warning against the pitfalls of city life as well as extravagant Christmas gifts. Zoe's friend Elbert Hubbard attracted more than 100,000 subscribers to *The Philistine* (1895–1915), "A Periodical of Protest . . . Printed Every Little While" by the Roycrofters in East Aurora.

Zoe also knew members of the little-magazine sisterhood. Elizabeth Towne, an Oregon-born motivational speaker, "pacifier, harmonizer, and steam roller," claimed that 175,000 people read *The Nautilus* (1898–1953), a Massachusetts-based monthly that she published with her second husband William, giving guidance for "Joyous Advance through Self-Knowledge, Self-Direction, Co-operation, and Confidence." Astors, Vanderbilts and "Crowned Heads of Europe" collectively worth $3 billion were said to be among the 25,000 subscribers of the periodical *Men and Women* (1903–1906), with "intimate, interesting items about distinguished people" from Mattie Sheridan, a Kentuckian turned Manhattan writer and saloniste. (See Chapter 17 for how Mattie's Hungry Club compared to Zoe's Klub.)

*The East Side* adhered to the field's norms with a small format (four by six inches), tan covers, 34 creamy interior pages, thrifty use of only red and black ink, and a price tag of 10 cents per issue and $1 a year ("One Plunk" was Zoe's slang). Printing 1,000 copies cost her $85 at first; she then bargain-hunted among lower Manhattan's print jobbing houses to pare the bimonthly expense down to around $35. She financed the first run by selling off some earrings, the last of her pre-Manhattan finery, thereby becoming "the first woman reported to have started a business by pawning her diamonds."[4]

Her bimonthly magazinelet would focus on the poor, she announced, although no one else thought that mission would be sustainable. "They are part of my life . . . There are none of them too humble for me" was her retort when "a great editor of a great New York paper" advised her not to waste her talents on anything sad, anyone but "those who are making their mark in the world." She expected no *East Side* profits, just a chance to channel other people's money in the right directions: "I can only fight for the poor with my pen."⁵

She wrote virtually every *East Side* word—"I hardly ever reject any of my own stories"—and granted herself all the masthead titles. She started with "Office Boy, Business Manager, Editor-in-chief, Managing editor and owner" (idiosyncratic capitalizations were an *East Side* hallmark) and then promoted herself to "Six Editors." She adopted ever-changing job titles from the printing and publishing trades: Circulation Liar, Compiler, Printer's Devil (a low-level apprentice), and Two-Thirder (a midlevel trainee). She came up with mouthfuls of corporate bureaucracy: "President, Vice-President and Assistant Secretary," and "Advertising Man, Advance Agent, Bureau of Statistics, Inquiries, Maid of All Work, Publisher and Boss." She imagined taking on construction work—Bricklayer, Hodcarrier, Hoisting Machine, Paperer, Plasterer—and service jobs: Bell-Hop, Bootblack, Bottle Washer, Bouncer, Common or Garden Waiter, Ironer, Laundry Boy, Porter, Scullery Maid.⁶ There were references to sports—"Bookmaker, Umpire and Referee"—and utter nonsense: "T' Tilly Tired Foot." She lowered herself to "All Around Drudge" and slangily asserted power as Pooh Bah, High Muckamuck, Big-Wig, Big Chief, The Whole Shebang, T' Main Guy, T' Whole Cheese, or "De Whole Ting! See!" One entire masthead (my favorite) was slightly menacing: "If You Want To See What She Is, Start Something."

The first issue credited its inspiration to Marion Miller, whose many books included studies of ancient Greek and Latin texts. Zoe called him a "delver into ancient lore of Iliad and Idiocy, I mean Odyssey," thus debuting an *East Side* tradition of teasing or insulting friends, biting hands that fed her. As was typical of magazinelets, she addressed readers directly, promising her "Dear Children" that her first-person prose would "bristle with as many 'I's" as Hubbard's *Philistine*. Hubbard opened his issues by free-associating for his "dear friends" with "Heart to Heart Talks with Philistines by the Pastor of His Flock," and Zoe's introductory essays likewise jumped around in topics, from reminiscences to reflections on politics, religion, and societal ills. But few other Big-Wigs would have published the newborn *East Side*'s descriptions of tenement conditions.

From issue no. 1 onward, Zoe gave trigger warnings—"This is not a nice subject, Dear Children"—for readers living complacently elsewhere. In her neighborhood, trashcans swarmed with flies and spread deadly diseases. Children were killed in blazes caused by stoves, fireplaces, or mattress bonfires, but landlords went unpunished for not supplying heat. She was haunted by an evening sighting of two shivering preschoolers, locked out of their Bowery home; she had been too afraid to confront "the ogre who had shut them out. . . . I dream of them and wake and wish I had broken open the door with my bare hands." She felt "cold horror" upon seeing the face of an emaciated, eyeless woman—on her face, "the flesh had been sewed in two straight lines"—who headed into Stuyvesant Square Park, "walking blind in all the hideous dangers of the dark night!" Individual destinies—like Zoe's own, as the descendant of vicars—were fixed by "the great unseen skeleton hand of a malicious ancestry." But could she not help her neighbors combat their fates, "when a great and cruel wrong is done collectively"? The poor patiently awaited upward mobility, nearly suffocating, like fish for sale in mongers' barrels: "in spite of it all, they live!"

Issue no. 1 ran the nearly stolen *Everybody's* submission about masquerading as a scrubwoman to seek a cot for the night at the Salvation Army's Bowery shelter for women.[7] The staff stayed behind closed doors as hungry women dozed all day in the waiting areas, hoping for a chance to pay 15 cents for a bed. The Salvation Army provided no meals or washtubs, so the women scavenged for food and bathed in the rain. "If you come to this place for charity, you'll find it cold, daughter," one bonneted woman warned Zoe, but then snapped, "You ask too many questions." (Zoe loved pointing out how poorly she disguised her undercover reporting.) A feisty elder named Katie, "perfectly reckless" in her chattiness, had one piece of jewelry left to her name, "a little coral ring, old as time," and tearfully told Zoe about its giver: "She's been dead a long while." Zoe pressed a quarter into dozing Katie's hand upon fleeing the place, and the Salvation Army became an *East Side* bête noire, "the Giant Fake of the Twentieth Century." She accused its founding family, the Booths, of giving unchristian pittances to the poor while granting themselves millions of dollars in alms. "I hate the sound of tambourine and drum" from the charity's musicians, "whose discordant shrieks for alms afflict the Universe" in performing hymns and ballads in barrooms and outdoors. The Booths lived in mansions, tempting Zoe to go undercover as "Scrubwoman in the palace."[8]

She leavened issue no. 1's bleakness—"let me tell you something gay"— with paeans to her humane piano supplier George Schleicher, "who won't take your piano from you when a panic comes on," and the hospitable Hungarian eateries that she frequented on lower Second Avenue. She hyperbolically likened Alexander Balogh, whose restaurant was at Sixth Street, to an emperor, charging 35 cents for dinners with wine flowing from "the roof and the floor and the refrigerator and every other article of furniture to which a faucet can be attached." Café Boulevard at 10th Street (where she dined with Ragged Edgers to the end) festooned its rooms and balconies with real and fake flowers and grapevines. Its orchestras sent "plaintive Magyar melodies" down the avenue. Waiters, rumored to have been noblemen in their homelands, poured wine from "long-necked bottles" (which the Queen of Bohemia turned into scepters). Uptowners—tuxedoed men, behatted women with "the glitter of jewels at ear and throat"—took long carriage rides to linger at the tables with literati. Haggard newsboys and soap and bread peddlers circulated during Café Boulevard's bacchanals. Zoe gathered stories about the regulars, which issue no. 1 promised to share "if it should occur that there is another issue of this magazine."

It was at Café Boulevard that she first met the illustrator William Oberhardt (1882–1958), who sketched her in profile for *The East Side*'s debut cover. The only child of a German-born cabinetmaker, he grew up partly on the Lower East Side, so he knew well the haunts of Zoe's "beloved poor." As a teenager he took night classes at the neighborhood's free art school, the Cooper Union, and then trained at the National Academy of Design and Munich's Academy of Fine Arts. By the time Zoe officially dubbed him "the Artist," he was prolifically freelancing in easeful strokes of pen, pencil, charcoal, pastel, and paintbrush for some of her former employers (*Success, Everybody's,* Funk & Wagnalls). He portrayed celebrities like Woodrow Wilson, William Howard Taft, and John D. Rockefeller as well as threadbare Ellis Island arrivals and sweatshop "little toilers," boys and girls dazed by want. Obie, as he was nicknamed, sometimes recycled other clients' Lower East Side images for Zoe while squeezing her into his schedule.[9]

She could not afford to pay him. He worked in exchange for sharing her free press passes to Broadway shows. "Personally I care very little for the stage," she admitted, but the tickets served to "repay him slightly for doing my drawings for nothing." Motivated also by a "love of the uplift" of the poor, he supplied her with hundreds of atmospheric sketches, related and unrelated to her topics: "There's nobody else who pictures the East Side as he pictures it." On the magazinelet covers and full pages, Zoe ran his views of skyscrapers, clotheslines, market stalls, peddlers, pawnshops, synagogue worshipers, laborers used as beasts of burden, and herself. His drawings of garlic strands, ashcans, pawnshops, washtubs, laundry lines, fire escapes, breadlines, wine goblets, hatracks, and Yiddish shop signs filled her page margins, and she incorporated them into her stationery and brochures. Many of his original *East Side* drawings and lithographs were a few feet tall, so they retained their intricate details and sense of depth once reduced for printing on four-by-six-inch pages.[10]

Few of Zoe's competitors ran any illustrations, and none rivaled her everchanging stream from an observer as keen-eyed as Oberhardt. Bruce

Calvert of Pigeon-Roost-in-the-Woods envied her artwork from a "sympathetic wizard of the brush and pencil." Hubbard's *Philistine* in East Aurora printed various artists' work, typically on the back covers alongside poems, aphorisms, and witticisms ("A Corkscrew Will Never Pull a Man Out of Trouble"). *The East Side* "beats the Sage of East Aurora at his own game," due to Oberhardt's "very artistic little marginal sketches."[11]

The proceeds from the pawned diamonds dwindled as Zoe mailed out sample issues nationwide. Her press releases explained that from the East 15th Street aerie, "I see enough any day to make me keep writing forever." She believed her work would bring "better times . . . to submerged folk of the East Side, and if the good times don't come, well, at least I will have said some things that have been a long time on my mind." She had *East Side* stacks delivered "wherever magazinelets are sold on the Earth above and in the Subway below," including newsstands, bookstores, and "every classy department store in New York and Brooklyn." (That is, as if provincial Brooklyn was not part of the city—that was the start of her five-year series of jokes about Brooklyn, which some friends considered "an outlying section of Weehawken.") She reluctantly signed up with the industry's dominant distributor, the American News Company, a greedy "Giant Octopus" that pocketed half of her newsstand revenue. People told her that they could not resist finishing each issue, and some returned copies did look as if a shopper had in fact devoured it "Then walked off without Buying It." Although she wanted to maximize $1 annual subscriptions, to pocket the plunk, she hesitated to ask friends "to contribute yearly . . . I don't want to find out how few real friends I have."[12]

Issues reached the desks of newspapermen who remembered her; a Kentucky paper reminded readers that she was "formerly of Harrodsburg." A syndicated profile of the newly self-appointed "Pooh Bah of the Shop" was illustrated with a sketch of entrepreneurial Zoe typing under a sign, "This Is My Busy Day" (similar to the motto of the frazzled stork that she interviewed in 1902). Errors cropped up in *East Side* coverage, which would persist into her obituaries and beyond. She was described as the widow of the writer Frank Norris, and a snide joke ran in syndication:

> Miss Zoe Anderson Norris has started a magazine in which, as she says, 'to speak her mind.' A magazine is a costly proposition; why not get married at 1-10 the price and have a constituency to which you may always speak your mind, Zoe?

This commentary on the news bizarrely kept resurfacing into the 1920s. How enraged was Zoe when strangers suggested that marriage would bring "Miss" Norris a more affordable, dependable audience?[13]

She hired a clipping service to gather evidence of her newspaper mentions. During a visit to the company's office, she interviewed the people who were alerting her that she was being written about for writing. She watched "hundreds of young women and girls . . . marking paragraphs . . . rustling among the leaves that had come from Maine to California." It seemed as though all newspapers were simply machines for "grinding out the voluminous news of the world for the press clipping bureaus to clip."[14]

Although she feared her magazinelet would last "one consecutive night," plunks poured in. Fan mail arrived from David Starr Jordan, Stanford University's first president, and *Collier's* editor John Milton Oskison, Stanford's first Native American graduate. Hubbard sent her a picture of himself, suitable for framing, and he "mopped a few" (tears, that is) while immersed in her "fine little publication . . . extra choice in a literary way." She was compared to Nathaniel Hawthorne's daughter Rose Lathrop, a writer turned Manhattan nurse and Catholic mother superior. (Rose lived among the dying cancer patients in her care and published a small magazine, *Christ's Poor*, about her work.) Zoe's issue no. 2 excerpted the rave reviews, including from merry dinner companions who asked, "who'd ever think you had any religion in you?" She promised not to quote quite as much praise as her friend Monahan's *Papyrus* did under the headline "Indifferent Modest!"[15]

Men offered to write for her—one potential contributor showed up at her apartment and, while she was still in her pink kimono, kept nervously calling her "Sir." But her pages typeset with her own long-pent-up thoughts left "room for nothing more besides." The Office Boy—every male editor had one on guard duty—protected her from would-be protégés: "If I don't want anybody to see myself they get to me over my dead body." A dashing young philanthropist surprised her with a check, no strings attached, to "help keep the Printer from the Door." When she went incognito to a newsstand that stocked her brainchild, the newsboy turned out to be an *East Side* doubter: "I didn't see nothin' to it," yet it was selling well. One of the few other *East Side* faultfinders was Zoe. Obie's "perfect pastel" sketch of her, when adapted for printing on no. 1's cover, made her look too old for her tastes; the engraver had overcharged ($1.50 for 10 cents worth of work), while taking pains "to ruin my portrait." That was the start of a five-year series of complaints about men who were putting her words and images on the page. How did the printers feel upon typesetting the insults?[16]

Monahan celebrated her debut by treating her to a sandwich lunch and some pessimism: "It was two years before I got a cent from 'The Papyrus.'" Newsstand sales would lead only to some advertiser appeal and opportunities to market her other writings, he warned. She tried to work with a female ad rep, "a purring Englishwoman" who generated nothing but unwanted advice on hairstyles, leaving Zoe feeling "once more living with a husband!" A promising male ad rep kept her waiting for hours while he was actually in Kalamazoo. "I see your finish, unless you find him," Monahan said, wishing her luck.[17]

How was she planning to remunerate her ad reps? Issue no. 2 had just four advertisements—an *East Side* record that she never surpassed—including for the restaurateur Alexander Balogh. Did he take out page space to thank her for no. 1's flattery, or did she barter with ads for meal discounts? (See Chapter 18 for her attempts to rescue Balogh's failing business with her pen.) Her 29-issue run brought in a total of only about two dozen ads, ranging from classifieds to full-pagers. Most were for small-timers: "Pandora Meta-Psychic Delineator of Character and Destiny," at $5 per consultation; Zoe's midtown beautician Caroline Boughton; *The Idler*, a short-lived "little magazine of ideas for the idle hour" (issued from New Jersey by Robert J. Shores, a Cornell-educated Montanan). Smith College-educated publisher Gertrude Ogden Tubby filled half a dozen *East Side* pages with excerpts from two novels about slums and settlement houses by Donna R. Cole, a globe-trotter and saloniste in northern California. Publishing giant Doubleday, Page offered Zoe's readers a money-back guarantee for an anti-stress self-help book, with chapters on the likes of "Pain—The Danger Signal," of minimal use to slum dwellers.[18]

Zoe provided copy for some advertisers. Her Belgian-born violinist friend Ovide Musin, offering instruction by mail, could win over even Kentucky gunfighters, replacing violent feuds with "Violent lessons." Zoe told the Office Boy that she was "out on important business" while joyriding to the Plaza Hotel in "a dear little car," a fringe-trimmed wicker prototype from the Kosmos Electric Runabout Company. (Expected to conquer cities, parks, and resorts from Brussels to Havana, the vehicle was in production for only about a year.) She advised any woman about to get hitched to see if the fiancé could pull one of New Jersey carriage maker James H. Birch's rickshaws, "before you hitch him up for life." Wives could please husbands by turning their lawns into "a new bit of clean green velvet" with mowers from the Coldwell factory in upstate New York. *The East Side* endorsed beauty treatments that could retrieve "the husband who has wandered away," and rubber corsets that created hourglass curves, "the envy of all your friends." The beautician Caroline Boughton's customers could enter her premises "looking like the Wrath of God, and come out so beautiful your Best Friends hardly recognize you." Did Zoe receive discounted or free phone service for Stuyvesant 1078, or hope to, in exchange for her long odes to "The Girl at the Switchboard . . . who never sleeps at the switch"? Phone operators protected customers by placing calls to patch up quarrels or track down errant husbands, or phoning police "when the burglar comes climbing stealthily into your window." Zoe's landlord would not give her a rent break, despite her pleas: "Look at all the free advertising you get through my magazine!" When a despondent spendthrift husband showed up drunk at her apartment, brandishing a pistol and threatening suicide, she convinced him to spare his life, although he speculated that the notoriety "will advertise you."[19]

Hubbard penned his *Philistine* ads, for example promising intellectuals that the grain-based beverage Postum could help brains "take on added ability." At $100 per ad page, he reeled in the likes of Tiffany & Co. and Anheuser-Busch. *The Philistine* touted Roycrofter products, too: mahogany footrests ($6), "wondrous wearing" leather handbags ($20), red crepe neckties "Full Fra Elbertus Size" ($1.50), and copies of Hubbard's bestselling 1899 poem, *A Message to Garcia*, lauding a soldier's dedication to duty. Zoe claimed to rival the Fra for the title of "best writer of advertisements in captivity." But she resented other comparisons to him, and she eventually switched from tan to white cover paper, to differentiate *The East Side*'s "entire complexion" from the sepia *Philistine*. She mocked Hubbard's cash-cow Garcia poem as a "message to somebody or other," and she pleaded with a historian compiling profiles of Kentucky literati: "For the Lord's sake don't call me an imitation of Elbert Hubbard." She was amused when her British friend Philip Riddell, a chess-playing insurance broker (nicknamed Honey, and born humble Peter Riddle), suggested that she build a Fra-like empire. She could stock a shop with furniture bought on installment, "call it the Zoecroft furniture and sell it to the Select Few Only."[20]

One market that she could realistically corner was women readers. With her maternal instincts and feminist outrage, she set out to "roast the men" by name, numbering them among the world's "seven original jokes." She trusted none but enjoyed their company, given "the exceeding variety of their lives" (as Nancy Yanks and Polly Locke had envied men footloose in "the gay, laughing, rollicking world"). On issue no. 2's cover, Zoe ran her own photograph of a "kindling wood woman," resigned and calm yet grimacing, balancing weathered planks on her head and hauling a barrel-size wooden pail.[21] If the pail contained beer for the kindling wood woman's husband, he might finish it off and beat her that night. But if the wife cooked "Very Nice Things" and made money peddling, to keep their home "more pleasant than the barrooms," maybe he would not emulate his wealthier counterparts and flit without supporting his family.

Laws written with "no regard whatever for the rights of women" enabled New York men in Zoe's time to escape alimony requirements. They could move out of state (New Jersey was a favorite haven) or spend six months in a jail on Ludlow Street known as "the Alimony Club," where the amenities included a billiard room. Zoe was repulsed when an unnamed male friend—did he recognize himself in print?—invited her to dine with his lover, "a cheap little actress," and then with his saintly wife, who just wanted to escape "the false gaiety of it all" and go home: "My baby wants me." In Zoe's syndicated short story set at a nightclub full of married couples, a singer flirts with the husbands, while she and the embarrassed wives all long to go home, thinking along similar lines: "My baby is crying for me. I know he is." Zoe told readers of her own planet-spanning bond with Clarence: "nothing holds the note of Eternity so much as Maternity." The only Lower East Side mothers seen "flying the coop when the Stork comes along" were forgivable, unwed outcasts, like the bonnet-wearing girls around Clarence and her newborn Bambino at the East 86th Street hospital. Zoe urged self-reliance on mothers and daughters; work, whether as lawyers or organ grinders, "dries the tears and heals the heartache." Children should take their mothers' maiden names, giving families "a permanent Head where the Body is."

Marital happiness must exist somewhere, Zoe thought, while scanning her court's living windows. She saw a disgruntled wife napping all day, building up energy to fling irons at her husband every evening. In an apartment wallpapered in "fiery, quarrelsome red," a couple guzzled beer and argued away a beautiful Saturday, as their puny son tried to protect his mother from his razor-wielding father's "ungovernable temper." An illicit romance seemed to be brewing across the court, as an elderly wife tenderly hugged a handsome blond doctor who arrived to tend her dying husband, "bent and broken and bald." But then mortified Zoe discovered that the May-December pair in sight were son and mother, reunited after a long separation. (Did she miss Clarence as she spied at the windowsill?) Zoe had hopes for one young couple reading contentedly in adjacent windows, night after night, back to back. The illusion dissolved as she realized the windows were separated by thick masonry walls. The man and woman lived alone, in different buildings: "They are strangers. I doubt if they would know each other if they met on the street."[22]

By issue no. 3, Zoe found her stride, establishing a structure of features and columns. She framed her introductory essays as secular sermons—she was an evangelist's daughter, after all—concluding with amens and pleas for God's blessings. The openers were titled "A Chat with My Friends in the Light of the Blind Man's Candles." She imagined typing by the light of candles from her neighborhood's blind peddler, only stopping when they "burned to the sockets." She stocked up on candles in anticipation of sermonizing on "a subject which so vitally touches me," such as why Christianity "damned the woman, who dares to separate herself from her husband, no matter how unworthy he may have proven himself." A brown-wigged competing peddler, a "little old fiendish orange woman," drove the blind candle seller from a well-trafficked curb corner that he had occupied for 12 years. When he uncomplainingly took over a newsstand instead, Zoe bought a few papers from him and then slipped them back into his inventory piles: "why read the papers when you write for them?" (A syndicated version of this *East Side* tale, "The Corner on the Curb," appeared in publications as improbable as *The Boston Cooking-School Magazine*.[23])

Her own experiences of "poverty and suffering" helped her feel at home in the neighborhood's "wildly scrambling jungle of every nationality... Italians, Hebrews, Arabs, Syrians, Hungarians, Choctaws and Greeks." Like everyone living near First Avenue's pushcart line, "a living, writhing, snapping serpent between side streets," she was shoved and insulted by conductors on 14th Street's crosstown streetcars—not until her last issue would she get undercover revenge. Slum oculists ruined patients' eyesight with defective discount lenses, and dentists implanted brass crowns that "deliberately kill the nerves of these people who need all the nerve they have." A few blocks away, liveried servants hoisted employers into upholstered carriages.

Reactions from readers gentle and harsh provided *East Side* copy, plus "balm to my weariness," as she waited "till the Crack of Doom for the Returns from the Sales." She rejected advice to focus on other neighborhoods, although founding a magazine called *Hell's Kitchen* was tempting. She remained a "Near-Optimist," convinced of "the Finality of Justice," which prevented her from joining "those human logs" who preferred the East River's "everlasting peace and forgetfulness." But she was called pessimistic and depressed: "You never know what you are till people tell you." When called pithy, she replied, "There is nothing so conducive to conciseness, kind friend, as having to cough up so much a page for what you write."

She filled *East Side* pages with "indifferent modest" quotes from 1902 rave reviews for *Soul*, "my book which was suppressed." Fenno had handed her the *Soul* inventory after marketing it haphazardly over the years (some ads misspelled her maiden name as "Andersen"). She charged 50 cents with a money-back guarantee for "as good a specimen of a book as possible," printed on "English box moor paper" (an imaginary import also touted by Hubbard's Roycroft publishing house) and shipped in "a cute little box." The novel was still being read and critiqued. The left-leaning painter John Sloan, not noticing that both Zoe and *Soul's* Dolly shared his sympathy for wage slaves, called the book "a poor screed directed against Courtenay Lemon, who was at one time the 'Boy Socialist.'" By then, "Cecil Mallon" was still thundering for "the Great Revolution" and comparing married couples to "prisoners manacled together," while working on a literary opus that he never finished, drinking heavily, and losing his knack for womanizing. One of his so-called affinities "only shrugged her beautiful shoulders when he accused her of unfaithfulness." Lemon still maligned Zoe with libel accusations, but *The East Side* defended *Soul's* portrayal of Cecil/Courtenay: "Truth makes a noise so much like libel, you can Hardly tell the Difference."[24]

*East Side* no. 3 introduced a theater column, with uncharacteristically perfunctory prose: a Shakespeare scene was done "remarkably well," a slapstick act with a live kangaroo "tickles me." Through 26 more issues, Zoe never managed any deeper stagecraft analysis. She went through the motions of reviewing just to persuade press agents to fill seats with "people who Push the Pen," sharing her press passes with Obie. She published publicist-pleasing mini-profiles and photos of stage talents: the actress Mae Simon was "the Hebrew Sarah Bernhardt." Zoe pitied actors, poor as pushcart peddlers but trying "to keep up appearances." The plays' plots, involving deceived wives and American frontier life, reminded her of dark times: "I lived a million years in the West—it seemed that long, I was married then." Shows gave her a platform for gossiping about celebrities she had interviewed. Nat Goodwin moved on to yet another wife—his "steenth," by Zoe's count—as his third ex, Maxine Elliott, became the first American woman to run her own eponymous theater, a delicate neoclassical building near Times Square, "beautiful as she is." (One of Zoe's most widely quoted witticisms: "I'd rather have a theater than a husband—you know where a theater is of nights!") A drama critic fictionalized in *The East Side* enjoys her "thrice blessed work," as she is welcomed courteously by theater managers: "Nobody has the right to treat me otherwise." The impresario David Belasco, however, was befuddled when a woman interviewer showed up, since he expected Joe Anderson Norris.

*The East Side* apologized when Obie, despite steady Broadway ticket supplies, missed his bimonthly deadlines. "The Artist is the Finest Ever, but you hesitate to hurry One who is drawing for you free gratis for nothing. Whose Beautiful Work is a Gracious Gift." To entice him into starting his assignments, Zoe had to "crawl around on all fours and bite the dust." When her poet friend William J. Lampton suggested that she stay on schedule by publishing her own sketches—she had taught art and painted portraits in Harrodsburg and Wichita, after all—she worried that he enviously wanted "to see my little mag collapse." Oberhardt was useful as a source of quotable reactions to theater as well. He hoped for Tristan and Isolde "to die and be done with it, so we can go home." When Zoe sobbed over female characters committing suicide onstage, he reminded her, "It's only make-believe!" Her retort in print: "what does the Artist know of Sorrow? He has never been married." (Not until the 1920s did Obie end his bachelorhood, marrying Josephine Sonnleitner, a German immigrant half his age.)[25]

Zoe started expecting readers to remember her literary pearls, or to leaf through back issues (which she sent to new subscribers), as she typed phrases like "As I have remarked before" and "I will say it again." Her apartment attracted tourists, curious to see the ebony piano and Borglum's grinning gargoyle mentioned in the magazinelets, and the "little blue kitchen, the view of the roofs and the Magic City." She detailed how she invested the profits from working "as hard as I'd work to support a husband," splurging on a new pottery coffeepot. As libraries requested *East Side* subscriptions, she grew convinced that her pen pictures of pushcart people would hold up as well as George Sand's novels about peasants: "how they live!" The Library of Congress paid her postage for magazines to be shelved "in a substantial binding for permanent preservation." She knew all periodicals were granted such immortality, but she still felt "Mine was Special." Reporters quoted her "Rose Colored Dream" of the British Museum uniting her publications with work by her father and the Anderson vicars, tending Britain's poor since 1502, "whose shades keep watch with me." (The British Library did finally acquire *The East Side* in 2008.) A newsboy told her, "An unbacked magazine! The thing's impossible!" She resisted lying that her readership was already in the millions, her subscriber network stretching from the Bowery to Budapest, from Hong Kong to Honolulu. Office boys dug into their pockets to subscribe, and Zoe swept aside twinges of guilt: "Doesn't my Office Boy need new buttons and a little spare change?"[26]

There were new slum horrors to report with every issue, as she pleaded with God: "Why sleepest Thou?" Women garment workers panted and stumbled while balancing "almost insupportable burdens" of clothing on their heads—they were handed cupsful of water, like "tired and thirsty animals." Little waifs slept on trash piles in the park and the marble floors of morgues. When a Jewish boy in Zoe's building was nearly killed by a band of "Early Christians" (teenage thugs flashing knives and tossing rocks from rooftops), no policeman could be distracted from sunning himself or seeking bribes to intervene or investigate. Still, the unfairness of it all did not tempt her to join Courtenay's Socialists, who would "Burn the House Down."

Issue no. 4 introduced a page of poetry, which put daily drudgery in a big-picture context: "You find Pins when you want Needles, and Needles when you want Pins. And That is Life." Subsequent *East Side* poems reflected on how fate treats us all like knives and scissors needing sharpening, straphangers awaiting streetcars full of lost loved ones "Bound for the Silent Places," laundry sent home "wrung out and rubbed and scrubbed," peddlers' fruit inventory exhausted at day's end, and fabric scraps sorted by ragpickers. No. 4 also had the magazinelet's first long piece of fiction, about a ragpicker named Anton, who works alongside a pitiful elderly woman in a Broome Street attic. Their throats ravaged by dust, and her brain benumbed, they separate scraps into piles: "the white to go through the mills for the raiment of the rich, and the black for the clothing of the poor." When a gold purse containing $200 turns up in the detritus, Anton sneaks out at lunchtime to invest it. He soon rises to bank executive, living in a white marble palace, but then he bets on "iridescent bubbles of speculation." Defrauded investors chase him back to the Broome Street attic, where the coughing old woman looks up from her piles: "You took a long time to eat your luncheon." *The East Side* ran a few other obviously imaginary tales, but Zoe never disclosed how much else she made up as her own Muckamuck. Reading her magazine would yield "about as much truth as you get about anything in this large and complicated city."[27]

She reinforced her credibility partly by describing her accurate premonitions. After a fire broke out at Caroline Boughton's beauty parlor, Zoe told readers that the beautician, while dying of her burns at the Flower Hospital (where Zoe herself had once lain delirious), had sent a dream message: "Don't put the little ad in your magazine . . . I can never treat you any more." In fall 1909, Phil Thompson, the murderous Kentucky Colonel, a "cheery humorist" who called the world an opera bouffe "with a Great Deity managing it and laughing at us," visited Manhattan. (His daughter Mattie, a belle with "the bluest of Kentucky blood," had married into New York's Pulitzer publishing dynasty—see Chapter 18 for Zoe's litigious interactions with that family.) During Phil's usual treat of a Waldorf meal, Zoe told him bluntly, "I dreamed you were dead." A few weeks later, he suffered a fatal hemorrhage outside his Washington hotel.[28]

Yet while confessing constantly in print and feeding off of the reactions—what might now be called "grabbing the mic"—she only wrote privately about sensing the imminent death of her estranged sister Mattie Thompson in early September 1909. Mattie had been sent to a Cincinnati sanitarium for the insane, where she died of typhoid, the scourge that had killed her brother, Louis Anderson, and Zoe's ex, Spencer. Obituaries called Mattie a devout congregant of her father's church, "gifted with unusual intellect . . . characteristic of her family," including artists (Jessie, Pickett), writer-scholars (Zoe, Henry), and civil servants (Nannie, Nettie). Zoe sent a long condolence letter to newly rewed Clarence in Harrodsburg. (Fletcher Chelf and Clarence had snuck off by train to marry quietly at the Lexington courthouse in early July 1909—nine years after the Morrises' London ceremony—and then immediately "telephoned the news" to surprised friends and family.) Mattie had helped Clarence resettle with her schoolboy-age son Robert. "I wrote her a letter while she was at the hospital thanking her for being good to you and the Bam," Zoe told her Cissy. Before anyone phoned Stuyvesant 1078 with news of Mattie's passing, Zoe had already felt telepathic grief from Madonna con Bambino: "All day long I couldn't work. . . . I was sure the Bam was terribly ill." Zoe "freely forgave" Mattie's behavior that caused the early 1900s rupture, that inspired writings about blonde, blue-eyed, icy, rich, violin-playing, deceived wives of teetotaling distillers at Clay Hill. "All that is lost in the memory of her kindness to my babies, you and the Bam. . . . Not a bitter memory of her is with me," only mourning for "a great strong fine woman . . . the head of the family to me." Zoe wept at the literary sanctum while playing one of Mattie's favorite hymns on the ebony piano, as rain fell on the window-box flowers and blurred the Magic City. She wondered what the weather had been like during Mattie's burial at Spring Hill Cemetery, where already lay so many Andersons and their friends and relatives: "I hate to think of her out in the rain. . . . I was going to say send me a little flower from her grave, but don't do that. I should kill myself crying." Ghosts approached the East 15th Street apartment as she typed to Cissy: "my beloved father . . . my poor little mother, Louis, Willie, Lucy, Charlie. Where are they? . . . Perhaps my sister's spirit is near me now. Maybe she sees me here in my lonely little flat crying about her and knows that my love for her never changed." Zoe sent love and condolences to Mattie's son Philip (but not apparently to John Thompson) and "great armsful" of love to Cissy, the Bam, and Fletcher Chelf. "I am so glad you have a good husband who loves you," Zoe wrote, for once uncynical. "Love is so scarce. Be good to him. Never say anything unkind to him. I am so glad you are sheltered in his home, you and the baby. The world [is] so big and hollow and cruel sometimes." Zoe signed the letter Momsey, and her postscript revealed that her son Rob had cut off contact. (Clarence had visited him and Eva in Memphis, where he was climbing the railroad's corporate ladder.) "Tell me where Rob is," Zoe pleaded with his sister. "I must write to him. Tell him to write to me. We must have no resentment. Life is too uncertain. What if he should die?" It is certain that he received *The East Side* (he read the 1914 premonition just before finding out that it was accurate), but not whether it was Zoe who mailed it to him.[29]

No other correspondence from the literary sanctum is in the papers that Clarence later hid "quite carefully . . . in an upstairs closet."[30] Why was this one raw letter saved? According to descendants of Andersons and their friends, Clarence and Robert spoke little of their time in London and Manhattan, although Zoe's publications were displayed on family bookshelves and her fight for the poor remained a point of pride. Did the Bam know anything about the fatherless Kentucky childhood of his grandfather Spencer, originally named Weedon Spenny Norris? Did anyone gossip about absent Harold Morris, Robert's British namesake at birth? Did anyone tell the boy that he was expected to "compensate for all the imitation men" who scarred his mother and grandmother? What did he remember of the apartment mice, raiding his toddlerhood savings to pay the gasman?

Mattie's spirit kept sending premonitions to East 15th Street. The night before Zoe was mowed down by a car on Second Avenue and badly gashed (see Chapter 18), she dreamed of sewing companionably alongside Mattie at Clay Hill on a terrifying dress, in satiny white, with "the look of a shroud." Mattie's widower John treated Zoe to Waldorf meals, where he opined that women seeking the vote and other rights would "push the men to the wall" and wipe out incentives for chivalry and marital fidelity. Women risked ending up vulnerable, "elbowed good and hard," in the workplace. "You give me a weariness," Zoe replied, pointing out that she had already overcome elbowing. She wondered if women's suffrage would lead instead to "big, strong, splendid" policewomen, demanding $10 bribes from men and jailing anyone who resisted. John subscribed to *The East Side*, in which she complained about his "terrible temperance" and longed for Christmas gifts of Old Jordan—the Waldorf exorbitantly charged 40 cents a glass.[31]

John Thompson paid $10 for a lifetime subscription, a patronage level that Zoe confidently introduced in issue no. 5. She listed "My Distinguished Life Preservers," who protected her from another economic panic, alongside her mastheads in no particular order. The headcount eventually swelled to about 60, barely fitting on one page: writers, musicians, politicians, physicians, lawyers, businessmen (some worked for her former employers, like Street & Smith), professors, philanthropists, restaurateurs, movie and theater personalities, Zoe's dentist, and her electrologist. She shared their happiness and hurt "in the cruel grinding Mill of the Gods," hoped they would all "come into fortunes," and promised to stop sending issues "when I cash in my checks." A male competitor sneered, "Fictitious names, I suppose." Some names came and went as the issues ticked past, suggesting that they were not true lifers. How did she keep track anyway? Her writings do not mention ledgers or other sensible bookkeeping tools. She followed the Jewish custom of lighting memorial candles on anniversaries of the death of her first life preserver, the Netherlands-born philanthropist Esther Herrman. The life preserver Abraham Gruber, a politician and lawyer who warned that Roosevelt's reckless warmongering was "turning the Executive Mansion into a shooting gallery," was named among *The East Side*'s "Wise Men of the East Side." Other steadfast preservers included Ignatz Rosenfeld, Café Boulevard's owner, and the Episcopalian minister John von Herrlich, Zoe's self-ennobled "Sky Pilot" from Wichita. (He was working at Trinity Church on lower Broadway—he led services at 2:30 a.m., for nightshift laborers—while his much younger wife Mathilde, formerly Tillie, sought fame as an opera singer.) *The East Side*'s early fans Elbert Hubbard and Stanford's David Starr Jordan apparently never sent $10, since they do not appear on preserver lists. Did Jordan, a eugenicist, regret his initial support after looking closely at her writings, so contrary to his stance that immigrants imported crime, disease, and "hereditary unfitness" to American shores? Zoe defended the Kentucky-born attorney James Clark McReynolds from corruption accusations, noting that he was among her longtime subscribers, but he was not on the preserver lists—did he ask to be left off, since he was a racist and antisemite?[32]

A lifetime magazinelet supply for $10 was the industry's going rate, and Zoe's competitors came up with preposterously overblown names for their higher-level patrons. Hubbard gave them nonstop *Philistines* plus membership in his American Academy of Immortals and daily telepathic doses of "Success, Health and Love Vibrations." Bruce Calvert welcomed *Open Road* supporters into his Society of the Universal Brotherhood of Man. Monahan named himself Patriarch of the Society of the Papyrites, which dated back to the imaginary "King Noh-Wrot of the fourth Egyptian dynasty." Papyrites would "have the privilege of unloading their sorrows on the Patriarch"— that is, he would read and perhaps publish their letters in *The Papyrus*. They could regard their lifetime *Papyrus* subscriptions "as a mere Business proposition or a Spiritual investment—psychically it is *up to you!*"[33]

*East Side* no. 5 introduced another column, with random thoughts, news snippets and club gossip (shades of Nancy Yanks). The clubbable John Francis Tucker (*Soul*'s "Tucket") kept attracting "a smart and interesting crowd" to his dinners, and the Hungry Club's Saturday soirees were hosted by the "witty and sarcastic" Kentucky native Mattie Sheridan. Zoe gave a new name to the Manhattan group that had welcomed her in 1898: "the Woman's Pressless Press Club." Few writers and *East Side* subscribers belonged, so it was no longer worth $5 in annual dues, but she paid nonetheless. In her copy of the club's 1910 membership directory, she checked off the names of eight other writers, including Mrs. Frank Leslie aka the Baroness de Bazus. Zoe scrawled on the directory's cover that she may have missed a few legitimate pen pushers: "There are also a few among the dead—that's why I stay in the club—So I can be with the real ones . . . when I shuffle off"—that is, she hoped to reunite with presswomen in the Undiscovered Country.[34]

With issue no. 6 and *The East Side*'s first birthday, its impact was detectable, including in the form of "a nice bunch of enemies." Zoe attended a charity dinner, where one corrupt Tammany politician warned another to avoid her: "she'll roast you in her magazine." The vindictive Salvation Army evicted *East Side* devotees from its premises, and Zoe's chatty elderly interviewee Katie resorted to selling soap to pay for someplace else to sleep. A sermon in issue no. 6 sent women readers into Zoe's kitchen for a while, so they could not overhear her lacerating more men garbed in an inherited "thick coat of Untruth." Paul the Apostle dealt a 2,000-year setback to feminism by commanding women "to keep a Still Tongue." Zoe described her own helplessness at her kitchen window, shouting "let her alone!" while an Italian immigrant neighbor, "fiendish in temper," beat his wife (who died in childbirth) and sister-in-law (who became his second wife). The man's oldest son, "almost as beautiful as a certain boy I know and love" (meaning the Bam), confided in Zoe across the court, as the bruised, cowed second wife tried to keep the window blinds closed. The dead first wife's favorite "little lilting cheery song" for washdays haunted Zoe: "How slow I am to learn life's lessons! . . . It is impossible to change the nature of a man without decapitating him."

She documented her own charitable acts gone awry. Her gift of coins to a tramp in Union Square wakened and shamed him; he drowned himself in a park fountain, "tangled up in the waterlilies." An elderly woman preferred the shelter of Stuyvesant Square Park's trees, "the kindly people," instead of an uptown refuge that Zoe found for her, "a Home for aged, indigent, infirm, and respectable females." Zoe understood her friend's choice to live in open air, rather than end up "branded for life as a respectable female!"[35]

She announced that a self-published novel (that is, *Wind*) was in the works, and that bound volumes of the first six issues were ready in cream-colored "toggery" bindings, "one nice green dollar" apiece, autographed by the Office Boy. She was more surprised than her readers that the magazinelet had lasted a year, due to "sheer nerve, pluck, endurance and hard work." On a typewriter with the overworked e key failing, she typed a poem, "The Song of the Typewriter," imagining a typist's motivational cries at the keyboard: "Now, Work, damn you, Work!" (In her time, the word for the machine and its usually female operator were the same.)[36]

No managing editor toned down or smoothed anything, as she careened from graphic reflections on injustice to lighthearted sniping and epigrams: "I believe in the Survival of the Fittest, but why Survive when you must have so many Fits." Given the South's "Curse of Slavery," its hereditary lusts and bloodlusts, Black men accused of assaulting white women were "tarred and feathered and hanged and cut in pieces and burned" by white husbands who, "each and every one of them," had Black maids and cooks for mistresses. Policemen, whose families had been persecuted in Ireland, publicly cudgeled immigrants into unconsciousness, toppled pushcarts into the gutters, and attempted sexual assault. "A nice place you live in," a night watchman told Zoe, while following her into the East 15th Street lobby, and she scrambled to slam the door on him. "A Woman's magazine," Zoe was willing to call hers, and it would cover fashion by reproducing her own dress patterns, stabbed with pins separating "the line of Joy . . . from the drab old track of tears." No underling pointed out inconsistencies, as this champion of the oppressed fumed about her building's elevator operator, insolently demanding tips, "an illiterate foreigner" ignorant of her work. She burned a few more professional and personal bridges. "You Must get some new stories," she told the orator Lee Fairchild, best man at her second wedding, when he urged her to write about him. Her former *Home* magazine editor Arthur Vance was rejecting her work, since he could only recognize a good story "now and then in a lucid interval." The error-prone typesetters of Biblical times rivaled her own printers, handing her page proofs only after "the Mistakes are past all Remedy."[37]

While she was taking down more guardrails, she added another recurring column: news of subscribers who belonged to her intentionally disorganized Klub.

Fig. 23: 1911 Ragged Edge Klub dinner at Café Boulevard (156 Second Avenue at 10th Street) celebrating writer Leita Kildare's new novel. At foreground central table, Leita is dressed in white and smiling broadly, and a man separates her from hatless Zoe in a dark gown and white gloves. AC, Nicole Neenan photo

# 17

# A Raggeder Edge than We, 1910–1913

SOMETIME IN FEBRUARY 1910, a casual suggestion at one of Zoe's dinner parties turned into an institution that inspired *East Side* prose and poetry and made national news.

She wanted to meet more subscribers by socializing more, without depleting her profits by picking up the dinner tabs or endangering her apartment furnishings. During her pre-*East Side* years of entertaining at home "in a fantastic way," guests might be found "acting like raving maniacs and sitting on everything but the ceiling and chandeliers," as well as "jumping up and down on the piano keys." So she invited her friends to a restaurant one fateful night, "at their own expense, $1.08 with wine, tip and dance . . . and it worked like a charm." Trading witticisms at one table were two writers, J. Herbert Welch and William J. Lampton. Welch, a Pennsylvanian turned Nevadan turned Brooklynite, was a prolific freelancer; among his Zoe-related journalistic topics over the years were new parks near Manhattan tenements and cyclones devastating American prairies. Lampton, who published hundreds of short rhymes called "yawps" (one would be Zoe's obituary), called himself "merely a Yawpist yawping his simple yawp." Born in Ohio, he had spent enough of his youth in Kentucky to earn honorary Kentucky Colonel status from the state government. (Zoe's amused reaction: "these Kentuckians never can tell just where they are to be born.") A gangly, penniless bachelor, Lampton lived in a YMCA cubbyhole piled with manuscripts, books, magazines, and toys. Welch and Lampton joked over dinner that Zoe should make this kind of evening a habit, maybe call it the Ragged Edge Klub. She and the guests promptly took out their printed invitations and "tore off the Ragged Edges." The Klub's mission: "alleviating the Condition of those who are on a Raggeder Edge than we (if any there be) and then in the Joy of the Evening, to forget the Ragged Edges."[1]

No structure was imposed on the weekly gatherings, starting at "Seven O'Klock." Dinner fees were "collected somewhere between the salad and coffee at the point of the gun" (yes, a Kentucky feudist joke). About $1 a head covered wine, storytelling, singing, and dancing—before and after meal courses, and in between. "No rules, no regulations, no manners and no dues," no officers, committees, agendas, motions, constitutional amendments, minutes, admissions interviews, membership directories. "No Gavel, no Scolding, no Calling Down. Only the Killing of Kare . . . with Komfortable exklusiveness." No dress code: "Glad Rags" or overalls welcome. No customized menus, no place cards for assigned seating, no paperwork at all except for postcard invitations illustrated by Oberhardt that encouraged RSVPs: "Kindly put the Humble Hostess wise," by mail or Stuyvesant 1078. If two people were expected but 125 showed, chairs were pulled up for "Any Live and Cheerful Body, carrying an East Side Magazine." Issues were handed to anyone emptyhanded: "They read it when they get home, out of sheer politeness; and end by loving it, the women especially."[2]

Zoe sent announcements of upcoming Edger meetings to newspaper society columns to tuck amid notices of cotillions and tariff reform lectures. Did anyone unsuspectingly come to Klub nights expecting some normal proceedings? Did Zoe remember her less scintillating Conversazione dinners in Wichita? Did newspapermen recall her membership in "the happy family" of regular freelancers and subsequent banishment? She held Klub dinners on Wednesdays or Thursdays, trying to avoid conflicts with competing organizations' sessions. New coed groups with "no permanent clubhouse" (which *Soul*'s Dolly had frequented) were gathering for meals with lectures, discussions, and music. They could not access the palatial homes of all-male clubs, so they reserved dining rooms at hotels and restaurants—Café Boulevard was considered particularly clubbable.[3]

Most of the Klub's counterparts took themselves quite seriously, setting up leadership hierarchies and taking minutes. John Tucker's highbrow Twilight Club brought in the likes of politician William Jennings Bryan and blueblood suffragist Augusta Belmont, pondering "How to Obtain Health and Longevity" and "Why Are Not the Churches More Active in Civic Affairs?" The Sunrise Club (*Soul*'s "Sunset Club") came up with the motto "eat to think and think to eat." Members debated "The Hypocrisy of Puritanism" and "Man's Inhumanity to Woman," with activist speakers such as W. E. B. Du Bois, Courtenay Lemon, and Emma Goldman (whose anarchist monthly *Mother Earth* was headquartered on East 13th Street). The Pleiades Club published illustrated yearbooks, with contributions from Lampton, Lee Fairchild, and Courtenay's artist brother Jo Lemon. The Thirteen Club, aimed at "combating dire and mischievous superstitions," started dinners at 8:13 p.m., hired 13-person orchestras, spilled salt and walked under ladders.[4]

A few of the coed groups were women's brainchildren. The Gotham Club was founded by Missouri-born songwriter Anita Comfort Brooks (who had been a friend of Katherine Stuyvesant Van Ness Roberts, aka con artist Mabel Tinley). She organized events in the realm of "art, music, literature and hygiene," such as vegetarianism campaigns and "Ghost Dances" with Native American performers. Zoe attended some Saturday gatherings of the Hungry Club, which Kentucky-born newspaperwoman Mattie Sheridan dedicated to "good nature, wit and appetite." Mattie, who had flattered her own club's members in her short-lived periodical *Men and Women*, was blonde, just over four feet tall, "a bubbling spring of life, love, wisdom and wit." She charged her club's "well bred, well dressed" members an exorbitant-by-Edger-standards $2 in annual dues and $1.25 per hotel meal. Lampton served as her club's "poet laureate," and she welcomed European barons and counts to the ballroom, but not women smokers—Zoe, by contrast, would anoint her own peerage, as her female guests simultaneously downed spaghetti and dragged on cigarettes.[5]

The Klub did follow the field's norms by celebrating holidays. Members handed out valentines and danced around springtime maypoles. At Thanksgivings, anyone was welcome who had "no home ties"—whether because they were poor, or they simply could not stand their relatives. At Christmastime, Edgers hung gifts for each other on trees at restaurants—one year, Lampton received a telephone, for help contacting girlfriends. At the Klub's masquerade balls, hardly any Kontrarians wore masques—they did not pretend to compete with the bejeweled gowns at costume parties of the upper-crust 400. On the Edgers' calico-theme nights, Zoe's red bandana handkerchief was "the only scrap of calico to be seen." A princess from Siam might be Zoe, and a captivating blonde in spangled yellow silk might be a bewigged female impersonator. Hannah Wyle, a French-born Pennsylvanian theater aficionado, cross-dressed to give the Klub some vaudeville-worthy impersonations of Buffalo Bill, Cardinal Richelieu, and Napoleon.[6]

Zoe named weekly guests of honor from her growing circle of male and female activists, artists, authors, aviators, composers, dancers, musicians, physicians, politicians, publicists, singers, and theater producers. Honorees were expected to cover their own tabs plus partygoers' drink rounds, and many also paid $10 to become *East Side* life preservers. No speeches were required—"why talk, when we can dance?"—not even attendance. "Lampton Dodged the Feast" was one headline after he showed up at the tail end of his banquet, "convoying a number of poetesses he had been entertaining in another room." Zoe printed her own yawp on one of Lampton's party invitations, calling him the "only Colonel from Kentucky" living in a YMCA unarmed: "Powder and shot. / He cares for not."[7]

The Klub, as contradictory as *The East Side*, toasted and roasted adulterers and other fun-loving scoundrels. Zoe called the artist Ferdinand Pinney Earle Jr. "greatly misjudged"; he had abandoned so many newlywed wives for younger "affinities" that his home in upstate New York was called Affinity Hill. Klub honoree Richard Le Gallienne, the Liverpool-born writer, was "really sorry about his divorce" from his journalist wife Julie Nørregaard, left behind in Europe. *The East Side* reported that he filled a scrapbook with news clippings about his misdeeds and fended off mistresses with the refrain, "Dear little girl, I should like to marry you; but it is impossible. I have a wife in Paris."

Le Gallienne, a brewery manager's son, had aggrandized his name during his youth, inserting a "Le." The poet Shaemas O'Sheel, born James Shields in Illinois, became the Ragged Edge's "Shameless O'Sheel," fervently supporting Irish independence without setting foot on Irish soil. Ardeen Foster, a Michigan-born poet sometimes known as Ardennes Jones-Foster Esq., posed as a Londoner in white spats for his Klub self-fundraising lecture as "International Commissioner of the British Federation for the Emancipation of Sweated Women, Girls and White Slave Victims." Other Klub honorees with rich imaginations included "Euthimios X. Tchor-Baj-Oglu of Constantinople," a rug importer turned founder of the International Society of the Orient and the Occident; Baroness von Schomberg, specialist in "Russian fancy dances" (actually Edith Jane Schomberg Howlett, a British whip maker's daughter turned Long Island horseman's wife); and Mrs. Albert Jones, "Queen of the Husbandettes." Countless divorced female Edgers, like Zoe, called themselves widows on documents, including census forms.[8]

The Klub also discussed serious issues, especially calls for government reform. It honored the self-made, newly divorced authors Mabel Herbert Urner, Leita Kildare, and Sophie Irene Loeb, whose fiction and journalism explored the sufferings of abused wives and recent immigrants. (Leita collaborated with her ex-husband Owen Kildare, "the Bowery Kipling," who wrote about his brutal, impoverished Irish American childhood but was actually a Russian-born poser—see Chapter 21.) Suffragists including the British-born actress Beatrice Forbes-Robertson told Edgers that granting voting rights to women would not wreck marriages but rather "bring about better conditions for our children." An actress, masked for anonymity, told the Klub about the profession's hazards; she had fended off a manager's sexual assault at his office by tossing an ink bottle out the window, "which hit the stationary policeman on the street below, who came up and rescued her." David Healy, an Irish American journalist turned Ellis Island administrator (and one of Zoe's eulogists), "gave the Klub an air of distinction from which it has never recovered," by describing the resourcefulness of new arrivals. One "wise little child," sent alone in steerage, had not seen her father since infancy, yet she claimed to recognize the man who came to retrieve her—forewarned that she would otherwise be deported as "LPC" ("likely public charge). The Russian-born, tenant-friendly Judge Leonard A. Snitkin earned a Klub dinner by "defending the poor from the tyranny of the East Side Landlords." Zoe saw him preside at Municipal Court, lenient on gaunt single parents who pawned their overcoats to pay tenement owners swaddled in furs. (One evictee's absconded husband was hiding at his mother's home, which made Zoe long to digress in *The East Side*: "the things I know about mothers-in-law would fill a library!") Klub honoree Rabbi Jacob Goldstein, a prison chaplain, advocated decriminalizing suicide attempts. He introduced Zoe to a teenage boy "with big brown melancholy eyes," whose mother had threatened to disown him after he lost his job. The teenager tried to die by gas inhalation at his cramped apartment and then was "thrown among the criminals" listening to the rabbi's prayers at the turreted downtown prison known as the Tombs. Zoe, who had stood at the East River's banks resisting its oblivion, firmly believed that none of us should be punished for wanting "to go home to your God."[9]

She published a transcript of her Ragged Edge talk jokingly pitying Mormon husbands, who shuttled among families in Brooklyn, New Jersey, and the Bronx, creating "an Alimony-less harem." Zoe dreamed that someday working women, while pursuing "other matrimonial ventures" in Mormon style, would magnanimously support their frowsy, balding ex-husbands. In spring 1910, she tried to speak to the Klub about her friend Lee Fairchild, "who had only just gone into the Big Silence." But she fell into silent tears, feeling "the presence of the Unseen." Fairchild had died of pneumonia. An obituary was headlined "Poet Dies Penniless." A charity paid for him to be buried in a Brooklyn cemetery section reserved for "friendless journalists." Zoe numbered him among the loved ones whose spirits posthumously kept her company, "not sufficiently weaned yet from earthly affections." She knew that her living friends were apt to cluck "Poor Little Zoe!" and doubt her sanity.

The Lebanese-born writer Ameen Rihani typed the text for his 1910 Klub speech. He was newly returned from long exile in his homeland, having offended fellow Arab Americans with calls for religious tolerance. He told the Edgers and their Humble Hostess that crassly materialistic, shoddily modern Americans had achieved a "studied raggedness . . . neatly canned and cleverly advertised." His countrymen authentically lived at the ragged edge, "woven by the Poets and Prophets, and tinged and scented by Time. . . . My people come to your Country for money, you go to ours for inspiration, for spiritual solace, for an indefinable something." Western merchants and missionaries were pouring into Lebanon, attempting to use "their big scissors . . . to cut off the ragged edgings of our Garment." Giddy heights of wealth had not yet emerged there, Rihani intoned, "nor the squalid poverty which huddles and groans in your slums." He reached a "ragged edge truth": the clubgoers only differed from his countrymen by being "better clothed, better lodged, better fed, and better faked."[10]

Zoe kept changing the Edgers' venues, in case anyone tired of Café Boulevard: "A Klub is like a woman. . . . the longer you stay at a place the worse you are treated." But postmen bungled deliveries of her meeting notices: "If you don't get this, please let me know," she wrote wryly on the cards. Cheap wine ("red ink") was on the tables, with a multicultural mishmash of "soup, deviled crab, spaghetti and a salad, baked chicken, ice cream and coffee demi-tasse." The Klub tried out Italian, German, and Hungarian spots that "don't mind if we jostle the soup." Zoe perhaps received restaurant discounts in exchange for gushing *East Side* reviews. Edgers ordered blueish cocktails and chili con carne at dawn at Joel's Bohemia near Times Square, run by the philanthropist-philosopher Joel Rinaldo, an *East Side* life preserver and "a real prince in manner, hospitality and generosity." He roamed his tables quoting his anti-Darwinist, "polygeneric" theory of evolution, which he self-published. It attributed species diversity to "latent electricity," among other forces, which sent Zoe into reveries about whether her friends had originated "on the wings of the wind." At Hofbrau Haus on Broadway at 30th Street, German-born restaurateur August Janssen, another *East Side* life preserver, "genial, smiling and ever obliging," served the kind of hearty "Imborted Peer" that helped keep Germans even-keeled, "of excellent judgment and of good sound sense." Zoe convinced uptowners "to wander through the picturesque maze of pushcarts" to reach Little Hungary on East Houston Street, run by life preserver Max Schwartz. He electrified its outdoor sign "in letters of fire," and tourists flocked to his dining rooms full of "rich bric-a-brac," where orchestras emitted "weird and wistful Hungarian music of cymbal and tambour." One kindly waiter at Little Hungary told Zoe, "I like your little magazine. I have read every number."

In the summer, when normal clubs hibernated, the Klub kept "running with brilliant crowds" at Brooklyn and Staten Island beach resorts, enticed by Zoe's hyperbolizing: "I will furnish the moon." Attendees navigated mazes of twilit streets from subway stations to coastal hotels, only to be "pretty badly stung by the mosquitoes and the waiters; but oh! So gay!" She soured on dining spots where Edgers were overcharged—15 cents extra for ice, for instance, which would "keep a corpse some hours"—and where, toward closing time, impatient waiters stabbed Klub-goers "with disappearing tables at the height of the dance." Zoe saw an "impudent and mean" waiter kick a pet black cat at Peter Galotti's Italian restaurant in Greenwich Village. Her dining companion begged her not to write about the incident, for fear of reprisals from the staff such as undercooked spaghetti. So she published her unkept promise: "I won't tell Galotti that the little fat waiter kicked the cat."[11]

Dance tunes for Edgers were often supplied by Harry S. Huggs, a New York-born, Black pianist and ragtime composer sometimes called Professor Harry Huggs and known to the Klub as Kalathumpian. Some Ragged Edgers preferred the professor's fast tempos, and others asked for slow waltzes while grousing, "We are galloping ourselves to death." Classical musicians also played; Texas-born Gustave Becker could "coax some marvelous music from most any sort of old piano," as could Zoe. Klub members took to the floor, "gripped together and whirling madly" in pairs, trios, quartets, and other "terpsichorean oddities." Dance instruction was offered by Louis H. Chalif, a Russian-born performer and educator whose school near Carnegie Hall was called the Temple to Terpsichore. Edgers tangoed, foxtrotted, and experimented with the Airship Quadrille, Tarpon Squirm, and Banana Peel Slide—the latter required side-slit yellow gowns with white stockings underneath, which showed as the dancers flowed across the floor. The vaudeville singer Libby Arnold Blondell (a former Wichitan) brought her troupes to serenade Zoe's guests into forgetting whatever remained of their troubles off the dancefloor. Libby sometimes spelled her stage names Libbie and Blondelle (her first husband's real surname was Bluestein).[12]

Zoe was repaid manyfold for the logistics of scheduling performers, bribing maître d's, and hoping for premonitions of how many dinners to serve, although during those hours she "might accidentally be writing a $100 story." After all, the impresario of "a very serious little magazine" should make public appearances in appreciation for "its many million subscribers the world over (Oh! You Circulation Liar!)." The Klub helped "hold up my hands for my work" (a phrase her father used for colleagues girding him for translation labors) and rejuvenated her in middle age: "Having suffered marriage, I have in my life spent many lonely hours; but I am no longer lonely. . . . Little Zoe never really knew how fine it was to live till she met these friends of hers." She estimated that 2,000 people kaleidoscopically came through her "frivolous frolicking Klub," whether weekly for years or just once, drawn to "its spontaneity, its good fellowship, its brilliancy and éclat." *The East Side* named talented Edgers by the score, ran photos and sketches of them, and noted their accomplishments, only stopping at "the End of the Page." Zoe recommended reading "beautiful little poems" by Italian-born Francesca di Maria Palmer Spaulding, published by Zoe's former employers like *The Smart Set*. The Ohio-born writer Eustace Hale Ball was summed up as "one of the few Harvard graduates who isn't driving a horse car or clerking in a candy store." As for the Detroit-born philosopher-orator-publisher Murray Schloss, "nobody knows exactly What he does." Zoe congratulated Klub members for relationship milestones: "Bless you, my children, may it be a long, long while before you take your journey to Reno" (where new government policies made divorce easier), she told newlyweds. At Zoe's birthday celebrations, "the politest Klub in the world . . . never once asked me my age." Other clubs were "Full of Snobs," spying, slandering, making sarcastic toasts, and droning in lectures that would "make a fine Nerve Tonic." Twilight Club attendees would drift off, so Tucker "has a gong . . . to wake them up for the next speech." The Thirteen Club made Zoe a guest of honor, but she never came around to believing "in smashing mirrors, sitting under black umbrellas or lying in your coffin till you have to."[13]

Many newspapermen fell under the Klub spell. Zoe was said to polish the stars with her "East Side dust rag," bringing out "light tripping" kindred spirits in all kinds of weather, to dining rooms that resembled "the foot of all rainbows." Klub members of all ages applauded each other for improvising at any piano pace: "My goodness, but they CAN dance, those Ragged Edgers!" A typical evening's "last thrill of exhilaration didn't pass into gloominess until after midnight."

But the Klub also developed a reputation for decadence and disorganization. It was listed among world's "queerest clubs," charging "bargain counter" fees. Speakers were seen hiding from Zoe, "looking half scared to death," as carpets were rolled up to make room for "freak dances." Ardeen Foster never finished persuading no one to contribute to his fictitious British Federation for protecting vulnerable women; Edgers snored through his speech, "drowned out by the grand finale of three kinds of ragtime at once from the bunny hug party next door." The Humble Hostess was said to know "all about the color of souls," as conversations lurched from a woman's right to smoke in public to "whether a pushcart man has a soul if he hasn't got a license."

The writer Sallie Toler, from Wichita's Hypatia circle, visited New York and reported for the *Eagle* that Zoe was "making good" in New York but the "pseudo-Bohemian" Klub was inferior to Hypatia. Sallie had paid for her Edger meal and therefore was "violating no hospitality" by harshly evaluating the evening. Its honoree, Euthimios X. Tchor-Baj-Oglu, "made a stupid little talk," followed by "exceedingly raw . . . impertinent questions." Scrawny dancers performed to uninspiring piano tunes played by "a 'Countess' in spangles." The Wichitan tourist noted that Zoe's "rollicking, independent, impudent" *East Side* was fueled by "the perverse, mischief-loving muse that inspires much of her writing, that prompts her to make copy out of her friends and their foibles. . . . Some of her most brilliant writing is the cruelest. But she is a rugged, indomitable little iconoclast, who laughs at her own hurts when the debris from the falling pillars bruises her own head."

The new monthly *Columbian Magazine* portrayed Zoe's circle as unattractive, underemployed, pretentious, self-indulgent to the point of debauchery, and annoyed that the world did not recognize their genius. Desperate for attention, they would set up "a dining club with a rakish name—say, 'The Starved Slobs'" and gather at "greasy little claret-and-spaghetti hotels." (*The Columbian*'s freelancers, by contrast, such as Edgers like Herbert Welch and Mabel Urner, considered Zoe "clever, deep-thinking and almighty plucky" and subscribed to her "delightful tabasco seasoned" magazine.) Soon after savaging "The Starved Slobs," *The Columbian* collapsed in financial shambles—its leaders were indicted for mail fraud—and Zoe felt "fiendish delight."[14]

Male writers tried to "sting the life out of her," roasting the Klub "in the fiery furnace of criticism." She was accused of pitting Democrats against Republicans, although she tried to ban political discussions among Edgers, dreading "sneers from people you have loved." The *New York Press* reported that at a birthday party for George Washington, Zoe cakewalked disrespectfully and shushed Edgers by wielding a hatchet, like the one "used by young George on the cherry tree"; that *Press* report, she retorted, was "a staggerer to those who knew the truth." She was said to encourage shockingly lewd dances, while "striving to think of some way of increasing her dinner list." But there were no indecencies in sight, just one mischievous young Edger who, during a dance floor demonstration by Louis Chalif, jumped up to caricature the Turkey Trot "how it shouldn't be danced." Newspapermen who enjoyed Zoe's hospitality claimed the Turkey Trot parody brought Klub-goers to the brink of arrest by anti-vice police forces. "It was hardly fair of the boys to treat a sister reporter so," she wrote. "When I worked for the papers, if I lied too glibly, I lost my job; but it doesn't seem to be so any more. The lyinger the merrier." She could understand why journalists were despised: "They'd sacrifice their grandmothers," not to mention their Humble Hostess, on deadline for "a good half column skit."[15]

Within a year or so of the Klub's founding, "vicious and malicious" enviers sarcastically dubbed her the Queen of Bohemia, who ruled over a dissolute realm. Although she hated the title at first, she admitted to a form of bohemianism, caused by her Southern legacy of "nonchalant recklessness in the matter of spending, without the money. . . . the Divine Creator could conceive of no greater irony than that of sending an aristocrat into the world without money." Enriched instead with "gaiety of heart and brains," she theorized that America's "only aristocracy is the aristocracy of brains. . . . and I am its Queen! Ha! Ha! What ho!" As she claimed the title of New World royalty—"isn't my own phone a Stuyvesant?"—she dreamed up official Court Presentation protocols.

Klub members cobbled together a throne at Little Hungary, draping American flags on some wine barrels. The queen caped herself in a rose-pattern cotton bedspread and assigned minions to hold her train. With a long-necked Hungarian wine bottle for a scepter, she "touched the heads of her kneeling friends lightly . . . and they arose Sir Knights, Barons, Counts and Lords and Ladies of the Court of Bohemia." At dawn, a tipsy peerage of "tried and chosen ones" spilled out into the streets of the Lower East Side: Countess Ella Bosworth of Brooklyn (a printer's widow and a respectable leader of the Professional Women's League, a support group for actresses); Lady Betty Rogers of the Bronx (wife of the comedian Will Rogers); the Duchess of Dingleman (Harriet Dingleman, an apartment "renting specialist"); and Baron Bernhardt of Hoboken. Lord Callahan was born humble Daniel H. Callahan, an ice-company paymaster. The antiquarian book dealer Christian Gerhardt, serving in the National Guard, was known to the Klub as a Lieutenant or Henchman. The restaurateur

Joel Rinaldo was dubbed a prince, as was Jack H. McPike, a cigar dealer from Missouri (who took over the Klub reins after Zoe's death). One *East Side* subscriber cluelessly complained that Zoe catered "too much to the wealthy classes, to the nobility." No king or prince consort was ever designated, as Zoe remained as chaste or discreet as any empire's virgin queen: "I live alone and shall, in all probability, die in the same way."[16]

The queen's coronation robe was one of a number of not terribly convincing disguises that helped her dig further into undercover reporting, slipping into strangers' skins.

Fig. 24: *East Side* bound volumes (top row: 1 and 2; lower row: 3 and 4) with Zoe's white paint highlights on Oberhardt illustrations. AC, Nicole Neenan photo

# 18

# The Best in the Land, 1910–1913

TRYING ON PERSONAS, conducting investigations, and finding glimmers of hope in the slums made for compelling *East Side* copy. Zoe turned readers into confidantes and shared her friends' secrets, but she only hinted at how much autobiography she wove into *Wind*, her last book, unprofitably published by "meself."

Her spring 1910 experiment in pretending to be a blind immigrant musician was perhaps the most visceral immersion in poverty of her career. She rented an accordion from a secondhand shop, borrowed a neighbor's checked shawl, wrapped a new floral bandana around her head, and veiled her eyes with blue goggles. She stationed her campstool near Café Boulevard just before a Sunrise Club dinner—its members "being, according to their speeches, especially philanthropic." Sunrisers paid no heed as she wheezed out Stephen Foster's "My Old Kentucky Home." So she tried her luck southward, in a shadowy doorway on Grand Street. (A few blocks away was the Bowery hotel where hard-drinking Foster, who had spent hardly any time in Kentucky, had fallen into fatal decline in 1864.) All around were street musicians with actual disabilities: a one-armed organist played "one tune that had but one note." Garbagemen, beggars, and a bootblack dropped coins into Zoe's cup. Her eyes misted over behind the blue lenses when a boy offered her a dollar to play "My Old Kentucky Home," not realizing that she was trying, and then gave her a quarter for the effort. The cup filled with nearly $1.50 (which she promptly gave back to the poor), more than her magazinelet would have generated for a day's work. Edgers, unsurprised to see her undercover again, plunked buttons into her cup and sighed, "Oh, you Zoe!" She blew whatever remained of her cover by reaching, "like a lunatic," for a candy proffered by a chocolate seller. Canny little girls announced, "Aw! She ain't blind!" Zoe's clothing had been too clean, among other signs that her disguise could not fool immigrants' cunning Manhattan-born children. The next day, when she tried to return the accordion, the deceitful storekeeper would not accept it nor refund her $5 deposit. No policemen cared, and she longed for the likes of the efficient London bobby who had retrieved her diamond ring in 1901, as she and Clarence slipped away from the Morrises' landlady at dawn.[1]

Zoe looked for employment undercover at firetrap sweatshops, reachable via dimly lit stairs with cracks between steps "you could throw a dog through." Boys and girls polished buttons and wove cords on cacophonous machinery resembling "instruments of the Inquisition." A shirtwaist factory had a paper door, perhaps "so that the flames could light more easily" if arsonists set out to help the owners file insurance claims. In asking for work there, Zoe truthfully stated that she was skilled at stitching, leaving out her follow-up thought: "but oh! how I hate to do it." The man in charge offered her 90 cents per dozen silk shirtwaists—a month's work, she estimated. She promised to start the following morning, knowing that she would never return, since the Klub would keep her out late that night. She wondered if a month on the job would ingratiate her enough with the seamstresses to find out "how they managed to live on 90 cents."[2]

Rewrapping herself in a shawl, she feigned homelessness to seek aid from the interrelated benevolent institutions that she called the Charity Trust (her progressive readers knew that she used the word "trust" disparagingly, meaning a destructive monopoly). Dozens of organizations, ranging from the still-extant Russell Sage Foundation to the now-forgotten Working Girls' Vacation Society and New York Milk Committee, filled the behemothic, multi-dormered United Charities Building on Fourth Avenue (now Park Avenue South) at East 22nd Street. Zoe spent a morning eavesdropping at the charities' communal waiting room, as the staff interrogated "the flotsam of the street." Supplicants were sent away with permits to work for their meals by chopping firewood at the charities' profitmaking woodyards. Zoe's interviewer was unmoved by her sob story of being stranded, penniless, and married: her "up in the air" husband had invited her to join him in New York but then (like Harold Morris) never showed up at the train station. Giving "almost" her real age in her act, she explained that a friend had taken her in but could no longer "afford to.

She could hardly keep herself, and that was true enough, for the friend to whom I alluded was meself." Zoe was directed to the upstairs office of the Guild of the Infant Saviour, a Catholic charity that found homes for abandoned infants. The young woman on duty, determined to leave punctually for her lunch break despite ailing babies in her care, curtly advised Zoe to return the following day "and we *May* get you something to do."[3]

At a charity-run woodyard, a cheerful salaried foreman mistook Zoe for a kindling customer and gave her a tour. "Frail pallid fellows, weak from the want of food," some reduced to "a living skeleton" by morphine addiction, earned their meals by splitting and stacking wood. Many were too weak to finish the daily minimum required for handouts. The foreman called it "a fine paying business," charging $1.50 per basketful of logs. When she asked if any wood was donated to the poor on bitter winter days, he unhesitatingly replied, "Oh, no. Not at all."[4]

The Charity Trust should be renamed "the Society for the Prevention of Cruelty to Landlords," she suggested, or "the Society for the Paying of Salaries to Philanthropists Who Need the Money." Alms were frittered away on bureaucracy and glossy books full of "stupid speeches about the condition of the poor." A fraction of the trust's revenue spent well "would more than wipe out the misery of the slums," putting up airy new apartment blocks with beflowered rooftop playgrounds.[5]

In 1911, New York's charity coffers ballooned with donations for the families of 146 workers killed in the Triangle Shirtwaist Factory Fire, on the top floors of a ten-story building near Washington Square Park. The garment company's greedy owners had locked the exits, to deter employees from stealing or taking breaks, so the only escape route for many when the fire broke out was to take a fatal leap out the window in front of horrified onlookers. The victims were mostly young daughters of Italian and Eastern European Jewish immigrants. They were sisters, cousins, neighbors. Some bodies were unidentifiable except for familiar shoes, jewelry, or hairstyles. Entire streets near Zoe's home echoed with families in keening grief.

A newspaperman told Zoe that his editors, fearful of New York's most powerful benefactors, would not publish his findings that philanthropic "sharks" had squandered much of the money destined for the families. But no one could intimidate *The East Side*'s Bureau of Inquiries. Armed with a list of addresses of the dead, Zoe walked for miles, "from tenement to tenement," to research how charities had cheated the needy. By the time she knocked, many bereaved relatives had already returned to Europe: "the horror of the tragedy had driven them from their homes. It haunts a house to have a burned body brought into it." She kept thinking of her

Wichita servant Mary McEachran, whose death had cursed the house that the Norrises built.

At a tenement entryway on East 3rd Street, Zoe met an elderly Black janitor from Tennessee, cleaning an iron staircase. She greeted him as Uncle. He smiled upon hearing a familiar Southern accent and called her Missie. What flickers of kinship were there for these two immigrants from faraway adjacent states ravaged during the Civil War, one of them a laborer descended from the enslaved and the other a sophisticate descended from slaveholding, abolitionist, impoverished intellectuals, she and he both eking out a living amid European-born families crushed by industrialists' greed?[6]

An Italian-born boy on Cherry Street, a cousin of Josie Del Castillo, killed at age 21, had seen the corpse: "We didn't know whether it was Josie or not." A charity's paltry grant had covered funeral costs for teenaged Beckie Koppelman, but her shirtwaist factory coworker and older sister Gussie was expected to keep supporting herself, "very delicate because of the wound on her head." Louis Altman, whose daughter Anna, 16, had jumped from a factory window, apologized to Zoe for his poor English while confessing that his family had relied on the dead girl's earnings: "now we have no hopes at all."

Triangle employees had earned pennies per hour, yet charity workers spent thousands of dollars researching which families deserved donations. One "summer excursion" to Russia was organized to verify which Old Country relatives had received wages from Bertha Wendroff, killed at 18. "The daughter of William Zuscofski was brought home to him, a charred bit of flesh," and while he was "frantic with grief" at her side, charity agents showed up offering handouts. "Leave me with my dead," he cried.[7]

In a 12-page *East Side* feature, Zoe pleaded directly with the Charity Trust: "give these people the money that has been placed in your charge for them. Give it to them! Give it to them! In the name of all that is good and just and holy, give it to them and help them to forget." For the issue's cover, a friend working at the District Attorney's office supplied a close-up photograph of the disfigured face of a fire victim in her coffin. I can find no record that this picture appeared anywhere else, nor any information identifying the girl. One can only wonder how it shocked people on the newsstand.

William Zuscofski brought the issue to the United Charities Building, hoping that some aid might be left for him. But he was "haughtily refused," told to "quit bothering" the staff. He wept while telling Zoe that he was going blind and unable to work, and his family was about to be evicted.

She accompanied him back to the trust's headquarters, magazine in hand, hoping an indignant American-born advocate could give him more clout. Down the hall from the Guild of the Infant Saviour, a Jewish charity's supercilious young woman on duty repeated that the Zuscofski case was closed: "He refused help when we offered it." She would not look through *The East Side* with the dead teenager's photo on the cover.

But the building was full of Zoe's readers, rushing to the newsstand every other month, worried about what she would expose next. She confirmed with the District Attorney's office and the Charity Trust's own records that thousands of dollars in Triangle relief money had simply been folded into the general reserves, in case of, heaven forbid, "another such fire." *The East Side* published a page-long fan letter for her Charity Trust excoriation from the Columbia-educated lawyer (and Ragged Edger) William DeWitt Tyndall, ranking Zoe "among the Immortals" for exposing the truth about the trust's supposed "tender mercies." She longed for her own foundation funds to draw on, "in my self appointed task of fighting with my pen for the rights of the poor." But her unbacked magazine was too close to nonprofit: "Sometimes I also have not my rent till it drops from the skies."[8]

Rich clubwomen asked Zoe to help distribute handmade baby clothes in the slums: "they couldn't find the poor, so they sent for me." But various charity offices, suspecting "some deep ulterior motive" of grifting, turned away her gifts at the door. She tried to help protect young women newly arrived in New York by cofounding a Society for the Prevention of Homesickness, providing gathering places for the vulnerable, to stave off "evil influences." But it never got off the ground.[9]

She tried to donate one *East Side* issue's print run to newsboys, "just hatched" but already supporting families. For the giveaway issue's "beautifully illumined" cover, Oberhardt portrayed a cherubic brunet newsboy, about age 8, his face framed in crumpled paper. She would let the boys keep the 10-cent cover price, half of which would otherwise have gone to the American News Company. She credited her magnanimous idea to her imaginary Printer's Devil: "He's a boy himself, so he loves boys." *The East Side* censored his "blankety blank" curses at the American News Company, which "eats the little magazines alive. They are tender, these little idiot magazines, and their backs are hardly ever green." The news company kept delaying her payments, but when she complained, an executive replied, "Why don't you ask some of your Life Preservers?" In returning unsold *East Side* inventory, it overcharged her for postage, accidentally weighting down the packages with her competitors' leftover *Philistine*s, *Papyruse*s, *Open Road*s, and *Idler*s.

To contact newsboys about the giveaway, she made phone calls and ran newspaper announcements nationwide. "A great scramble for copies" ensued among literate and illiterate boys everywhere except New York, where the underage salesmen jadedly responded to Zoe's offer of freebies, "Ah! Quit yer kiddin'!" Men were sabotaging her, to keep *East Side*s away from impressionable youths: "They might learn something by reading and break away from the Charity Trust."[10]

News of Zoe's anti-trust activism reached Wichita. The *Eagle* editorialized that by urging philanthropies to reduce administrative costs, she could help put "the legitimate objects of charity on Easy Street." A *Beacon* contributor met with her in New York, praised her "splendid work" battling the trusts, and somehow came away persuaded "Mrs. Norris is still very fond of Kansas, especially Wichita." But the poet Ella Wheeler Wilcox (a friend of Edwin Markham and Courtenay Lemon) syndicated a screed about Zoe's misguidedness. Charities needed to vet applicants, to weed out "professional beggars," Ella Wilcox opined (prefiguring modern complaints about "welfare queens"). The tenderhearted Queen of Bohemia did not understand that donating to "the sufferers of the earth," without confirming their worthiness or strengthening their bootstraps, would only lead to "thousands of idlers and loafers. . . . If Zoe Anderson [sic] owned billions," she should buy up farmland for the unemployed and give prizes for the finest harvests. "And she should transport all the homeless people from our great cities" to new towns along cross-country highways, where they could find work as builders, decorators, "sculptors and artists." No newspaper would print Zoe's retort to Ella's "Idiotorial. . . . it would remain unanswered till the Crack of Doom" if not for *The East Side*. Ella had lopped "Norris" off Zoe's name, so she feared that soon, "I shall have only the Zoe left." Her editor friend Marion Miller reassured her: "That's enough . . . You are the only Zoe."[11]

Whenever Zoe felt the inertia of "such lazy Southern natures as mine" coming on, evidence of intolerance and callousness chained her to the keyboard again: "so many thoughts come surging, so many wrongs that should be righted even by so small a might as mine . . . I haven't half enough room in my little publication." Zoe saw a starving teenager in front of posh clothing stores on lower Fifth Avenue, leaning on his skeletal horse, "being severely lectured" and threatened with arrest by an elegantly dressed representative of an animal-protection society. A single mother of three was found emaciated and freezing, her baby dead in her arms, and while she was carried to an ambulance, "she struggled for possession of the little corpse." On streetcars and subways, Northerners who branded Southerners like Zoe as racists would give wide berth to Black passengers, so she went out of her way to defy stereotypes and "sat by and talked with them, I pitied them so." During a Sunday morning errand, she saw the begrimed, bleeding corpse of a newly emigrated workman, who had fallen from First Avenue's elevated train track. She called out to the crowd of onlookers: why did no one at least bring the body inside the corner drugstore, why was he left dying on the pavement "as if he were an animal?" The reply: "Oh, he is only a workingman." While she was waiting on the Bowery for a downtown train, a blaze briefly flared up on the third rail. A workman had been electrocuted, his clothes turned to ash, his bared shoulders "scarred with great red scars." Zoe found no newspaper report of his death and was sure that the railroad company had paid off witnesses, throwing "a wonderful cover of silence over their burnt sacrifices."[12]

Just south of "the gray and spidery skeleton" of the Williamsburg Bridge's Manhattan footings, Zoe asked 1,000 children in a settlement house classroom to tell her about their grievances, "and I would right them by writing of them in my magazine." But no one dared speak: "It is others who grieve for them." Zoe joined mourners sitting shiva at the midtown tenement home of a teenage laborer named Anna Borowsky; a few blocks away, "thousands of snobs" were paying $2 per snob for tours of a "great cream and gold palace" built by Vanderbilts. Anna had committed suicide by inhaling gas, a brochure at her side for a resort hotel in Maine—newspapers attributed the death to an unfaithful suitor in addition to thwarted wanderlust. At the midtown coffin factory where Anna and 15 other girls had stitched shrouds, a foreman told Zoe that he could not understand why making clothing for the dead would worsen anyone's despair: "What's there in a little piece of white cloth to scare you?"[13]

On East 14th Street, Zoe risked being arrested for prostitution while handing *East Side*s to streetwalkers, "my poor little shadow-like sisters," starving, sobbing, leprous, begging in doorways with "bloodless corpselike hands." Men told Zoe that streetwalking actually offered better working conditions—fresh air, flexible hours—than clerking in a department store "or forever writing to the dictation of a cantankerous employer." No one but Zoe believed the women's stories of having been trafficked, "driven by the blast of Fate to a life hardly fit for dogs, to a life that no sane human being would choose for herself." Zoe's vicar ancestors and Jesus himself would have forgiven these sinners, but unchristian Gilded Age women wanted the victims "shunned as a pestilence ... If we only stood by each other as men do, we women." Any pimp who lured in girls "with promises of love and protection" would go unpunished, "he clean in the eyes of the world, she forever unclean." Zoe urged prostitutes to start anew in the West, "where the air is pure and wholesome and sweet," and have a chance to marry big-hearted ranchers and join them in herding cattle "on a swift little broncho, your curls to the wind!" (She did not mention her own miseries in Kansas.)[14]

European-born businesspeople ranted xenophobically to Zoe, and she quoted them verbatim—did she warn away any immigrant customers? A wine merchant longed for his unspecified Old Country, where no Jews or Italians had brought "poverty and squalor." A deli owner with a thick German accent waved "her pudgy wienerwurst hand" in mourning for her countrymen, "the only clean people in the world," fleeing lower Manhattan for the Bronx, "movink and movink . . . as if bound for the wilderness." They were disgusted by "Eyetalians" throwing bombs, Irishmen guzzling whiskey, and Jewish peddlers dropping "roddon banana peelinks" from "der bushgarts." Zoe listed other examples of bigotries that had coursed through Manhattan's "seething cauldron" since Henry Hudson sailed in: from early colonists "burning their women for witches" and seizing Native American land, to 20th-century Christians excluding Jews from tony hotels, and Zoe's own aversion to thieving capitalists "who live in Brooklyn." The deli owner warned that Jewish sweatshop operators trying to "own the zitty" would be thrown from the housetops "if they don't look out," which gave Zoe nightmares and then determination: "Not while there's an East Side magazine, little Wienerwurst woman."[15]

In spring 1911, on the night before Easter, Zoe had a nightmare that she and Mattie were sewing a glossy white shroud together at Clay Hill: "even in the dream, I knew she was dead." At dusk on Easter, Zoe went out to mail some Klub invitations. As she crossed Second Avenue, a car barreled into her: "I dropped like a dead fly." Badly bruised everywhere, blood from a headwound streaming down her long hair, she nonetheless felt compelled to console the distraught chauffeur: "I am not much killed." Hospitals kept turning her away, but she did not distress the driver by admitting that she feared bleeding to death. A hospital finally took her in, and fistfuls of her matted hair were shaved away. She was relieved to learn that no metal had penetrated her skull, so she would not spend her remaining years "a driveling idiot behind the bars of some insane asylum." The doctor delegated "a young and unfledged nurse" to stitch up the scalp gash with "long, rude horsehairs," despite Zoe's protests: "Please don't let her practice on me . . . it's the only head in the world that I've got to write with." To demonstrate how much she needed her brains, she brought out some of her battered magazines. The doctor saw a pageful of praise for *The East*

*Side* from his mentor, Stanford's David Starr Jordan, who was "profoundly impressed with the truthfulness, the brightness, the justice" of Zoe's work. The doctor, taken aback, told his bleeding patient that Jordan "taught me all I know!" Zoe had minimal hope that the doctor then regretted how his staff had treated her. Their indifference helped her better understand the life of any ordinary "poor woman from the East Side. . . . What else must I experience to see how it is with the poor."[16]

She sued the driver for $2,000 in damages, somehow hiring a lawyer, "the best in the land"—did he expect a percentage of a jury award? Her team's expert witness, Dr. Frederick S. Kolle, a German-born plastic surgeon and X-ray pioneer (and *East Side* life preserver), testified to the severity of her wound. But the car's insurers brought in alleged eyewitnesses, who were nowhere near Second Avenue that night yet willing to "lie like pickpockets." Their version of Zoe's encounter with the car: "I had attacked it and fallen in a spasm of rage because I couldn't devour it whole," wresting away "a valuable piece of its shining metal" to gouge her own scalp. Zoe made mistakes in court: she admitted that she had likely jaywalked that night rather than used the crosswalk, and she took off her hat, showing that her hair had grown back. The bald judge insured her defeat by sarcastically advising the bald jurymen, "weigh well the fact that the loss of her hair served somewhat to mar the beauty of this plaintiff." She slunk away from the courthouse in debt after the verdict, realizing that she had come across in the courtroom as "a writer who hadn't sense enough to keep out of the rain or she wouldn't write." The only way to ensure pedestrian safety, she decided futuristically: "erect paths for us from skyscraper to skyscraper." She hardly ever crossed avenues alone thereafter, relying instead on policemen as escorts, though she had seen them pummel the poor in the streets.[17]

She did find a few local heroes. The restaurateur Joel Rinaldo, known to Edgers as Prince Joel of Bohemia, helped poor families cover their rent "all Unbeknownst to the general public"—well, unbeknownst until *The East Side* announced it. Dr. Joseph Bissell, a "Wonder Wizard" physician, helped Prince Joel recover from an ailment so dire that the Jewish businessman woke up at the hospital as a Catholic chaplain showered him with holy water for last rites. The chiropractor Alma C. Arnold (a Klub dinner honoree), whose profession was widely dismissed as quackery and technically illegal, cured paralyzed children yet had been "thrown for a while into the Tombs." Dr. William Sirovich, a Columbia grad and *East Side* life preserver, brought Zoe back from the brink of the Land of the Lilies after she ate some low-budget tainted meat, "worse than dynamite."

He volunteered as head of the People's Hospital on lower Second Avenue (where Zoe would spend her last day). A briskly efficient nurse let Zoe shadow her on house calls in the slums, to advise immigrant parents and hand out fresh milk. At one tenement, the nurse revived a starving mother found unconscious on her couch, having set aside the milk donations for her chubby baby, setting his cradle on a table like a centerpiece, "a glow of radiant and beautiful healthfulness."[18]

A malfunctioning furnace in Zoe's building spurted flames and smoke: "I could have hugged the fire laddies" who rushed to extinguish the blaze. She could not afford to lose her uninsured apartment, full of "painfully accumulated" possessions: the ebony piano, heirloom silver candlesticks, grinning gargoyle, stacks of *East Side*s "bound and unbound." *The East Side* fictionalized a toddler on Hester Street, a "little mother" who saves her infant brother's life after their washerwoman mother locks them inside the apartment and heads out to work. The girl is confused at first to hear neighborhood alarm bells clanging furiously but then, as "little yellow flames licked in at the door," she throws herself on the cradle to protect the boy. A fireman breaks in through the window and rescues them, calling out, "A baby taking care of a baby!"[19]

At Ellis Island, Zoe met a blue-eyed young Episcopal chaplain, known as Padre. He comforted a frail, sobbing, elderly Irishwoman, about to be deported in steerage, abandoned by her violent alcoholic son in Rhode Island. She was clearly so close to death that Zoe longed to kneel and beg her to report from the afterworld, "what flowers grew there and how it was with those mute travelers who had never returned." The chaplain, his "clean limbed strength" evident under his vestments, begged Zoe's forgiveness for wanting to track down and flog the Rhode Island drunk. (A handsome Episcopal priest known as Padre appears in a freelance short story, too; he tends poor immigrants and loves, of course, a beautiful agnostic divorcée from the West, who illuminates her apartment with "dim, soft, radiant light" from heirloom silver candlesticks.)[20]

Just in case readers thought they knew what to expect every other month, *The East Side* took frivolous and contradictory turns. During a subway trip uptown, Zoe confused a companion by jokingly sobbing at each stop: "I lived near here once with a husband . . . it was a different husband every station." At a Manhattan pier, she toured a battleship, admiring 900 men in uniform: "How beautiful to walk through rows of saluting navies! Oh, the brass buttons! What wonderful guns, primed and ready in case one is quick tempered!" She flirted with aviators, known for "swoops mighty near the ground," but declined to take a test flight: "The Ragged Edge needs me yet a little while." In her comic playlet "The Elopement," a mansion-dwelling woman, bored by her husband—"Always either working or reading the papers!"—plots to run off with a lover unwilling to live with her toddler son, known as the Bambino (of course). Her French maid steps in to break off the affair with the child-hater: "Nevaire!" would she let Madame go off "with a man si brute as of it." (See Chapter 19 for moviemakers' theft of this plot.) Zoe swaggeringly invented words like "pushativeness" (ambition) and parodied figures as revered as Walt Whitman. Where his "Mannahatta" teemed with "the most courageous and friendly young men," her poem of that same title found "the arrogant motorman" accelerating streetcars past passengers "who with timid finger implore him to stop," and chauffeurs honking while "running down those who fail to get away." In place of Whitman's "hurried and sparkling waters," lined in bustling offices for "ship-merchants and money-brokers," Zoe poeticized electric signage with "Kittens and Klocks," agleam at the feet of "skyscrapers stabbing the clouds." Her Mannahatta's infrastructure marvels enabled men to reach New Jersey via the Hudson River's "great tunnels which speak also of Escape from Alimony."[21]

She nonetheless loved "wickedly interesting!" men and encouraged married women to flirt, "find a mental affinity," and slough off "prudish scruples." She denied outright manhating: "I like men. I just hate husbands." She gave aphoristic advice for resisting underminers—"The Encomiums of the Whole Wide World will not give you self respect, if there is one beside you who continually Belittles you"—and maintaining friendships: "Be a Live Wire, but try not to be a Third Rail." In the Garden of Eden, Zoe suspected, Eve must have bitten the serpent's apple because of "something wrong about that Adam," off dreaming about his dead first wife Lilith. "Write on!" was women's response as the magazinelet urged them to support themselves upon evicting cruel, jealous, deceitful, or dull husbands: "Money means so much in this disastrous matter of matrimony." For twice-married Zoe, marriage and home were somehow sacred, "to be kept intact at any sacrifice." A cuckold should forgive his unfaithful wife: "wrap her warmly with your love and win her back." Working divorcées, "out somewhere scratching for worms," risked neglecting their children: littler ones tended "by some yawning nurse girl," older daughters barhopping unchaperoned with college boys or shipped off to boarding schools "bound about by ironclad formalities." (Did Zoe regret Clarence's time at Nazareth Academy?) But then she pretzeled herself into respecting anyone who would hire nannies: "I'd rather maul rails than take care of a baby. It's easier."[22]

She named men who drove wives to alcoholism or morphine addiction, "to sleep away the years," or fatal gunshots or leaps out of skyscraper windows. She walked in the funeral procession for Second Avenue restaurateur Alexander Balogh, who committed suicide in his wine cellar by inhaling gas, after "terrible years of brooding over his financial condition." She had tried to help him with *East Side* speculations on how many "Barons or Counts or Emperors" were on his payroll and at his tables, alongside deaf revelers "flourishing madly" in sign language. Yet she condemned newspapers that quashed her morning optimism by delivering reports to her doorstep of "Suicide upon Suicide, Divorce after Divorce." The Pulitzers' million-subscriber *World* maligned the city as "vile and perverted," besieged by thieves and murderers, a target for anarchists' bombs, ruled by "gangs searching only for graft." Zoe and her Office Boy still idolized New York as "a glorious Garden of the Gods," although besieged by corrupt, hypocritical bureaucrats like the anti-vice czar Anthony Comstock ("how fat he is!") and leftist rabblerousers like Emma Goldman, "crazy to get arrested and written up in the papers." The justice system, "a screaming farce," sent innocent Italian immigrants to the electric chair at Sing Sing. But a candy store owner in Zoe's neighborhood went unpunished after sexually abusing little girls; he terrified them into silence on the witness stand with threats from his "cruel, sharp, long" knife.[23]

Zoe inconsistently insisted that women should stay out of politics—"they can't keep from quarreling"—yet she endorsed William Randolph Hearst for president (he was an *East Side* reader and "Very good to the Poor").[24] She despised Roosevelt ("a boob entirely devoid of manners") and his successor Taft (a mollycoddled "fat slob"). Her vendettas were partly personal, as she hinted in a 1912 *East Side* feature, "The Copyist," published after her sister Nettie Cheeks was found dead in a bathroom at her Washington boardinghouse. *The East Side* described sifting through "pitiful effects" in the estate of an unnamed government copyist—without explaining that she was Zoe's sister. Nettie, who had earned $1,000 a year as a clerk in her 1880s prime, was relying on pittances from her dead husband's pension. "Give us this day our daily bread" was underlined in her Bible. As overwork had ruined her eyesight, oculists' bills piled up in her neatly organized papers. She begged for employment from Roosevelt and Taft, while denying rumors of her incompetence: "Please appoint me by an Executive order . . . I am in the most urgent need . . . I have been persecuted all these years and kept in poverty . . . on slander from vile enemies." Her frantic letters left her "awful sorry" afterwards. Politicians rejected her pleas with "insolent letters, couched in the most insulting terms."

The government did pay for Nettie to be interred between her father Henry and her sister Lucy. (There were erroneous reports that Peter Cheeks' grave was adjacent; he was buried in northern California, where he had moved with Nettie's niece and nephew turned stepchildren.) Zoe attended the funeral with her brother-in-law John Thompson. It was probably the last time she saw relatives, and her last trip outside New York. Nettie, "robbed of all hope," had chosen to end her life, *The East Side* theorized (heart failure was listed on the death certificate and in obituaries). The men who broke her spirit "will have to answer for her death at the Throne of God."[25]

More compassionate and humane politicians would be elected if women could vote, Zoe was told, but she was not convinced at first. *The East Side* quoted the suffragist Helen Hamilton Gardener bluntly asking why Zoe, "a woman of such brains," did not support the cause. Zoe defended her inactivism: "this is no time for Isms here on the East Side. We need help now." In Kansas, she was appalled by "the ranting militant Suffragette," and she was repulsed at the literary sanctum when "a simpering idiot in silk and velvets," a rich suffragist "from the swell part of Stuyvesant Square," paid a visit: "Came over slumming to convert me. She hadn't the brains of a stuffed toad." And yet Zoe was infuriated by the *World*'s portrayals, "scathing to the point of insolence," of suffragists as fools or violent menaces.[26]

In spring 1912, as the *World* devoted page after page to the doomed Titanic's wealthy passengers, Zoe pointed out how little ink was allotted to "the poor of the steerage . . . who were drowned, like rats in the hold." John Jacob Astor VI, who had been a fetus on the Titanic, was such a frequent headline topic, even when teething, that Zoe and the Office Boy went picnicking to celebrate "when the last tooth was out." She threatened a libel suit and won an apology when Roy McCardell, a *World* columnist, inaccurately called her a "shining member" of the unphilanthropic Sunrise Club. Yet she worked for the writer and publisher Walter Pulitzer, a first cousin of the *World*'s brother-owners. (In the small world category, the brothers' maternal uncle William Davis was married to Zoe's niece-in-law Mattie, daughter of Phil Thompson, the Kentucky Colonel.) For Walter's short-lived weekly *Satire*, Zoe turned her Second Avenue car accident into short fiction about a male poet felled and bloodied by a chauffeured car near his tenement home. The distraught driver brings him to a hospital, and an inexperienced nurse stitches the victim's scalp as he implores her to be careful, since his head is all "that I have to make my living with." The poet tries to sue the car owner for $5,000 in damages, but authorities conclude that no money was owed anyone, since the uninsured car had been damaged while clobbering the poet. *Satire* never paid Zoe the promised $10 for the story: the magazine's "most Satirical thing . . . is the way it pays." She took Walter Pulitzer to court, representing herself. He was represented by "a seedy little associate editor, who testified that I was Nobody and my work was worth Nothing, which won me the case" and brought in "considerably More" than $10. She did not specify the amount of the manna. She must have been pleased when *Satire* folded, amid accusations that its salesmen were hardened criminals, "well known and flagrant."[27]

*Satire* was among her last freelance clients, along with publications as obscure as *Choice-Bits*, a short-lived poetry monthly published by a New Jersey hardware dealer. Thumbnail biographies of Zoe in "Who's Who" directories gave impressive lists of her past outlets, but then she was sent the exorbitantly expensive books and expected to buy them. She carted them back to the publishers' office, longing to add a caveat to her future Who's Who entries: "she wouldn't cough up the Dough for the Books!" A few of her decade-old stories were recycled in places as unglamourous as the monthly *Railroad Telegrapher*, sometimes with happy endings tacked on and without her permission. Male colleagues, while job hunting themselves, "beating the turf," were undermining her opportunities: "She thinks she can run a magazine. Well, then, let her sink or swim by it!" She invited freelancers to pay $50 per page for the privilege of writing for *The East Side*. *Harper's Weekly*, "a journal of civilization," ran her long-shelved story about some drunken neighbors neglecting their son. But the piece might as well have appeared in "the Killiommiletre of Kalamazoo," for all it mattered to her by then: "I am prouder of the East Side than of anything I have ever done or ever will do."[28]

Her confidence swelled that her bimonthly "pamphlet, as some call it . . . has come to stay." God destined her to spread enlightenment, "to awake those who are slower to awake" (a quote that she attributed to Ye Yen, a nonexistent ancient Chinese sage). Her readers, and anyone else interested in the poor, "are the Real People . . . the Best in the Land." Oberhardt illumined her pages despite "the Great work he is doing for the Big Magazines," like her plagiaristic former employer *Everybody's*. Yet she called herself "full of faults . . . prone to evil as the sparks fly upward." Her neighborhood's Jews, "hounded to desperation" in their homelands, maintained unwavering faith in God, which she pleaded with them to share: "Teach me to humbly bow unto His will."

Her Oberhardt-illustrated *East Side* brochure quoted about 30 fan letters, including from David Starr Jordan, Elbert Hubbard, some Edgers (Lampton, the Prince of McPike, writer Mabel Urner, violinist Ovide

Musin), life preservers and nobodies. "Send the East Side there Forever," one Thomas E. Perkins added with his change of address note. The magazinelet "smites you full in the face and sends your prim conventionalities reeling," one W. H. Given wrote. The writer and reformer Sophie Irene Loeb called Zoe a "universal inspiration dispenser." The poet Francesca Spaulding reported having hung a framed portrait of *The East Side*'s Pooh Bah on her wall. Bruce Calvert, the back-to-nature advocate issuing *The Open Road* from his Indiana farm, damned Zoe's magazine for irresistibly distracting him "when I should have been hoeing my potatoes." The pianist Gustave Becker subscribed "to see how long you can keep up such effervescence. Long may the champagne bubble." One fan was identified only as Don: "The story of the way your printers treated you brought a lump to my throat. . . . The more we see of men, the more we like dogs."[29]

Did the pressmen read her brochure and magazines savaging them? One printer, "absolutely heartless," tried to trim away "my very best words . . . I had to stand over him with a gun." Typesetters made errors as galling as "Wiohita" and left out the plural in men sowing wild oats: "As if I would accuse any man of sowing one oat!" She insisted on whimsical layouts, leaving a page half empty except for a sketch of high-stepping dancers: "It is against every artistic rule for these people to be dancing off the page; but why not? The story is at an end." Paper dealers overcharged her—"Would they treat a man so? No!!!"—and bookbinders made her magazine spines look "finished by the rats." Department stores treated her as badly as they did Black people, shunting her to the loading docks, where she navigated through delivery wagons pulled by draft horses, "their big feet ready to trample and kill."[30]

Not even her close male friends were immune from *East Side* criticism. She longed for her "Sky Pilot" John von Herrlich's vastly wealthy landowning employer, Trinity Church, to alleviate its downtown neighbors' "most insufferable poverty" by giving away just one of its skyscrapers' monthly rents. *East Side* advertiser Robert Shores' frothy periodical *The Idler*, which published letters from fictitious readers like Barbara Bluestocking and Seth Shirtless, sold surprisingly well: "Maybe because he's a man." (Her *East Side* would outlive his magazinelet, however; he gave up after three years of Sisyphean battling against a Cerberus with three heads: the printer, "The Retailer, and The Newsagent.") The lawyer and newspaperman George Harrison McAdam praised Zoe's poetry as "more melodious and rhythmical" than Walt Whitman's, but in return she called him "a fussy old hen"; he had accused Kentucky feudists of laying in cowardly ambushes to shoot enemies, rather than the actual statewide practice of getting acquitted for murders in broad daylight. Sydney Rosenfeld, a Virginia-born theater impresario, *East Side* distributor, and Klub honoree,[31] set a play in the South Seas, and Zoe nitpicked when a performer tossed a rose at the backdrop, hitting it with "a dull and sickening thud" and spoiling its illusion of depth. Edgers including her wunderkind "special protégé" Henry McHarg Davenport (while still a Columbia undergrad, he published fiction and poetry as well as reviews lauding Zoe's work) gave their new books to Zoe and her Printer's Devil, during feasts of Prince Joel's tamales and chili con carne "at the table of the Literrotti." Her response in print: "Must I read them? Oh, how short life is!"

Calvert's *Open Road* told Zoe that New Yorkers were "blind moles in the underworld of darkness." She told him to stay in the woods, "full of poison ivy for me." She preferred Broadway's "stream of humanity," flowing between the boulders of granite skyscrapers veined with windows goldened by sunsets, and Central Park's cedar groves kept company by apartment buildings "scintillating with lights." She invited Calvert to join her under the Brooklyn Bridge during a storm, as winds transformed its cables into "a great aeolian harp," sending songs, wails, moans, and sobs "sighing out to the sea." (Bruce Calvert, known as "the Indiana Thoreau," soon moved to Brooklyn with his singer wife Anna Gulbrandsen, known as "the Norwegian Nightingale.") The Queen of Bohemia told readers, "I'd rather be a peanut vendor in New York than a Queen in the Country." Then she contradicted herself with paeans to Mother Earth's woodland glades, comforting the city's "wandering Child of Toil" with singing nightingales, "sighing willows . . . peace and rest . . . all things best." She saw families spending nights on Coney Island beaches, gratefully cradled in sand while "gentle lullabies sang the waves." In an *East Side* short story, immigrant children slave at their Hester Street tenement, making artificial violets infested with scarlet fever germs, until a philanthropist sends them "out under the blue skies with the real violets . . . to run and play and rest."[32]

Critics leafing through *East Side* bound volumes noticed Zoe's mood swings, in "colloquially delightful style," juxtaposing "poignant pathos" with "saucy little obtrusions of herself," on pages "warm with the bubbling of the melting pot." Zoe was said to philosophize vivaciously, earnestly, unconventionally, perkily, opinionatedly, with "no end of perverse ideas." She was considered such a neighborhood expert that a Unitarian group from New Jersey took her guided tour, "Little Journey Through the Ghetto and Yiddish New York." They stopped for a kosher lunch, synagogue services, and a Yiddish play about angels debating the virtues of a Russian tobacco merchant's family. (How one longs to know what the Unitarians thought while sitting through a melodrama incomprehensible to them!) Zoe's leap-year birthdate, February 29, attracted attention, too; she had celebrated "nine birthdays in my whole life. It's the one rule I know for keeping young." She was unabashedly flattered at "how lovely" she looked in a pastel portrait by Brooklyn-based artist Mary Theresa Hart, a daughter of the painter James McDougal Hart (whose cattle tableau Zoe had copied at Wichita's Lewis Academy).[33]

For just "One Plunk," Zoe mailed out copies of her self-published *Wind*, "beautifully printed as may be," with Oberhardt's sketches of Kansas's "thirsty treeless plains." Some of its characters and incidents had recurred in her fiction since the 1890s: cyclones sending houses flying across state lines; British émigré tenderfeet falling in love with cowgirls. Zoe told *East Side* readers that she based the book on her own experiences, exchanging her native Kentucky's "gentle zephyrs" for the frontier's ceaseless wind that "blows the feathers off the chickens."[34] But only her innermost circle would have known about the book's other autobiographical aspects. Like *Wind*'s villain Celia Lawson, Zoe grew up in a gossipy Kentucky hamlet, was dragged to Kansas as a young bride, watched her husband's business fail, and fled nostalgically homeward upon leaving behind her only son. Like Zoe's sister Mattie, Celia is an icy blue-eyed blonde with a colonnaded ancestral home. Like Celia's husband Seth, Zoe was a dreamer who grew to love her hardscrabble existence in a faraway unfamiliar land (Manhattan). One of *Wind*'s Wichita millionaires, Will Low, has nearly the exact name of the Kentucky-born testifier about adultery in the Norrises' 1898 divorce proceedings. Zoe's mother Henrietta descended into madness, as do Seth and his neighbor Cyclona, a cowgirl who tends the Lawsons' doomed son Charlie and turns down a British expat's marriage proposal. Seth, while plowing his inhospitable Kansas fields, hums "My Old Kentucky Home." At the novel's end, Seth returns in despair to Kentucky, and as he inflicts a fatal pistol wound in his temple, he sends a telepathic farewell to Cyclona that she receives in a dream—just as Zoe heard from loved ones in the Undiscovered Country.

A number of publishers had gone out of business at the verge of releasing the novel, *The East Side* explained, without mentioning how drastically Zoe had revised the plot over the years. In one previous version, Charlie outlives his father, builds the Wichita mansion that Seth envisioned, and then reunites in Kentucky with his estranged mother Celia, "a wreck . . . like the house she lives in." (It is this draft that Houghton Mifflin described as "not well enough done to bear up under its load of sorrow and blundering," see Chapter 13.)

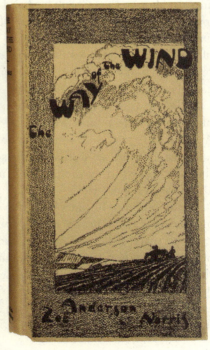

Fig 25: Oberhardt-illustrated last novel, *The Way of the Wind* (Zoe dabbed white paint on some covers), with author portrait and press release clipping. AC, Nicole Neenan photo

When boxfuls of freshly printed *Wind*s reached Zoe's literary sanctum, she and the Printer's Devil giddily perched on the stacks, "made into window seats and such." On the pinkish-tan covers, "Little Zoe's Own Hand" applied opaque white streaks to Oberhardt's outlines of clouds dwarfing a prairie farmer (she similarly dabbed highlights on her bound volume covers). Her magazinelet quoted *Wind* reviews from "Her Ever Increasing Circle of Friends." Herbert Welch, the writer who suggested that she found the Ragged Edge Klub, admired the novel's poignance and pace: "you have kept time on your typewriter with the beating of your heart." Marion Miller wrote that her somberly realistic book, with humorous interludes rivaling Mark Twain's, merited "a permanent place in American literature." The California novelist Donna R. Cole called it a "wonder word painting!" Backhanded compliments came from Yonkers newspaperman Edwin Austin Oliver ("Somebody must have helped you with That book") and Ohio-born *World* editor Frederick Boyd Saumenig ("I don't see why a woman capable of such work isn't rich").[35]

New York critics largely ignored the novel, which Zoe blamed on Funk & Wagnalls' "moneyed influence" (did anyone at the company even remember the *Soul* debacle?). *Wind* was lionized in a few other places. "The spirit of the undying winds" was said to have steeled this "famous writer of New York City" to self-publish the "almost epic" tale, "set in an atmosphere of Thomas Hardy relentlessness." The *Eagle* serialized *Wind*, predicting it would "touch the tender chords of the heart of every Kansan." People noticed how the plot veered away from Zoe's usual gender tropes: stoic, browbeaten, non-adulterous Seth is martyred by "heartless, unseeing, selfish" Celia.[36]

Some reviewers found *Wind* depressing, "long on shadows and short on sunshine," and unflattering to hardworking families "on Kansas' ragged edge . . . it isn't a good story to go to bed thinking about." Or perhaps Zoe's "mighty bad stories on Kansas" were not unflattering enough, "not quite so bad as if they were true." Zoe hoped for profits to share with the Office Boy and perhaps buy a new swimsuit for summer Klub outings. But few copies sold. By late 1913, she largely gave up publishing *East Side* advertorials for *Wind, Soul*, and even her bound volumes.[37]

That was only one sign of her waning faith in her ability to change the world, which was disappointingly changing around her.

## Art—?

I have always threatened to illustrate my magazine. Now I will. I am determined on it. The Exhibition has filled me with courage. I may become in time a Cubist. Who knows? At any rate, watch me! And if you don't like my drawings, it's not my fault. It is yours. You don't understand my drawings. However, I will sign my work, so you may not think that Oberhardt, who will continue to draw for me, has also gone mad.

Tom Powers reeled through the Picabia exhibit, his head in both hands.

"They're kidding us!" he stammered. "They can't really mean it. No!"

"Rotton!" cried Block, his bodyguard.

"I saw it first in Paris," said Fornaro. "It is all right."

"There must be something to it," Andre Tridon declared. "A man could make money much easier another way."

And just then they made room for the carrying out of a young artist whose reason had temporarily tottered.

This girl had wasted her time at the Academy, learning to draw.

We, too, emerged into the fresh air before it was too late. It was around Washington's Birthday. We passed a lovely portrait of George, framed in the flag.

"How thankful we ought to be," said Oberhardt, "that the Father of Our Country was not painted by a Futurist."

Fig. 26: 1913 *East Side* curmudgeonly review of Armory show. AC, Nicole Neenan photo

# 19

## Lest They Fade from Affection's Bliss, 1913–1914

SOME OF ZOE'S entrenched opinions shifted as a few con artists sought her help promoting their causes. *The East Side* had some impact—albeit never enough—as her friend circle shrank and omens plagued her.

Addressing readers ever more maternally as "Little Ones," she warned, "you'll be unlucky in the year 1913 if you don't renew your subscription, but you won't be so unlucky as I will." She introduced an art review column, which lasted two issues. The advent of abstract art left her practically speechless. After visiting the 1913 Armory show, which imported modernism to America, she wrote a curmudgeonly critique illustrated with her own sketches of polygons and amoebas. She reduced George Washington's bewigged head to a triangle, slashes, and squiggles. "The What is it?" was her title for an eyeball on a stalk dangling over a staircase. "The Exhibition has filled me with courage. I may become in time a Cubist. Who knows? . . . And if you don't like my drawings, it's not my fault. It is yours. You don't understand my drawings." She signed her artwork, lest anyone think Oberhardt "has also gone mad."[1]

A few dozen other drawings by Zoe, mostly bust portraits of Edgers, appeared in her last issues. Was Oberhardt preoccupied with paying work, or was her stream of free theater tickets for him drying up? Or did she simply like dusting off her 1880s skills? "The Right Honorable Hannah Wyle" posed for Zoe's sketch while impersonating mustachioed Cardinal Richelieu. Alongside portraits of young Edgers, Zoe published their inflated mini biographies. The filmmaker Wray Physioc, "distinguished and promising," was supposedly a descendant of President Andrew Johnson. Zoe wished for "a Fairy with a Magic Wand" to ensure a life of gilded leisure for Sidonie Devereux Pur-Don, who was becoming known for giving lectures on medicine and designing prizewinning wallpaper. Lampton wrote a yawp for "lithe and fair" Sidonie (it was one of *The East Side*'s few contributions from a non-staffer), calling her "our one best bet," a talented singer and graceful dancer who "stands by Zoe, strong / And helps the Ragged Edge along / To raise the right and down the wrong."[2]

Due diligence on new friends, however, was never Zoe's forte, as she unwittingly lionized some unsavory characters. The Hungarian-born, NYU-trained lawyer Elias B. Goodman, an Edger along with his wife Lottie, told Zoe that he was "running to earth these human beasts of the East Side" who sexually abused girls. (Goodman, who had been disbarred over the years for misconduct, actually preyed upon "wayward girls" in his care—he installed two as his mistresses at a Greenwich Village hotel.) Zoe called the German physician Dr. Friedrich Franz Friedmann "the Great Healer of the White Plague," unjustly persecuted by regulators and other doubters as he injected his new turtle-based tuberculosis cure into patients at the People's Hospital. (His serum actually did no good.) The Italian-born opera impresario Gaetano D'Amato convinced Zoe that Italian immigrants bombed each other's businesses during rather harmless family feuds. "Fool reporters" were overreacting to Italian Americans' disputes, D'Amato explained, just as Zoe's Kentucky Colonel stories had exaggerated gunmen killing off "nearly the whole population of the state." (D'Amato, who also worked for a city licensing bureau, was caught demanding bribes from businessmen.) Zoe suggested the downtrodden could find pleasant work at a New Jersey farm owned by Evelyn Wentworth Murray, a paragon of "Sisterly Love" who fed farmhands well and kept their workloads "light as possible." (The farmwoman, a former actress sometimes known as the Countess de Grasse, made headlines for her divorces, litigiousness, cruel treatment of servants, and suspicious housefires.) When Lady Evelyn's chauffeur took Zoe home in the rain, the car spun out of control. Zoe imagined her mangled corpse described in newspaper reports, which would also give her real age—"that's the worst of being killed."[3]

She wanted "to lie in ambush and take a shot at" John Wilson Townsend, a young Kentucky historian, who disclosed a number close to her real age in a two-volume opus, *Kentucky in American Letters, 1784–1912*. It was her only write-up in a scholarly book in her lifetime. Townsend gathered about 200 profiles of culturati and examples of their writings; for Stephen

Foster's entry, the text was the lyrics to "My Old Kentucky Home." About a third of Townsend's subjects were women, including Maria Thompson Daviess, a novelist, suffragist, and Ragged Edger from Harrodsburg (and an in-law of the Thompson twins; her namesake grandmother had been a writer and Zoe's colleague at Daughters College). Zoe sent Townsend her books, an *East Side* brochure and the bound volumes, and a one-page typewritten memoir with some untruths—those Northumberland vicars! *Kentucky in American Letters* ran two *East Side* excerpts: a poem longing to be "rocked in a cradle again," and a short story about unhappy young mothers at a nightclub longing to go home to their babies. Townsend called the magazinelet "almost bursting with love, sympathy, and understanding," giving the poor "a voice in the world worth having."

Townsend quoted some of Zoe's memoir confessions: she had expected, "like an idiot," that resettling in London would increase her literary fame. But he left out some of the best lines in the typescript (which survives in his papers): she had married as a teenager, "like an idiot," and after the divorce, "got alimony but didn't got it." Zoe had asked Townsend, "for the Lord's sake," not to compare her to Elbert Hubbard, but instead he noted that her periodical was smaller in size than the Fra's *Philistine*. Townsend did comply with her requests to mention Oberhardt, "her one best friend," as well as "the loveliest Klub in the world," organizing dinners "that delight the diners—and the newspapers!" If it was "absolutely necessary" to publish her birth year, then Townsend should eliminate her entry altogether, she told him; the world only needed "to know that I was born." So he asked for research assistance from a Harrodsburg pastor, Robert N. Simpson, who headed the congregation descended from Henry's Disciples. Simpson in turn asked Clarence, by then raising two boys (her second son, Francis Chelf, was born in 1910). Clarence leafed through some heirlooms and found a textbook with Zoe's 1878 scribblings about preparing to marry Spencer upon graduating from Daughters College. Townsend then misestimated that Zoe was born in 1861. By then she told people, including census takers (one was handed an *East Side* when he asked to speak with "the man who pays the rent"), that she was in her early 40s.

A profile of Ohio-born Lampton appeared in Townsend's book, along with a yawp for champagne that ended with "Gee whiz, Fizz!!!" No birthdate was given for Lampton, since the YMCA-dwelling yawpist had insisted, "NEVER will I tell my age until I am safe in the arms of some estimable woman of means." When copies of *Kentucky in American Letters* reached New York, Lampton saw Zoe and dashed off a warning to

Townsend: "take to the tall timber." Watch out for her "white hot" wrath in print: "If there is anything left of you when she has finished pull it together please and let me know how the remnants feel."[4]

*The East Side* tore into Townsend as a "chronological fiend," stealing "the youth of the heart" that she had earned by surviving "the torture of marriage . . . in these progressive days where an up-to-date woman is any age she looks and thinks and feels." Zoe wanted to make a bonfire out of Townsend's volumes, no matter how much status they brought her in the company of Foster's "Old Kentucky Home." She compared Townsend to *Who's Who* scammers, who now left her out of their overpriced sets, though she felt "more alive than I ever was." (Editions of *Who's Who*, despite her refusal to cough up the dough, kept mentioning her among notable women through 1914.)[5]

Zoe strived for immortality on her own terms by giving up on copyrighting her magazine. "All who wish may copy it, provided they give me credit," rather than plagiarizing. She stopped shipping her work to the Library of Congress, but she hand-delivered her novels and bound volumes to the New York Public Library. The staff pasted labels inside noting that the books were personally "presented by Mrs. Zoe Anderson Norris." She predicted that someone would profit someday from reprinting her uncopyrighted magazine, after she followed her pushcart people to "the Happy Hunting Ground," since it was "invaluable as history" and illustrated "generously and beautifully" by pro bono Obie. The newborn movie industry plagiarized her, while stealing ideas from many of her era's best writers, "everything that is lying around loose . . . copyrighted or uncopyrighted." Her 1912 playlet "The Elopement," about a French housemaid scuttling her boss's adultery attempt, was adapted into a screenplay without Zoe's permission and "thrown on the screen." A film company manager brought her to see the comedy and offered her a well-paid screenwriting job stealing other writers' plots: "But I had suffered too much myself to accept."[6]

The Magic City started grating on her nerves. Upwardly mobile children practiced "Interminable two-finger exercises" on pianos and defied parental rules, turning into stereotypes of the "disagreeable and impossible little American child." As prospering immigrants fled for greener pastures, the windows of empty apartments stared back at Zoe, "meaningless as mindless eyes." Neoclassical and neogothic skyscraper designs were derived "not any too well" from Old World precedents. Construction noise from Second Avenue—"They open up a new hole every day to see what it's stuffed with"—still could not blot out "the cry of the child of the poor for bread."[7]

Zoe peered into brownstones' dreary cellar apartments, exposed as landlords modernized by lopping off stoops. She stayed loyal to pushcart vendors, as department stores hired ever haughtier clerks for their confusing miles of new aisles. Edgers' favorite restaurants were razed to make room for shirtwaist factories: "How cruel a big city is!" On the brick walls of half-demolished tenements, fireplaces clung in midair, with "the wreck of mantels upon which have stood clocks, wearily watched for the homecoming of husbands." One of the few visible improvements near the literary sanctum were some flowerbeds in Stuyvesant Square Park, inspired by Zoe's *East Side* urgings: "That side of the park was like a wilderness before I wrote about it."[8]

She deprecated herself—by age 175, "I'll be a very wise woman"—even as a fawning young Bostonian headed home from the literary sanctum to "start a Zoe Anderson Norris Cult." The *Wichita Beacon* still listed her among former Kansans thriving in New York, along with the lecturer and writer Mary Lease and the Levy brothers, Jewish bankers who had attended the Norrises' parties as children. *Wind* sank out of sight, but reviewers kept reading *The East Side*, a "diminutive freak" of an unfiltered magazine, "terribly cynical on men and marriage," serving "meaty views in a nutshell," reporting on "divorced couples, cabaret shows and other up-to-datenesses."[9]

After one more presidential election—Woodrow Wilson was "a Southern gentleman" but dull—Zoe ranted against the industrial, corrupt North for impoverishing the postbellum nation and leaving Black people in the South worse off than ever. She compared sweatshop overseers to antebellum enslavers (echoing repellent Lost Cause rhetoric), sadistically wielding "the lash of the wage" to motivate malnourished tailors hunched over businessmen's vests. She emptied her purse to help a shawled mother sifting through an ashcan on the street, looking for "enough coals to keep her and her children alive." Zoe's sketch of the woman appeared alongside a final vow to keep battling the Charity Trust, with help from the Office Boy, although she suspected "its strength is too great for us to cope with."[10]

Friends invited her to join them in exile in Canada, India, Australia, or the Bronx, but she loved waking up to downtown towers "a-gleam against the tender sapphire of the early sky." Klub diners left chairs empty and overturned wineglasses at their tables in memory of those moved away or turned highbrow or married. Ghosts of those lost in "bitter parting" glowed in Zoe's mind like lightbulb loops "left on the retina after the light is out" (a metaphor she had used since the 1890s). A poem described feeling "mem'ries kiss" at twilight from departed "dear ones . . . Lest they fade from / Affection's bliss." The literary sanctum filled with relics: a German baroness's punchbowl, a dentist's tall-case clock, Hannah Wyle's handsewn rag rug, Lady Evelyn Murray's "Magic Trunk, so full of silks and velvets and laces!" A Bronx farmer sent some chickens "fit for a Queen," but otherwise her refrigerator was largely bare: "Once in a while a small bottle of beer stands in a lonely way in there against the ice." She sought new friends—"I should be glad to meet some Crack Chess Players"—even as she insulted existing ones in print. Philip Riddell exasperatingly critiqued the Klub management, and Hannah Wyle gossiped the night away. One of the magazinelet's crankiest last aphorisms: "Others will give you the gratitude due you for the kindnesses that you have lavished on someone else."[11]

Zoe danced around one more Klub maypole and enjoyed one last moonlit summer of "gay parties . . . just past the honeysuckles" at Brooklyn waterfronts. She kept changing the Klub's weekly meeting places, while longing for some "rich railroad men . . . to build us a Klub House." Two more Edger sweethearts tied the knot; the ceremony was held at the Episcopal church on 29th Street where Zoe and Jack had been turned away as divorcés. Zoe blessed the couple but inwardly prayed for "the stork to forget you in his rounds" (that is, stave off babies who could cause disenchantment and quarrels)—but she did not pray inwardly enough to stop her from publishing that prayer. She made fun of herself for devoting too much ink to male readers' flaws: "My Dear Men Children, for you are dear to me, very dear in that sisterly comrade-like way which is the only way a woman should care for a man, I think, indeed, I believe that eventually it will be the only way and men will be entirely sidetracked as husbands, they have made such a fizzle at it,—my dear Men Children again (what an awfully long sentence this is. I don't seem to be able to finish it at all) I have something to say to you."[12]

Bohemia's Queen worried that her friends, overly ennobled, "are beginning to look down on me a little . . . to sort of scorn me." Philip Riddell wondered if "they think a lot of money ought to go along with the title." On October 9, 1913, she handed out her last ennoblements: "The Court Presentation at the Calico Ball at Little Hungary was a Scream." Minions including F. Emil Gramm, a Columbia-educated composer of saccharine love songs, held up the trailing corners of her rose-covered bedspread cape as she "sailed down the Ballroom to the throne." The peerage titles got jumbled in her enthusiasm to tap her friends lightly with another long-necked wine bottle: Dowager Chessman or Lady Chessman, Sir Leon Bachenheimer or Baron von Bachenheimer, what did it matter? Another group of Edgers was slated for Court Presentation in 1914, "if we live and nothing happens."[13]

She bobbed for more Halloween apples, and on one last steakhouse Thanksgiving, Libby Blondell sang torch songs for Edgers who had "no home ties or families." As Zoe knew well, "A big city is worse than the prairies for loneliness." There was time for another Turkey Trot contest, another faux highbrow ball with Hannah Wyle playing Napoleon, one more reading of Prince Joel Rinaldo's "polygeneric theory." Newspapermen stayed on the Klub's trail, struggling to describe the dance floors' "novel evolutions in the Terpsichorean line which have not yet received appropriate names." The *Brooklyn Eagle* noticed that "the favorite prince," cigar dealer Jack McPike, "ably assisted his ruler in providing pleasures for the courtiers." The prince's wife, Emma, and daughter Antoinette lived overseas during his Edger years—was the *Eagle* rumormongering that he was Zoe's lover?[14]

As she prepared to hang gifts for Edgers on a restaurant's Christmas tree, aided by Lady Betty Rogers and the Duchess of Dingleman, one invitee begs off: "I must go home for Christmas." The friend died a few days later. Zoe interpreted "going home" as a premonition of death. She reminded readers to "live God fearingly and as if every moment may be your last," just as she lived, plaiting her hair nightly so her corpse would be found "pretty as possible." When she told Edgers that she was well prepared to die, Lampton teasingly "offered to write her an obituary poem which she would consider quite good enough to print." She laughed, took his word for it, and then printed her own obituary.[15]

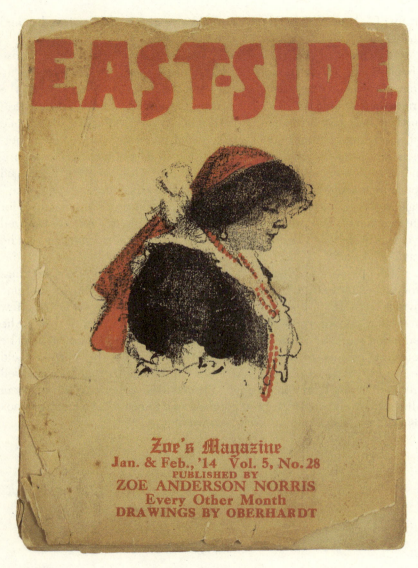

Fig. 27: Zoe's last issue cover, portraying her reporting undercover as an immigrant transit passenger. AC, Nicole Neenan photo

## 20

# Land of the White Lilies, 1914

IN THE LAST issue, which Zoe predicted would be her last, she regretted how few years she had spent in her prime, reported undercover a few more times, and prepared for the hereafter. Some of the fondest wishes on its pages were granted posthumously.

No. 29's cover image was "a portrait of Zoe, the Immigrant from Kentucky . . . dressed as a peasant," in a long red headkerchief and a longer necklace of red beads. (The cover mislabeled the issue as no. 28—did Zoe miscount, or did her typesetters fail her one last time?) She donned the peasant disguise to experience how the poor were abused on streetcars. She intentionally carried the wrong kind of transfer ticket on the 14th Street crosstown car, to entrap "conductor 4574" into cursing at her and throwing her off, as he had done even when she was not in costume. Since her dark eyes and hair suggested that she was foreign born, and therefore "helpless, not knowing the language," she knew that he would never suspect she was a troublemaker who would publish his badge number.

For the issue's investigative report on working conditions at textile factories, she spent a day trudging in and out of enormous brick-walled silk mills in Paterson, New Jersey. The town's months-long strike had just been broken; unemployed breadwinners were sending their children to foster homes, as industrialists imposed ever more grueling production demands that "turn men into machines." Foremen and forewomen blocked Zoe at the factory doorways, mistaking her for a corporate spy pilfering pattern ideas: "I encountered frowns that would have driven a less experienced writer away." Zoe wormed her way into workplaces where managers blamed the recent unrest on foreign-born laborers, who "come to this country just to make trouble," and on detectives, inciting violence to make work for themselves. Zoe could not help admiring the rainbows of thread on looms operated by "the prettiest rosy cheeked girls," who did not mind the machines' deafening noise and had taken higher paid men's jobs. An emaciated widowed weaver from Belfast, mistaking Zoe for a job applicant, warned that heavy lifting on the factory floor was causing constant chest pain. "If ye can do ennything else in the world, don't weave," she told the visitor. A union organizer, "idling in the office" of the Industrial Workers of the World, told Zoe that she would find still worse workplaces at a nearby flax mill and dyeworks. She wandered into its workrooms, with mucky floors and steamily unbreathable air. Shirtless men, hoisting flax rolls into the vats, "looked at me dully, sullenly, like animals of dull and deadened brain." One worker told Zoe that he did not expect to live long, given the toxins airborne and seeping into his socks and skin: "There is acid in this water, an acid that kills."

Issue no. 29 abruptly switched gears to compare Paterson's looms to Klub management techniques, an enjoyably arduous form of weaving with "wonderful silks of all colors, the silks of loving kindness, of humanity, of cordiality, of humility, of anti-snobbishness." Edgers' quarrels and departures weighted her chest "with lonely sadness . . . almost too heavy to bear," much as the Irishwoman ached in Paterson. Zoe nonetheless loved "to stand before a loom, weaving threads of joy and gladness."

As she admired her friends' "mesh of most exquisite pattern," she told readers about another recurring pattern: the deaths in her family, mostly spaced two years apart. She did not name the lost, just gave a rough timeline of the departures: Henry (1872), Lucy (1877), Willie (1879), Charlie (1881), Louis (1882), Mattie (1909), and Nettie (1911). Between Louis and Mattie's passing there had been "a long stretch of years without deaths," Zoe wrote, leaving out her mother (1897) and half-siblings Lelia (1901) and Clarence (1902).

In Zoe's recent dream, Henrietta's ghost swept into the literary sanctum through doors opening "as if blown by winds." Zoe hugged her mother's bedside apparition, dressed in black silk, barely taller than the bedframe, "such a tiny little thing to have borne thirteen children." Zoe, who by then had only four living siblings, asked, "Am I the next?" Henrietta's spirit replied, "Yes," and then shushed Zoe's scream. Dawn brought relief and gratitude. Zoe no longer needed to fear aging into a wizened peddler or an asylum inmate. She had tired anyway of men's untruthfulness and women's "poisonous tongues," and she felt "fortunate to have been given time to prepare" for her trip to the Land of the White Lilies. "Maybe the skies are green there, just for a change, and the grasses are blue." She hoped that she had helped women resign themselves to men's unbreakable habits and "interested anybody in the poor," her calling: "I have made my life worth living, have cut out a work for myself, have found myself, as it were, after long and most unhappy wandering." She looked forward to learning whether Jesus accurately prophesied that the afterlife would allow for "no marriages nor giving in marriage." She planned to spend her remaining days emulating Jews' "unfaltering unquestioning faith in God." Her persistent questions would go unanswered: "why some lead the lives of butterflies and others go barefooted, why the world is a fairy palace for some and a prison for others," why so many animals prey upon the weak, and "the man upon the woman." At her ideal "real and beautiful funeral," long-tailed black horses would pull the hearse, and her court's German oompah band would accompany a procession of Ragged Edgers. There was a chance that Henrietta was wrong, so no. 29's premonition ended with a disclaimer: "Lest mine enemies rejoice too gleefully . . . this may be one of those dreams that go by contraries, and I may yet have the pleasure of following them to the Happy Hunting Grounds."

The issue fictionalized one more deceived wife, dissolving in "despairing sobs of a lost soul" as her sculptor husband stays out late lusting after his model. There was a final review of Sarah Bernhardt, a septuagenarian "hobbling about the stage . . . holding on to the furniture and the actors." Page 17 explained that an envious Brooklynite had persuaded Zoe to stop running pages full of "press compliments" for her work. Yet page 31 quotes a newspaperman's compliments for Zoe's flawless, invaluable, "real, vitalizing literature" and Klub friends with "a real purpose in life." A poem, framed in Oberhardt's sketch of a January 1914 calendar page, asked the New Year to "Expel the pain, let gladness reign, / Let sorrows cease and bring me peace." There was one more tirade against disappointing men, especially the men paid to put that tirade on the page. Printers misogynistically delayed women's orders, typesetters slapped down *East Side* lines "waving as in a high wind," and a conscienceless binder mutilated Zoe's issues "with fiendish crookedness. . . . If I had been a man I would have gone down there and cut him with a whip as he had cut and slashed my poor little helpless East Side. . . . There is murder in my heart when I think of the Binder." She hoped to cleanse her soul of binder bloodthirst to prepare for journeying to "the gates of Paradise." But she likely did not have time.

She mailed out the fiendishly crooked print run of no. 29 and then, back at her ink-stained desk overlooking the Magic City, briefly pausing the song of the typewriter, she snipped some red crepe paper into hearts to hand out at the Edgers' upcoming Valentine's Day party. A physician advised her to stay home, since she was suffering from bronchitis. After sundown on February 12, as skyscraper windows glowed disembodied against sapphire skies, she put on some nearly Glad Rags, left her desk strewn with red crepe, and braved subzero winds along the Second Avenue blocks where she had played accordion and survived a direct hit from a chauffeured car, to reach Café Boheme. (Café Boulevard had been renamed, under new management.) She told friends how Henrietta had prophesied: "I saw her beckoning . . . and heard her say, 'It is your turn next.'" At midnight, an Edger emerged dressed as Saint Valentine, but Zoe did not feel well enough to enjoy his company for long. On her way home, or at the apartment, she collapsed. She was brought, "much against her will," to the People's Hospital, across Second Avenue from Café Boheme. Dr. Sirovich, the *East Side* life preserver who ran the hospital, who had once saved Zoe from a low-budget restaurant's tainted meat "worse than dynamite," declared the prognosis grim.[1]

Despite no. 29's fatalism, "she laughed over the idea of being ill. . . . her old buoyant spirits held sway." Someone brought *East Side*s to the hospital room, along with invitations for the next Klub dinner—the honoree, Lady Lottie Goodman, was divorcing the unmasked predator Elias B. Goodman. On the cards, Zoe wrote "In the People's Hospital" as her return address, and she gave magazinelets to the nurses. At 5 p.m. on Friday the 13th, the nurses "closed her eyes and laid her back upon the pillows in her last sleep." The death certificate's list of ailments—"mitral stenosis," kidney failure, an embolism—suggest that a childhood bout of rheumatic fever had damaged her heart. She would have been pleased that the death certificate gave her age as 47 and her profession as "Author," but not that her marital status was "married." (Julius Lempert, the young Russian Jewish surgeon who filled out the form, would go on to develop innovative cures for deafness and finance Broadway shows—interesting people surrounded Zoe to the last.)[2]

Rob and Clarence were alerted by telegram that night. Rob's arrived while he and Eva, who had just received and read issue no. 29, were hosting a bridge party. The siblings had not yet boarded trains for New York when the news spread of the Queen of Bohemia's accurate premonition. About 230 newspapers reported her death, sometimes on front pages: her former employers like New York's *Sun* and *Times* and Wichita's *Eagle*, along with the *Los Angeles Times*, *Atlanta Constitution*, *Alaska Citizen*,

*Reno Gazette-Journal*, *Dubuque Telegraph-Herald*, *Oklahoma State Register*, and Ontario's *North Bay Nugget*. The headlines were enigmatic ("It Was Her Turn Next") or patronizing ("Girl Dies As She Predicted") or poetic ("Ghetto Queen Dies Death She Dreamed") or exhaustive: "No Hand Hurried Her End / Mrs. Zoe Anderson Norris' Dream of Death Had No Hidden Meaning So Nurse Reports. / She Caught Cold at Valentine Party. / Walked Home From Midnight Event and Was In Hospital Soon Afterwards—Blood Clot Stopped Heart."

Syndicated obits were illustrated with no. 29's cover image of Zoe kerchiefed as the Immigrant from Kentucky. Henrietta's warning was quoted as "undeniable proof" that the dead can communicate and "dreams have warning power." Zoe's reporting in disguise, including on conductor 4574's misdeeds, conveyed the misery of the poor "in such a way that all the world might understand and sympathize." Her account of begging while playing "My Old Kentucky Home" on the accordion, receiving pennies from "the humblest and the poorest," was ranked among "the classics of description of the life of the city." Widespread mourning for her was cited as evidence of compassion in "heartless, rushing, bustling Manhattan," its residents often maligned for "seeming cruelty and neglect." Pleaides Club members remembered her among their "early friends," who then helmed her own Klub. The *Times* ran Lampton's obituary poem that he hoped would be worthy of *The East Side*: Zoe's weary, "worried soul" had passed at last "from earth's darkness to the Great Light . . . Quickly, easily, and unafraid. / At last her heavy burden has been laid" in God's strong arms.[3]

Reporters near Zoe's former homes tailored the news for their readers. Kentuckians ranked her among Daughters College's "most brilliant graduates . . . in its palmiest days" and pointed out where she and other Andersons had lived, preached, worshipped, photographed, and painted. Kansans noted where Harry homesteaded and gambled, and where Zoe taught art, offended friends with her "snappy gossip column," and headed off with her "piquant, original and mercurial" prose to the literary speedway.[4]

No *East Side* could combat the posthumous errors and criticisms. "Queen Zoe" was called embittered, wealthy, a social worker, and "a typical Kansan." Given her "strange combination" of emotional extremes, she could never have thrived in Kentucky or Kansas, and her work sometimes showed "flashes of genius equal to those of any writer in the country, at other times being inane and affected." It was said that she came from San Francisco and called her magazine *Outside*, that she and her friends were "the mongrel few" or "doubtful notables" or "blessed failures," accustomed to looking at "the seamy side of life." Her surname was given as Anderson or Morris, and Rob was called her brother or brother-in-law. He was interviewed on his way eastward—had he reconciled with Zoe by then? He called death premonitions "the family tradition" and "a legend of our people"—the only time that he was mentioned in the press sharing any aspect of his mother's worldview, coming across as anything but a pragmatic railroad executive shunning the limelight.[5]

It was reported that Zoe's will bequeathed *East Side* drawings to Oberhardt, and indeed he ended up owning many. But I can find no evidence that a will existed, let alone was probated—she owned so little of value, except great stories.[6]

Philip Herrlich, a German-born undertaker headquartered on Avenue A at East 7th Street, laid Zoe's body in a "lavender hued coffin." He was immediately "besieged by telephone inquiries" about when the funeral would take place. His premises could not hold the expected audience, so a larger room was reserved at a tenement across the avenue; its lower floors housed a community center for German Americans called Leppig's Hall. On February 17, 1914, customers for Leppig's bowling alley and saloon paid little heed as Zoe's friends trudged in through the snowdrifts—a blizzard had pummeled the city on Valentine's Day.[7]

The German oompah musicians, as she had wanted, played at Leppig's Hall. They wheezed and wailed, "somewhat out of tune and time," alongside a bust of Beethoven. Rob and Clarence sat in heavy carved chairs at the front of the room. The coffin was laden with violets and calla lilies—would Zoe have objected to the luxurious flowers, the money that could have gone to feed the poor? The hall overflowed with Edgers, life preservers, reporters, wastrels, Triangle Fire victims' relatives, Oberhardt's portrait sitters, "men and women of wide reputation and some of no reputation . . . unlike in all save sorrow." One journalist spotted "there a scrubwoman with a shawl over her head, yonder a playwright, a writer or an artist." When no seats or even standing room remained, "Many who could not get inside knelt in the snow in the street and prayed in their own languages."[8]

The pastor John von Herrlich, Zoe's "Sky Pilot" since the 1890s, recalled how "she brought sunshine into the lives of those forlorn and ministered to those of the hungry heart." The Irish American activist David Healy testified to her good deeds as "the self-appointed missioner to the neglected." Sidonie Pur-Don, lauded in Lampton's *East Side* poem for helping Zoe right wrongs, fought back tears as she eulogized her role model: "as a woman she was proud to have known one who had made her feel how noble a thing it was to be a woman." An unnamed man bid fond farewell to the Queen but could not help mentioning that the last time he saw her, "she had rebuked and chastened him" (he was not quoted explaining whether he deserved that). Journalists coldly appraised her embalmed face, "a little disfigured by the marks of late evenings and many dinners, a little twisted by mirth that came near to pain in her late years."[9]

People unflatteringly mentioned in *East Side*s were seen grieving, including newspaperman George McAdam (Zoe had labeled him "a fussy old hen"). Stalwarts like Oberhardt, singer Libby Blondell, clubman John Francis Tucker, cross-dresser Hannah Wyle, Klub criticizer Philip Riddell, writer Mabel Urner, Countess Ella Bosworth of Brooklyn, the Prince of McPike, Lady Lottie Goodman, Henchman Christian Gerhardt, and Lady Betty Rogers of the Bronx mingled with attendees not known as Edgers or subscribers, such as Mary Sargent Hopkins, a bicycling advocate who used the pen name Merrie Wheeler. Clarence Norris Morris Chelf gathered up the attendees' calling cards, with handwritten inscriptions: "Blessed sleep from which none wake to weep" (Sidonie Pur-Don), "In loving memory of our little Queen" (Lady Mary Callahan). Jack Bryans was not spotted in the crowd, nor were Zoe's friends from the Woman's Press Club, nor any Lemons.[10]

At the funeral, McPike announced that he would keep the Klub alive, gathering on Thursdays at Café Boheme. He formally incorporated it, to perpetuate Zoe's memory, "to study her writings and to continue her philanthropic work." Officers were elected, including Gerhardt, Lord Daniel Callahan, Sidonie Pur-Don, and the Duchess of Dingleman—how the Queen would have hated Klub bureaucracy![11]

Issue no. 29 called for the Edgers to follow the hearse to her gravesite, along the asphalt riverbeds that humanity carved between the boulders of window-veined skyscrapers, to make her a permanent New Yorker. Instead, Rob and Clarence accompanied the coffin by train to Harrodsburg, for interment at Spring Hill. As the railcar reached Kentucky, newspapers there mangled her name as "Joe Anderson Norris" and "Mrs. Anderson" and misreported that her body would be buried in Washington with her father and sisters. The coffin-laden train rolled past Henrietta's asylum, the riverbanks that gave poison ivy to young Zoe, the first Brooklyn Bridge that she crossed, her childhood farm where Henry spread his reference books on the lawn, oblivious to his offspring's "noisy romp." Her body was unloaded at the tiny station where her Daughters College classmates took the Great South Western line's maiden voyage, where Spencer took his family to Kansas, where divorced Zoe headed to New York, where her last novel's doomed Seth hauls baggage. Her second funeral was held at Henry's old church, led by Robert Simpson (the pastor who had just persuaded

## LAND OF THE WHITE LILIES, 1914

Fig. 28: Harrodsburg tombstone lists Zoe's professions but not her birthdate. AA

Clarence to help him research Zoe's real age, on assignment for the chronologically fiendish historian John Townsend). Newspapers listed attendees including the Chelfs, Zoe's sisters (Pickett Timmins, Nannie Cardwell, Jessie Rue), and Mattie's widower John Thompson. Zoe was buried "beside her little mother who came to her in dreams and whispered 'you are next.'" Spring Hill's nearby permanent residents included Mattie, more

Thompsons and their feud victims, Nannie's murdered husband Creed, the infants of Nannie and Jessie, John Williams of Daughters College and his family, the historian Maria Thompson Daviess (a Daughters College colleague of Zoe), and Spencer Norris's mother Mariah and grandmother Patsy (who had both soured newlywed Zoe's happiness). They would be joined by Will Lowe (who had verified Spencer's adultery in court), teetotaling distiller John Thompson and his hapless alcoholic son Philip, John's girlfriend Georgia Redford (who inherited Clay Hill), the writer Maria Thompson Daviess (an Edger and her grandmother's namesake), Rues, Cardwells, and Chelfs—Madonna con Bambino are at Zoe's side.[12]

What spectral conversations are ongoing at Spring Hill? People who broke Zoe's heart or paid her bills, embraced or terrified her in dreams, does peace reign for them all in the Happy Hunting Grounds?

The cemetery's oddest epitaph was carved on a gray slab, designed by Clarence: "MUSICIAN / ARTIST / WRITER / ZOE ANDERSON NORRIS / DIED FEB. 13, 1914 / ERECTED BY HER FRIENDS / OF THE RAGGED EDGE / CLUB OF NEW YORK. / IN LOVING MEMORY." Why were musician and artist, not her fortes, listed above writer? It is clear why nothing on the tombstone hints at her birthdate. As she admonished Townsend, the only historian who published an essay on her in her lifetime, "It is only necessary for the world to know that I was born."

Not even the Edgers could stop the world from forgetting her.

Fig. 29: Zoe's granddaughter, Mary Chelf Jones, at the Harrodsburg theater that she founded and named after Zoe's Ragged Edge Klub. AA

## 21

# To Break Through the Silence, 1914–2000s

PIECING TOGETHER ZOE'S posthumous legacy is like trying to reassemble a smashed windshield. I am left with far more gaps than wholes.

Who emptied her apartment? Who swept up the valentine snippets? Was her father's New Testament open to page 238, "Let not your heart be troubled"? Who canceled the clipping bureau service that alerted Zoe to newspapers' misreporting? What happened to the wicker observation chair, the ebony piano paid for in installments, worn-out typewriter, grinning gargoyle, dolls' heads on pedestals, silver and brass holders for candles that burned until Zoe ran out of words, the ceramic coffeepot paid for with early magazinelet profits, the German baroness's punchbowl, the pink kimono that Clarence wore before leaping back "into that great uncertain chasm of Marriage"? What happened to the rented accordion that Zoe could not return? Who cleaned the fridge of beers and chickens fit for a Queen? Her family did take home some Edgers' books that Zoe never read, plus unsold inventory of *Soul*, *Wind*, and *The East Side* (Clarence gave some to "my beloved mother's friends and admirers"[1]). Were any records lost from the Klub or the Circulation Liar?

The Prince of McPike kept the Klub going for about two years, changing venues often. Café Boheme, the site of Zoe's last supper, was razed to make way for an apartment house—did anyone salvage architectural fragments that reverberated with the orchestra's Magyar tunes, Zoe's accordion, and Harry Huggs' ragtime? In 1915, just after Valentine's Day, the Edgers held a mock trial at dinnertime to "to settle a momentous question": would happier marriages result if women could vote? The judge was bewigged, McPike played court clerk, and the jurors never reached a verdict, distracted by "a swirling mob of tangoers and fox-trotters." Or so said newspapermen who, according to Zoe, would "sacrifice their grandmothers" for attention-grabbing Edger copy. After the Klub folded, parts of its "beautiful mesh" of friendships survived. McPike became a lodger at Countess Ella Bosworth's Brooklyn apartment, and he wrote an advice column for cigar salesmen in a trade magazine—did Zoe and her "Literrotti" inspire him to take up his pen?[2]

The antiquarian book dealer Christian Gerhardt, the Klub's Lieutenant, claimed he had served as Zoe's business manager and was appointed her literary executor. (But her family has never heard of him.) At Gerhardt's midtown bookshop, Zoe's publications occupied "a place of honor in his den." Reporters interviewed him, misreporting that "Miss Anderson" had "ended her own life" and was buried in Harrisburg. Gerhardt never created much of a market for her work; *East Side* bound volumes, for instance, long sold at auction for about $10 each. His other inventory included mild erotica, "spicy stuff" that eventually landed him in a penitentiary—a vice squad detective infiltrated the bookshop, disguised as a bohemian poet. How Zoe would have loved that undercover sting![3]

A few friends and acquaintances reminisced accurately about her in print. The historian Rea Woodman, in a memoir of her 1880s youth in Wichita, mentioned clubwomen including the orator Mary Lease and physician Nannie Stephens; Zoe was among the very few who then "made a name for herself" in New York. Gertrude Tubby, the book publisher who had taken out full-page *East Side* ads, wrote in a psychical research journal that Zoe often spoke about forebodings of troubles and deaths and telepathic connections, sensing faraway Clarence's "physical or mental anguish." The columnist Charles B. Driscoll recalled his 1898 teenage purchase of a paradisiacal milkshake at Spencer Norris's store on Main Street, illuminated by "wondrous tales" of Zoe's literary accomplishments in the East. Her last feat, Driscoll noted, was publishing the warning conveyed by "a vision of her mother."[4]

The pastor and writer James Corrothers, while working on his autobiography, learned "with genuine sorrow" of Zoe's death. His book described first meeting "the friend of 'Ragged-Edgers'" in 1901, when he was the only Black guest at the banquet honoring Elbert Hubbard. By the 1910s, Corrothers had come to "regret exceedingly" his 1902 *Black Cat Club*, written in dialect that he had uncomfortably adopted, that did not uplift his people, that Funk & Wagnalls considered saleable, that Jack Bryans illustrated.[5]

Jack outlived his second wife by four decades. Despite his dislike of children, his only notable publications after her death were two children's books about "Shadowkids," silhouettes who play with pets, dolls, and siblings. (The 1950 census lists him as a "widower," and he died in obscurity in 1955.) Among Zoe's other male persecutors who fell by the professional wayside—"injustice unravels itself if you wait long enough," as she foresaw—was *Satire*'s deadbeat owner Walter Pulitzer. He became notorious for trading in "obscene pictures" and violently abusing his first wife. Courtenay Lemon, who had censored Zoe's novel, railed against censorship while descending into crippling alcoholism. "Tell her that I am not an ordinary drunkard," he begged a friend about to introduce him to the rising literary star Rebecca West. During World War I, Courtenay was briefly married (possibly as a draft-dodging technique) to the celebrated writer Djuna Barnes.[6]

Wartime tragedies derailed or ended the careers of some *East Side* readers. Hubbard was killed in 1915 on the torpedoed ocean liner *Lusitania*; he had been headed overseas to interview the kaiser. Zoe's wunderkind protégé McHarg Davenport never regained his health after mustard gas damaged his lungs on French battlefields. He earned a French government medal for carrying civilians in his arms to find shelter from German shelling, while taking notes on conditions that "would horrify the most war-hardened of us all."[7]

Some of Zoe's "baby life preservers" did realize their early promise, especially in Hollywood and on Broadway. The filmmaker Wray Physioc became the first major experimenter with Technicolor. Harvard-educated Eustace Hale Ball wrote dozens of screenplays and put daredevil airplane stunts on the screen. At least a dozen movies were based on writings by Mabel Urner, who lived in Gramercy Park splendor (her second husband was the wealthy book dealer Lathrop Colgate Harper) and adopted Zoe's habit of constant eavesdropping, resulting in stories "like camera-plates in their flawless reflections" of real life. The reformer Sophie Loeb, who called Zoe an "inspiration dispenser," ran children's welfare advocacy groups, spearheaded legislation to protect poor families from eviction, lectured internationally, and made a movie whose heroine crusaded in Washington to ban child labor in factories. A fountain in Central Park is named for Sophie, as is a playground tucked under the Manhattan Bridge, today amid Chinese immigrant peddlers' pushcarts. Her motto is on her tombstone in a Westchester County cemetery: "a chance for every child." Dr. Sirovich, Zoe's deathbed caregiver, became a congressman, who combatted child labor alongside Sophie Loeb, and wrote plays. After the press savaged one of his shows, he went before Congress to denounce theater critics as "malicious, wanton, unfair and abusive"—how Zoe would have loved that high-profile self-defense move![8]

William Oberhardt became nationally celebrated for sketching portrait sitters such as Ameen Rihani, Thomas Edison, Theodore Roosevelt, Irving Berlin, Ralph Bunche, Salvador Dali, and Dwight Eisenhower. He illustrated *Time* magazine's first covers, and at New York ports, he volunteered his services to sketch servicemen headed overseas. But he disliked portraying women, given their resistance to depictions of "lines and wrinkles."[9] Was that lesson imparted by Zoe?

As Prohibition dampened New York nightlife, many Edgers led quieter lives. During Little Hungary's closing party, prohibited drinks were free, and "the orchestra played as if its collective heart would break."[10] Prince Joel shut down his Bohemia, published a psychoanalytic study of prohibitionists as sadistic perverts, and pragmatically went into the real estate trade. Harry Huggs kept performing and composing, but not at any high-profile Klubs. Libby Blondell remarried to an actor and retired from vaudeville. Sidonie Pur-Don, who helped Zoe "raise the right and down the wrong," became an interior decorator. The terpsichorean Louis Chalif battled unsuccessfully against popular tastes for "suggestive dances," such as the Charleston and the shimmy.

There were ironic twists of fate in store for some brazen posers and loud fulminators in Zoe's circle. Ardeen Foster, a Michiganian aka Ardennes Jones-Foster Esq., who pretended to be a British savior of trafficked women during his ineffectual Klub fundraiser, became an actual Brit, helping run theaters around London. Bruce Calvert, whose back-to-nature *Open Road* magazinelet accused Zoe of unhealthy fondness for cities, died of heart failure at a midtown Manhattan subway station. The writer Leita Kildare, a Klub honoree, stripped away "the shroud of myth" from her long-dead collaborator and ex-husband Owen, "the Bowery Kipling," who claimed to have dissipated his youth among illiterate Irish American roughnecks. As rumors circulated that Owen was actually Russian-born (which census records corroborate), Leita fabulized even further: he was Count Loris Carroll Jean Stanislaus Poninsky, or maybe Prince Peter Loris Poninski, who had disguised himself in the slums while on the run from Czarist and Soviet enemies.[11]

By the 1920s, the achievements of Zoe's father Henry had resurfaced. His Chicago-based youngest daughter, Pickett Anderson Timmins, persuaded a Christian publishing house in Cincinnati to release the work left in his estate, which had been entrusted to her by his friend John Williams. The 1918 edition of *The New Testament: Translated from the Sinaitic*

*Manuscript Discovered by Constantine Tischendorf at Mount Sinai* was affordably priced at $1.50—around what Henry's 1860s publishers had exorbitantly charged. Pickett's preface paraphrased her father's preface, without mentioning that he was her father; she dedicated the book "to all lovers of Truth," since its translator had "desired to find the truth of God." Reviewers praised Mr. [sic] Pickett Timmins for "a labor of love . . . a worthy monument" to Henry's piety and skill, making ancient prose "perfectly clear and intelligible to the modern mind . . . eliminating all obsolete words." The text, which diverges in places from the original Greek, is not considered a literal translation, but it remains in print, and contemporary scholars use it to navigate digitized versions of the codex.[12]

Why did John Williams not entrust the manuscript to Zoe, a Daughters College star, her family's only other published author? Was she considered too renegade and agnostic, based in New York, where editors were unlikely to care about a 19th-century Kentucky pastor's scholarship? Who inherited the reference books that Henry spread out on the bluegrass? Pickett was a skilled portrait painter and world traveler, who scaled glaciers in Canada and explored temples in Japan. She was not particularly religious, and she and her family little mentioned their roots in Kentucky and Kansas. "They just didn't talk about anything negative," one descendant told me. Pickett was age 11 when her father died, so she would have had few memories of him in good health, physically, emotionally or financially. What balm was there for her, five decades later, in bringing to light the last translation that consumed him, that he expected to make his fortune?

Zoe's descendants inherited aspects of her creativity, theatricality and adventurousness. Rob and Eva vacationed as far afield as Monaco and Algeria, and they criss-crossed the U.S. and Canada via the train lines that employed him, visiting attractions including the 1933 world's fair in Chicago. Did they remember Zoe's painted porcelain displayed at the dazzling 1893 Chicago fair, or her critiques of its Paris counterpart in 1900? Or her visits to Monte Carlo's casinos, "known as the American who was waiting patiently to see somebody shoot himself at play"? Or her train rides along the Mediterranean, homesick for Manhattan, the seawater reflecting "her own two startled eyes"? In Harrodsburg, Clarence Chelf performed as a singer, organist and pianist, accompanying silent movie showings, and she displayed her inherited Obie drawings. Her husband Fletcher marketed his farm products, including seeds for "Chelf's White Dent, the earliest maturing big eared white corn in existence."

Robert Morris, Zoe's Bambino, trained at the U.S. Naval Academy in Annapolis, Maryland, and he rose to admiralty rank with postings scattered from New York to Korea. His application for membership in the Sons of the American Revolution listed many prominent Anderson ancestors in Virginia, along with the long-absconded Harold Morris. Did anyone recall that in the 1890s, Zoe fictionalized a sniveling Revolutionary War deserter, whose great-granddaughter was too embarrassed to join the Daughters of the American Revolution? Robert had three daughters with his Indiana-born wife Adelia Ball, a member of a philanthropic family of industrialists (their fortune was made in food containers). During World War II, he helped command the armada that landed battalions on Mediterranean beaches. What did he remember of his Nona's stories about Vesuvius's rim, the disabled beggars, and the women and children used as beasts of burden in coastal towns? In the 1950s, the admiral dined with his teenage daughter Ann at a German restaurant near Manhattan's Union Square, where Zoe had seen sleeping men "petrified in misery." He reminisced about his Nona's determination to help the poor, her diverse Klub friends, and the peace she felt the morning after the last "strange dream."[13]

In Harrodsburg, a replica of James Harrod's fort opened to the public, and Adelia's mother Bertha Crosley Ball financed construction of another tourist attraction, the Lincoln Marriage Temple, a steepled brick building that shelters the tiny log cabin where Abraham Lincoln's parents Thomas Lincoln and Nancy Hanks were married in 1806. Pleasant Hill, the Shaker community where Zoe saw windowpanes scrubbed to "diamond-like brilliancy," also became a museum.[14] A statue of a Confederate soldier was installed atop a pedestal near the entrance to Spring Hill Cemetery. Jim Crow segregation was imposed throughout the region. The Ku Klux Klan paraded through towns. Who remembered all the contradictions: that some Andersons and their neighbors supported abolition, trained Black missionaries, aided the Underground Railroad, prevented whippings of the enslaved, and served in Federal forces, that Zoe deplored the Civil War's ravages on the South, befriended Black people, and considered Lincoln "the Greatest Man in the Nation's History"?

Robert Morris's half-sister Mary Clarence Chelf, born in 1918, showed talent early on for music and acting; she described herself as "a great imitator of people." At her youthful singing recitals, her piano accompanist was her mother Clarence. Mary also made an appearance bonneted and on horseback in a 1941 educational film, *Kentucky Pioneers*, about 18th-century settlers from Virginia "of dauntless courage" who carved out farmsteads in a new "land of promise" (aided by enslaved people). Mary won a scholarship to a Cincinnati conservatory after the dean heard her sing at Harrodsburg's luxurious Beaumont Inn—the "much be-ivied" neoclassical

Fig. 30: Oberhardt's 1940s portrait of Zoe's naval officer grandson, Robert Morris. NDC

building that housed Daughters College. With her pianist husband, Lawson Jones, as her accompanist, Mary traveled as a contralto, mezzosoprano, and teacher from Carnegie Hall to Topeka, from London to Michigan's Interlochen academy. She credited her success partly to "the Zoe in me," which inspired her "to seek the best in art, music and writing." Mary became known in the family as Cissy, and Clarence became Nona for her son Robert's daughters Patricia, Barbara, and Ann Morris—just as Zoe had been the Bam's Nona, and Clarence, her supposed sister, was Cissy.[15]

Around 1980, widowed Mary (her husband and her mother had died weeks apart in 1967) semiretired in Harrodsburg, and she became Zoe's torchbearer. An Art Deco movie theater, where *Kentucky Pioneers* had originally been screened, was decrepit on Main Street, and Mary tirelessly fundraised to turn it into the nonprofit Ragged Edge Theater Klub. She drove around in a vintage blue Mercedes, firmly telling bankers and other potential donors, "Here's what you're going to do for me." She toured them through the crumbling building: "Let me show you my dream." Her determination to create performing opportunities for "young people out there with talents . . . laid on them by God" arose from "sort of stirrings within. It's a spiritual drive to do something good for people." Naming the building after the Klub paid tribute to her grandmother's "bravery and 'stick-to-itiveness' in New York." It has thrived on Main Street as the Ragged Edge Community Theatre.

Mary pored through Zoe's books, magazines, newspaper clippings, photos, and other "prize materials" that Clarence had "hidden quite carefully" in an upstairs closet at, yes, "my old Kentucky home." A dozen of Zoe's typescripts, published and unpublished, were in storage, along with a Woman's Press Club directory, the Edgers' cards from Leppig's Hall, and a pressed calla lily from the funeral bouquets.[16] Mary drafted a book titled *Zoe*, interweaving family lore with fact and fiction mainly gleaned from *Soul* and *East Side* issues. Mary's biographical essay for *Zoe* speculates that in girlhood, "She was already seeking her own creative identity," learning insatiably, "pursuing ideas, then taking action." Mary wrote that although mature Zoe's proposed solutions to social problems might seem "sometimes flimsy and other times naive" by current standards, she merited a biography as a trailblazer who documented "the hazards of being female, intelligent, and artistic with unfailing humor and sensitivity." *Zoe*'s title character tends doomed teenage Elsie at the Catholic maternity hospital, unmasks Cecil Mallon as a predator and hypocrite, and writes about pushcart peddlers, ragpickers, orphans, icemen, and chorus girls. She strives to purge her prose of the kind of "undue lecture or scolding" spewed by firebrands like Cecil. "She wondered what it would be like to sell candles for a living like the blind man," Mary wrote. *Zoe's* heroine, while playing accordion on a Second Avenue curbside, watches the indifferent Sunrisers "loping along in bunches and pairs." Beggars fill her cup with coins as she draws "such dismal sounds from the sighing instrument that she, herself, was well nigh brought to tears." *Zoe's* title character resolves to keep writing about "the people of the East Side, people like Elsie. I'm going to show them the good they are" and brace them "to deal even with the exploiters, the people who pretend to change the world."

*Zoe* went unpublished. Of its planned 23 chapters, seven are in family files. A scholar at Penn State, meanwhile, proposed an anthology, *Zoe Anderson Norris' East Side Diary*, but then dropped the idea. "There just isn't enough material to do anything in-depth biographically," he told her descendants. Harrodsburg historian Anna Armstrong (of blessed memory) told me that her friend Mary "kept trying and never succeeded" in telling Zoe's "unique and wonderful story. Mary was not happy with anything that had been done." Anna showed me Mary's page-long handwritten reflection on Zoe: "My, the world is really better because of her. . . . Perhaps she is quite near me, now—trying to break through the silence."[17]

By the 1990s, Zoe was little remembered outside her hometown and family. She was mentioned in scholarly studies of, for instance, Sarah Bernhardt's Hamlet and Mark Twain's cat Bambino. A bibliographer of circa-1900 magazines listed Elbert Hubbard, Michael Monahan, and Bruce Calvert as editors of their publications, but Zoe's official title was given as "T'Whole Cheese." Bibliographers of 19th- and 20th-century religious books placed Zoe's *Soul*, amusingly, in the "Soul" subject category. Booksellers cataloged *The East Side* as "written and published by a talented, idiosyncratic lady, much in the style of Elbert Hubbard's Philistine" (which no doubt caused Zoe to take another spin in her Spring Hill grave). Zoe's great-granddaughter Ann Morris Stack, based in Indianapolis, published art and literary magazines between the 1970s and 1990s, dedicated to the memory of ancestresses including Clarence and Zoe. In 1996, Dr. Steven Lomazow's *American Periodicals: A Collector's Manual and Reference Guide* described *The East Side* as Zoe's "solo production . . . containing humor, anecdotes, stories and 'shtick' pertaining to the Jewish community of the Lower East Side."[18]

It was in Steve's basement, as noted in this book's Methodology section, that my 2018 encounter with Zoe's writings about my own ancestors led me down a very long rabbit hole.

Fig. 31: Joao Fazenda's 2023 *New Yorker* portrait of author. AC, Nicole Neenan photo

# 22

# You Wouldn't Believe What's Going to Happen, 2018 Onward

MY INTERVIEWEES KEEP accidentally calling me Zoe—that's how far I have slipped into her skin. Flukes of fate have directed my research, making it seem inevitable, as I became known as the woman writing about a woman who wrote about being written about for writing about writing and righting wrongs. As I traveled in her footsteps, and saw New York anew as "Zoe country," I wondered what she would make of my interpretations.

"Ragged Edge roots studied by well known author and historian" was the *Harrodsburg Herald*'s headline during my first research trip, in 2021. The newspaper photographed me in the foyer of the art deco cinema on Main Street that Zoe's granddaughter Mary Chelf Jones revived as the Ragged Edge Community Theatre.[1] That morning, before my plane had landed, town historian Anna Armstrong had announced my imminent arrival at Mary's Spring Hill grave: "Mary, you wouldn't believe what's going to happen this afternoon." When I was brought later that day for my own introduction at the cemetery, Anna told the tombstone, "Mary, this is Eve. She's going to do it for you." Anna and I agreed that *Queen of Bohemia Predicts Own Death* was not the title that Zoe or Mary would have wanted. But it could be catchier and more saleable than, perhaps, *Zoe: Fighter for the Poor with Her Pen Who Also Ruled Bohemia*. Mary "would be ecstatic" about my progress on the trail, Anna said, and she added that for her own career battles, educating people about history and trying to preserve buildings, "Mary taught me, you never give up."

At the Spring Hill grave of Zoe's mother Henrietta, I told her spirit, "I am so sorry for what you went through," bearing 13 children and dying at an asylum. Encrustations on Zoe's slab had reduced "Musician Artist Writer" to illegibility. I had much to tell her: "You got the hell out of here and ended up back here. You wrote a lot of words, and many of them were great. You're going to like this book. I'm going to quote you, a lot. But I need to warn you, it will reveal your real age."

I stayed at the Beaumont Inn, where baby Zoe's family took refuge in the tearoom while Henry translated, where schoolgirl Zoe ignored advice to delay marriage and her classmates used a diamond to scratch their names into the windowpane glass, where young mother Zoe taught art. I pored through memorabilia at the inn and the local historical society, including photos by Zoe's brother-in-law Archibald Rue, paintings of Henry Anderson and John Williams, and bottles of John Thompson's Old Jordan. His distillery has been razed, along with the nearby Great South Western railway station. Freight trains miles long now slice through town at top speed, their howls reaching my inn bedroom, half a mile from the tracks. A drainage ditch runs alongside a drugstore parking lot, where antebellum mineral springs coursed, enslaved teenage musicians plotted escape to Canada, and Civil War casualties' amputated limbs were piled in a ballroom.

The Thompsons' Clay Hill had fallen into disrepair, but the white-washed interior woodwork still gleamed, carved with reeding and rosettes by Zoe's first grandfather-in-law, Matthew Lowrey. I imagined schoolgirl Zoe stitching with Mattie in a sunny upstairs bedroom, and divorced freelancer Zoe mortified but taking notes at the top of the staircase, overhearing Mattie scornfully wonder how long the homesick visitor from Manhattan would stay.

Zoe's birthplace at the town outskirts is prosperous farmland, with endless velvety bluegrass—local historian Amalie Preston plucked a bluegrass stem for me, which has never left the front pocket of my favorite notebook (black, like Zoe's). At the Shaker community turned museum, I was told about real-life lovers like Zoe's fictional pair, fleeing from celibacy at nightfall. Locals explained their intertwined family trees—"It's amazing we're not stranger than we are," one descendant of 18th-century settlers joked—and pointed out where their kin lived in Greek Revival brick houses named after owners long dead.

I kept asking, why would someone from this dog-kennel hometown come to care so much about the hordes of starving urban poor? Zoe would likely have been shocked at first to witness starvation, Amalie suggested. Any rural 19th-century Kentuckian with a gun could hunt to keep meat on the table. But I remain mystified that Zoe became so confessional in print. Harrodsburg can be as long-winded and gossipy as any Ragged Edge dinner ("It's a regular Peyton Place here," I was told), but public soul-baring is not the norm. If an ancestor was said to have died suddenly when "his heart gave out," you might find out later that was technically true: his heart stopped when he shot himself in the head.

In Wichita, I visited a museum's recreations of the kind of fringe-bedecked parlors where Zoe played whist and painted on porcelain, socialized with suffragists and Lemons, and took notes on frontier pretensions. In a pinnacled brick building that housed Garfield University (named for Henry Anderson's martyred congregant), I peered into a barrel-vaulted auditorium, where Zoe played piano and little Rob and Clarence danced in costume. A low-slung brick railway station still stands, where Zoe made multiple escapes from Spencer, where Rob started his career, as does a mansard-roofed hotel where Clarence and her infant Bambino lived until Harold Morris dragged them back to London. The Norrises' clapboarded homes are all gone (one was razed just before I arrived), along with Spencer's grocery stores, the *Eagle* headquarters that published Nancy Yanks' gossip columns, and Lewis Academy, where Zoe bluffed that she could teach mechanical drawing. Spencer's gravestone is a few feet from a noisy roadside, in the same cemetery as the family of Rob's wife Eva—Illinois country people satirized by Zoe. I toured the limestone courthouse where Spencer admitted adultery, relinquished custody of his daughter, and promised to pay alimony. In an austere courtroom with cocoa-colored woodwork, I sat in one of the wooden folding chairs used by reporters and gawkers who saw newly divorced Zoe's face beam "like a summer day."[2]

During my hours-long ride from Wichita to the Andersons' homesteads in Ellsworth, the prairie horizon turned oceanic, punctuated with oil pump jacks. Horsethief Canyon, where Zoe's brother Harry turned vigilante and chased intruders, is now a nature preserve, with egrets and turkey vultures soaring over cliffs etched in ancient petroglyphs. At Henrietta's farm, no buildings are left, just a ghost of a creek fishpond—did the Andersons stock it with salmon spawn from Maine? During my summer visit, drought threatened, as usual: "You notice the corn is suffering for water," a farmer said. At the tiny cemetery where Henrietta buried her sons Louis and Charlie under a sheared stone column, the wind tore at my sun hat, yanking the chin strap and pinning back the brim. About three dozen people are interred there, half of whom had not reached adulthood.

Ellsworth's historical society owns some Anderson family photos and a newspaper ledger, which shows that Harry and Henrietta subscribed to the papers that reported on his scandals. I visited a farm's intact 19th-century dugout, a stone block hut no bigger than the staircase bulkheads that Zoe saw on Lower East Side rooftops. In the dugout's windowless depths, homesteaders had cowered as cyclones turned the skies lurid colors and sparks from locomotives caused wildfires. At the horizon, miles away, I could make out gigantic white turbines spinning at a wind farm. I was gob-smacked at the poetry of it all: the blades are channeling, subduing, making useful power out of the winds that maddened and drove away Zoe and her relatives and fictional characters, the wind that crept into her dreams on East 15th Street.[3]

In eastern Virginia, my daughter Alina Kulman drove me around for days to the Andersons' ancestral lands. In the Fredericksburg Area Museum's basement, we saw a graffitied chunk of tawny sandstone, shaped like an armless chair, which had been removed from a downtown curb. Enslaved people had stood upon it while for "sale" by merchants like Zoe's paradoxical uncle Thomas Lipscomb, who had rescued a Black child kidnapped from Massachusetts. In the nearby hamlet of Guinea Station, underbrush blocked our views of Henry's property, where schoolgirl Zoe waded in mud puddles, shed uncomforted tears, and listened to Mattie's violin hymns at twilight.

In rural Maryland, I tracked down William Oberhardt's descendants, whose attic was stacked with boxfuls of his artworks, writings, and memorabilia. Dozens of *East Side* sketches and lithographs turned up, even an invitation to a Klub calico ball. Among his daughter Lorianne's reactions to my initial inquiry about Zoe was, "You know, she predicted her own death." The family (bless them) donated everything to the New-York Historical Society. Among the few items that the society did not accept was a beastly heavy lithograph stone, with a 1913 *East Side* portrait of Zoe. I had to bring it back to New York, where she felt most at home. The family put it in three tote bags for me, and it tore through all three on the Amtrak ride back to the Magic City.

In Washington, D.C., I paid respects at the plane of grass over the graves of Henry and his daughters Lucy Cheeks and Nettie Cheeks. In a warehouse near Dulles Airport, boxfuls of Anderson papers surfaced in Alexander Graham Bell's massive archive. In 1905, Bell sent Mary S. Breckinridge, a Kentucky teacher and historian, to research Zoe's uncle Robert Anderson's school for the deaf in western Kentucky. "In my quest I am remorseless," Mary told Bell, as she traveled around the South. She interviewed Andersons (but not Zoe) and their friends, dug into courthouse files, and hiked through overgrown graveyards (finding traces of Robert's obelisk gravestone today requires slogging through a cornstalk jungle—yes, I speak from experience). Mary at times coped with a "pathetic lack of documentary evidence": all that was left of one storied trunkful of family papers was the trunk's lid. She brought back dozens of photos for Bell as well as relics, including a myrtle sprig from Robert's grave. The interviewees sent long, grateful letters to Mary—one called her a "pure gold little worker" for caring about the Andersons. She drafted a book about Robert, his family and the school, which Bell never published. During my few Covid-era hours of warehouse access, I scanned and photocopied hundreds of pages, as a world opened up to me: idealistic, slaveholding, antebellum Andersons, stocking their libraries with intellectual books and trying to spread enlightenment. I realized that Mary Breckinridge and then Zoe's granddaughter Mary blazed a trail for me, although their plans went unrealized. If, dear reader, this book is in your hands, someone has finally gotten at least part of the remarkable Andersons' story in print.[4]

My discoveries have been maddening at times: on Rob Norris's 1948 death certificate, who wrote his mother's maiden name as "Joe Anderson"? At libraries, as I leafed through rare, brittle magazines with Zoe's stories, tiny fragments of page edges fell off, and I took them home as talismans (but shh, don't tell anyone).[5] I felt gut-punched by dry antebellum papers, listing enslaved people by first names or no names, putting "prices" on their heads—they were more "valuable" than the acres they were plowing. I interviewed the Missouri-based historian Dr. Traci Wilson-Kleekamp, who has heroically traced her ancestors enslaved by Spencer Norris's family. During a Zoom call with Traci, my whole scalp tingled upon discovering that both of us, by happenstance, have become fascinated by Zoe's underappreciated writer friend James Corrothers.

Zoe's direct and collateral descendants turned up by the score, sharing memories and heirlooms with me. There's a strong family resemblance: high cheekbones and wide-set, sparkly eyes—an inner fire. In Indianapolis, Zoe's philanthropist great-granddaughter Ann Morris Stack and great-great-granddaughter Patricia Ganter Pelizzari (an art historian, advocate and philanthropist) let me pore through treasures dating back to a baby picture of Zoe, already looking steely and determined. Patricia Long-Moss, a descendant of Zoe's brother Harry and his wife Sarah, used an app to colorize and animate family photos; I would open an email and lo, Aunt Zoe blinked and smiled at me. Jacquelyn Bean Hall, another descendant of Harry and Sarah, gave me a priceless copy of *The Way of the Wind*. It belonged to Sarah, who survived the terrors of homesteading documented in the book—she signed it inside no less than four times, and it has been read so often that its spine is broken. Jackie summed up *Wind*'s plot through a descendant's lens: "the absolute loneliness of a Kansas wife on a windy plain completely disassociated from her previous life of greenery, friends, family and human connection."[6]

Linda Rue Allen, a Harrodsburg-born great-granddaughter of Zoe's artist sister Jessie and the photographer Archibald Rue, long lived nine blocks from me on the Upper West Side. She had worked as an actor, real-estate broker and psychoanalyst—her patients told their stories on a daybed made by Shakers at Pleasant Hill. She grew up visiting Clay Hill, where the ceilings were still stained by hams hidden away for protection from Federal raiders, but she did not know that her great-great-aunt Mattie Thompson lived there. She was told during her childhood about her theologian ancestor Henry, but not much about the backgrounds of the neighboring Chelf cousins—"old Mary Clarence" and "young Mary Clarence," as mother and daughter were distinguished in conversation. Linda knew by age 10 or so that she loved performing. In the theater world, she told me, "Nobody cared who your family was." You could be quirky and express yourself, without worrying about small-town judgmentalism: "The only thing that mattered was how good you were, and how hard you worked." She could relate to Aunt Zoe's feeling that New York was home. My eyes misted over when she gave me two photos from her family album, of aged Henry and blooming young Pickett.[7]

Ann Morris Stack's son Chris Stack is an actor in New York, and I was mesmerized to see him in the Broadway blockbuster *Stereophonic*, playing a high-strung, drug-addled British drummer in a 1970s band loosely based on Fleetwood Mac. His journalist cousin J. Carl Ganter told me that while growing up in small-town Michigan, he became fascinated by his great-great-grandmother's *East Side* portrayals of "bustling dramas playing out on the streets of a big city far away." In his career contributing to outlets including *The New York Times*, sharing Zoe's curiosity and "pull for justice," one highlight has been helping an Illinois man wrongfully convicted of murder walk free. Carl identified the real killer after a stakeout calling for "the type of invisibility that Zoe might have contrived." Is there no end to the hereditary impact of her talent for pretending in the workplace?

Zoe's estranged nephew Charles Cheeks, Lucy's son and Nettie's nephew turned (briefly) stepson, became a musician in California, playing piano and organ, including for the Pantages chain of theaters and cinemas. His Californian great-granddaughter Catherine Segurson grew up going to Pantages shows with her father Frank, but she had never heard of the

Andersons until I reached out in 2022. She has run a literary and visual arts quarterly, *Catamaran*, and published poems and short stories and written a novel. When I explained that Zoe, too, battled magazine typos, met deadlines, commissioned artwork, and fielded subscribers' reactions, Catherine wondered, "Is there a genetic memory?" She related to Zoe's *East Side* masthead titles, from Office Boy to Advertising Man. Running a literary magazine now is just as hard as in the 1910s, but rarer. "I did it out of passion, not really knowing where that drive might come from until I found out about Zoe," Catherine told me. While juggling publishing and event-organizing—*Catamaran* issue launch parties at museums, galleries, and bookstores attract Klub-like crowds of writers and artists—Catherine has been reminded, "you can't help it, you're reliving the life of your ancestor and her Ragged Edge tradition." My *Catamaran* article about Zoe concluded that although economic disparities remain pernicious, she would be pleased at how much conditions have improved for many of our poorest and "how many women, like Catherine, edit their own magazines."[8]

Catherine visited me, and we toured the Lower East Side. Someone leaving 338 East 15th Street held the door open for us (bless those research gods!). On the iron staircase that Zoe trudged up after Klub dinners, I imagined the cacophony of German oompah musicians and phonographs blaring ragtime and opera. On the seventh floor, where Zoe's four-room luxury contrasted with desperation below, I hesitated to knock at an apartment door, though we could hear people inside. "You need to just do this," Catherine said, and so I did. The door was opened by the father of an NYU student who was finishing her studies in musical theater and packing up her belongings. He assumed we were scammers until I showed him "338 East 15th Street" on an *East Side* masthead. Catherine and I photographed each other in the kitchen, peering at the partly blocked views of a hundred living windows. I introduced Catherine to her Manhattan-based cousins Linda Rue Allen and Bridget Goodbody, an art historian, critic, and tech entrepreneur (her mother Barbara Morris Goodbody, Admiral Robert Morris's daughter, was a Maine-based photographer, artist, collector, and philanthropist). When Catherine and I described our East 15th Street adventure, Bridget replied, "What a great story that will make for the NYU student: 'I was living in the apartment of the Queen of Bohemia.'" We pondered how much went unsaid in their families—why did so few relatives, even those living close by, know of each other's existence?

Every day, I scour the internet for more insights into Zoe. Sometimes I come across something juicy moments after it was posted, just as serendipity fueled Zoe's father Henry in his search for reference books: "It is wonderful how works flow to my hand—the very works I want."[9] In spring 2023, I exhibited a fraction of my Zoeiana collection at the Grolier Club, two years after that Manhattan institution displayed a fraction of the 83,000 American periodicals owned by my obsession-inspiring friend Steve Lomazow. I gathered family photos, views of Kentucky and Kansas, Henry's New Testament editions, and a bottle of Old Jordan to complement evidence of Zoe's versatility: *Smart Set* and *American Agriculturist* stories, *Soul*, *Locke*, *Wind*, *East Side* articles on peddlers, skyscrapers, accordion playing, the court of a hundred living windows. As an exhibition handout, I had letterpress versions made of "The Song of the Typewriter."[10] In vitrines devoted to Ragged Edgers, I combined their poetry that Zoe never read with postcards and dinnerware from their hangouts.[11] There is nothing, I often say, that brings you closer to the feeling that you are in the room with the spirit of someone you have been researching, writing and lecturing about for years than to hold a talismanic pickle fork in your hand from a restaurant where you know they dined.

People ancestrally connected to Zoe poured in during the Grolier run: Andersons, Norrises, Oberhardts. (Catherine Segurson flew in from California, after having a dream that her late father Frank encouraged her to make the trip.) During my Grolier lecture-musicale, live performers belted out some of Libby Blondell's favorite songs about dreamlands, peddlers, and deceitful lovers.[12] While giving tours of my exhibition, I polished answers to FAQs that have shaped this book. Yes, to modern eyes the Ragged Edgers look too well dressed to be at the ragged edge, but they dined in shirtwaists and other daywear, not the bejeweled gladdest rags of their era. No, I found no evidence that Zoe met Jacob Riis, although the two reformers documented the same horrific tenement conditions. Nor did she know L. Frank Baum of *The Wizard of Oz*, despite their shared interest in Kansas cyclones. Yes, virtually all of Zoe's work is available digitally, with a handful of unfiltered passages about ethnic groups that might, if she were writing today, bring her to the brink of "cancellation." But I believe her huge range of friends would stand up for her, given her words and deeds combating bigotry. No, I cannot credit Zoe with any specific legislative reforms, but she was a springboard for more successful activists like Sophie Loeb. Zoe, unable to vote or give away money, was empowered just by publishing stories of icemen, chorus girls, newsboys, leprous prostitutes, ragpickers, and seamstresses, and those who preyed upon them.

Yes, the movie and theatrical rights are still for sale; the narrator should be Harry Huggs, observing Zoe as heroic and complicated while he plays ragtime, aware that he is one of the few Klub members using his real name. In flashbacks, Spencer Norris and Jack Bryans could be played by Zoe's great-great-grandson Chris Stack. And imagine a flashback to antebellum Harrodsburg, as Zoe and Harry realize that their families knew each other there, that her abolitionist slaveholding theologian ancestors heard his enslaved musician ancestors perform at hotel ballrooms on their way to Canada.

As for what I would ask Zoe over dinner at Café Boulevard: "What would you write about me, how would you portray me? That uptown nitpicker, trying to get at the truth? And would you ennoble me for the Klub? Could I please be Baroness, Duchess, or maybe even Princess Nitpicker?"

Reporters interpreted and misinterpreted my Grolier show. "Wichita's 'Queen of Bohemia' celebrated in New York City" was the *Eagle* headline (Zoe would have hated being called Wichita's anything). "The Nellie Bly You've Never Heard Of" were the headlines for an in-depth blog post on the website Hell Gate and for a Talk of the Town piece in *The New Yorker*. "See? The research gods are looking out for me," I told *New Yorker* writer Hannah Goldfield, as someone leaving 338 East 15th Street let us in. At the literary sanctum's doorstep, where men were handed an *East Side* upon asking to speak with the man of the house, Zoe would have loved the welcome mat's inscription: "COME THE FUCK IN OR FUCK THE FUCK OFF."[13]

I kept hoping the building's owners would grant me formal access, given my dedication to studying a famous past tenant. Zoe, after all, speculated that people would someday "stop as they go by and point out the place" as a literary muse. But no one at the owner's office returned calls and emails. So I resorted to subterfuge that Zoe would have enjoyed, to see where pigeons nibbled her geraniums as she settled into her wicker observation chair. I pretended to be scouting apartments for my niece and my daughter (not my worst lie, since they both have rented apartments in New York, just not in the ridiculously overpriced East Village). I felt twinges of guilt, as Zoe did, while conning nice gullible real-estate agents. I hereby extend official apologies to StreetEasy's staff for wasting moments of their time on East 15th Street. I also went undercover as a potential renter at the Upper West Side apartment house where Zoe tired of watching Jack Bryans "grind out fun"; Courtenay Lemon's Harlem apartment building where he claimed that women could not understand his speeches; and the former United Charities headquarters, which she found so uncharitable. At one of her former homes near Madison Square Park, where she watched humanity stream down Broadway, a psychic's neon ad was glowing on the second floor. I was tempted to pay to inquire whether the spirit of bohemia's Queen was on site, especially since Pandora Meta-Psychic Delineator of Character and Destiny advertised in *The East Side*. It took me a few months to work up the nerve to walk in, and by then, the psychic was gone—should I have made up an undercover séance report for this book?

I was granted formal scholarly access at only one of Zoe's homes, the brownstone on East 126th Street where she rented a room while writing *Soul*. The sisters Hallia and Shkigale Baker have adapted it into a Pentecostal house of worship, the United New Church of Christ Deliverance Unto the Lord. The Bakers were thrilled to learn that a previous occupant fought for the poor with her pen. The Gothic church on the corner whose bell pealed for Zoe is gone. But backyards that her bedroom overlooked are still beflowered, contrasting with her East 15th Street views of fire escapes with immigrant children gasping for breath during heatwaves. I trod the Bakers' wooden staircase painted glossy crimson, where Zoe's skirts rustled as she rushed down to see if the mail brought checks or rejections. I attended the Bakers' Sunday services; how pleased Zoe would be that there was not a moment of boredom, sanctimoniousness, or misogyny as the church's women leaders sang while pounding drums. I felt weirdly fated to be there, called Beautiful Sister Eve, swaying and trying to belt out gospel while taking notes. "God takes you exactly where you need to go," Hallia preached. She encouraged me from the pulpit: "Keep on writing that book! Don't get tired!"

I keep taking notes in my black notebook wherever Zoe walked. The Catholic charity hospital on East 86th Street, where *Soul*'s teenage Elsie and her baby died, where teenage Clarence gave birth to Harold-turned-Robert Morris, has been demolished. Across the street, 19th-century brick rowhouses witnessed the nuns praying for terrified girls in slatted bonnets and newborns destined for early career training. "It shines for all" is still emblazoned on the long-shuttered *Sun*'s clockfaces at its downtown headquarters, where deadbeat, plagiarizing editors insisted that Zoe write about "something cheerful," rather than overcrowded Catholic orphanages that resulted from "the loving weakness of woman, the perfidy of man."

Stuyvesant Square Park is still shaded by the trees that Zoe considered "kindly people," and colorful with flowerbeds planted after *The East Side* drew attention to the bare patches. A few eateries survive where she dined with Ragged Edgers, including Keens Steakhouse near Herald Square; its rooms are packed with photos of Gilded Age parties, and I keep looking for signs of Klub diners who shed their home ties over Thanksgiving steaks.[14] When I cross bridges over the East River, blue skies mirrored in the water are still "showing kaleidoscopically" through criss-cross railings. "Peoples Hospital" is inscribed on the foyer floor at Zoe's deathplace on Second Avenue, now a headquarters for Ukrainian immigrant groups. In the 1980s, the former Leppig's Hall on Avenue A, Zoe's funeral site, was converted into the Pyramid Club, a haven for experimental punk and drag performers. In 2023, it became the Knitting Factory, a performance space, bar, and clubhouse. In its chicly battered downstairs space called the Feverdream Lounge, I spotted a Remington noiseless typewriter—just what Zoe hoped someone would invent, to prevent neighbors from knowing when freelancers were home.

I wonder what topics would have called to her if she had lived longer. Would she have borrowed a Red Cross nurse outfit to report from World War I battlefields? Reconnected in wartime Paris with her boardinghouse friend Doddy, to apologize again for telling the world about his youthful accidental buzzcut?[15] Protested against Prohibition with Prince Joel of Bohemia, written screenplays for talkies (with music by Harry Huggs) about Southern women reformers in New York, hosted Harlem Renaissance poetry readings, given tours of the Lower East Side's vanishing Jewish landmarks, gathered with the Algonquin Round Table's "Vicious Circle"? During the Great Depression, would she have queued in Hooverville breadlines, or interviewed the families of people killed by the Dust Bowl? If her doppelganger were alive today, would she report on working at chicken slaughterhouses, or dress as a Latin American migrant to peddle candy in New York subway cars? How would she react to the never-ending news of immigrants terrified, villainized, assaulted, and deported; the loudest anti-sin campaigners revealed as the worst sinners; men in power going unpunished for public cruelties; and persistent economic gaps, in an age of "wildest extravagance," between those who "go barefooted" and those who "lead the lives of butterflies"?

I hope readers agree with Zoe, and me, that *The East Side* is "invaluable as history." Yet I welcome fresh eyes and suggested revisions. What did I miss? I do not want mine to be the last word on the personas that Zoe adopted while trying to kill kare, with komfortable exklusiveness.

Sometimes I remember how lucky I am to be typing these words. My ancestors evaded Cossack slaughter and Ellis Island rejection, leaving behind relatives who were murdered by Nazis and Soviets. My mother's parents and their siblings scrounged for jobs in America, selling cigars, hauling baggage, manning elevators, stitching shoes and clothes, singing onstage in Yiddish, playing the cornet, not talking about the past. They tried to stay married, sent their surviving children to free schools, and somehow did not fall victim to the wrongs that mowed down the poor in front of Zoe.

Did she make any *East Side* copy out of my relatives, battered by policemen and streetcar conductors, sewing menswear in firetraps, discouraged and tempted to return to unsafe but familiar Odessa, dozing or weeping at synagogues while losing their faith, dodging chauffeured cars, delirious in charity hospitals, grabbing ice shards falling off delivery trucks, flying kites from fire escapes? Did anyone in my bloodline ever bewilderedly walk past a shawled accordionist playing "My Old Kentucky Home," and give her a quarter just for trying?

## ACKNOWLEDGMENTS

THIS BOOK WOULD not have been possible without the nonstop joyous interest and insights of my daughter, Alina Kulman, and the steady support of my husband, Brad Kulman. Inexpressibly deepest thanks also go to my friends Martha Pavlakis, Julie Lasky, Alexandra Shelley, George Calderaro (and Romeo and the late Bill Megevick), Marcia Ely and Andy McKey, Elizabeth Harris and Mark Fox, Nora Demeter and Kristóf and László Földényi, and Linda and the late Gaston Vadasz; my family Andrew Kahn and Janet Schneider, David Freudenthal and Ken Jockers, and Renee and Dana Jacoby; Fordham University Press's team (Fredric Nachbaur, Kem Crimmins, Courtney Lee Adams, peer reviewer Jennifer Putzi); Grolier Club bibliophiles (especially Dr. Steven Lomazow and Suze Bienaimee, Gretchen Adkins, Lisa Baskin, Denise Bethel, Natalie and John Blaney, Nancy Boehm, Mildred Budny, Sarah Funke Butler, Reid Byers, Julie Carlsen, Fern Cohen, Bruce and Mary Crawford, Deirdre Donohue, Mindy Dubansky, Basie Gitlin, Henrietta Hakes, Cheryl Hurley, Jerry Kelly, Rhiannon Knol, Mark Samuels Lasner and Margaret Stetz, Chris Loker, Miko McGinty, Ellen Michelson, PJ Mode, Olivia Loksing Moy, Marie Oedel, Beppy Owen, Jim Periconi, Corina Reynolds, Nancy Rosin, Ellen Rubin, Michael Ryan, Caroline Schimmel, Mary Schlosser, Ken Soehner, David Solo, Susan Tane, Irene Tichenor, Mark Tomasko, Cathy Vanderpool, and Henry Voigt; staff members Dionis Afric, Maev Brennan, Shira Buchsbaum, Meghan Constantinou, Jamie Cumby, Scott Ellwood, Ilir Pervizi, Kate Rowland, Tammy Rubel and Jennifer Sheehan;

consultant Amanda Domizio); photographer Nicole Neenan; supporters at CUNY's Women Writing Women's Lives, Society for the Study of American Women Writers, BIO (including Sara Catterall, Christine Cipriani, Cathy Curtis, Allison Gilbert, Elizabeth Harris, Carla Kaplan, Janice Nimura, Alison Owings, Diane Prenatt, and Amy Reading), Margaret Fuller Society, Poster House, Victorian Society New York, Tin Pan Alley American Popular Music Project (especially Bob Lamont and Gabrielle Lee), Art Glass Forum (especially Paul Doros and Lindsy Parrott), Bank Street and IPS moms, and Center for Book Arts (Roni Gross). In Kentucky my gratitude goes to Amalie Preston, Nancy Hill, Helen Dedman, Rebecca Soules, Jeff and Becky Bischoff, Sarah Lowe, Jerry Sampson, Yvette Holmes, William Turner, Wynn Radford III, and the late Anna Armstrong; in Kansas, to James Mason, Kenneth H. Yohn, Jami Frazier Tracy, Vernon and Phyllis Dolezal, and Tracy Andringa; and in Missouri, to historian Dr. Traci Wilson-Kleekamp. Also the Oberhardt family (Heather Kelly Woodburn and the late Lori Oberhardt Kelly), Ken Cobb at NYC Department of Information Records & Information Services, Hallia and Gale Baker on East 126th Street, New-York Historical Society (Margi Hofer, Marilyn Kushner, Allison Robinson, Valerie Paley), Periodyssey's Richard West, Museum at Eldridge Street (Nancy Johnson, Maya Locker, Adrienne Ottenberg), Woodlawn Cemetery's Susan Olsen; Zoe's relatives including Linda Rue Allen, Barbara and Bridget Goodbody, the Stacks (Ann Morris Stack, Chris and his family), J. Carl Ganter, Patricia Ganter Pelizzari, the Norrises (Dixie and Lynda), Catherine Segurson, Jacquelyn Bean Hall, and Patricia Long-Moss; kindred spirits Lauren Drapala, Carl Raymond, John Stuart Gordon, Phyllis Ross, Paul Carlos and Urshula Barbour at Pure + Applied, Clara and Emily Bingham, Penelope Green, Sarah Lyall, Yuri Kim and Benoit Ludwig, David Lowden, Cristina Martinez, Rich Dana (University of Iowa), Lahnice Hollister, Karen Strickland, Zeva Oelbaum, Hilly Dunn, Susan Tunick, Rivka Schiller, Sandra Howland Smith, Anne Stewart O'Donnell, Matthew Algeo, Robin Eiland (Daughters of the American Revolution), Warren Ashworth (Victorian Society in America), Vincenzo Rutigliano (New York Public Library), Allison C. Meier and Rebecca Rego Barry (*Fine Books & Collections*), Hannah Goldfield (*New Yorker*), Ann Lewinson (Hell Gate), and Steve Heller (Daily Heller). And the lifesavers at Mike's Tech Shop.

To my BIO sisters, my debt surpasses words. Countless times they helped me turn seemingly insurmountable obstacles into opportunities. Countless times I wanted to jump up from my seat during virtual or in-person gatherings, when a sister-biographer expressed just what I was working through but couldn't express, or felt as down on herself as I'd felt the week before but had been cheered up by sisterhood, or shared my frustration with people asking the same questions or not answering any, or exulted with me over some great detail out of the blue, or sympathized with my sense of slipping into someone else's skin to the point that my eyes sting when I talk about hard times in the lives of my subject and her subjects. I feel like we women writing about women have all been chefs, giving each other input on the best seasonings for our stews and soufflés in progress, preparing a banquet of women's words. Or no, it's more permanent than that: we are collaborating on a glorious quilt of women's narratives, stitching amicably side by side, teaching each other the best techniques to make something that will endure.

And to the feline deities Sneferu and Cleopatra Kahn, who never left my side nor passed judgment while dozing in sync.

# APPENDIX I

Zoe's friends, Klub and funeral attendees, and *East Side* readers (including Life Preservers), in addition to those explored elsewhere in this book:

Charles Albert Adams, Navy captain (Leita Kildare's husband)
John F. Ahearn, politician
Theresa M. Avery, real-estate developer
Alexander S. Bacon, lawyer, politician
Stephen H. Bacon, broker
Abe Baerman, literary agent
Arthur Bairnsfather, artist
Laura Baker, wife of writer George Barr Baker
Georgia Sawyer Baxter, activist
Rex Beach, writer, and his wife Edith Crater Beach
Lincoln Beachey, aviator
Jessie Tarbox Beals, photographer
Mildred Beardslee, illustrator
Zoe Beckley, writer
Carrie Behr, actress
Clark Bell, lawyer, editor
Lloyd Bingham, theatrical manager
James H. Birch, carriage maker
Ada Barton Bogg, journalist
William Goodrich Bowdoin, newspaperman

Grace Duffie Boylan, writer
Platon Brounoff, conductor, arranger, composer
Lewis Sayre Burchard, attorney
Katherine Butler, suffragist
Dr. Joseph Caccavajo, engineer
Benjamin de Casseres, writer
Charles Chapin, editor, murderer
Stephen G. Clow, gossip writer
Bird S. Coler, politician
Harry Coldwell, lawnmower maker
Marie Conners, pianist
Jane Corcoran, actress (wife of J. Emmett Baxter)
David A. Curtis, writer
H. Gail Davis, plow works magnate
Beatrice deMille, writer, theater impresario
Mortimer Delano, aviator
Bernard S. Deutsch, lawyer, alderman
Helen Diers, vaudeville harpist
Ruth Crosby Dimmick, writer
Frank Dotzler, alderman
Jack Doyle, singer
Walter Bronson "Bide" Dudley, critic, playwright
Henry M. Duncan, appliance and automotive executive
Robert Lee Dunn, writer
William Hanford Edwards, "Big Bill," football player, politician
Leonard Brooks Elms, salesman
Lillian English, actress
Renee Florigny, pianist
Maud Flowerton, suffragist
Lee de Forest, inventor
Carlo de Fornaro, illustrator, revolutionary
Arthur L. Fullman, lawyer
Lucy Gantt, journalist
Dr. Samuel Gilmore, electrologist
Dr. Frank Sargent Grant, surgeon
John Temple Graves, newspaperman, politician
Maida Gregg, journalist
Moses and William Grossman, lawyers
Harry J. Haon, inventor
Henry DeWitt Hamilton, politician, military officer

Caroline Harding, journalist
Clifford Harmon, aviator
Sadie Harrison, composer, singer
Jerome A. Hart, historian, publisher
Mary Theresa Hart, artist
Sadakichi Hartmann, writer
Isabel Hauser, pianist
Beckwith Havens, aviator
Frank Heine, sculptor
F. Harrison Higgins, aviator
Alberta Hill, suffragist
Ichiro Hori, artist, photographer
Burling Hull, magician
Edgar F. Ingraham, advertising executive
Alfred Jackson, vaudevillian
George Johnson, female impersonator
Adolph Kmetz, Karatsonyi & Kmetz restaurateur
Irene and Harry Tobin Lamkin, cotton broker
James Liebling, cellist
Peyton R. McCargo, beauty products magnate
Richard M. McCann, editor
John R. Meader, writer
Charles Meeker, dentist
Dr. Anna Mercy and Henrietta Mercy, sister suffragists
Herman A. Metz, politician
Seth Moyle, writer, agent, producer
Paul F. Myers, lawyer, politician
Maude H. Neal, writer
Harry W. Newburger, deputy police commissioner
Louis Hasbrouck Newkirk, lawyer
Maurice Nitke, violinist
Lillian Wells Ogle, singer
Ladislas d'Orcy, aviator
Charles M. Payne, cartoonist
Roland Phillips, writer
Tom Powers, artist
Edward Raffin, engineer
Nellie Revell, writer
Jancsi Rigó, violinist
Jacob Rosenbloom, biochemist

Ignatius/Ignatz Rosenfeld, Café Boulevard restaurateur
Helen Rowland, writer
Edward Schermerhorn, military officer
Max Schwartz, Little Hungary restaurateur
John P. Scrymser, veterans' group leader
Edwin Seligman, economist
Harriet Shonts, wife of Theodore P. Shonts, railroad magnate
Laura Simmons, poet
Ida Vera Simonton, writer
G. C. Smith, Street & Smith publishing executive
Eleanor Smithe, dancer
Winthrop Morton Southworth, aviator
Clinton Stagg, writer
Arthur Stilwell, railroad magnate
Sam Tauber, theater manager
Laurette Taylor, actress
Edward Owings Towne, writer
James Bliss Townsend, editor
Andre Tridon, writer, translator, psychoanalyst
John Curtis Underwood, poet
George Vermilye, Countess Ella Bosworth's son-in-law
Commodore George J. Vestner, Waterways League leader
Theodore Waters, writer
Minnie Graves Watson, composer (sometimes under pseudonym Alfred Norman)
William Jennings Weakly, poet
Agnes Wedgewood, writer (wife of Clinton Stagg)
Daniel de Wolf Wever, lawyer
Benjamin Ide Wheeler, academic
Dr. William DeCourcy White, dentist
Frank White, press agent
Horace B. Wild, aviator
Mornay Williams, lawyer, reformer
Carrie Astor Wilson, philanthropist
Charles Witmer, aviator
Racia Wood, artist, writer
Lola Wright, dancer
Arthur Young, illustrator

# APPENDIX II

Partial list of publications that Zoe contributed to:

Newspapers:
*Brooklyn Life*, 1905
*NY Press*, 1897–1908
*NY Sun*, 1898–1906
*NYT*, 1904–1908
*Wichita Eagle*, starting 1893
*Wichita Democrat/Mirror*, 1895

Periodicals:
*Ainslee's*, 1902
*American Agriculturist*, 1902
*American Monthly Magazine*, 1896
*Arena*, 1898
*Argosy*, 1907–1908
*Bankers Magazine*, 1912
*Bohemian*, 1906–1909
*Book-Lover*, 1904
*Bookman*, 1907
*Boston Cooking-School Magazine*, 1909
*Boston Ideas*, 1897
*Bostonian*, 1896
*Clack Book*, 1897

*Cosmopolitan*, 1910
*Criterion*, 1899–1900
*Current Literature*, 1898, 1909
*Demorest's Family Magazine*, 1899
*Etude*, 1897
*Ev'ry Month*, 1899
*Everybody's*, 1908–1909
*Four O'Clock*, 1897–1898
*Frank Leslie's Monthly*, 1901–1902
*Harper's Weekly*, 1913
*Home Magazine of New York*, 1897–1903
*Ladies' World*, 1897–1898
*Manuscript*, 1901
*Midland Monthly*, 1895
*Mirror*, 1901–1903
*Monthly Illustrator*, 1896
*Munsey's*, 1898–1908
*New Age*, 1904–1906
*New Bohemian*, 1896
*Pearson's*, 1910
*People's*, 1907–1909
*Peterson Magazine*, 1897
*Puritan*, 1899
*Quaker*, 1899
*Red Letter*, 1897
*Rough Rider*, 1901
*Satire*, 1911
*Smart Set*, 1901–1904
*Success*, 1907
*Symposium*, 1896
*10 Story Book*, 1903–1909
*Thistle*, 1902
*Valley Magazine*, 1903
*Vanity Fair*, 1901
*Wisdom Monthly*, 1902
*Woman's Home Companion*, 1902–1903
*Woman's World*, 1898
*Writer*, 1899–1904

# NOTES

### Prologue: Weep No More

1. TES 18 (1912).
2. TES 8 (1910).
3. ZAN, "A Southern Woman's Decoration Day," *NYT*, June 26, 1904.

### Methodology: Why Zoe, and How, and Why Me?

1. ZAN, "A Christmas Truce," copyrighted 1900; Michael Monahan, *Papyrus*, Sept. 1903; Sallie Toler, "Saw Wichita Authoress," *Eagle*, July 17, 1910.
2. TES 20 (1912).
3. TES 4 (1909), 15 (1911).

### Chapter 1. A Sort of Waif, 1860–1873

1. "Mr. W. N. Ducker," *Hopkinsville Kentuckian*, Jan. 14, 1902. Henry's wife Jane Buckner Hawes was widowed when they married in 1832.
2. Sarah Ann Tompkins Garnett, *Cursory Family Sketches* (New York, NY: 1870); William Henry Perrin, ed., *County of Christian, Kentucky. Historical and Biographical* (Chicago and Louisville: F. A. Battey, 1884); Zoe's cousin LaVece Ganter Hughes, *The Dickinson Family of Glasgow, Kentucky* (Wind Publications, 2005). Zoe is also descended from Sir Edmund Anderson, a 16th-century judge who presided over trials of Sir Walter Raleigh and Mary, Queen of Scots. I am deeply grateful to Harrodsburg historians Amalie Preston and the late Anna Armstrong.
3. JWT; ZAN, "A Daughter of the Revolution," *American Monthly Magazine*, Dec. 1896.
4. TES 4 (1909).
5. MSB.

6. Sarah Ann Tompkins Garnett, *Cursory Sketches*; David Fiske, *Solomon Northrup's Kindred* (Santa Barbara and Denver: Praeger, 2016). Per Fiske, Lipscomb may have aimed to cast his profession in a less unsavory light, or to thwart a competitor obtaining cheap "inventory" by kidnapping.

7. MSB; "The Deaf Hear, and the Dumb Speak!!," *The Baptist*, Feb. 13, 1847; "Colored," *Hopkinsville Kentuckian*, Dec. 16, 1890. Robert and Martha Anderson were cousins. The now-vanished hamlet, Garrettsburg, is near Hopkinsville.

8. James Ross, *The Life and Times of Elder Reuben Ross* (Philadelphia: Grant, Faires & Rodgers, 1882); Hopkinsville historians William Turner and Yvette Holmes ("H. T. Anderson" is painted on windows commemorating past leaders at Hopkinsville's First Christian Church); ZAN, "Decoration Day."

9. HTA, "Prospectus of the Christian Disciple," *Millennial Harbinger*, Jan. 1845.

10. Susan E. Lindsey, *Liberty Brought Us Here* (University Press of Kentucky, 2020); research by Hopkinsville historians William Turner, Yvette Holmes, and Wynn Radford; University of Kentucky's Notable Kentucky African Americans Database entries for antebellum Disciples pastors including Samuel Buckner, Alexander Campbell Sr., and Alexander Cross.

11. HTA's writings: *Herald of the Future Age*, late 1848; *British Harbinger*, Jan. 1, 1864, July 1, 1867; *Millennial Harbinger*, May 1849, June 1860; Wingfield (whereabouts of original correspondence unknown); Disciples of Christ papers, Butler University, Indianapolis. On Henry's brother Albert and sister-in-law Louisa Anderson (he became a Christadelphian leader, and they both wrote for religious periodicals): David Lertis Matson, *Stone-Campbell Journal*, Spring 2008, Fall 2011.

12. Her birthplace is in the vicinity of what is now Montgomery Lane off Burgin Road.

13. John Augustus Williams, *Reminiscences* (Cincinnati: F.L. Rowe, 1898). The school's name had various apostrophe configurations over the years including Daughters' and Daughter's.

14. HTA, *Millennial Harbinger*, Jan. 1864; Moses E. Lard, "Reply," *Lard's Quarterly*, Jan. 1865; Wingfield. Henry's publishers: Franklin Type Foundry, Cincinnati (1864); John P. Morton & Co., Louisville (1866); David King, Birmingham, UK (1867). Henry's texts, in keeping with Disciples dogma, used "immersion" for "baptism." His volumes' prices ranged from 50 cents (pocket edition) to $3 (library edition).

15. TES 23 (1913); ZAN, "The Story of a Dream," copyrighted 1901, syndicated; "Jim Leverin's Daughter," copyrighted 1903, syndicated; "A School Ma'am," *NY Sun*, Dec. 4, 1904 (reprinted TKCS).

16. "Burned to Death," *Louisville Daily Democrat*, April 16, 1861.

17. Maria Thompson Daviess, *History of Mercer and Boyle Counties* (Harrodsburg, KY: Harrodsburg Herald, 1924); Stuart W. Sanders, *Perryville Under Fire* (Charleston, SC: The History Press, 2012).

18. HTA, *British Harbinger*, Jan. 1, 1867; W. T. Moore, ed., *The Living Pulpit of the Christian Church* (Cincinnati: R.W. Carroll & Co., 1868); TES 1, 4 (1909); ZAN, "Decoration Day."

19. "Mrs. Jessie Anderson Rue," *Kentucky People*, April 5, 1872; "Mrs. Jessie Rue," *Lexington Herald-Leader*, Aug. 2, 1925. The mansion, Glenworth, was built by Robert Mosby Davis on land that had belonged to the family of President Andrew Jackson's future wife Rachel Robards. Jessie's sitters included Kentucky governors and her sister Mattie Thompson.

20. Mattie Anderson to President Johnson, Sept. 1, 1868 (National Archives).

21. TES 13 (1911); QPL; ZAN, "Seeing Manhattan: Poverty Hollow's Pathos," NYT, July 9, 1905; Sept. 1909 letter to Clarence Chelf, NDC.

22. TES 21 (1912). 29 (1914); QPL; ZAN, "Is Up On Her Ear," *Eagle*, Feb. 11, 1894; "On the Rim of Manhattan," NYT, June 4, 1905.
23. Wingfield.
24. ZAN, "Story of a Dream," syndicated 1901.
25. Garfield to Burke A. Hinsdale, May 3, 1868, Library of Congress; Isaac Errett, "Henry T. Anderson," *Christian Standard*, Sept. 28, 1872; "Eld. Henry T. Anderson," *Kentucky People*, October 11, 1872. Henry's Codex translation reverted from "immersion" to "baptism."
26. QPL; ZAN, "Story of a Dream," 1901.

## Chapter 2. Mineralogy and Constitutional Law, 1874–1878

1. ZAN, "The Carved Initials," copyrighted 1900, syndicated.
2. TES 22 (1912).
3. ZAN, "Andrew Jackson's Romance," *Home*, Nov. 1898; *Wind*; Daviess, *History of Mercer and Boyle Counties*.
4. ZAN, "They Too" (unpublished NDC manuscript, MCJ published 1989).
5. Anne Shanks Bourne, *History of Daughters College (1856–1893) and Its Founder John Augustus Williams*, (Harrodsburg, KY: Hutton Publishing, 1907). Legal wranglings over the musicians George, Reuben, and Henry, who escaped in 1841, reached the Supreme Court as *Strader v. Graham*. Interviews with Anna Armstrong; Paul Finkelman, *Slavery in the Courtroom* (Library of Congress, 1985); Ron Bryant bio of Graham, *Kentucky Ancestors*, Jan. 2006; Allan W. Vestal, *Marquette Law Review*, Summer 2019.
6. TES 8 (1910).
7. ZAN, "Cappie's Boy," *Mirror*, Jan. 8, 1903; "On the Rim of New York," NYT, May 14, 1905.
8. TES 14 (1911). Archibald Rue was an inventor (he patented a reins-protecting device for horse-drawn vehicles) as was Clarence Anderson's brother-in-law Benjamin Spilman (x-ray photography, a photographic plate holder).
9. ZAN, "The Carved Initials," copyrighted 1900, syndicated; "Our War Veteran," *Arena*, June 1898. The title character of "Our War Veteran" attributes his deafness to battlefield blasts, but what he cannot mainly hear are his family's money pleas. *Arena* then published enraged letters from injured veterans who did not appreciate Zoe's humor. Florence Anderson Clark's works include a novel, *Zenaida* (Philadelphia: J. B. Lippincott, 1858), about a genteelly impoverished (but still slaveholding) Southern family of intellectual dreamers. Her brother Henry, while fighting for the Confederacy, was known as an erudite, cynical critic and dialectician, defending the most "audacious assumption," per George Dallas Mosgrove, *Kentucky Cavaliers in Dixie* (Louisville: Courier-Journal Job Printing Co., 1895).
10. TES 8 (1910).
11. Beaumont Inn memorabilia. The Williamses' sons and John's father, Charles, helped run the business.
12. Williams, *Reminiscences*.
13. Martha Stephenson, "A Unique Railroad," *Register of Kentucky State Historical Society*, May 1922. Stephenson was a Daughters College alumna and teacher.
14. TES 14 (1911), 23 (1913).
15. TES 13 (1911). Re Southern schoolgirls: Anya Jabour, *Scarlett's Sisters: Young Women in the Old South* (Chapel Hill, NC: University of North Carolina Press, 2007).
16. "The Concert," *Kentucky People*, Aug. 7, 1874.

17. Emphasis mine, based on multiple copies of this text in print that I have seen with the italicized phrase underlined, undoubtedly by women readers.
18. TES 26 (1913).
19. "Harrodsburg," *Cincinnati Daily Star*, Oct. 7, 1879.
20. TCKS; ZAN, "The Kidnaping of Poggioreale's Twins," *Munsey's*, April 1908, syndicated. The Thompson twins' older brother Davis was imprisoned during the Civil War and then became a physician, trained at New York University.
21. Re feud: see for instance "Thompson Trial," *Interior Journal* (Stanford, KY), Jan. 9, 1874.
22. MCJ.

## Chapter 3. Of the Best Families, 1878–1887

1. JWT; "Harrodsburg, Kentucky," *Cincinnati Enquirer*, June 12, 1878.
2. With postwar surnames, they were Addison Diggs, Amanda, Augustus Joplin, Catherine, Charles, Charlotte, Daniel, Eliza Diggs Tyman, George, Henry Diggs, Jane Diggs Hall, Lucy Wright, Phillip Diggs, Sandy Diggs, William Plaiter, and Winnie Diggs. They were related to people enslaved by the Spennys' neighbors. The historian Dr. Traci Wilson-Kleekamp, a descendant of these people, has done heroic research on them.
3. "No. 8," *Kentucky Gazette*, June 22, 1827. I am grateful to Spencer's descendants Lynda Norris and Dixie Norris Koontz for their insights. Descendants of the successful Meaux litigants include the actor Maya Rudolph, per her appearances in the TV show *Finding Your Roots*.
4. "Extensive Rascality," *Louisville Daily Courier*, Nov. 2, 1857; "Died," *Daily Missouri Republican*, Oct. 30, 1858.
5. Harrodsburg Historical Society has Lowrey family Bible with genealogical information and newspaper clippings.
6. TES 2 (1909); 24 (1913). Robert Norris was likely given his middle name after Harrodsburg's Grimes family, prominent in pursuits including publishing.
7. Henrietta's modern-day address is near the northwest corner of Avenue H and 22nd Road.
8. "Mrs. Henrietta Anderson," *Ellsworth Reporter*, March 11, 1880.
9. "Local & Miscellaneous," *Ellsworth Reporter*, March 9, 1882.
10. TES 11 (1910), 29 (1914); *Wind*; ZAN, "The Hot Winds," *Frank Leslie's Monthly*, Sept. 1901; "On the Rim of Manhattan," NYT, June 11, 1905.
11. Emails about 1870s legal proceedings from Ellsworth officials; ZAN, "'Bat' Masterson Vindicated," NYT, April 2, 1905.
12. TES 11 (1910); Harry Anderson in *Ellsworth Reporter*: "To the People of Ellsworth County," Nov. 14, 1878; "Mr. Anderson Explains," March 20, 1879; "Communicated," Oct. 31, 1878; *Lincoln Banner*: no headline, Nov. 17, 1882; "The Register," April 6, 1883.
13. No headline, *Lincoln Banner* (Kansas), April 16, 1879; 1882: "A Wife's Bill for Divorce," *Evening Star* (DC), Feb. 20; "In the Divorce Case of Nettie A. Cheeks," *Evening Star*, April 3; "Peter C. Cheeks Replies," *National Republican*, April 4; 1890 ads in *Cloverdale Reveille* (CA) for "Dr. Wilford Hall's Health Pamphlet" with colon-cleansing regimen; NARA Cheeks pension file 92702966; ZAN, "A Government Rat," *Arena*, Feb. 1898; TES 6 (1910). Peter and Lucy named their son after Charles Ewing, a Federal general who had been one of Peter's commanding officers.
14. *Ellsworth Reporter*: "At Rest," June 16, 1881; Nov. 23, 1882.
15. ZAN, "Bred in the Bone," copyrighted 1899, syndicated.

16. Pickett's Corcoran training is documented in curator William MacLeod's diaries. Corday painting was by French artist Charles Louis Müller.

17. ZAN, "Copying from the Original," *Red Letter*, April 1897.

18. No headline, *Ellsworth Reporter*, Dec. 21, 1882; "An Artistic Display," *Topeka Daily Capital*, Oct. 2, 1886.

19. ZAN, "The Fate of a Missionary," *Home*, March 1897; "Through the Glass Door," *New Age*, Oct. 1904.

20. "Harrodsburg," *Kentucky Advocate*, March 28, 1884; Daviess, *History of Mercer and Boyle Counties*. Daviess also noted women writers with Harrodsburg roots, including Zoe's newspaperwoman cousin Florence Anderson Clark and playwright and magazine contributor Hannah Daviess Pittman (Maria Daviess's daughter). Among the Choctaw students ("In the Territory," *Fort Worth Daily Gazette*, July 4, 1886) were Norma Standley, who became a newspaper editor, and her younger sister Jennie, who drowned at 16.

21. "Harrodsburg Tragedy," *Tennessean*, May 4, 1883. The Davises owned the mansion where Zoe's sister Jessie took refuge during the Civil War.

22. ZAN, "The Carved Initials," copyrighted 1900, syndicated; "Our Neighbors," *Kentucky Advocate* (Danville), Oct. 26, 1883; "Local News," *Harrodsburg Democrat*, Oct. 17, 1884; "Personal" and "A Gentlemens' Feast," *Harrodsburg Democrat*, Dec. 5, 1884; "Harrodsburg's Interesting Fire History," *Harrodsburg Herald*, Feb. 27, 1925; "100-Year-Old Invitation," *Lexington Herald*, May 25, 1947.

23. "Falls Fever," *Courier-Journal*, Sept. 2, 1883; no headline, *Evening Bulletin* (Maysville, KY), May 23, 1885. "The matter has been kept very quiet," the newspaper unquietly reported about Nannie's suicide attempt. The candidate was James Blaine, a Republican controversial in Kentucky for supporting Black suffrage.

24. ZAN, "Which?" *Clack Book*, Feb. 1897.

25. "Personal," *Interior Journal* (Stanford, KY), July 27, 1886.

## Chapter 4. To Nourish the Temperament, 1887–1893

1. "Married in London," *Eagle*, July 15, 1900.

2. ZAN, "At Halloween," undated (c. 1897, return address Wichita) short story typescript, NDC; "Bellepointe," *Frankfort Roundabout*, Aug. 27, 1887; James E. Mason, *Wichita* (Charleston, SC: Arcadia Publishing, 2012). Norris addresses in Wichita included East Oak, 704 North Fourth, North Topeka's 600 block, North Market's 300 and 400 blocks.

3. MCJ; TES 19 (1912); "With Eagle Eyes," *Eagle*, Nov. 30, 1910; Clarence Sousley, "An Indian Santa Claus," *Dry Goods Reporter*, Dec. 26, 1914; Charles B. Driscoll, "The World and All," Feb. 23, 1932, syndicated column; Victor Murdock, "Marvel of Evolution," *Beacon*, June 22, 1932. Spencer at first ran a store with James M. Cook at 517 East Oak St. (where the Norrises at first lived) and then solo at 104 North Main St., at the northeast corner of East Douglas Ave.

4. George R. Smith, "Lewis Academy," *Church At Home and Abroad*, June 1894; Lewis Academy in *Eagle*: Aug. 25, Sept. 4, Nov. 12, 1887; April 29, June 2, 1888.

5. ZAN, "After Long Years," copyrighted 1902, syndicated.

6. 1888: "Personals," *Eagle*, July 20; "Political Chips," *Ellsworth Reporter*, Sept. 13.

7. "Died at the Asylum," *Courier-Journal* (Louisville), Jan. 18, 1897; emails from Kentucky state officials; Alma Wynelle Deese, *Kentucky's First Asylum* (Cheyenne, WY: Stratton Press, 2017).

8. TES 7 (1910), 14 (1911), 29 (1914).

9. MCJ; "Just Like Mother's," *Wichita Journal*, April 16, 1890; ZAN, "Wichita Writer in London," *Eagle*, Aug. 12, 1900; "Rests in 'Land of Lilies,'" *Eagle*, Feb. 15, 1914.

10. "Social Swim," *Eagle*, March 4, 1888; "In Society," *Beacon*, March 14, 1891. Joseph Lemon is also listed among Wichita's lauded dance performers and instructors: "Local Brevities," *Wichita Star*, Jan. 19, 1889.

11. *Lexington Herald-Leader*, May 6.

12. *Eagle*, Oct. 9, 1892.

13. See for instance "Mrs. Cardwell Suspended," *Courier-Journal*, June 1, 1906.

14. "The Hypatia," *Democrat*, Sept. 11, 1887. Hypatia was modeled after Sorosis (named for fleshy fruits) in New York, the U.S.'s first professional women's club, founded in 1868 by the journalist Jane Cunningham Croly—one of Zoe's Manhattan idols.

15. MCJ; "Personal," *Beacon*, Feb. 9, 1892; "In Vanity Fair's Domain," *Democrat*, March 5, 1892; "Rests in 'Land of Lilies,'" *Eagle*, Feb. 15, 1914.

16. *Report of the Kansas Board of World's Fair Managers* (Topeka, KS: Hamilton Printing Co., 1894); *A History of Kentucky's Distilling Interests* (Lexington: Kentucky Distillers' Bureau, 1893); "Announcements," *Eagle*, Aug. 9, 1893.

17. ZAN, "Life's Fitful Fever," copyrighted 1899, syndicated; "A Woman at the Paris Exposition," *Home*, July 1900.

## Chapter 5. She Has a Halo, 1893–1895

1. MCJ; "Boudoir Gossip," *Democrat*, July 15, 1893, 4; "Personals," *Beacon*, Jan. 27, 1894, 3. The house, no longer extant, was at 430 North Market Street, on land that cost $1,000.

2. Julia Golia, *Newspaper Confessions: A History of Advice Columns in a Pre-Internet Age* (New York: Oxford University Press, 2021).

3. Lemon, *Wichita Journal*: "Woman's Tidings," Dec. 24, 1888, March 23, 1889, May 9, 1889; "New York Gossip," May 7, 1890; "Correspondence," *Democrat*, March 23, 1895.

4. "Look At This," *Eagle*, Jan. 13, 1894; ZAN, "Beware That Man," *Eagle*, Jan. 7, 1894, 6. This appeared under Yanks pseudonym, as did other 1893 and 1894 *Eagle* articles credited to ZAN in this chapter's footnotes.

5. ZAN, *Eagle*: "Has Music Charms?," Dec. 24, 1893; "Poetry Saved Her," Feb. 25, 1894; Margaret Lemon, "A Flying Trip to Florida," *Godey's*, Dec. 1893.

6. ZAN, *Eagle*: "Blames the Waltz," Dec. 31, 1893; 1894: "Beware That Man," Jan. 7; "She Has a Halo," March 4; "It Is Indeed Sad," March 11.

7. ZAN, *Eagle*, 1894: "Dodges His Dove," Feb. 4; "Is Up On Her Ear," Feb. 11.

8. ZAN, "Mrs. Lease is Seen at Home," *NY Sun*, Sept. 25, 1904.

9. ZAN, *Eagle*, 1894: "Rises to Explain," Jan. 28; "Poetry Saved Her," Feb. 25; "Ripped Them Off," March 18.

10. "Letter to Nancy Yanks," *Eagle*, Feb. 15, 1894; Molly Warren, *Topeka Daily Capital*, "Wichita," Sept. 22, 1907; Toler, "Saw Wichita Authoress," *Eagle*, July 17, 1910; "Rests in 'Land of Lilies,'" *Eagle*, Feb. 15, 1914.

11. 1894: "The Gayer World," *Beacon*, April 7; "The Auditorium Opened," *Eagle*, June 16; "Town Topics," *Beacon*, Aug. 4.

12. 1894: "Terrible Burns," *Beacon*, Sept. 27; "Her Sad Death," *Beacon*, Sept. 28; "Died of Her Burns," *Eagle*, Sept. 28. I am grateful to Wichita historian James Mason for finding these articles, among other insights into Zoe's Wichita life.

13. TES 20 (1912); ZAN, "Women Tell of Dreams," *NY Sun*, Sept. 11, 1898, syndicated.

14. *Eagle*: "Entertained the Boys," Dec. 13, 1894; "Very Successful Exhibition," June 4, 1895; *Beacon*: "In Society," Dec. 15, 1894; "Birthday Party," Feb. 16, 1895; "Society," June 1, 1895.

15. ZAN, "Janet," *The Midland Monthly*, Sept. 1895. Reviews included "A Kansas Romance," *Eagle*, Sept. 6, 1895.

16. Syndicated after appearing in *Eagle*, Dec. 1, 1895.

17. ZAN, "Two Waifs," *The Mirror*, Dec. 21, 1895.

## Chapter 6. Norris vs. Norris, 1896–1898

1. "Must Tell Stories," *Eagle*, Nov. 13, 1895; "Town Topics," *Beacon*, Apr. 29, 1896.

2. ZAN, "The Reason Why," *Home*, Dec. 1897.

3. ZAN, "Georgiana's Mother," *Symposium*, Dec. 1896. *The Symposium*'s editor, George Washington Cable, was a Confederate veteran from New Orleans who fled northward after coming under fire for supporting African Americans' rights.

4. "Editorial," *The New Bohemian*, Jan. 1896; same issue, ZAN, "Our First Mandolin." ZAN, "A Daughter of the Revolution," *American Monthly Magazine*, Dec. 1896; "The Wrong Nest," *Boston Ideas*, April 24, 1897.

5. No headline, *Eagle*, May 5, 1896; "Social Happenings," *Wichita Democrat*, March 7, 1896; "Mrs. Norris' Story," *Beacon*, Dec. 9, 1896.

6. 1897: "Near to Death," *Morning Herald* (Lexington, KY), Jan. 16; "City in Brief," "Coming Local Events," *Eagle*, Jan. 19; obituary, *Sayings* (Harrodsburg), Jan. 20; ZAN, 1909 letter, NDC.

7. Celeste's husband Will Ewing, a veterinarian, was related to Harrodsburg's Lowrey clan—another sign of the densely intertwined gene pool that Zoe escaped from.

8. *Iroquois* (*NY Press* magazine), June 13, 1897.

9. ZAN, May 1897: "Aliens from God's Country," *Home*; "Her Only Son," *Four O'Clock*. The Thompson brothers' mother Martha was a Montgomery. Zoe was lauded for using nasturtiums as party decorations.

10. ZAN, "Women Tell of Dreams," *NY Sun*, Sept. 11, 1898, and syndicated; "Wichita and Vicinity," *Saturday Evening Kansas Commoner*, July 8, 1897.

11. ZAN, "Miss Liz'beth" *Bostonian*, July 1896; *Home*, 1897: "Emily's English Lord," July; "Number 9," Aug.

12. "A City Bred Girl's Attempt to Climb Pikes Peak," *Philadelphia Inquirer*, Oct. 10, 1897; syndicated news reports on her "fearful climb"; ZAN, "A Woman Friend," *Smart Set*, Oct. 1902.

13. MCJ; "Norris vs. Norris," *Beacon*, Jan. 15, 1898.

14. TES 23 (1913); ZAN, "The Little Cross," *Pearson's*, March 1910. The property buyer, George Bohon, a carriage factory tycoon, razed the building to make way for a mansion, per historian Amalie Preston.

15. JWT; TES 8 (1910); ZAN, "The Chimney Corner," unpublished typescript copyrighted 1910 (Library of Congress, D 20491). Similar language about preferring menial tasks appears in her writings including "The Picture of Her," *Smart Set*, Dec. 1901.

16. ZAN, "At the Musicale," *Etude*, Oct. 1897; "Our Contributors" and "A New Year's Resolution," *Home*, Jan. 1898.

## Chapter 7. Beetles in Her Biscuits, 1898–1899

1. Jane Cunningham Croly, *The History of the Woman's Club Movement in America* (New York: Henry G. Allen & Co., 1898). She used the pseudonym Jennie June.

2. ZAN, "Merely a Loan," *Woman's World and Jenness Miller Monthly*, Feb. 1898; "The White Scars," *Home*, March 1898; "Regrets," *The Ladies' World*, Oct. 1898; "Her House of Bondage," *Demorest's Family Magazine*, April 1899; *Ev'ry Month*, 1899: "The Veil Between," Jan.; "Cupid=Cashier," April.

3. TES 16 (1911); ZAN, *Home*, 1898: "The Cat on the Wall," July; "The Second-Hand Book-Store," Aug.

4. ZAN, "Our War Veteran," *Arena*, June 1898; "An Unimportant Error," *Home*, Oct. 1898; "The Face on the Canvas," *Criterion*, May 15, 1899, and syndicated. Nannie's son Creed Cardwell, Jessie's son Insco Rue, and Mattie's son Philip Thompson (a hard-drinking Harvard dropout) served. Among the typhoid casualties was the Norrises' friend from Harrodsburg, Robert Grimes Sea (1871–1898), who had moved to Kansas. *Home*'s lynching story is apparently not based on any particular crime; in a related incident, Seay J. Miller of Illinois was lynched in Bardwell, Kentucky, in 1893, while protesting his innocence, and even the father of the murder victims, Mary and Ruby Ray, doubted his guilt.

5. Charles Johanningsmeier, *Fiction and the American Literary Marketplace: The Role of Newspaper Syndicates, 1860–1900* (Cambridge University Press, 1997).

6. MCJ; ZAN, "Women Tell of Dreams," *NY Sun*, Sept. 11, 1898, and syndicated.

7. MCJ; HTA, *Millennial Harbinger*, May 1849; Nazareth Academy ad, *Courier-Journal* (Louisville), July 16, 1899.

8. "Writers of the Day," *Writer*, July 1898; ZAN, *Puritan*, 1899: "The Deformed Thumb," March; "Without Counting the Cost," Dec.

9. Charles B. Driscoll, "The World and All," syndicated Feb. 23, 1932.

10. 1898: "Norris Fails," *Beacon*, Aug. 19; "New Feature," *Beacon*, Aug. 20; "Going to Europe," *Eagle*, Aug. 21; "In Charge of the Sheriff," *Saturday Evening Kansas Commoner*, Aug. 25. Ray W. House & Bro. ad, *University Life* (Wichita), Dec. 1, 1901. Spencer was hired by Casey & Garst and remained in their employ until a few months before his death.

11. ZAN, "The Widow McClane"—the name also appeared as M'Clane; "John's First Wife," both copyrighted 1898; Julia Guarneri, *Newsprint Metropolis: City Papers and the Making of Modern Americans* (Chicago: University of Chicago Press, 2017).

12. TES 27 (1913); ZAN, "The Whereabouts of the Lost Manuscripts," *Writer*, March 1899; "The Happy Family," *Bohemian*, Aug. 1907. Her beloved "Big Chief" at *Sun* was likely Edward Page Mitchell.

13. "Tea at Woman's Press Club," *NY Tribune*, Jan. 29, 1899; Columbia RBML, Woman's Press Club of New York City, Box 3, Volume IV, minutes April 9, 1898–Jan. 27, 1900.

14. ZAN, "Letter from Mrs. Norris," *Eagle*, April 16, 1899. Per MCJ, Clarence also attended Potter College, now Western Kentucky University.

15. ZAN, syndicated and sometimes copyrighted: "Letitia's Daughter," 1899; "When the Door Opened," 1901; "The Sound of the Sea" and "Into the Dark," 1902.

16. JWT. Woman's Press Club of New York City papers at Columbia RBML list Zoe's address while overseas as care of Margaret Lemon, 270 West 119th Street.

## Chapter 8. Champagne or Skyrockets, 1899–1900

1. MCJ; ZAN, "The Passing of Rebecca," *Home*, Sept. 1899.

2. MCJ; TES 4 (1909); ZAN, "The Story of a Dream," copyrighted 1901, syndicated; "Letter from Mrs. Norris," *Eagle*, April 16, 1899, written March 31, 1899, at 21 Woburn Place, Russell Square.

3. ZAN, *Criterion*, 1899: "Sarah Bernhardt in Hamlet," July 8; "The Cowboy and the Lady," Aug. 19; "Mrs. Langtry in 'The Degenerates,'" Oct. 14; "Outside the House of Kipling," Dec. 2.

4. ZAN, "The Blessed Peace," *Criterion*, Oct. 7, 1899; "In the Old Steine Road," copyrighted 1901, syndicated; "The Chorus Girl," *Mirror*, April 9, 1903; "The Telegram," unpublished typescript in NDC (address 35 West 21st St.), c. 1905. Syndicated stories set in Manhattan or rural America from this period include "John Doolan's Christmas," "Their Aunt Clorinda," "Bill Scraggin, Civilized," "Letitia's Daughter," "Bred in the Bone," "Their Golden Wedding," "The Passing of a Soul," and "Life's Fitful Fever."

5. ZAN, "Americans in London," *The Criterion*, Sept. 1900, and unbylined syndicated news item, "As Others See Us," British and Australian newspapers, Oct. and Nov. 1900.

6. *Soul*; ZAN, "Dealing with London Editors," *Writer*, Sept. 1902.

7. MCJ; JWT; QPL; ZAN, "Tea in the Latin Quarter," *Criterion*, Dec. 30, 1899; "The Carved Initials," copyrighted 1900, syndicated; "Influence of President's Death," *Eagle*, Sept. 29, 1901; "A Free Show," *Argosy*, Feb. 1908.

8. TES 13 (1911); QPL; ZAN, "A Cheerful Liar," "The Girl from Omaha," "A Fair Hobgoblin," copyrighted 1900, syndicated; "A Little Penance," *Frank Leslie's Monthly*, June 1901.

9. MCJ; TES 3 (1909); *Soul*; ZAN, "Wichitans in Paris," *Eagle*, Nov. 10, 1899; "Cheerful Liar."

10. ZAN, "The Carved Initials," copyrighted 1900, syndicated.

11. ZAN, "A Christmas Truce," copyrighted 1900, syndicated; "Her Paris Gloves," syndicated 1902. Real-life William Dodsworth remained a Paris expat and died there in 1943.

12. MCJ (which erroneously dates Zoe's fall 1900 Riviera and Italy trip to spring 1900); no headline, *Eagle*, Sept. 14, 1900; ZAN, "The Gentleman," copyrighted 1901, syndicated; "A Window in Lausanne," copyrighted 1901, syndicated; "Ferney, Where Voltaire 'Made His Peace with God,'" *NY Press*, March 12, 1905.

13. ZAN, "Wichitans in Paris"; "Good Money and Bad" (syndicated as "Tricks With Money"); *Eagle*, March 8, 1900.

14. ZAN, "A Woman at the Paris Exposition," *Home*, July 1900; "Americans in Paris," *Criterion*, Nov. 1900; "Girl from Omaha," syndicated; "Influence of President's Death," *Eagle*, Sept. 29, 1901; Vance Thompson, "Americans in Paris," *Saturday Evening Post*, Sept. 8, 1900.

## Chapter 9. A Wealthy Silk Merchant, 1900–1901

1. MCJ; "Married in London," *Eagle*, July 15, 1900.

2. The Morris marriage certificate's boardinghouse address was 52 Charleville Road. "S. W. Norris Married," *Beacon*, July 4, 1900.

3. TES 12 (1911); ZAN, "Americans in London," *Criterion*, Sept. 1900; "Wichita Writer in London," *Eagle*, Aug. 12, 1900. Zoe also reported on mausoleums with "snowy domes and gray domes" at Paris's Montmartre cemetery: "A Parisian Instance," *Criterion*, April 1900.

4. TES 2 (1909); ZAN, "The Man in the Chair," "From Dieppe to Newhaven," both copyrighted 1901, syndicated.

5. ZAN, "The Closed Doors," *Thistle*, Nov. 1902; "On the Rim of Manhattan," NYT, May 28, 1905.

6. TES 14 (1911); MCJ; "Zoe Anderson Norris Coming," *Eagle*, Dec. 9, 1900; emails from curator Bram Beelaert, Red Star Line Museum, Antwerp.

## Chapter 10. Sisters of Misery, 1901

1. ZAN, *Home*: "The Coming Home," April 1901; "Out of the Dark," March 1902, illustrated by Jack Bryans. *Vaderland* arrived in NY on Jan. 22, 1901; "Mrs. Z. A. Norris" and "Mrs. Morris" listed in saloon passengers, #4126 and #4127, both "married." Among the other passengers were John Getz, "commissioner of decorations," and Fred Brackett, "disbursing agent" ("Return of World's Fair Officials," *Washington Post*, Jan. 23, 1901). No evidence suggests that stokers died on Zoe's trip.

2. MCJ; 1901: "Personal," *Wichita Star*, Feb. 22; "Harrodsburg," *Kentucky Advocate* (Danville), April 24; "Concerning People," *Danville News*, April 26. In TES (15) 1911, Marion Mills Miller praised Zoe's depiction of the E. 86th Street hospital.

3. *New York Charities Directory* (New York: Charity Organization Society, 1900); T. J. McGillicuddy, "Notes on Some Interesting Cases," *Journal of the American Medical Association*, July 23, 1892.

4. ZAN, "A Literary Harlequin," *Writer*, May 1902.

5. Copyrighted on July 27, 1901, for instance: "The Man in the Chair," "A Window in Lausanne," "Miss Simpkins, Spinster," and "In the Old Steine Road."

6. Francis Henry Allen, reader's report, July 1901, Houghton Mifflin Company correspondence and records, ms no. 9111, Houghton Library, Harvard University, Cambridge, Mass.

7. ZAN, *The Manuscript: Issued Every Month in the Interest of Book-Builders & Book-Buyers*, 1901: "The Telepathy of Manuscripts," May; "The Dog and the Manuscript," Sept.; "The Editor as Friend," Oct.

8. ZAN, "The Picture of Her," *Smart Set*, Dec. 1901.

9. ZAN, "A New Woman," *Vanity Fair*, Sept. 1901. Divorce proceedings Oct. 17, 1895 coverage: "A New Woman's Way," *St. Joseph* (Missouri) *Daily News*; "The 'New Woman,'" *Beacon*.

10. ZAN, "The Hot Winds," *Frank Leslie's Monthly*, Sept. 1901; "The Chimney Sweep," *Ainslee's*, July 1902 (she was paid $30, slightly above her career's average rate).

11. 1901: "Personal," *Daily Register* (Red Bank, NJ), April 3, 1901; "Two Items," *Star of Zion* (Charlotte, NC), Dec. 19; James D. Corrothers, *In Spite of the Handicap: An Autobiography* (New York: George H. Doran Co., 1916).

12. "Hypatia," *Wichita Democrat*, April 4, 1892; "A Former Mattooner Heard From," *Mattoon Gazette*, Oct. 27, 1893; "Woes of One Wichita Author," *Eagle*, May 4, 1902; Konrad Bercovici, *It's the Gypsy in Me* (New York: Prentice-Hall, 1941); "Solution of Problems," *The Literary Digest*, June 18, 1898; Ella Wheeler Wilcox, "Assertion," *Salt Lake Herald*, Oct. 24, 1901. Mrs. Mallon is portrayed as going deaf, and it is not clear if Margaret Lemon suffered from that condition.

13. "Influence of President's Death."

14. Emma Goldman, *Living My Life*, vol. 2 (New York: Alfred Knopf, 1931).

15. ZAN, nearly identical interview unbylined: "Confessions of a Chorus Girl," *NY Sun*, July 7, 1901.

16. Dolly appallingly compares immigrants enjoying one another's company to impoverished southern Blacks, socializing affably while steeped "in uncleanliness, in shiftlessness." Polly Locke describes Europe's poor with similar stereotypes. They are jarring in otherwise compassionate passages, but common in Zoe's time, and so puzzling today—why, while defying so many other

expectations of her time, and befriending Black cultural leaders, did Zoe not shed this terrible legacy of antebellum Kentucky?

## Chapter 11. Threat to Pretty Girl Novelist, 1902

1. MCJ; "City in Brief," *Eagle*, Aug. 30, 1901. She stayed at the Carey hotel, 525 East Douglas Ave.
2. MCJ; "Woes of One Wichita Author," *Eagle*, May 4, 1902. According to Zoe's great-grandniece Linda Rue Allen, elderly Clarence reminisced in Harrodsburg about playing piano in London accompanying the actress Beatrice Tanner, known onstage as Mrs. Patrick Campbell.
3. Divorce records from NJ archives; J. Dempster Carter, "Bryans, Silhouette Artist," *Broadway Magazine*, Dec. 1903.
4. ZAN, "Buying the Hat," syndicated and *Eagle*, Dec. 22, 1901; "Into the Dark," syndicated 1902; "The Mockery of It," *Smart Set*, June 1903; "The Letter She Sent," copyrighted 1904, syndicated.
5. "Books and Men," NYT *Book Review*, Jan. 25, 1902; "Honors an Author," *Bookseller*, Feb. 1902. The party was at Hecker's, 172 Fifth Ave.
6. 1902 reviews and news items: "The Ring of True Metal," *Literary Digest*, Feb. 1; "Books & Writers," *Evening Star* (Washington), Feb. 22; "Phases of Home Life," *Good Housekeeping*, April; "Darkness and Light," *Commercial Advertiser* (NY), Feb. 15; "Recent Fiction," *Northern Christian Advocate* (Syracuse, N.Y.), April 2; "The Color of His Soul," *Courier-Journal* (Louisville), Feb. 1; "A Hero," *Mirror*, Feb. 20; Tudor Jenks, "What the Books Say," *Pearson's*, June; "New Books," *Minneapolis Journal*, Feb. 8; ZAN, "What's in a Publisher's Name?," *Writer*, May 1904.
7. 1902 reviews: "Fiction," *Book News*, March; "Books and Authors," *Living Age*, April 5; "Here & There," *Current Literature*, April; "Current Fiction," *Standard*, July 19. Corrothers, *Handicap*.
8. TES 27 (1913); "Woes."
9. TES 6 (1910); "Woes."
10. 1902: "Authoress to Fight Hero," *Sunday Telegraph* (New York), Feb. 9; "Quarrel Over Book," *Eagle*, Feb. 18; Fairchild, "Thistle Points," *Thistle*, March; Monahan, *Papyrus*, Sept. 1903. Ouida was one of Winstock's own literary idols.
11. 1902: Joseph Edwards, "Edenia Club Jealous Over Squeezed Lemon," *Morning Telegraph* (New York), Feb. 8; "Threat to Pretty Girl Novelist," *Evening World* (New York), Feb. 10; "A Hero," *Mirror*, Feb. 20.
12. "Woes."
13. Wagner College, Staten Island, Edwin Markham papers, Zoe's letter in Bookcase D's binders. Markham had met Margaret Lemon at a Woman's Press Club event.
14. "J. K. Bryans Weds Author of 'Color of His Soul,'" *Morning Telegraph*, March 28, 1902.
15. "Sues for Divorce," *St. Helena Star*, Aug. 3, 1900; *The Tippler's Vow* (New York: Croscup & Sterling, 1901), illustrated by Romanian artist Paleologue and extravagantly priced at $10; "Life," *Medical Mirror*, Oct. 1902; Edwin Emerson, "Lee Fairchild," *Scroll of Phi Delta Theta*, May 1910. Fairchild was briefly married to Anna Ashim, a widowed storekeeper in California—they tied the knot on impulse during a steamship voyage. *The Thistle* presciently published a poem about falling leaves by a recent Lombard grad named Charles (later Carl) Sandburg: *Ever the Winds of Chance* (Urbana and Chicago, IL: Univ. of Illinois Press, 1983).

16. "Mrs. White Goes for the Head," *Butte Miner*, April 6, 1896; "Morton Club's Meeting," *Brooklyn Eagle*, Nov. 1, 1900; "Levi P. Morton Club," *Brooklyn Times*, Nov. 1, 1900; "Woman Will Combat Bryan's Arguments," *Evening World*, Jan. 29, 1901; Grace Miller White, *A Harmless Revolution* (New York: J. S. Ogilvie, 1902). Grace went on to publish newspaper columns about economics, play novelizations, and romance novels. The film based on her novel *Tess of the Storm Country*, set in an impoverished Ithaca fishing community, was the actress Mary Pickford's first major movie role.

17. ZAN, *Mirror*: "The Strange Faces," March 27, 1902; "Cappie's Boy," Jan. 8, 1903; "Thompson," *Kentucky Advocate* (Danville), May 7, 1900; "Local Round-Up," *Harrodsburg Herald*, April 3, 1902; Sept. 1909 letter to Clarence Chelf, NDC; TKCS; John J. McAfee, *Kentucky Politicians* (Louisville, KY: Courier-Journal, 1886); emails from Harvard University Archives; conversation with Helen Dedman, former Beaumont Inn owner. Zoe remained on civil terms with siblings Harry, Nannie, Jessie, Nettie and Pickett (or at least did not roast them in print).

18. TES 6 (1910); JWT; "Affinities!," *Washington Times Magazine*, Dec. 1, 1907.

19. ZAN 1902: "A Literary Harlequin," *Writer*, May; "A Woman Friend," *Smart Set*, Oct.; "The Closed Doors," *Thistle*, Nov.; "Her Ultimate Conclusion," *Mirror*, Feb. 12, 1903; "A Household Hobgoblin," *Smart Set*, Oct. 1903; "In Andalusia," *Book-Lover*, April 1904; "My Little Syndicate," unpublished typescript, NDC. Syndicated 1902 and 1903: "Her Beau from Hartford," "The Ways of Women," "Wrinkles or No Wrinkles," "The Perfect Man," "The Cake Walk," "The Loneliness Of It," "The Boat," "The Yacht." Among her new outlets was *Mirror* spinoff *Valley Magazine*; *Woman's Home Companion* (edited by former *Home* editor Arthur Vance), and Chicago-based syndicator Daily Story Publishing Co.

20. TES 11 (1910); ZAN, *American Agriculturist*, 1902: "The Little Windowpanes," Feb. 8; "A Metropolitan Maid," June 14 and 21, July 5; "The Cinderella of the Flat," copyrighted 1904, syndicated. The boardinghouse colleague's sexual menacing was described in TES but not in *Agriculturist*.

## Chapter 12. The Useless Tears, 1902–1903

1. TES 27 (1913); 1902 reviews: "Fiction," *NY Sun*, Aug. 16; "Fiction New This Week," *Detroit Free Press*, Sept. 13; "Books of the Hour," *Saint Paul Globe*, Sept. 13; "New Books," *Nebraska State Journal* (Lincoln), Sept. 15; Fairchild, *Thistle*, Sept.; William H. Hills, "Book Reviews," *Writer*, Oct.; no headline, *Mirror*, Dec. 18; 1903: "Some Minor Fiction," *Chicago Tribune*, Feb. 14; "New Publications," *Argonaut* (San Francisco), May 11; ZAN, "Sun Roasted Her Novel," *Eagle*, Sept. 14, 1902; "Literary Chat," *NY World*, Dec. 13, 1902.

2. TES 14 (1911); 1902: "'Zoe Norris' Greets Her Son," *Beacon*, Dec. 12; *Eagle*: "Mrs. Bryans Visiting," Dec. 13; "Electricity in Wichita," Dec. 21.

3. ZAN, "The Only Thing Worth While," *Valley Magazine*, March 1903, syndicated.

4. The Morrises arrived March 9, 1903, on the *Philadelphia*; Harold's $200 and Zoe's 78 W. 82nd St. address are on ship manifest.

5. MCJ; ZAN, "A Talk with Mark Twain's Cat," NYT, April 9, 1905.

6. TES 16 (1911); ZAN, 1903: "A Household Hobgoblin," *Smart Set*, Oct.; "The Parting of the Ways," *Valley Magazine*, Oct.; ZAN, 1904: "The Useless Tears," *Smart Set*, April; "Through the Glass Door," *New Age*, Oct.; "The Trial Separation," *Bohemian*, Jan. 1908; "The Chimney Corner," unpublished typescript copyrighted 1910 (Library of Congress, D 20491). Re divorce: emails from NYC archivists.

7. TES 7 (1910), 14 (1911), 21 (1912).
8. "Book Reviews," *Bookseller*, Sept. 1903; "His Soul Was Black," *Cleveland Leader*, Sept. 6, 1903; "The Color of His Soul," *Washington Post*, Aug. 10, 1903; "Color of His Soul" in *NY Herald*, March 8, 1902 and July 11, 1903; "What's in a Publisher's Name?" *Writer*, May 1904.
9. TES 4 (1909), 6 (1910).

## Chapter 13. On the Rim of Manhattan, 1904–1906

1. ZAN, "A Free Lance Symposium," *Bookman*, Sept. 1907; NYU Fales Library, Pleiades Club collection MSS.035, series III, correspondence, box 2, ZAN undated note to club secretary Howard Neiman: "I expect to bring one fellow on Saturday and hope to bring two—Thank you for remembering me."
2. 22 and 38 East 21st and 35 West 21st appear in documents. ZAN, "When the Cows Come Home," *New Age*, April 1906; "Born Again," *People's*, April 1908; "Building the House," *Success*, Oct. 1907.
3. MCJ; ZAN, "The Mice," *People's*, May 1907.
4. ZAN, *NY Press*: "The Peeping Turtles" (also syndicated), May 28, 1905; "The Little Girl in White," June 17, 1906.
5. ZAN's syndicated and sometimes copyrighted circa-1904 stories include "Not Yet," "The Tramp on the Park Bench," "The Marquis Brand," "The Cinderella of the Flat," "The Twin Brothers," and "The Princess"; also "Her Lucky Suit," *New Age*, Dec. 1904, in which Froken, the tall Swedish stenographer from Paris, found work as a library researcher in New York and then married her handsome boss.
6. Herbert R. Gibbs (also initialed by George Harrison Mifflin and William Stone Booth), reader's report, Sept. 15, 1904, Houghton Mifflin Company correspondence and records, ms no. A1340, Houghton Library, Harvard University.
7. Harry's reminiscences: "Market Letter," *Salina Herald*, Aug. 9, 1906; he spent his last years estranged from family in a Kansas veterans' home. A. B. Rue, *Historical Sketch of Mercer County, KY* (Harrodsburg, KY, 1904) for Louisiana Purchase Exposition, where Jessie Anderson Rue exhibited paintings at the "New Kentucky Home," complete with bluegrass lawn. Among researchers focused on Andersons: teacher and historian Mary Breckinridge, assigned by Alexander Graham Bell to document Zoe's uncle Robert's school for deaf children, unpublished notes at A. G. Bell Association, Washington, D.C. I am grateful to Spencer's descendants Lynda Norris and Dixie Norris Koontz for their insights. Ruth had no children with her second husband, Howard Gleason, who died of tuberculosis two years after they married in 1911.
8. TES 13 (1911); among her celebrity profiles (some unbylined originally but bylined in syndication or mentioned in later writings) and reflections on the genre: NYT 1905: "What Women Have Done in the Field of Invention," Feb. 5; "Stained-Glass Workers," March 21 (profile of French-born Gabriel Chênes, a La Farge and Tiffany protégé); "A Woman 'Promoter' in Action," March 26 (Ella Reader's stories do not hold water, per George Robb's *Ladies of the Ticker*, University of Ill. Press, 2017); "'Bat' Masterson Vindicated," April 2; "A Talk with Mark Twain's Cat," April 9; "Oscar Hammerstein Getting Ready," May 14. *Sun*, 1904: "Does New York Keep Sunday?," May 8 (interviewees: clergymen Charles H. Parkhurst, George C. Lorimer, and George Roe Van De Water; lawyers Clark Bell, John J. Delaney, J. L. Sullivan, William T. Jerome), "Mrs. Lease is Seen at Home," Sept. 25; 1905: "New York's Roof Gardens," July 9; "Mourns His Lost Angels," Oct. 15; "Angels in Stained Glass," Nov. 19 (interviewees included Chênes; Tiffany staffer Bond Thomas, who became a glassworkers' union leader; and

a caretaker at Church of the Ascension in Greenwich Village); "Paul Nocquet Talks of Art and Balloons," Feb. 25, 1906. *NY Press* 1905: "Would a Jury of Women Acquit 'Nan' Patterson?," April 30; "What Belmont Thinks of the Subway," June 18; *Bohemian:* "The Common-or-Garden Reporter," Dec. 1906; "The Omar of the Persian Kitten," Jan. 1907. Also "The Penny-a-Liner," *Argosy*, Nov. 1907, later syndicated. Unbylined features by a newspaperwoman with Zoe's self-deprecation and arch tone, which cannot be definitively attributed: NYT 1905, attempted interview of Chinatown gangster Mock Duck (April 2), profile of circus cat wrangler Louise Morelli (June 18); *Sun*, "Causes of the Bachelor," March 5, 1899. Articles lauding Zoe as profiler include "Lady Gay," *Morning Telegraph* (NY), Feb. 2, 1906; "A Sad, Sad Story," *Hutchinson News* (KS), Feb. 15, 1906. Isabel Lyons: June 28, 1905 diary entry.

9. ZAN, "Heard Between Slaps," syndicated 1905; NYT: "Decoration Day," June 26, 1904; "One Woman's Impression," April 16, 1905; "What a Woman Saw," April 30, 1905.

10. TES 4, 5 (1909); ZAN, NYT, 1905: "On the Rim" series, May 14 and 28, June 4 and 11; "Land of Wooden Indians," June 18; "A Night's Lodging at the Deep Sea Hotel," *NY Sun*, March 12, 1905.

11. ZAN 1905: NYT: "Life As You See It in New York's 'Goosetown,'" June 25; "'Seeing Manhattan," July 2 and 9; also "West Side Urchins," *NY Press*, March 26 (Zoe met blind Annie Ortega through the philanthropist Cynthia Alden).

12. ZAN, "No Bread Riot" (syndicated Aug. 1905); *NY Press*: "Shopping in Little Syria," July 23, 1905; "The Woman Who Went to Chinatown," Nov. 11, 1906 (she visited restaurants at 24 Pell St., which today serves excellent vegetarian dim sum, and 18 Mott St.); "The Smoke of the Nargileh," c. 1904–1905, unpublished typescript in NDC (mailing address: 22 E. 21st St.).

13. ZAN, "Orphans Sign Plea to Land," *NY Sun*, Aug. 28, 1906; "Case of a Little Jeweller," *NY Sun*, Sept. 23, 1906; "The Common-or-Garden Reporter," *Bohemian*, Dec. 1906; "The Little Jeweler," *People's*, Aug. 1907; "The Replica," *Pearson's*, June 1910. Among the offices where she inquired about the jeweler's post-Ellis Island fate: Industrial Removal Office (174 Second Ave.), United Hebrew Charities (356 Second Ave., 149 Rivington St.), and *Forward* newspaper. Re Harkavy: "The Ellis Island Gateway," *Sunday State Journal* (Lincoln, NB), March 24, 1907.

14. ZAN, *NY Sun* 1905 interviews: hippo, June 25 (baby Petey would go unsold and remain in New York); rhino, July 2; alligator, July 23; giraffe, July 30; wolf, Aug. 6; clam, Aug. 13; tortoise, Aug. 20; seal, Aug. 27; Arctic sled dog, Sept. 3; serpent, Sept. 17; stork, Sept. 24; elephant, Oct. 1; hound, Oct. 8.

15. ZAN, *Brooklyn Life* 1905: "Love's Mask," Feb. 11; "The Blessed Sleep," March 11; "The Knout of Pain," March 18; "The Poem About Her," July 15.

## Chapter 14. Those Were Hungry Days, 1906–1907

1. "Personal," *Harrodsburg Herald*, July 25, 1907; ZAN, "The Japanese Kimono," *People's*, June 1908; TES 7 (1910); Columbia RBML, Woman's Press Club of New York City, Box 11, 1908–1909 directory; "Storage," *NY Tribune*, Nov. 21 and 28, 1906. The storage unit was on West 90th St. at Amsterdam Ave.

2. *Courier-Journal*, 1906: "Mrs. Cardwell Suspended," June 1; "Mrs. Cardwell Exonerated," July 27; NARA Hitchcock files 7269080. Nannie's defenders included the Kentucky politician William Bradley, one of Jessie Anderson Rue's portrait sitters.

3. TES 3, 5 (1909), 13 (1911), 22 (1912); "The Way of the Wind," *Kansas City Star*, Nov. 5, 1911.

4. TES 5 (1909), 7 (1910), 13 (1911); ZAN, "Celebrating the New Year," *NY Sun*, Sept. 21, 1906; "The Happy Family," *Bohemian*, Aug. 1907. Deportees she named included Jacob Salomon and Ahron Nachimsohn. The "doctor" was probably Lee Kaufer Frankel, a charity executive with a chemistry PhD.

5. TES 2 (1909), 13 (1911), 26 (1913); Ullman, probably ghostwritten by Zoe: "A Day with Santa Claus" and "Christmas of the Down and Out," syndicated Dec. 1907.

6. TES 5 (1909); ZAN, "The Bread Line at Close Range," NYT, Feb. 16, 1908.

7. "Beset by Bills and Lawsuits," *NY Press*, Jan. 4, 1908.

8. ZAN, "A Shattered Ideal," *Ladies' World*, June 1897, recycled for syndication as "The Little Laundress"; "A Household Hobgoblin," *Smart Set*, Oct. 1903, recycled as "Hunting a Flat"; "His Younger Brother," *Smart Set*, Jan. 1904, reappeared 1909.

9. ZAN: "The Bird Imitator," *Bohemian*, Nov. 1907; "The Girandoles," *People's*, Dec. 1907; "Gwendolin's Histrionic Talent," *Munsey's*, July 1908; "The Disturbing Element," *10 Story Book*, Aug. 1908; *Argosy*, 1908: "A Case of Chilled Cupid," Jan.; "A Free Show," Feb. (heavily trimmed for syndication); "A Shuffle in Flowers," April; "To Please the Prince," July; "Bad for the Boon Companions," Aug.; "Wives of a Mormon Elder," *10 Story Book*, Jan. 1909; "Barnet's Second Wife," syndicated 1909.

10. ZAN, *People's*: "The Little Jeweler," Aug. 1907; *Bohemian*, 1908: "The Cross," March; "Born Again," April. Per Alexander Harkavy, *Memorial of Bella Harkavy* (1931), in 1884, jilted teenage Bella had attempted suicide by leaping off a Manhattan pier, and then he proposed to her after teaching her English and nursing her back to health.

11. TES 11 (1910); ZAN, "Building the House," *Success*, Oct. 1907.

12. TES 17 (1910).

## Chapter 15. That Great Uncertain Chasm, 1907–1909

1. "Private Sales Market," *Real Estate Record and Guide*, Sept. 12, 1908. The building was designed by prolific Russian-born architect Michael Bernstein and commissioned by Shaff & Silberman, cloak makers.

2. TES 11, 14 (1911).

3. Kate Masterson, "New York's Latin Quarter," NYT, July 21, 1912.

4. TES 3 (1909); *The Long Day* (Century Co.).

5. TES 10 (1910), 13 (1911), 21 (1912).

6. TES 14 (1911), 19 (1912), 26 (1913); ZAN, *Everybody's*: "The Vampire of the Slums," April 1908; "Among the Chimneys," Sept. 1909.

7. TES 12 (1911); ZAN, "Vampire"; "The Tiny Window Washers," *NY Press*, July 14, 1907.

8. TES 1, 2 (1909), 8 (1910); ZAN, "The Line-Up Man," syndicated 1907.

9. TES 2, 3 (1909); ZAN, "Yom Kippur," *People's*, Jan. 1909 (fictionalizing a synagogue at Ave. A and 7th St., probably Beth Hamedrash at 242 E. 7th).

10. ZAN, "The Kidnaping of Poggioreale's Twins," *Munsey's*, April 1908 (syndicated through the late 1920s).

11. TES 6 (1910).

12. TES 1, 2, 3 (1909), 7 (1910), 18, 21 (1912); "Mr. and Mrs. Hudson Maxim Entertain," NYT, March 10, 1908; ZAN, "The Blond Lunatic," *Argosy*, Sept. 1908. Zoe was probably Oberhardt's guest; she left no other trace in Maxim's voluminous papers (NY Public Library). Her piano came from the dealer George Schleicher on West 14th Street.

13. TES 11 (1910); ZAN, "The Japanese Kimono," *People's*, June 1908.
14. TES 11 (1910); ZAN, "A Phone Message to Santa Claus," syndicated 1907. Clarence called the Christmas story "very dear to me" in a 1924 inscription on an *East Side* issue in a private collection.
15. ZAN, "My Search for Aid at the Y.W.C.A.," *NY Press*, Sept. 27, 1908; the shelter was at 6 Rivington St.
16. TES 8 (1910); MCJ; "Sale of Tags," *Standard Union* (Brooklyn), Dec. 19, 1908 (the charity was headed by Cynthia Alden); ZAN, "The Happy Hunting-Ground," *People's*, Nov. 1908.
17. TES 5 (1909).

## Chapter 16. Dear Children, 1909–1910

1. TES 4 (1909).
2. TES 1 (1909), 21 (1912).
3. Kirsten MacLeod, *American Little Magazines of the Fin de Siècle* (University of Toronto Press, 2018).
4. MCJ. TES 9 (1910) has a mark from her only identifiable printer, short-lived Monarch Press, 38 Cooper Square.
5. TES 1 (1909), 11 (1910).
6. She appallingly prefaced porter with the n-word.
7. The 1880s building, originally used for hospital storage, was at 243 Bowery.
8. TES 1 (1909), 9 (1910), 14 (1911).
9. Oberhardt's pre-*East Side* images of Lower East Siders include "The Ghetto Market," *Leslie's Weekly*, Nov. 30, 1905; "Turning Children into Dollars," *Success*, Dec. 1905.
10. Oberhardt descendants donated his archive, including *East Side* sketches and lithographs, to New-York Historical Society. I am grateful to historians Paul Shaw and Irene Tichenor for insights into the era's printing methods. One *East Side* cover depicts the interior of the synagogue at 60 Rivington St., from the vantage point of the two-tiered women's galleries. Anyone reading this footnote who gains me access to the building through its owner, the artist Hale Gurland, gets a free inscribed copy of this book.
11. TES 4 (1909), 28 (1913); "Has Own Magazine," *Eagle*, June 14, 1911; "The Way of the Wind," *Kansas City Star*, November 5, 1911; Calvert, "Way Side Chats," *Open Road*, March–April 1913.
12. TES 1 (1909), 6 (1910), 21 (1912); MacLeod; "G. Washington's Hatchet," *NY Press*, Feb. 23, 1911.
13. TES 2 (1909); "Grave to Gay," *Buffalo Evening News*, March 17, 1909; "Troubles of the Push-Cart Man," *San Francisco Examiner*, Aug. 15, 1909.
14. "Mrs. Norris Writes About Clipping Bureaus," *Eagle*, April 11, 1909. She visited Henry Romeike company; its tags are in NDC.
15. TES 2 (1909); Stanford University, David Starr Jordan papers, SC 58 Series I-A 65–628, 1909, Dec. 20–31 & n.d.; Patricia Dunlavy Valenti, *To Myself a Stranger: A Biography of Rose Hawthorne Lathrop* (LSU Press, 1999).
16. TES 2 (1909); NDC has original profile portrait.
17. TES 4 (1909), 13 (1911).
18. Doubleday book: Luther Halsey Gulick's *The Efficient Life*. Gertrude Tubby masculinized her name to G. O. Tubby and Donna Cole went by D.R.C.

19. TES 2, 5 (1909), 7, 8 (1910), 12 (1911), 20 (1912), 24 (1913).
20. TES 3 (1909), 22 (1912); MacLeod; JWT; Bruce White, *Elbert Hubbard's The Philistine* (University Press of America, 1989).
21. Zoe's photos also appeared with her newspaper feature on "little fathers," sallow and underfed, ducking from her camera while pushing strollers full of "rosier and healthier" infant siblings: "With The Little Fathers," *Chicago Examiner*, Sept. 5, 1909.
22. TES 2 (1909); ZAN, "The Long Gray Sock," *Cosmopolitan*, Jan. 1910; "The Cabaret Singer," TES 21 (1912), syndicated as "At the Cabaret Show"; "His Little Tan Shoes," *Harper's Weekly*, Aug. 9, 1913.
23. TES 2 (1909), 7 (1910); *Current Literature*, Sept. 1909; *Boston Cooking-School Magazine*, Nov. 1909.
24. TES 6 (1910); Bruce St. John, ed., *New York Scene: 1906–1913 / John Sloan* (New Brunswick, N.J.: Transaction Publishers, 2013); Lemon, "Socialists and the Sex Question," *International Socialist Review*, Feb. 1909; Konrad Bercovici, *It's the Gypsy in Me* (New York: Prentice-Hall, 1941). Sloan was a friend of Albert Ullman, who had allowed Zoe to use him as a pseudonym. Fenno took out an ad for a crime novel in *The East Side*.
25. TES 3, 5 (1909), 6, 7, 8 (1910), 14, 16 (1911), 28 (1913).
26. TES 4, 5 (1909).
27. TES 4 (1909), 7 (1910), 14 (1911), 19 (1912), 27 (1913).
28. TES 10 (1910), 29 (1914); "Noted Washington Society Women," *Peterson's*, Aug. 1892; "Beauty Parlor Fire Mars Beauty," NYT, Sept. 18, 1910.
29. "Marriages," *Harrodsburg Herald*, July 16, 1909; ZAN, Sept. 1909 letter to Clarence Chelf, NDC; "Death's Touch on Lovely Brow" *Courier-Journal*, Sept. 9, 1909; *Harrodsburg Herald*, Sept. 10, 1909. Mattie's grave is unmarked.
30. MCJ.
31. TES 7 (1910), 14 (1911), 17 (1912), 28 (1913).
32. TES 5 (1909), 12 (1911), 17 (1912), 25, 26 (1913); Jordan, *The Heredity of Richard Roe* (Boston, MA: American Unitarian Association, 1911). Zoe's 1911 letter requesting $10: Stanford's Jordan papers, SC 58 Series I-A 71–673, 1911, Feb. 25–28 & n.d.
33. MacLeod; Monahan, *Papyrus* ads.
34. NDC.
35. Building is extant at 891 Amsterdam Avenue.
36. According to typewriting historian Richard Polt, Zoe probably used a Yost machine.
37. TES 6, 7 (1910); "Journals and Books," *Medico-legal Journal*, March 1910.

## Chapter 17. A Raggeder Edge than We, 1910–1913

1. TES 7, 9 (1910), 19 (1912), 25 (1913). Re Welch, for instance *Demorest's*, 1896: "The Fury of the Winds," Aug.; "Regenerating the Slums," Oct. Lampton was a cousin of Mark Twain's mother Jane Lampton Clemens. The K in Zoe's time had no Ku Klux Klan implications, it was meant as a self-mockingly childish, memorable misspelling. Other groups of the time called themselves, for instance, the Klef Klub Orchestra and the Kodak Klub, and the cartoon character Krazy Kat debuted in 1913.
2. TES 7 (1910), 15 (1911), 18 (1912); Toler, "Saw Wichita Authoress," *Eagle*, July 17, 1910. Oberhardt's invitation is at N-YHS.
3. Fred Millar, "Club Life," *Smart Set*, Dec. 1911.

4. "Mild Goldman Talk," NYT, May 25, 1909; "Race Problem," *NY Tribune*, March 1, 1910; "Man's Inhumanity," *Medico-Pharmaceutical Critic & Guide*, Dec. 1911; "Hoodoo 13," *Brooklyn Eagle*, June 14, 1913.

5. "Is Love Really," *Courier-Journal*, March 4, 1917; Elizabeth Towne, "The Hungry Club," *Nautilus*, Dec. 1908; Norman, "Ragged Edgers," syndicated 1913. Hungry Club met at Hotel Flanders near Times Square.

6. TES 22 (1912); ZAN, "A Dinner for the Homeless," NYT, Nov. 19, 1913.

7. "Lampton Dodged," NYT, Dec. 2, 1910; "Col. Lampton," *Winchester News* (KY), Dec. 8, 1910.

8. TES 12, 15 (1911), 17 (1912); "Ferdinand P. Earle," *Orange County Times-Press*, March 21, 1911; "City Social Notes," NYT, Feb. 11, 1912; "Ardeen, Uplift Man," *NY Tribune*, April 11, 1913.

9. TES 9 (1910), 18, 19 (1912); "Woman's Suffrage," *NY Press*, April 6, 1910 (speakers included the Austrian-born sisters Henrietta and Anna Mercy, who had endured politicians' taunts); "It Is a Wise Child," Healy news item, syndicated June 1910; "Masked Actress," *NY Sun*, Jan. 10, 1913. Mabel Herbert Urner, *The Journal of a Neglected Wife* (New York: B. W. Dodge & Co., 1909); Leita and Owen Kildare, *Such a Woman* (New York: G. W. Dillingham Co., 1911).

10. TES 8 (1910), 12 (1911); Rihani typescript, "Dear Ragged Edgers," NC State University, Moise A. Khayrallah Center for Lebanese Diaspora Studies, Rihani2018AR39_440. NY Press Club plot, Cypress Hills Cemetery, Brooklyn.

11. TES 8, 11 (1910), 15 (1911), 18, 20, 21, 22 (1912), 24, 26, 27, 28 (1913). Joel Rinaldo, *Rinaldo's Polygeneric Theory: A Treatise on The Beginning and End of Life* (New York, 1910). Galotti's was at 64 West 10th St. Klub favorites in addition to Little Hungary, Joel's and Hofbrau Haus included Italian venues (Moretti's, 51 West 35th St., the Carlos, 25 West 24th St., and Maria's, 121 West 21st St.), Hoffman House's roof garden overlooking Madison Square, the Parisienne, 945 8th Ave., Keens, West 36th St., Brighton Beach Hotel and Reisenweber's Casino (at Brighton Beach).

12. TES 9 (1910); Norman, "Ragged Edgers," syndicated 1913; "'Frisco Sends Us Banana Peel Slide," *Evening World* (NY), April 25, 1913. *The East Side* used "Koon" once as a preface for Harry Huggs's title; he also used the term in his music, and Zoe emphasized in print that he was a composer as well as a musician. Among his copyrighted works were the musical comedies *Coontown Coronation* and *In Beulah Land* and the songs "Spiritual Man," "The Colored Masquerade," and "Jule: A Lover's Declaration." As the Harlem-based historian John Reddick has pointed out, many Black performers, writers, and composers in Zoe's time used the term "coon" to describe themselves, including as a marketing tool to differentiate themselves from white performers in blackface. Huggs's half-brother Abram, known as A. B. Comathiere or DeComathiere, was a prominent actor in plays and movies including works by Oscar Micheaux. For more on Libby Blondell: Hutchins Hapgood, "The Story of a Singing Soubrette," *The Trend*, 1914. Her first husband Ed Blondell fathered the celebrity Joan Blondell with his subsequent wife Katie.

13. TES 10 (1910), 12, 15 (1911), 20, 21 (1912), 23, 24, 26, 28 (1913).

14. 1910: Toler, "Saw Wichita Authoress," *Eagle*, July 17 (Toler's son and sometime collaborator was the actor Sidney Toler, known for playing Charlie Chan); Mrs. P. Adolphus Ragan, "Greetings," *Anaconda Standard* (MT), Oct. 23; *Columbian*, 1911: Henry McHarg Davenport, "Critic's Book Shelf," Jan.; Harris Merton Lyon, "Bo! Hemia," Sept.; 1912: Eleanor Ames (pen name of Louise Hitchcock Puckrin), "Are You an 'Edger?'," March clip in NDC; "George H. M'Adam," *NY Press*, March 7; "Queerest Clubs," *Colorado Springs Gazette*,

Sept. 15; "Comic Artist," *NY Ledger*, Nov. 23; 1913: "Ardeen, Uplift Man," *NY Tribune*, April 11; *NY Sun*: "Masked Actress," Jan. 10; "Ragged Edge Club," Feb. 23.

15. TES 13, 15 (1911), 18, 22 (1912), 25 (1913); "G. Washington's Hatchet," *NY Press*, Feb. 23, 1911; Jan. 18, 1912: "Policeman Shut Out," *NY Sun*; "Diners See 'Turkey Trot'," NYT.

16. TES 18 (1912), 23, 26, 28 (1913).

## Chapter 18. The Best in the Land, 1910–1913

1. TES 8 (1910).
2. TES 17 (1912).
3. TES 13 (1911). United Charities headquarters is extant, divided into micro-offices.
4. TES 25 (1913). She likely visited the charity woodyard at 516 West 28th St.
5. TES 13 (1911).
6. "Uncle" would have been considered more of a familiar title than an insult for a Black man descended from enslaved people in the South, encountering a white fellow Southerner in the North in the 1910s. My insights come partly from a talk by the Kentucky historian Bruce Mundy about the Black craftsman "Uncle" Phil West, who worked at the Shaker community near Harrodsburg. Per 1910 census records, Blacks from Tennessee and Kentucky made up a very small fraction of the population from the South resettled in New York; did that increase the sense of familiarity and shared homesickness for Zoe and the janitor?
7. TES 20 (1912). Zoe visited the homes of Anna Altman, 33 Pike St.; Josie Del Castillo, 155 Cherry St.; Beckie and Gussie Koppelman, 161 Madison St.; Gussie Rosenfeld, 414 E. 16th St.; and Bertha Wendroff, 205 Henry St. She looked in vain for "Anna Goulo" at 437 E. 10th St., which may refer to fire survivor Annie Gullo, 439 E. 12th St., who testified against the Triangle factory owners. It is not clear which victims' families Zoe sought at 257 East 3rd St. (perhaps Fannie Hollander or sisters Rosie and Sarah Brenman) and 747 East 5th St. (perhaps Annie Pack). Zoe never settled on a spelling of Zuscofski or Zuscofsci, and the girl killed was likely Ida Jukofsky, 294 Monroe St.
8. TES 13 (1911), 20, 21 (1912).
9. "Homesick Girls' Haven," *NY Press*, Feb. 20, 1911. The anti-homesickness society was the brainchild of Anita Comfort Brooks, who also ran the Gotham Club. The Little Mothers' Aid Society, 236 Second Ave., one of the charities suspicious of Zoe's clothing gifts, was run by her Woman's Press Club friend, the philanthropist Marie Burns—Zoe had interviewed her in 1905 about the showgirl Nan Patterson's fate.
10. TES 13 (1911), 18, 19 (1912); 1912: "Times Newsboys," *Washington Times*, Feb. 20; ZAN, "Where's the Newsies' Union," NYT, Feb. 4.
11. TES 20, 22 (1912); 1912: "Conserving Administrative Expenses," *Eagle*, Aug. 16; "What One Wichita Woman is Doing," *Beacon*, March 9; Wilcox, "The Charity Trust," syndicated. Wilcox is known for her 1883 poem beginning "Laugh, and the world laughs with you, / Weep, and you weep alone." She battled with a Kentucky Colonel named John Joyce who claimed authorship of those lines, even having them inscribed on his grave marker.
12. TES 8, 10 (1910), 13, 15, 16 (1911), 26 (1913).
13. TES 15 (1911), 19 (1912). The classroom was at the Educational Alliance, 197 East Broadway.
14. TES 10 (1910), 28 (1913).
15. TES 15 (1911), 21 (1912). Her list of bigotries also included her own "scorn of the bullying Irish, and an inherent dislike to the thought of sitting at table with a negro," which

directly contradicted her documented strong friendships (and frequent meals and conversations) with Irish and Black people. Was she trying to be a provocateur, mocking the supposed inherent prejudices expected of small-town Southerners?

16. TES 14 (1911).

17. TES 20 (1912). *NY Herald*, June 5, 1912, reported that Zoe A. Norris owed $74.88 to insurer C. L. Despard.

18. TES 9 (1910), 16 (1911), 18, 22 (1912), 25 (1913).

19. TES 13 (1911), 25 (1913).

20. TES 10 (1910); ZAN, "The Little Cross," *Pearson's*, March 1910. Zoe likely met Ellis Island's young chaplain Rev. Thomas McCandless.

21. TES 11 (1910), 14, 15 (1911), 19, 20, 22 (1912).

22. TES 14 (1911), 17, 20 (1912), 23, 24, 25 (1913); "Because Men Are Stupid," syndicated news, Aug. 8, 1910; Ames, "Edger," March 1912 clipping, NDC.

23. TES 11 (1910), 14 (1911), 19 (1912), 24, 26 (1913). The Italian-born workers had participated in a robbery-murder near the Croton Reservoir in 1911; five accomplices were executed along with the confessed killer.

24. TES 11 (1910). Hearst's *East Side* bound volumes from San Simeon are now at UC Berkeley's Bancroft Library.

25. TES 18, 22 (1912); Taft papers, Library of Congress, series 5, #407, series 6, #1371; NARA 92702966; "Well Known in Danville," *Advocate-Messenger* (Danville, KY), Nov. 28, 1911.

26. TES 11 (1910), 17 (1912), 26 (1913).

27. TES 19, 20 (1912), 26 (1913); ZAN, "The Accident," *Satire*, Oct. 18, 1911; "Family Disturbance Among Publishing Pulitzers," syndicated news May 1912.

28. TES 12, 14 (1911), 17 (1912), 27 (1913). Her c.-1910s resuscitated stories include "The Widow M'Clane" (syndicated 1898), renamed "The Widow's Opinion"; "A Woman Friend" (*Smart Set*, Oct. 1902); "The Tramp on the Park Bench" (syndicated 1903); and "The Science of Captivating" (*Munsey's*, April 1905). *Choice-Bits* was published in Hackensack, NJ, by hardware dealer Daniel Mallett. Among her other freelance outlets was *The Bankers Magazine* (March 1912).

29. TES 7 (1910) 14, 15 (1911), 18, 21, 22 (1912). Brochures survive in N-YHS and JWT. Other brochure blurbs came from the writers and editors Grace Duffie Boylan, Waldemar Kaempffert, Edwin Markham, Kate Masterson, John R. Meader, and Roland Phillips; illustrator Mildred Beardslee; politicians Herman A. Metz and Bird S. Coler; chemistry professor Jacob Rosenbloom; dentist Charles A. Meeker; physician Frederick S. Kolle; lawyers Moses and William Grossman, Arthur L. Fullman and Daniel de Wolf Wever; California businessman C. Beyfuss; M. M. Hansford (possibly the music writer Montville Morris Hansford), May M. Robson (perhaps the actress) and one Frank Solomon.

30. TES 9 (1910), 12 (1911), 26 (1913).

31. His wife, British-born writer and singer Genie Holtzmeyer Rosenfeld, was a Woman's Press Club member, and his brother, Monroe, was a journalist and songwriter.

32. TES 9, 10, 11 (1910), 14 (1911), 17, 18 (1912), 23, 24, 25, 28 (1913); Shores, "The Idler to His Readers," *Idler*, c. 1910; Calvert, "Way Side Chats," *Open Road*, March-April 1913.

33. TES 19 (1912); 1911: MCJ (*Book Chat*); "The East Side," *Kansas City Star*, Sept. 3; NYT *Book Review*: "The East Side," April 2, "Mrs. Norris," Sept. 17; Unity Church, Montclair, NJ, 1912 archives; Ames, "Edger," March 1912 clipping, NDC. I am grateful to Rivka Schiller for translating Dr. Jacob L. Snitzer's *The Last Proof*, the Yiddish play that Zoe attended at David

Kessler's theater on Second Avenue with a Unitarian tour group. NDC has original Hart pastel portrait.

34. TES 15 (1911).

35. TES 19 (1912), 25 (1913). Other blurbs came from Lampton, McAdam, McCardell ("There's no more wind left in the West"), British writer Charles Rideal (suggesting she adapt it into a play), and newspaperwoman Madame Jule de Ryther ("I have always said you are the finest living woman writer").

36. TES 18 (1912); 1911: *Eagle*, "Wichita Woman's New Book" Oct. 11; "Way of the Wind," *Kansas City Star*, Nov. 5; *Eagle* ad, Dec. 28.

37. "Way of the Wind," *Atchison* (KS) *Daily Globe*, Dec. 1, 1911; "Evening Gossip," *Winfield* (KS) *Daily Courier*, Dec. 30, 1911; William Towne, "Anent Books," *Nautilus*, Nov. 1912.

### Chapter 19. Lest They Fade from Affection's Bliss, 1913–1914

1. TES 24 (1913).

2. TES 24, 25 (1913).

3. TES 25, 26, 28 (1913). Goodman: "Disbarred Lawyer's Wife Sues," *Standard Union* (Brooklyn, NY), Aug. 19, 1914; "'Rescued' Wayward," *Brooklyn Eagle*, Aug. 19, 1914. D'Amato: "Impresario of the Masses," *The Delineator*, Oct. 1907; Roberta E. Pearson and William Uricchio, "Corruption, Criminality, and the Nickelodeon," in Henry Jenkins III et al, eds., *Hop on Pop* (Duke University Press, 2002). Murray: "Woman of Wealth, Beauty and Much Eccentricity," *St. Louis Republic*, Sept. 1, 1901; Greg Gillette, "On Hillsborough," cnhillsborough.blogspot.com, March 27, April 3, 2018.

4. JWT; "Six in One," *The Chat* (Brooklyn), Oct. 25, 1913. Townsend also received poems for consideration from Zoe's Texas-based first cousin Florence Anderson Clark, who did not make the final cut.

5. TES 28 (1913). It is not known whether she supplied the information for a listing in John W. Leonard's *Woman's Who's Who of America* (NY: American Commonwealth Co., 1914), which called her a member of her father's church, despite her self-described apostasy.

6. TES 12 (1911), 18 (1912), 26 (1913).

7. TES 8 (1910), 16 (1911), 19, 22 (1912).

8. TES 22 (1912), 26, 27 (1913).

9. TES 26, 27 (1913); 1913: "Here's a Book," *Washington Times*, June 5; Frank Jarrell, "Kansas Folk," *Beacon*, Oct. 20; Winnifred Harper Cooley, "Minneapolis Woman," *Minneapolis Star Tribune*, Dec. 7.

10. TES 21, 22 (1912), 24, 27 (1913).

11. TES 21, 22 (1912), 24, 26, 27 (1913).

12. TES 26, 27, 28 (1913).

13. TES 27, 28 (1913).

14. TES 28 (1913); ZAN, "A Dinner for the Homeless," *NYT*, Nov. 19, 1913; "Ragged Edge Klub," *Brooklyn Eagle*, June 27, 1913. The last Thanksgiving was at Keens.

15. TES 29 (1914); Lampton obit, *NYT*, Feb. 27, 1914.

### Chapter 20. Land of the White Lilies, 1914

1. 1914: "Death Follows Her Obit," *NY Tribune*, Feb. 14; "No Hand Hurried Her End," *Eagle*, Feb. 21.

2. "'Queen of Bohemia' Dies as She Had Predicted," *NY Herald*, Feb. 14, 1914. For insights into Zoe's cause of death, and so very much else, I am grateful to Dr. Martha Pavlakis.

3. 1914: "Warning of Death Norris Tradition," *NY Herald*, Feb. 15; "Ragged Edge Club Loses Its Founder," *Buffalo Sunday Morning News*, Feb. 22; Winnifred Harper Cooley, "Feminism Has Struck New York," *Sunday Tribune* (Minneapolis), Feb. 22; "Her Vision of Death that Came True," *World Magazine*, March 29; "Twinklings," *The Pleiad*, March; Lampton obit, NYT, Feb. 27. Someone tucked Zoe's obit and a clipping of Lampton's poem into NYPL's copy of her fourth bound volume.

4. 1914: "Rests in 'Land of Lilies,'" *Eagle*, Feb. 15; "Mrs. Norris' Body," *Lexington Herald*, Feb. 16.

5. 1914: "Zoe Anderson Norris Dead," *Beacon*, Feb. 14; "Death Dream True," Feb. 15, *Kansas City Journal*; "Warning of Death Norris Tradition," *NY Herald*, Feb. 15; no headline, *Birmingham Age-Herald*, Feb. 20; Cooley, "Feminism Has Struck New York," *Sunday Tribune* (Minneapolis), Feb. 22; "Her Vision of Death," *World Magazine*, March 29; Will Allen Dromgoole, "Song and Story," *Nashville Banner*, April 11.

6. Emails from NYC probate records office; N-YHS.

7. I am grateful to the writer Ann Lewinson for pointing out that Herrlich's funeral parlor was at 100 Ave. A, and the funeral took place at 101 Ave. A. The latter was owned by John Leppig Jr., known as the Mayor of Avenue A.

8. 1914: "Last Goodby to Queen of Bohemia," *NY Herald*, Feb. 18; "Mourners Kneel in the Snow," *NY Sun*, Feb. 18; "Curb Band Plays Her Dirge," *Washington Post*, Feb. 19; "At Spring Hill," *Harrodsburg Leader*, Feb. 21. The German band was likely led by Rudolf Hoering ("Herring" was reported in *NY Herald*).

9. 1914: "Last Goodby," *NY Herald*, Feb. 18; "Her Vision of Death," *World Magazine*, March 29.

10. NDC has condolence cards and Romeike service clippings.

11. "Ragged Edge Club Incorporated," *NY Ledger*, Feb. 28, 1914.

12. *Lexington Herald*, 1914: "Body of Mrs. Joe Anderson Norris," Feb. 20; "Mrs. Anderson's Body," Feb. 21; "Came True," *Harrodsburg Herald*, Feb. 20, 1914; "At Spring Hill," *Harrodsburg Leader*, Feb. 21, 1914. Philip Thompson's 1923 death certificate lists a cause of death as "acute alcoholism."

## Chapter 21. To Break Through the Silence, 1914–2000s

1. JWT. I have bought books inscribed and owned by Zoe from eBay, bookstores, and Jerry Sampson's antiques store in Harrodsburg, Kentucky (he sold me her books by Lafcadio Hearn and Ameen Rihani).

2. "Tango Breaks Up Suffrage Debate," NYT, Feb. 19, 1915; McPike, salesmanship column, *Tobacco Record*, 1919.

3. Guido Bruno, "Mr. Gerhardt's Den," *Pearson's*, Dec. 1918; Charles B. Driscoll, "The World and All," syndicated 1932; Jay A. Gertzman, *Bookleggers and Smuthounds* (UPenn Press, 1999). Frank Munsey's company maintained some posthumous copyright control, syndicating Zoe's 1908 stories into the 1920s, including "Gwendolin's Histrionic Talent," "The Kidnaping of Poggioreale's Twins" and "Bad for the Boon Companions."

4. Tubby and James H. Hyslop, "Premonition," *Journal of the American Society for Psychical Research*, March 1920; Driscoll, "The World and All," syndicated 1932, "New York Day By Day," syndicated 1943; Woodman, *Wichitana 1877–1897* (1948).

5. Corrothers, *In Spite of the Handicap* (New York: George H. Doran Co., 1916).

6. "Walter Pulitzer Sued," *St. Louis Star and Times*, July 8, 1916; "Publisher Is Arrested," *NY Sun*, Sept. 26, 1917. Courtenay Lemon, "Free Speech in the United States," *Pearson's*, Dec. 1916; also Konrad Bercovici, *It's the Gypsy in Me* (New York: Prentice-Hall, 1941). Bryans: *Shadowkids: Pictures and Verses*, 1929; *Shadowkids at Play*, 1930 (both Platt & Munk). He is buried in his family's plot at Bronxville Cemetery.

7. Davenport, "The American Spirit," *Yorkville* (SC) *Enquirer*, Nov. 29, 1918.

8. Rosalie Armistead Higgins, "The Colorful Pep of Mabel Urner's Stories," *Editor & Publisher*, June 11, 1921; Kurt F. Stone, *The Jews of Capitol Hill* (Lanham, MD: Scarecrow Press, 2011).

9. Lyn Fernbach, "Oberhardt's Portraits of Notables," *NY Herald Tribune*, April 1957; Lorianne Oberhardt Kelly, *Obie the Artist* (Hunt Valley, MD: Brown & Ware, 2015). His other portrait sitters included Zoe's grandson Robert Morris in his naval uniform.

10. Max Schwartz obit, NYT, April 5, 1939.

11. O. O. McIntyre, "Chalif, Who Wars on Unclean Dances," syndicated Sept. 1920; Rinaldo, *Psychoanalysis of the "Reformer"* (NY: Lee Publishing, 1921); "Who Owen Kildare 'The Bowery Kipling' Really Was," syndicated 1926. Zoe's other friends turned real estate brokers included the poet Francesca Spaulding.

12. 1918: "A New Translation," *Christian Standard*, May 11; "Books," *Christian Century*, Aug. 15. Standard Publishing Co. released the book. Emails from British Library curator Peter Toth; codexsinaiticus.org.

13. Ann Morris, "In Loving Memory," *Abbot Courant* (Abbot Academy, Andover, Mass.), May 1959. Re the admiral's wartime service: Barbara Brooks Tomblin, *With Utmost Spirit: Allied Naval Operations in the Mediterranean, 1942–1945* (University Press of Kentucky, 2004).

14. Zoe's sister Jessie Rue painted a portrait of the Shaker community's last believer, Sister Mary Settles, a feisty suffragist.

15. Wedding announcements for Robert and Adelia's daughters Patricia, Barbara, and Ann Morris are the last known published references to Harold Morris.

16. Mary published Zoe's unpublished story, "They Too" (Harrodsburg Herald, 1989), set at the Shakers' Pleasant Hill, as a pamphlet with illustrations of the temporary Shaker couple who clandestinely embraced by moonlight at the riverbanks where Zoe caught poison ivy.

17. NDC; Carnegie Hall concert program, Dec. 7, 1964; Ronald L. Filippelli, "Author's Query," NYT, Oct. 31, 1971, and 1973 letter, NDC; Susanne Britt Craddock, "New York Woman is Inspiration," *Harrodsburg Herald*, June 2, 1983; Jo Witt, "Harrodsburg woman hopes to provide showcase," *Advocate-Messenger* (Danville, KY), Feb. 5, 1984; Rosalind Turner, "They Too," *Harrodsburg Herald*, Oct. 12, 1989; NDC's Phyllis Campbell 1991 typescript profile of MCJ; emails and conversations with Anna Armstrong. Mary's collaborator on *Zoe*, Loretta Randall Sharp, a Mormon poet, did not reply to my messages. The attempted anthologist Ronald Filippelli told me that he did not remember his 1970s proposal.

18. David Moss, "Bibliography," *Contact*, May 1932; Swann Galleries auction catalog, March 8, 1973; *Religious Books, 1876–1982* (New York: R. R. Bowker, 1983), which also lists Pickett Timmins' 1918 edition of HTA's New Testament translation; Lomazow, *American Periodicals: A Collector's Manual and Reference Guide* (West Orange, NJ: 1996); Gerda Taranow, *The Bernhardt Hamlet* (New York: Peter Lang, 1996); Alice Fahs, *Out on Assignment: Newspaper Women and the Making of Modern Public Space* (Chapel Hill: University of North Carolina Press, 2011); Mark Dawidziak, *Mark Twain for Cat Lovers* (New York: Rowman & Littlefield, 2016).

## Chapter 22. You Wouldn't Believe What's Going to Happen, 2018 Onward

1. *Harrodsburg Herald*, May 20, 2021.

2. Preserved buildings and interiors from Zoe's time include the Wichita-Sedgwick County Historical Museum (it owns Lewis Academy's 1886 cornerstone), Old Cowtown Museum, Old Sedgwick County Courthouse, Friends University, and Carey House. The last Norris home to vanish was at 626 North Topeka. Spencer's grave is in Maple Grove Cemetery, where Eva Leighton's family and Spencer's Kentucky-born storekeeping successor Ray W. House are interred. I am grateful for insights from the historian James Mason and the historical museum curator Jami Frazier Tracy.

3. I am grateful to Vernon and Phyllis Dolezal (historians and farmers living adjacent to Henrietta Anderson's homestead), Tracy Andringa at Ellsworth County Historical Society, and Kenneth H. Yohn at McPherson College. Kanopolis State Park is on Harry Anderson's land.

4. A. G. Bell Association, Washington, D.C.; George Morris McClure, "An Oral School in Kentucky One Hundred Years Ago," *American Annals of the Deaf*, May 1946. I am grateful to Hopkinsville historians Yvette Holmes and William Turner for archival discoveries, insights and cornfield navigation.

5. I cannot find, in print or digitized, a profile of "Little Zoe," *Book Chat* (NY: Broadway Publishing), Aug.–Sept. 1911. Anyone reading this footnote who finds it gets a free inscribed copy of this book.

6. For Patricia, a Democratic political activist and retired nurse, Zoe's battles for human rights have resonated with her own advocacy efforts for "the poor, the disenfranchised and disadvantaged, and the religiously persecuted," and against "the oppression of women's rights over their own bodies." Jackie traveled for genealogical research: Cheeks graves in California, Henrietta Ducker Anderson's ancestral hamlet, Duckers, in Kentucky, and the British haunts of 17th-century émigrés to Virginia who had "the basic guts it took to step out into the unknown," she told me.

7. Linda heroically researched family history, focusing on her 1940s childhood. Her father Edwin W. ("Skip") Rue and his younger brother Archibald, members of the federalized Kentucky National Guard's Harrodsburg Tankers, were sent to the Philippines. "They were part of a foredoomed holding action against the Japanese. When Bataan finally fell after a courageous defense, they were taken prisoner with 50,000 Filipino and about 12,000 other Americans," she told me. They endured the Death March and years as Japanese POWs. Harrodsburg erected memorials to the Tankers; 29 of the 66 enlistees, including Arch Rue, died in unspeakable conditions. Linda preserved the flowered, ruffled dress she wore as a toddler in 1942 when she was photographed for a *Life* magazine feature about a small town where many Tankers' families "were still waiting to hear if their young men were alive or dead." In 2023, Linda took on another acting assignment, reading a Kentucky-accented summary of Zoe's biography for the soundtrack of the Museum at Eldridge Street's exhibition about female changemakers, *On the Lower East Side: Twenty-Eight Remarkable Woman . . . and One Scoundrel, Portraits by Adrienne Ottenberg*.

8. *Catamaran*, Spring 2022.

9. Wingfield. I own the only complete *East Side* run known in private hands. Princeton University's librarians, bless them, digitized my five 1913–1914 loose issues that no institution had yet posted online.

10. The artist Roni Gross designed the letterpress version and printed it on a Vandercook machine at the Center for Book Arts. "The printing god is being nice to us, for whatever reason

we won't question," she said, as she let me try out the choreography of steps and lever pulls. I asked recipients of the broadside to give money in Zoe's memory to the International Rescue Committee, helping resettle refugees.

11. My exhibition labels pointed out odd coincidences: Zoe's friend Mabel Urner likely visited the Grolier Club, since her book dealer husband, Lathrop Colgate Harper, was a club pillar. The Harpers bequeathed funds to the club that it still draws on. They were donors to NYPL as well—their names are carved in stone on an entry hall wall. Mabel also donated a large embroidery collection to the Metropolitan Museum of Art.

12. My lecture-musicale accompanists were the incomparable Robert Lamont and Gabrielle Lee.

13. 2023 coverage included *Eagle*, Feb. 26; Ann Lewinson, "Meet Zoe Anderson Norris," Hell Gate, Feb. 28; Steven Heller, The Daily Heller, March 7; author's feature, *Fine Books & Collections*, spring; *New Yorker*, April 24–May 1.

14. Of other eateries in spaces where Zoe dined, I recommend Alta, 64 West 10th Street, where Zoe saw a waiter kick a cat (I saw no pets harmed there). Joel's Bohemia, 206 West 41st St., is a depressing, black-walled pub. Pokol, 69 Second Ave., is a grocery store with a pressed-tin ceiling that might have echoed with Edgers' speeches and tunes.

15. Zoe's NYT editor William J. Guard saw Doddy in wartime Paris, "still a decorative feature of Paris life," natty and working for American Express. Guard, *The Soul of Paris* (New York: H. Rogowski, 1914).

# SELECTED BIBLIOGRAPHY

Some secondary sources consulted:

Cockrell, Dale. *Everybody's Doin' It: Sex, Music, and Dance in New York, 1840–1917*. New York: W. W. Norton, 2019.

Evans, Brad. *Ephemeral Bibelots: How an International Fad Buried American Modernism*. Baltimore: Johns Hopkins U. Press, 2019.

Fahs, Alice. *Out on Assignment: Newspaper Women and the Making of Modern Public Space*. Chapel Hill: University of North Carolina Press, 2011.

Golia, Julia. *Newspaper Confessions: A History of Advice Columns in a Pre-Internet Age*. New York: Oxford University Press, 2021.

Guarneri, Julia. *Newsprint Metropolis: City Papers and the Making of Modern Americans*. Chicago: University of Chicago Press, 2017.

Johanningsmeier, Charles. *Fiction and the American Literary Marketplace: The Role of Newspaper Syndicates, 1860–1900*. Cambridge, UK: Cambridge University Press, 1997.

Kroeger, Brooke. *Nellie Bly: Daredevil, Reporter, Feminist*. New York: Crown, 1994.

———. *Undaunted: How Women Changed American Journalism*. New York: Knopf, 2023.

Lomazow, Steven. *Magazines and the American Experience: Highlights from the Collection of Steven Lomazow, M.D.* New York: Grolier Club, 2020.

MacLeod, Kirsten. *American Little Magazines of the Fin de Siècle: Art, Protest, and Cultural Transformation*. Toronto: University of Toronto Press, 2018.

# INDEX

*In this index, "ZAN" refers to Zoe Anderson Norris. Figures are indicated by "f" following page numbers.*

abolitionists, xii, 2, 4, 7, 112, 174, 214, 227
abuse: child sexual abuse, 182, 192; of immigrants on streetcars, 199; lack of punishment for, xxii, 182. *See also* domestic abuse
African Americans. *See* Black Americans
alcohol and alcoholism: inventions related to, 110; Lemon (Courtenay) and, 55, 211; marital problems due to, 43; maternal mortality rates and, 80; Thompson (Philip) and, 97, 207, 262n12; women and, 182. *See also* Prohibition; temperance movement
Alden, Cynthia Westover, 111, 254n11, 256n16
alimony, 54, 148, 163, 181, 193, 221
Allen, Linda Rue (great-grandniece of ZAN), 224, 225, 251n2, 264n7
Altman, Louis and Anna, 174, 259n7
American Indians. *See* Native Americans
American News Company, 144, 175
anarchists, 19, 96, 132, 161, 182
Anderson, Albert (uncle of ZAN), 2, 242n11

Anderson, Ann (aunt of ZAN), 2
Anderson, Anne (cousin of ZAN), 8
Anderson, Benjamin (uncle of ZAN), 2, 8
Anderson, Charles (brother of ZAN), xxvi, 10, 25, 28–29, 200, 221
Anderson, Clarence (half-brother of ZAN), xxv, 1, 6, 7, 15, 96, 200
Anderson, Cornelia Pickett. *See* Timmins, Cornelia Pickett Anderson
Anderson, Edmund, 241n2
Anderson, Garland (great-grandfather of ZAN), 1
Anderson, Henrietta (niece of ZAN), 26
Anderson, Henrietta Ducker (mother of ZAN), xxviiif; death of, xiii, 50–51, 200; at Kansas homestead, 10, 25, 29, 244n7; marriage and children, xxv–xxvi, 1, 3–9; in psychiatric facility, xiii, 36–37, 50; temporary home at Daughters College, 4–5; in ZAN's premonition of imminent death, xiii, 10, 28–29, 200–3
Anderson, Henrietta "Nettie." *See* Cheeks, Henrietta Anderson

269

Anderson, Henry Tompkins (father of ZAN), xxviii*f*; on Catholicism, 59; Codex Sinaiticus translation, 9, 243n25; death and gravesite of, 9, 222; Disciples of Christ and, 3–4, 7, 9; family background, 1–3; marriages and children, xxv–xxvi, 1, 3–9; New Testament translation, 4–5, 51, 66, 133, 212–13, 242n14; premonitions of, 4; temporary home at Daughters College, 4–5; in ZAN's dreams, 9–10, 66

Anderson, Henry Tompkins, Jr. ("Harry," brother of ZAN), xxviii*f*; birth and death of, xxv; Civil War service, 6–7, 26; gambling habit, 27, 36, 203; at Kansas homestead, 7, 10, 25–26, 29, 109, 203, 221; in Kansas veterans' home, 253n7; marriage and children, 7, 25–26; political career, 27; ZAN's relationship with, 252n17

Anderson, Jane (first wife of ZAN's father), xxv, 1, 241n1

Anderson, Jessamine "Jessie." *See* Rue, Jessamine Anderson

Anderson, John (uncle of ZAN), 2

Anderson, Kate (sister-in-law of ZAN), 25

Anderson, Lelia. *See* Trabue, Lelia Anderson

Anderson, Louis (brother of ZAN), xxv, 10, 25, 26, 28–29, 153, 200, 221

Anderson, Louisa (aunt of ZAN), 242n11

Anderson, Lucy. *See* Cheeks, Lucy Anderson

Anderson, Martha (aunt of ZAN), 2–3, 242n7

Anderson, Martha "Mattie." *See* Thompson, Martha Anderson

Anderson, Mary Spilman (sister-in-law of ZAN), 7

Anderson, Nannie. *See* Cardwell, Nannie Anderson

Anderson, Robert (cousin of ZAN), 8

Anderson, Robert (uncle of ZAN), 2–3, 6, 7, 222–23, 242n7, 253n7

Anderson, Sarah Hughes (sister-in-law of ZAN), 7, 25–26, 223–24

Anderson, Stella (niece of ZAN), 25

Anderson, Tabitha (aunt of ZAN), 8

Anderson, William, Jr. (nephew of ZAN), 25

Anderson, William, Sr. (brother of ZAN), xxv, 10, 25, 28, 200

Anthony, Susan B., 41

antisemitism, xx, 107, 119, 120*f*, 122–24, 155

Armstrong, Anna, 217, 219

Arnold, Alma C., 179

Arnold, Libbie. *See* Blondell, Libby Arnold

Astor, John Jacob, VI, 183

Baker, Hallia and Shkigale, 228

Ball, Adelia, 214, 263n15

Ball, Bertha Crosley, 214

Ball, Eustace Hale, 166, 211

Balogh, Alexander, 142, 146, 182

Barnes, Djuna, 211

Barnum, P. T., 42

Baum, L. Frank, 226

Bazus, Baroness de (Mrs. Frank Leslie), 57, 83, 156

Beaumont Inn as location of Daughters College, 214–15, 220

Becker, Gustave, 165, 185

Belasco, David, 150

Bell, Alexander Graham, 222–23, 253n7

Belmont, August, Jr., 111

Belmont, Augusta, 160

Berlin, Irving, 212

Bernhardt, Sarah, 66, 89, 201, 217

Bernstein, Michael, 255n1

Bienaimee, Suze, xix

Birch, James H., 146

Bissell, Joseph, 179

Black Americans: Civil War service of, 6; lynchings of, 58–59, 248n4; as New Yorkers, 174, 177; as pastors, 4, 16, 84; resettlement in Liberia, 4; segregation and, 36, 214. *See also* racism; slavery and enslaved people

Blaine, James, 245n23

Blondell, Ed, 258n12

Blondell, Joan, 258n12

Blondell, Libby Arnold, 37, 165, 197, 205, 212, 226, 258n12

Bly, Nellie, 98
Bohon, George, 247n14
Boone, Daniel, 13
Borglum, Gutzon, 110, 151
Borowsky, Anna, 177
Bosworth, Ella, 168, 205, 210
Boughton, Caroline, 146, 152
Brackett, Fred, 250n1
Bradley, William, 254n2
Breckinridge, Mary, 222–23, 253n7
Brooks, Anita Comfort, 161, 259n9
Brown, Ada (first wife of Jack Bryans), 90, 95
Bryan, William Jennings, 96, 160
Bryans, John Kennedy ("Jack," second husband of ZAN): death and gravesite, 263n6; as illustrator, 88*f*, 90–93, 91*f*, 96, 101, 117, 210; marriages and divorce, 90–92, 95, 103–5, 211
Bunche, Ralph, 212
Burbridge, Stephen Gano, 6
Burns, Marie, 259n9

Cable, George Washington, 247n3
Café Boulevard (New York), 85, 142–43, 155, 158*f*, 160, 164, 202
Callahan, Daniel H., 168, 205
Calvert, Bruce T., 140, 143–44, 155, 175, 185, 186, 212, 217
Cardwell, Henrietta (niece of ZAN), 31, 38, 59
Cardwell, Nannie Anderson (sister of ZAN): birth and death of, xxvi; as customs clerk, 38, 121; at funeral for ZAN, 206; marriage and children, 15, 31, 38; escorting mother to psychiatric hospital, 36; ZAN's relationship with, 252n17
Cardwell, Samuel Creed, Jr. (nephew of ZAN), 38, 248n4
Cardwell, Samuel Creed, Sr. (brother-in-law of ZAN), xxvi, 15, 31, 38, 207
Catholicism: boarding schools and, 59–60, 80; charity organizations and, 173, 228; churches, 75; Nazareth Academy and, 59–60, 60*f*; nuns and, 6, 59, 63, 78*f*, 80–81, 228

celebrity interviews, 27, 43, 109–12, 253–54n8
censorship, 66, 93, 105, 175, 211
Chalif, Louis H., 165, 168, 212
Chandler, Thomas and Mary, 8
charity hospitals, xxii, 78*f*, 79–81, 93, 126–27, 228, 230
Cheeks, Charles Ewing (nephew of ZAN), 27, 28, 224, 244n13
Cheeks, Eglina ("Lena," niece of ZAN), 27
Cheeks, Henrietta Anderson ("Nettie," sister of ZAN), xxv, 9, 27–29, 121, 182–83, 200, 222, 252n17
Cheeks, Lucy Anderson (sister of ZAN), xxv, 7, 9, 19, 27, 28, 200, 222, 244n13
Cheeks, Peter (brother-in-law of ZAN), xxv, 7, 27–28, 183, 244n13
Chelf, Fletcher Creed (son-in-law of ZAN), 135, 153–54, 213
Chelf, Francis (grandson of ZAN), 193
Chelf, Mary Clarence. *See* Jones, Mary Clarence Chelf
Chelf, Mary Clarence Norris Morris (daughter of ZAN): birth and childhood, 28, 37, 53, 221; carriage accident, 44; children of, 78*f*, 79–81, 89, 103, 193; education, 35, 54, 57, 59–60, 60*f*, 248n14; Europe trip with ZAN, 63, 65–69, 71, 73–74, 76–77; marriages and divorce, 73–74, 76–77, 102, 135, 153–54, 249n2; musical abilities, 39, 89, 213, 251n2; at ZAN's funeral and gravesite, 204, 205
Chenoweth, Alice. *See* Gardener, Helen Hamilton
Chicago world's fair (1893), 39, 70, 213
children: in charity hospitals, 80, 81; in immigrant neighborhoods, 114, 131; orphans, 4, 24, 78*f*, 96, 104, 115, 216, 228; sexual abuse of, 182, 192; in slums, 5–6, 67, 151–52; stereotypes of American children, 194; in sweatshops, 143; in tenements, 42, 113, 131, 141; welfare advocacy groups for, 211; ZAN's charitable acts toward, 135, 175–76. *See also* education

272 · INDEX

Chopin, Kate, 94
Civil War: Black recruitment during, 6; Daughters College during, 14; ailments contracted during, 15–16, 27; mass graves for casualties of, 19; memorial events, 112; prisoners during, 6, 8, 244n20; women's activities during, 6. *See also* Confederacy
Clark, Florence Anderson (cousin of ZAN), 15, 243n9, 245n20, 261n4
Clark, James B., 15
Clay Hill mansion (Harrodsburg), 15, 38, 96, 109, 153–54, 178, 207, 220, 224
Clemens, Jane Lampton, 257n1
Cleveland, Grover, 30
Cole, Donna R., 146, 189, 256n18
Cole, Nancy, xiv*f*
Comathiere, Abram, 258n12
Comstock, Anthony, 182
Confederacy: Black Americans targeted by, 6; Lost Cause ideology and, 8, 195; "My Old Kentucky Home" as eulogy for, xii; veterans of, 7, 15–16, 30, 243n9, 247n3
Conversazione, 49, 50, 160
Cook, James M., 245n3
Corday, Charlotte, 29, 245n16
Corrothers, James D., 84, 90, 93, 210, 223
Croly, Jane Cunningham, 57, 246n14
Crook, Ruth. *See* Norris, Ruth Crook

Dali, Salvador, 212
D'Amato, Gaetano, 192
Daudet, Alphonse, 93
Daughters College (Harrodsburg, Kentucky): Beaumont Inn as location of, 214–15, 220; in book on historical sites, 109; in Civil War, 14; costs of attending, 14–15; curriculum at, 16–17; description of, 12*f*, 14; establishment of, 14; homesickness of students, 17–18; name configurations, 242n13; Native American students at, 30, 245n20; rules and regulations, 16, 19, 23; as temporary home to Anderson family, 4–5; ZAN as art teacher at, 30; ZAN as student at, 10, 14–19, 23, 203

Daughters of the American Revolution (DAR), 50, 214
Davenport, Henry McHarg, 186, 211
Davidson, Grace L., 66
Daviess, Maria Thompson, 193, 207, 245n 20
Davis, Mattie Thompson, 152, 183
Davis, Robert Mosby, 242n19
Davis, Walter H., 30
Davis, William, 183
deafness: of Confederate veterans, 15, 243n9; innovative cures for, 202; school for deaf children, 2–3, 7, 222, 253n7
Del Castillo, Josie, 174, 259n7
Dickens, Charles, 94, 95
Disciples of Christ, 3–4, 7, 9, 15, 25, 193, 242n14
discrimination and stereotypes: of American children, 194; of Jewish community, 115; of Native Americans, 70; of Southerners, 176–77; xenophobia, 116, 123, 178, 259–60n15; in ZAN's works, 44, 155, 250–51n16. *See also* antisemitism; racism
Dodsworth, William, 68–69, 229, 249n11
domestic abuse, 13, 24, 27–28, 52, 132, 147, 156, 162, 211
Doyle, Arthur Conan, 105
dreams and nightmares. *See* premonitions and nightmares
Dreiser, Theodore, 94
Driscoll, Charles, 61, 210
Du Bois, W. E. B., 161
Ducker, Henrietta. *See* Anderson, Henrietta Ducker
Ducker, William (uncle of ZAN), 1
Dunbar, Paul Laurence, 94

Earle, Ferdinand Pinney, Jr., 162
*The East Side* (magazine): on adultery, 53–54; advertisements in, ii*f*, 145–47, 210; annual subscription price for, 3; on apostolic misogyny, 76; Armory show review, 190*f*, 191; on Bernhardt, 66; brochures promoting, 184–85, 193, 260n29; criticisms of, 93; establishment

of, 139; format of, 140–41, 147–50; on immigrant poverty, xx, 149; on Jewish community, xix–xx, 115; on male bureaucrats, 38; on marriage, 104, 144, 148, 181; masthead titles, xxii, 141, 154, 225; on Mormons, 125, 163; on motherhood, 25, 148; on Native Americans, 13; on *Sun* firing, 124; Oberhardt's illustrations for, x*f*, 138*f*, 143–45, 150–51, 170*f*, 175, 184, 204; poetry published in, 28, 105, 152, 159; portraits of ZAN in, ii*f*, x*f*, xix, 143, 145, 222; on psychiatric facilities, 36–37; reviews of, 145, 149; on slums, 151–52; subscribers to, 83, 105, 110, 145, 151, 154–56, 159, 184–85; on tenements, 141–42; theater column in, 150, 151; on Triangle Shirtwaist Factory fire (1911), 174–75; on women's employment, 18–19, 54; on xenophobia, 178, 259–60n15; ZAN's prediction of imminent death in, xiii, 29, 30, 201–3; ZAN's writings marketed in, 105, 145, 149–50, 157, 187, 189. *See also* Ragged Edge Klub; undercover reporting

Edison, Thomas, 212

education: in boarding schools, 4, 55, 57, 59–60, 63, 65, 80, 181; for deaf children, 2–3, 7, 222, 253n7; for enslaved people, 4, 16; of Native Americans, 30, 145, 245n20; in one-room schoolhouses, 8; for orphans, 4; at settlement houses, 177. *See also specific institutions*

Edward III (king of England), 1

Eisenhower, Dwight, 212

Elliott, Maxine, 66, 150

Ellis Island, 77, 106*f*, 115–116, 122–23, 126, 143, 163, 180, 260n20

Ellsworth (Kansas), Anderson family in, 10, 25–29, 221–22, 244n7

English, Maude, 35

enslaved people. *See* slavery and enslaved people

eugenics, 155

Ewing, Celeste, 51, 69, 247n7

Ewing, Charles, 244n13

Ewing, Will, 247n7

Exposition Universelle (Paris, 1900), 64*f*, 70–71, 79, 213

Fairchild, Lee, 92, 94–95, 101, 140, 157, 161, 163–64, 251n15

Forbes-Robertson, Beatrice, 163

Foster, Ardeen, 162, 167, 212

Foster, Stephen, xii, 171, 192–94

Francis, Sidney, 2

Frankel, Lee Kaufer, 255n4

Friedmann, Friedrich Franz, 192

Funk & Wagnalls (publisher), 89–90, 92–94, 102, 105, 123, 139, 143, 189, 210

Galotti, Peter, 165

Ganter, J. Carl (great-great-grandson of ZAN), 224

Ganter, Patricia Morris (great-granddaughter of ZAN), 216, 263n15

Gardener, Helen Hamilton (Alice Chenoweth), 57, 183

Garfield, James, 9, 27, 85, 121

Gerhardt, Christian, 168, 205, 210

Getz, John, 250n1

Gleason, Howard, 253n7

Goldfield, Hannah, 227

Goldman, Emma, 86, 161, 182

Goldstein, Jacob, 163

Goodbody, Barbara Morris (great-granddaughter of ZAN), 216, 225, 263n15

Goodbody, Bridget (great-great-granddaughter of ZAN), 225

Goodman, Elias B., 192, 202

Goodman, Lottie, 192, 202, 205

Goodwin, Nat, 66, 150

Gotham Club (New York), 161, 259n9

Graham, Christopher Columbus, 14, 15

Gramm, F. Emil, 196

Grolier Club (New York), xix, 226–27, 265n11

Gross, Roni, 264–65n10

Gruber, Abraham, 155

Guard, William J., 110, 112, 122, 265n15

Gulbrandsen, Anna, 186
Gurland, Hale, 256n10

Hall, Jacquelyn Bean, 223–24, 264n6
Hammerstein, Oscar, 110, 122
Harkavy, Alexander, 116, 122–23, 126
Harper, Lathrop Colgate, 211, 265n11
Harrod, James, 13, 14, 39, 214
Harrodsburg (Kentucky): Clay Hill mansion, 15, 38, 96, 109, 153–54, 178, 207, 220, 224; enslaved people in, 13, 14; establishment of, 13; feuds and gunfights in, 19–20, 30, 118; fire incidents in, 30; Great South Western railway in, 17, 205, 220; mineral springs in, 14, 220; Native Americans and, 13; postwar prosperity in, 15, 69; Ragged Edge Community Theatre in, 208f, 216, 219; ZAN's birth and childhood in, 4–9, 15, 220; ZAN's gravesite in, 20, 205–7, 206f. *See also* Daughters College
Hart, James McDougal, 29, 35, 187
Hart, Mary Theresa, 187
Hawes, Jane Buckner. *See* Anderson, Jane
Hawthorne, Nathaniel, 145
Healy, David, 163, 204
Hearst, William Randolph, 182, 260n24
Herford, Oliver, 111
Herrlich, John von, 49, 52, 59, 155, 185, 204
Herrlich, Philip, 204, 262n7
Herrman, Esther, 155
Herron, George, Mary, Carrie Rand, 85, 92–94, 105
Hoering, Rudolf, 262n8
homelessness, 4, 46, 62, 81, 87, 172–73, 176
homesickness: anti-homesickness society, 175, 259n9; at Daughters College, 17–18; in ZAN's works, 68, 71, 75, 79
Hopkins, Mary Sargent, 205
House, Ray W., 62, 264n2
Howlett, Edith Jane Schomberg, 162
Hubbard, Elbert: banquet in honor of, 83–84, 210; death of, 211; *East Side* and, 83, 145, 155, 184; *The Philistine* and, 83, 140–41, 144, 147, 155, 175, 193, 217; Ragged Edge Klub and, 84; Roycroft publishing house and, 83, 93, 150
Huggs, Harry S., 165, 209, 212, 226–27, 229, 258n12
Hughes, Sarah. *See* Anderson, Sarah Hughes
Hungry Club (New York), 140, 156, 161, 258n5
Hypatia Club (Wichita), 38, 42, 44, 73, 83, 167, 246n14

immigrants: Arab, 116, 164; assimilation of, 38, 115; Chinese, 115, 211; demonization of, xii; German, 49, 114; as homesteaders, 26–27; Irish, 178, 180, 259–60n15; Italian, 8, 79, 114–116, 130, 132, 156, 173, 182, 192, 260n23; Jewish, 4, 38, 115–116, 122–23, 130, 173; language barriers for, 68; poverty, xx, 114, 123, 132, 149; Russian, 79, 115; in slums, 126, 180; in tenements, 114, 129–31, 186; Triangle Shirtwaist Factory fire and, 173–75; xenophobia against, 116, 123, 178, 259–60n15; ZAN's undercover reporting on, xf, xi–xiii, 171–72, 198f, 199. *See also* Ellis Island

Jackson, Andrew, 14, 24, 242n19
Jackson, Stonewall, 8
Janssen, August, 164–65
Jaunt, Mademoiselle, 68, 69
Jewish community: *East Side* portrayals of, xix–xx, 115; immigrants in, 4, 38, 115–116, 122–23, 130, 173; memorials for death anniversaries in, 155; philanthropy of, 134–35, 175; poverty within, 132; stereotypes of, 115. *See also* antisemitism
Jim Crow segregation, 36, 214
Johnson, Andrew, 7, 9, 15, 192
Jones, Lawson, 216
Jones, Mary Clarence Chelf (granddaughter of ZAN), 208f, 214, 216–17, 219, 223
Jordan, David Starr, 145, 155, 179, 184
Joyce, John, 259n11

Kaempffert, Waldemar, 110
*Kentucky Pioneers* (film), 214, 216
Kessler, David, 260–61n33
Khayyam, Omar, 95, 115
Kildare, Leita, 158f, 162–63, 212
Kildare, Owen, 163, 212
Kipling, Rudyard, 66, 105
Kolle, Frederick S., 179
Koppelman, Beckie and Gussie, 174, 259n7
Kosmos Electric Runabout Company, iif, 146
Ku Klux Klan, 214

La Farge, John, 110
Lamont, Robert, 265n12
Lampton, William J., 151, 159, 161–62, 184, 192–94, 197, 203, 257n1, 261n35
Langtry, Lillie, 66
Lathrop, Rose Hawthorne, 145
Lease, Mary Elizabeth, 38, 43, 44, 109, 195, 210
Lee, Gabrielle, 265n12
Le Gallienne, Richard, 82, 84, 162
Leighton, Eva. *See* Norris, Eva Leighton
Lemon, Courtenay: alcoholism and, 55, 211; appearance and personality, 85; family background, 42; libel accusations against ZAN, 93, 97; Markham and, 94–95, 133; marriage of, 211; *Sun* and, 123; Sunrise Club and, 161; ZAN characters based on, 35, 55, 85–87, 93–95, 105, 150
Lemon, Joseph, 35, 42, 161, 246n10
Lemon, Margaret, 35, 38, 41–42, 57, 63, 85, 248n16, 250n12, 251n13
Lemon, William, 41–42, 84–85
Lempert, Julius, 202
Leonard, John W., 261n5
Leppig, John, Jr., 204, 229, 262n7
*Leslie's Popular Monthly*, 83
Lewinson, Ann, 262n7, 265n13
Lewis Academy (Wichita), 35, 36, 41, 187, 221
libel, 93, 97, 150, 183
Lincoln, Abraham, 7, 42, 85, 214
Lincoln, Nancy Hanks, 42, 214
Lincoln, Thomas, 214

Lincoln Marriage Temple (Harrodsburg), 214
Lipscomb, Thomas, 2, 222, 242n6
Little Mothers' Aid Society, 259n9
Loeb, Sophie Irene, 162, 185, 211, 226
Lomazow, Steven, xix, 217, 226
Long-Moss, Patricia, 223
Lowe, Will, 37, 45, 53, 207
Lowrey, James, 24
Lowrey, Mariah Meaux. *See* Norris, Mariah Meaux Lowrey
Lowrey, Martha Meaux ("Patsy"), 24, 25, 207
Lowrey, Matthew, Jr., 24, 25
Lowrey, Matthew, Sr., 15, 24, 220
Lyons, Isabel, 112

MacLeod, Kirsten, 139
MacLeod, William, 245n16
magazines in which ZAN published (partial list): *Ainslee's*, 83; *American Agriculturist*, 98, 98, 226, 226, 252n20; *American Monthly*, 50; *Arena*, 243n9; *Bohemian*, 106f, 115, 120f, 124, 125; *Boston Ideas*, 50; *Choice-Bits*, 184, 260n28; *Criterion*, 66, 72f, 74; *Everybody's*, 128f, 139, 142, 143, 184; *Four O'Clock*, 52; *Home Magazine*, 48f, 51, 55, 58–59, 64f, 65, 70, 157, 248n4; *Manuscript*, 81, 82, 140; *Midland Monthly*, 40f, 45–46; *Mirror*, 94, 96–97, 101, 252n19; *Munsey*, 59, 100f; *New Age*, 107; *New Bohemian*, 50; *Puritan*, 56f; *Satire*, 183–84, 211; *Smart Set*, 82, 100f, 122, 166, 226; *Symposium*, 50, 247n3; *10 Story Book*, 107, 125; *Thistle*, 95, 101, 140, 251n15; *Valley Magazine*, 252n19; *Vanity Fair*, 82–83; *Voice*, 89–90; *Woman's Home Companion*, 100f, 107, 252n19; *Writer*, 60–62, 98. See also *The East Side*
Markham, Edwin, 84, 94–95, 133, 251n13
Mary, Queen of Scots, 241n2
Masterson, Bat, 27, 109–10
Masterson, Kate, 130
Maxim, Hudson and Lilian, 133, 255n12
McAdam, George Harrison, 185–86, 205, 261n35

McCandless, Thomas, 260n20
McCardell, Roy, 183, 261n35
McClure, Samuel S., 59
McEachran, Mary, 44–45, 59, 174
McIlvain, Mary, 6
McKee, Ellen, 66
McKinley, William, 70, 85, 95, 96
McPike, Emma and Antoinette, 197
McPike, Jack H., 169, 197, 205, 209–10
McReynolds, James Clark, 155
Meaux, John, 24
Mercy, Henrietta and Anna, 258n9
Micheaux, Oscar, 258n12
Miller, Marion Mills, 81, 90, 92, 94, 139–41, 176, 189, 250n2
Miller, Seay J., 248n4
Millet, Jean-François, 84
misogyny, 30, 43, 76, 201, 228
Mitchell, Edward Page, 248n12
Moberley family, 24–25
Monahan, Michael, 84, 94, 140, 145–46, 155, 175, 217
Mormons, 125, 163, 263n17
Morris, Ann. *See* Stack, Ann Morris
Morris, Barbara. *See* Goodbody, Barbara Morris
Morris, Harold William (son-in-law of ZAN): family background, 73–74; gambling and debts, 76–77; marriage and divorce, 73–74, 135, 249n2; at Paris Exposition (1900), 71, 73; Robert as son of, 78f, 79–81, 89, 103, 154, 214, 221
Morris, Mary Clarence Norris. *See* Chelf, Mary Clarence
Morris, Patricia. *See* Ganter, Patricia Morris
Morris, Robert Melvin (grandson of ZAN), xxii, 78f, 79–81, 103, 133–34, 213–16, 215f, 263n9, 263n15
Morton, Fannie, 24
Müller, Charles Louis, 245n16
Mundy, Bruce, 259n6
Munsey, Frank A., 59, 262n3
Murdock family, 35, 44, 81
Murray, Evelyn Wentworth, 192, 196
Musin, Ovide, 146, 184–85

"My Old Kentucky Home" (Foster), xii, 3, 93, 171, 187, 193, 203, 230

Nachimsohn, Ahron, 255n4
Nation, Carry, 102–3
Native Americans: *East Side* on, 13, 178; education of, 30, 245n20; Ghost Dance performers, 161; Harrodsburg settlement and, 13; land seized from, 13, 26, 178; Pikes Peak scaled by, 53; stereotypical images of, 70; in Wichita, 33
Nazareth Academy (Bardstown, Kentucky), 59–60, 60f
Neiman, Howard, 253n1
newsboys, 117, 143, 145, 151, 175–76, 259n10
newspapers in which ZAN published (partial list): *Brooklyn Life*, 119; *New York Press*, xxi, 134; *New York Sun*, xxi, 43, 62, 102, 116–118, 122–24, 228, 248n12; *New York Times*, 27, 104, 110–113, 122, 124. *See also Wichita Eagle*
New York City: anarchist bombings in, 19, 132, 182; boardinghouses in, 18, 58, 81, 86; charity hospitals in, 78f, 79–81, 127, 228; gun violence in, 19; homes of ZAN in, 95, 103, 107–8, 121, 127–36, 128f, 225, 227–28, 252n4, 255n1; psychiatric facilities in, 37; slums in, 55, 129–30, 133, 151–52, 171, 180; sweatshops in, 80, 84, 122, 143, 172, 178, 195; textile factories in, 199–200; Triangle Shirtwaist Factory fire (1911), 45, 173–75, 259n7; ZAN feeling at home in, xii, 17, 43, 77, 112–113, 224; ZAN works set in, 58, 107–9, 126, 132, 249n4. *See also* Ellis Island; immigrants; tenements; undercover reporting
Nocquet, Paul, 111–112
Nørregaard, Julie, 162
Norris, Eva Leighton (daughter-in-law of ZAN), 103, 109, 154, 202, 213, 221
Norris, Frank (writer), 144
Norris, Mariah Meaux Lowrey (mother-in-law of ZAN), 15, 24, 25, 37, 51–52, 54, 59, 207

# INDEX · 277

Norris, Mary Clarence. *See* Chelf, Mary Clarence

Norris, Mary ("Mollie," sister-in-law of ZAN), 23–25, 30, 51

Norris, Robert Grimes (son of ZAN), 22f; birth and childhood, 25, 37, 221, 244n6; custody following divorce, 53; marriage, 103, 109; on premonitions, 204; railroad employment of, 54, 102, 154, 204; trips taken by, 213; at ZAN's funeral and gravesite, 204, 205; ZAN's relationship with, 70, 103, 154

Norris, Ruth Crook (second wife of Spencer), 74, 102, 109, 253n7

Norris, Sarah ("Sallie," sister-in-law of ZAN), 24–25

Norris, Spencer William (first husband of ZAN), 22f; birth and childhood, 23–25; caricatures published by ZAN, 51, 52; at Chicago world's fair (1893), 39; children of, 22f, 23, 25, 28; courtship with ZAN, 20; death and gravesite of, 109, 153, 221, 264n2; employment as salesman, 62, 74, 248n10; financial troubles, 49, 54, 57, 61–62; marriages and divorce, 23, 49, 53–54, 187; mistresses of, 34–35, 53–54; name change from Weedon Spenny Norris, 23, 25; stores owned by, 30–38, 32f, 41, 43, 61–62, 221, 245n3

Norris, William Walker (father-in-law of ZAN), 23–25, 51

Norris, Zoe Anderson ("ZAN" *in this index*): as art teacher, 19, 30, 33, 35–36, 203; birth and childhood, xxi, xxviiif, 4–9, 15, 99, 102, 220, 222, 242n12; charitable acts, 135, 156, 175, 195; children of, 22f, 23, 25, 28, 103; courtship of Spencer Norris, 20; death of, xiii, 202–3, 229, 262n2; education, 8, 10, 14–19, 23, 203; Europe trip, 62–77, 64f, 72f, 248n16, 249n3; family background, xii, xxi, xxv–xxvi, 1–9, 241n2; funeral services, 131, 201, 204–6, 229; gravesite in Harrodsburg, 20, 205–7, 206f; health challenges and injuries, 44, 126–27, 178–79, 202; marriages and divorce, xii, 14, 23, 49, 53–54, 92, 95–97, 102–5, 187; methodology for study of, xviiif, xix–xxii, 219–29; musical abilities, 33, 39, 113, 133, 221; obituaries, xiii, 144, 159, 197, 203–4, 262n3; photos of, 40f, 48f; photos taken by, 64f, 70, 147, 257n21; posthumous legacy, 209–14, 216–17; pronunciation of name, xx; pseudonym "Nancy Yanks," 41–44, 221; religious life, 8–9, 18, 25, 98; reputation of, 61, 112. *See also The East Side*; Harrodsburg; New York City; premonitions and nightmares; Ragged Edge Klub; undercover reporting; Wichita

Norris, Zoe Anderson, works by (partial list): "After Long Years," 35–36; "Aliens from God's Country," 51–52; *Color of His Soul*, 80–82, 84–90, 88f, 92–95, 97, 101, 105, 112, 139, 149–50, 217, 250n16; "The Common-or-Garden Reporter," 115; "The Copyist," 182; "The Corner on the Curb," 149; "A Daughter of the Revolution," 50; "The Elopement," 181, 194; "The Happy Hunting-Ground," 136; "Her Only Son," 52; "Janet," 45–46; "The Japanese Kimono," 133–35; "Mannahatta," 181; "A New Woman," 82–83; "Our War Veteran," 243n9; "The Passing of Rebecca," 65–66; "A Phone Message to Santa Claus," 134, 256n14; "The Picture of Her," 247n15; *Quest of Polly Locke*, 74–76, 87, 90, 91f, 94, 99, 101–2, 119, 250n16; "The Song of the Typewriter," 105, 157, 226; "A Starlit Sail," 51; "The Sunshine Within," 46; "They Too," 263n16; *Twelve Kentucky Colonel Stories*, 119; "Two Waifs," 46; *The Way of the Wind*, 16–17, 26, 29, 33–34, 36–37, 54, 109, 122, 157, 171, 187–89, 188f, 223–24, 261n35; "The Whirl of the Wheel," 82. *See also* magazines in which ZAN published; newspapers in which ZAN published

Oberhardt, Lorianne, 222
Oberhardt, William: background of, 143, 222, 256n9; *East Side* illustrations by, *xf*, 138*f*, 143–45, 150–51, 170*f*, 175, 184, 204; historical archive of works, 256n10; marriage to Josephine Sonnleitner, 151; at Maxim's soiree, 133, 255n12; portrait sketches by, 212, 215*f*, 263n9; Ragged Edge Klub and, 160; *The Way of the Wind* illustrations by, 187–89, 188*f*
Ogilvie, J. S., 101, 102, 119
Oliver, Edwin Austin, 189
orphans, 4, 24, 78*f*, 96, 104, 115, 216, 228
Ortega, Annie C., 114, 254n11
O'Sheel, Shaemas (James Shields), 162
Oskison, John Milton, 145
Ouida (Maria Louise Ramé), 94, 251n10

Panic of 1907, 121–22
Paris Exposition (1900), 64*f*, 70–71, 79, 213
Patterson, Nan, 111, 259n9
Pelizzari, Patricia Ganter (great-great-granddaughter of ZAN), 223, 264n6
Physioc, Wray, 191–92, 211
Pickford, Mary, 252n16
Pietrafesa family, 114
Pikes Peak, ZAN scaling, 53, 70
Pittman, Hannah Daviess, 245n20
plagiarism, 67, 93, 139, 184, 194, 228
Pleiades Club (New York), 86, 92, 94–95, 107, 115, 161, 203, 253n1
poverty: in Europe, 73, 75; of homesteaders, 26; immigrants and, xx, 114, 123, 132, 149; Jesus's mandate for alleviation of, 4; of Wichita families, 45; of ZAN, xii, xiii, 4–5, 108, 124–25, 149; in ZAN's works, 46, 75, 87, 108, 171. *See also* homelessness; slums
prejudice. *See* antisemitism; discrimination and stereotypes; racism; xenophobia
premonitions and nightmares (including ZAN's own death), xiii, xx, 4, 9–10, 28–30, 45, 59, 66, 152–54, 178, 197, 200–4, 222
Presbyterians, 25, 35, 52, 76, 95, 101

Preston, Amalie, 220, 247n14
Prohibition, 38, 89, 212, 229
prostitution, 68, 177–78, 226
Pulitzer family, 182–84, 211
Pur-Don, Sidonie Devereux, 192, 204, 205, 212

Quaint Club (New York), 86

racism: eugenics and, 155; Ku Klux Klan and, 214; language and, 65, 256n6, 258n12; lynchings, 58–59, 248n4; segregation, 36, 214; Southerners accused of, 177
Ragged Edge Community Theatre (Harrodsburg), 208*f*, 216, 219
Ragged Edge Klub (New York): activities of, 161–66, 196–97, 202, 209–10; criticisms against, 167–69; disorganized nature of, xii, 157, 160, 166; history and mission of, 159–60; management techniques for, 200; meeting venues, 85, 142, 158*f*, 160, 164–65, 196, 205, 209, 228, 258n11, 261n14, 265n14; members of, 37, 44, 82, 86, 115, 125, 195, 226; multiethnic nature of, 38, 86; name considerations, 160, 257n1; reputation of, 166–68
Ramé, Maria Louise. *See* Ouida
Ravenhill, Margaret, 111
Ray, Mary and Ruby, 248n4
Reader, Ella Rawls, 110
Reddick, John, 258n12
Redford, Georgia, 207
religion. *See specific denominations*
Richardson, Dorothy, 130
Riddell, Philip, 147, 196, 205
Rihani, Ameen, 115, 164, 212
Riis, Jacob, 226
Rinaldo, Joel, 164, 169, 179, 197, 212, 229
Robards, Lewis, 13
Robards, Rachel Donelson, 13–14, 24, 242n19
Roberts, Katherine Stuyvesant Van Ness. *See* Tinley, Mabel
Rockefeller, John D., 143
Roebling, John, 17

Rogers, Betty, xii, 168, 197, 205
Rogers, Will, 168
Roosevelt, Theodore, 85, 121, 122, 155, 182, 212
Rosenfeld, Genie Holtzmeyer, 260n31
Rosenfeld, Gussie, 259n7
Rosenfeld, Ignatz, 155
Rosenfeld, Monroe, 260n31
Rosenfeld, Sydney, 186
Rudolph, Maya, 244n3
Rue, Archibald B. (brother-in-law of ZAN), xxv, 7, 15, 109, 220, 243n8
Rue, Edwin W. ("Skip"), 264n7
Rue, Insco (nephew of ZAN), 29, 248n4
Rue, Jessamine Anderson ("Jessie," sister of ZAN): as artist, 7, 29, 242n19, 253n7, 263n14; birth and death of, xxv; during Civil War, 7, 245n21; education of, 15; at funeral for ZAN, 206; marriage and children, 7, 29; ZAN's relationship with, 252n17
Rue, Zoe (niece of ZAN), 29
runaway enslaved people, 14, 243n5
Runnymede colony (Kansas), 46, 53
Ryther, Jule de, 261n35

Saint-Gaudens, Augustus, 107
Salomon, Jacob, 255n4
Salvation Army, 139, 142, 156
Sampson, Jerry, 262n1
Sand, George, 151
Sandburg, Charles (Carl), 251n15
Saumenig, Frederick Boyd, 189
Schleicher, George, 142, 255n12
Schloss, Murray, 166
Schwartz, Max, 165
Sea, Robert Grimes, 248n4
Seawell, Molly Elliot, 79
Segalowsky, Bella, 126, 255n10
segregation, 36, 214
Segurson, Catherine, 224–26
settlement houses, 146, 177
Settles, Mary, 263n14
Shakers, 14, 17, 97, 214, 220, 224, 259n6, 263n16
Sheridan, Mattie, 140, 156, 161
Shields, James (Shaemas O'Sheel), 162

Shores, Robert J., 146, 175, 185
Simon, Mae, 150
Simpson, Robert N., 193, 205–6
Sirovich, William, 179–80, 202, 211–12
slavery and enslaved people: education for, 4, 16; emancipation of, 2, 4, 7, 24; in Harrodsburg settlement, 13, 14; in Norris household, 24; punishment of, 124, 214; runaways, 14, 243n5; in Spenny household, 23–24, 244n2; wage slavery, 84, 86, 87, 114, 150; ZAN's relatives and, xv–xvi, xx, 2, 3, 6, 73, 222, 227. *See also* abolitionists
Sloan, John, 150, 257n24
slums: children in, 5–6, 67, 151–52; *East Side* descriptions of, 151–52; immigrants in, 126, 180; in London, 67; in New York, 55, 129–30, 133, 151–52, 171; novels on, 146; oculists in, 149; women in, 119, 151; in ZAN's works, 75, 86–87. *See also* tenements
Smith, Orlando J., 59
Snitkin, Leonard A., 163
Snitzer, Jacob L., 260–61n33
Socialists, 81, 84–85, 92, 96, 105, 135, 150, 152
Sorosis Club (New York), 246n14
Spanish-American War (1898), 58, 70, 248n4
Spaulding, Francesca di Maria Palmer, 166, 185, 263n11
Spenny, Mary and Sarah, 23
Spenny, Weedon, 23, 24
Spilman, Benjamin, 243n8
Spilman, Mary. *See* Anderson, Mary Spilman
Stack, Ann Morris (great-granddaughter of ZAN), 214, 216, 217, 223, 224, 263n15
Stack, Chris (great-great-grandson of ZAN), 224
Standley, Norma and Jennie, 245n20
Stephens, Nannie, 38, 82–83, 210
Stephenson, Martha, 243n13
stereotypes. *See* discrimination and stereotypes
*Strader v. Graham* (1851), 243n5
suffrage. *See* voting rights

Sunrise Club (New York), 86, 160–61, 171, 183
sweatshops, 80, 84, 122, 143, 172, 178, 195

Taft, William Howard, 122, 143, 182
Tanner, Beatrice, 251n2
Tchor-Baj-Oglu, Euthimios X., 162, 167
temperance movement, 38, 43, 89, 102–3
tenements: children in, 42, 113, 131, 141; *East Side* descriptions of, 141–42; immigrants in, 114, 129–31, 186; in ZAN's works, 84, 86–87, 117. *See also* slums
*Tess of the Storm Country* (film), 252n16
textile factories, 199–200
Thackeray, William, 94
Thirteen Club (New York), 161, 166
Thompson, Davis, 244n20
Thompson, John Burton (brother-in-law of ZAN): distillery owned by, 17, 39, 220; *East Side* and, 154; at funerals for ZAN and Nettie, 183, 206–7; marriage and children, xxv, 7–8, 97; ZAN characters based on, 96; ZAN's relationship with, 15, 118–119
Thompson, Martha Anderson ("Mattie," sister of ZAN), xxviii*f*; birth and childhood, xxv, 8; death and gravesite, xxv, 29, 153, 200, 257n29; marriage of, 7–8, 15; as music teacher, 7; portrait painted by sister Jessie, 242n19; ZAN's relationship with, 31, 96–97, 153
Thompson, Philip (nephew of ZAN), 97, 153, 207, 248n4, 262n12
Thompson, Philip B., Jr. (brother of John Thompson), 15, 19, 27, 30, 118–119, 152, 183
Tiffany, Louis Comfort, 110, 111
Timmins, Cornelia Pickett Anderson (sister of ZAN), xxviii*f*; birth and childhood, xxvi, 6; death of, xxvi; education of, 15, 29, 245n16; at funeral for ZAN, 206; at Kansas homestead, 10, 25; marriage of, 38; New Testament translation, 9, 212–13; ZAN's relationship with, 252n17
Timmins, Harry (brother-in-law of ZAN), xxvi, 38

Tinley, Mabel, 125, 126, 161
Tischendorf, Constantin von, 9
Toler, Sallie, 38, 44, 167, 258n14
Toler, Sidney, 258n14
Tompkins, Robert Reade (great-grandfather of ZAN), 1
Towne, Elizabeth and William, 140
Townsend, John Wilson, 192–94, 206, 207, 261n4
Trabue, Benjamin (brother-in-law of ZAN), xxv, 7
Trabue, Lelia Anderson (half-sister of ZAN), xxv, 1, 7, 96, 200
travelogues, 42, 45, 53, 102
Triangle Shirtwaist Factory fire (1911), 45, 173–75, 259n7
Tubby, Gertrude Ogden, 146, 210, 256n18
Tucker, John Francis, 86, 92, 156, 160, 166, 205
Twain, Mark, 57, 111, 112, 116, 124, 189, 217, 257n1
Twilight Club (New York), 86, 160, 166
Tyndall, William DeWitt, 175

Ullman, Albert Edward, 124, 257n24
Umberto (king of Italy), 75, 85
undercover reporting: on homelessness, 172–73; as immigrant musician, *xf*, xi–xiii, 171–72; as immigrant transit passenger, 198*f*, 199; on low-cost housing for laborers, 113–114; as scrubwoman seeking shelter, 139, 142; on servants, 98–99, 135, 252n20; as stranded tourist, 134–35; on sweatshops, 172; on textile factories, 199–200
Underground Railroad, 4, 214
United Charities Building (New York), 172, 174–75, 227, 259n3
Urner, Mabel Herbert, 162, 167, 184, 205, 211, 265n11

Vance, Arthur T., 51, 55, 157
voting rights, 38, 45, 154, 163, 183, 245n23

wage slavery, 84, 86, 87, 114, 150
Washington, George, 1
Welch, J. Herbert, 159, 167, 189

Wendroff, Bertha, 174, 259n7
West, Phil, 259n6
West, Rebecca, 211
White, Grace Miller, 95–96, 101, 252n16
White, Homer, 96
Whitman, Walt, 181, 185
Whittington, Mary E., 17
Wichita (Kansas): Conversazione in, 49, 50, 160; economic hardship in, 39, 43; Hypatia Club in, 38, 42, 44, 73, 83, 167, 246n14; immigrants in, 38, 49; impoverished families in, 45; Lewis Academy in, 35, 36, 41, 187, 221; music scene in, 42, 54–55; Native Americans in, 33; Norris addresses in, 245n2, 246n1; Norris grocery store in, 32f, 33–38, 41, 43, 61–62, 245n3; social life in, 37–39
*Wichita Beacon* (newspaper): on anti-trust activism of ZAN, 176; on Kansan pride of ZAN, 102; on ZAN as thriving in NYC, 195
*Wichita Eagle* (newspaper): Dodsworth story published by, 69; on Grolier Club exhibition (2023), 227; on letter lost by Clarence, 89; on portrait painted by ZAN, 35; updates on ZAN in New York published by, 62, 167, 176; *The Way of the Wind* serialized by, 189; wedding announcement for Clarence in, 73; ZAN's column under pseudonym "Nancy Yanks," 41–44, 221, 246n4
*Wichita Journal*, "Woman's Tidings" column by Margaret Lemon, 41–42
Wilcox, Ella Wheeler, 85, 176, 259n11
Wilde, Oscar, 82
Williams, Abram and Lucy, 16
Williams, Charles, 243n11
Williams, J. Insco, 29
Williams, John Augustus: Daughters College founded by, 4–5, 12f, 16–19, 207; as father figure and mentor to ZAN, 16, 30, 133; New Testament translation and, 9, 212–13; weddings officiated by, 23, 38
Williams, Mary, 4–5, 16
Wilson, Woodrow, 143, 195
Wilson-Kleekamp, Dr. Traci, xvi, 223, 244n2
Winstock, Melvin G., 94, 251n10
Woman's Press Club of New York: Corrothers at event hosted by, 84; directory of, 156, 216; establishment of, 57; leadership of, 111; Markham at event hosted by, 251n13; ZAN as member of, 57, 62–63, 84, 107, 121, 156
women: alcoholism and, 182; angelic designs influenced by, 110, 111; Civil War activities of, 6; clubs organized by, 161; domestic abuse and, 13, 24, 27–28, 52, 132, 147, 156, 162, 211; employment of, 18–19, 54; feminism and, 147, 156; jury duty rights for, 111; misogyny and, 30, 43, 76, 201, 228; motherhood experienced by, 25, 148; as nuns, 6, 59, 63, 78f, 80–81, 228; Pikes Peak scaled by, 53, 70; premonitions and telepathy of, 59; professional clubs for, 38, 246n14; prostitution and, 68, 177–78, 226; Salvation Army shelter for, 139, 142; as servants, 98–99, 135, 252n20; in slums, 119, 151; in sweatshops, 80, 122; in temperance movement, 38, 43, 102–3; voting rights for, 38, 45, 154, 163, 183. *See also* Daughters College; Woman's Press Club of New York
Woodman, Rea, 38, 210
World's Columbian Exposition. *See* Chicago world's fair
Wyle, Hannah, 161, 191, 196, 197, 205

xenophobia, 116, 123, 178, 259–60n15

Young, Caesar, 111

Zuscofski, William, 174–75, 259n7

Independent scholar **Eve M. Kahn** is a regular contributor to *The New York Times* and author of a prizewinning monograph, *Forever Seeing New Beauties: The Forgotten Impressionist Mary Rogers Williams, 1857–1907* (Wesleyan University Press, 2019).

## SELECT TITLES FROM EMPIRE STATE EDITIONS

Salvatore Basile, *Fifth Avenue Famous: The Extraordinary Story of Music at St. Patrick's Cathedral*. Foreword by Most Reverend Timothy M. Dolan, Archbishop of New York

William Seraile, *Angels of Mercy: White Women and the History of New York's Colored Orphan Asylum*

Andrew J. Sparberg, *From a Nickel to a Token: The Journey from Board of Transportation to MTA*

*New York's Golden Age of Bridges*. Paintings by Antonio Masi, Essays by Joan Marans Dim, Foreword by Harold Holzer

Gerard R. Wolfe, *The Synagogues of New York's Lower East Side: A Retrospective and Contemporary View, Second Edition*. Photographs by Jo Renée Fine and Norman Borden, Foreword by Joseph Berger

Joseph B. Raskin, *The Routes Not Taken: A Trip Through New York City's Unbuilt Subway System*

Phillip Deery, *Red Apple: Communism and McCarthyism in Cold War New York*

*North Brother Island: The Last Unknown Place in New York City*. Photographs by Christopher Payne, A History by Randall Mason, Essay by Robert Sullivan

Stephen Miller, *Walking New York: Reflections of American Writers from Walt Whitman to Teju Cole*

Tom Glynn, *Reading Publics: New York City's Public Libraries, 1754–1911*

Craig Saper, *The Amazing Adventures of Bob Brown: A Real-Life Zelig Who Wrote His Way Through the 20th Century*

R. Scott Hanson, *City of Gods: Religious Freedom, Immigration, and Pluralism in Flushing, Queens*. Foreword by Martin E. Marty

*Dorothy Day and the Catholic Worker: The Miracle of Our Continuance*. Edited, with an Introduction and Additional Text by Kate Hennessy, Photographs by Vivian Cherry, Text by Dorothy Day

Mark Naison and Bob Gumbs, *Before the Fires: An Oral History of African American Life in the Bronx from the 1930s to the 1960s*

Robert Weldon Whalen, *Murder, Inc., and the Moral Life: Gangsters and Gangbusters in La Guardia's New York*

Britt Haas, *Fighting Authoritarianism: American Youth Activism in the 1930s*

Nandini Bagchee, *Counter Institution: Activist Estates of the Lower East Side*

Susan Celia Greenfield (ed.), *Sacred Shelter: Thirteen Journeys of Homelessness and Healing*

Andrew Feffer, *Bad Faith: Teachers, Liberalism, and the Origins of McCarthyism*

Colin Davey with Thomas A. Lesser, *The American Museum of Natural History and How It Got That Way*. Forewords by Neil deGrasse Tyson and Kermit Roosevelt III

Wendy Jean Katz, *Humbug: The Politics of Art Criticism in New York City's Penny Press*

Lolita Buckner Inniss, *The Princeton Fugitive Slave: The Trials of James Collins Johnson*

Angel Garcia, *The Kingdom Began in Puerto Rico: Neil Connolly's Priesthood in the South Bronx*

Jim Mackin, *Notable New Yorkers of Manhattan's Upper West Side: Bloomingdale–Morningside Heights*

Matthew Spady, *The Neighborhood Manhattan Forgot: Audubon Park and the Families Who Shaped It*

Marilyn S. Greenwald and Yun Li, *Eunice Hunton Carter: A Lifelong Fight for Social Justice*

Jeffrey A. Kroessler, *Sunnyside Gardens: Planning and Preservation in a Historic Garden Suburb*

Jean Arrington with Cynthia S. LaValle, *From Factories to Palaces: Architect Charles B. J. Snyder and the New York City Public Schools*. Foreword by Peg Breen

Boukary Sawadogo, *Africans in Harlem: An Untold New York Story*

Alvin Eng, *Our Laundry, Our Town: My Chinese American Life from Flushing to the Downtown Stage and Beyond*

Stephanie Azzarone, *Heaven on the Hudson: Mansions, Monuments, and Marvels of Riverside Park*

Mark Bulik, *Ambush at Central Park: When the IRA Came to New York*

Matt Dallos, *In the Adirondacks: Dispatches from the Largest Park in the Lower 48*

Brandon Dean Lamson, *Caged: A Teacher's Journey Through Rikers, or How I Beheaded the Minotaur*

Raj Tawney, *Colorful Palate: Savored Stories from a Mixed Life*

Edward Cahill, *Disorderly Men*

Joseph Heathcott, *Global Queens: An Urban Mosaic*

Francis R. Kowsky with Lucille Gordon, *Hell on Color, Sweet on Song: Jacob Wrey Mould and the Artful Beauty of Central Park*

Jill Jonnes, *South Bronx Rising: The Rise, Fall, and Resurrection of an American City*, Third Edition

Barbara G. Mensch, *A Falling-Off Place: The Transformation of Lower Manhattan*

David J. Goodwin, *Midnight Rambles: H. P. Lovecraft in Gotham*

Felipe Luciano, *Flesh and Spirit: Confessions of a Young Lord*

Maximo G. Martinez, *Sojourners in the Capital of the World: Garifuna Immigrants*

Jennifer Baum, *Just City: Growing Up on the Upper West Side When Housing Was a Human Right*

Davida Siwisa James, *Hamilton Heights and Sugar Hill: Alexander Hamilton's Old Harlem Neighborhood Through the Centuries*

Annik LaFarge, *On the High Line: The Definitive Guide*, Third Edition. Foreword by Rick Dark

Marie Carter, *Mortimer and the Witches: A History of Nineteenth-Century Fortune Tellers*

Alice Sparberg Alexiou, *Devil's Mile: The Rich, Gritty History of the Bowery*. Foreword by Peter Quinn

Carey Kasten and Brenna Moore, *Mutuality in El Barrio: Stories of the Little Sisters of the Assumption Family Health Service*. Foreword by Norma Benítez Sánchez

Kimberly A. Orcutt, *The American Art-Union: Utopia and Skepticism in the Antebellum Era*

Jonathan Butler, *Join the Conspiracy: How a Brooklyn Eccentric Got Lost on the Right, Infiltrated the Left, and Brought Down the Biggest Bombing Network in New York*

Nicole Gelinas, *Movement: New York's Long War to Take Back Its Streets from the Car*

Jack Hodgson, *Young Reds in the Big Apple: The New York Young Pioneers of America, 1923–1934*

Lynn Ellsworth, *Wonder City: How to Reclaim Human-Scale Urban Life*

Walter Zev Feldman, *From the Bronx to the Bosphorus: Klezmer and Other Displaced Musics of New York*

Larry Racioppo, *Here Down on Dark Earth: Loss and Remembrance in New York City*

Bonnie Yochelson, *Too Good to Get Married: The Life and Photographs of Miss Alice Austen*

David Brown Morris, *Ten Thousand Central Parks: A Climate-Change Parable*

Miriam Chaiken, *Creative Ozone: The Artists of Westbeth*

Stefanie Mercado Altman, Claire Altman, and Stan Altman, *Twice Blessed: A Story of Unconditional Love*. Foreword by Stephen G. Post

Stephanie Azzarone, *Fabulous Fountains of New York*

**For a complete list, visit www.fordhampress.com/empire-state-editions.**